Thoreauvian Modernities

Thoreauvian Modernities

TRANSATLANTIC CONVERSATIONS

ON AN AMERICAN ICON

Edited by

FRANÇOIS SPECQ

LAURA DASSOW WALLS

MICHEL GRANGER

THE UNIVERSITY OF GEORGIA PRESS

ATHENS AND LONDON

© 2013 by The University of Georgia Press

Athens, Georgia 30602

www.ugapress.org

All rights reserved

Designed by Walton Harris

Set in 10/14 Minion Pro by Graphic Composition, Inc.

Printed and bound by Thomson-Shore

The paper in this book meets the guidelines for permanence
and durability of the Committee on Production Guidelines
for Book Longevity of the Council on Library Resources.

Printed in the United States of America

13 14 15 16 17 P 5 4 3 2 1

Library of Congress Cataloging-in-Publication Data

Thoreauvian modernities : transatlantic conversations on an American icon /
edited by Francois Specq, Laura Dassow Walls, and Michel Granger.

p. cm.

Includes bibliographical references and index.

ISBN 978-0-8203-4428-7 (hardcover : alk. paper) — ISBN 0-8203-4428-1 (hardcover : alk. paper) —
ISBN 978-0-8203-4429-4 (pbk. : alk. paper) — ISBN 0-8203-4429-X (pbk. : alk. paper)

1. Thoreau, Henry David, 1817–1862—Criticism and interpretation. 2. Civilization, Modern, in
literature. 3. Transcendentalism (New England) I. Specq, Francois, 1965– II. Walls, Laura Dassow.

III. Granger, Michel, 1947–

PS3054.T59 2013

818'.309—dc23

2012024219

British Library Cataloging-in-Publication Data available

Contents

Illustrations

Acknowledgments

This book grew out of a May 2009 conference in Lyon, the first ever such meeting on European soil devoted to Thoreau. The editors would like to acknowledge the generous support of the different organizations, and the men and women who constitute them, that in various ways devoted time and expertise as well as funding to the organization of this conference: École Normale Supérieure de Lyon & Université Lyon 2, Centre National de la Recherche Scientifique (CNRS-UMR 5611 LIRE), Institut des Amériques, American Embassy, and the local authorities, Région Rhône-Alpes, Conseil Général du Rhône, and Ville de Lyon. This publication was made possible thanks to funds contributed by the Région Rhône-Alpes and by the William P. and Hazel B. White Foundation at the University of Notre Dame through the generous support of John McGreevy, Dean, College of Arts and Letters. The editors and authors also owe special thanks to friends and colleagues who have commented on earlier versions of various parts of the manuscript, and to Randall Conrad, who provided the index.

Abbreviations

CC   Henry David Thoreau. *Cape Cod*. Ed. Joseph J. Moldenhauer. Princeton, N.J.: Princeton University Press, 1988.

CompW   Ralph Waldo Emerson. *The Complete Works of Ralph Waldo Emerson*. Ed. Edward Waldo Emerson. Centenary Edition. 12 vols. Boston: Houghton Mifflin, 1903–4.

Corr   Henry David Thoreau. *The Correspondence of Henry David Thoreau*. Ed. Walter Harding and Carl Bode. New York: New York University Press, 1958.

CW   Ralph Waldo Emerson. *The Collected Works of Ralph Waldo Emerson*. Edited by Joseph Slater et al. 10 vols. Cambridge, Mass.: Harvard University Press, 1971–.

EEM   Henry David Thoreau. *Early Essays and Miscellanies*. Ed. Joseph J. Moldenhauer and Edwin Moser, with Alexander Kern. Princeton, N.J.: Princeton University Press, 1975.

Exc   Henry David Thoreau. *Excursions*. Ed. Joseph J. Moldenhauer. Princeton, N.J.: Princeton University Press, 2007.

Faith   Henry David Thoreau. *Faith in a Seed: The Dispersion of Seeds and Other Late Natural History Writings*. Ed. Bradley P. Dean. Washington, D.C.: Island Press, 1993.

J   Henry David Thoreau. *The Journal of Henry David Thoreau*. 14 vols. Ed. Bradford Torrey and Francis H. Allen. Boston: Houghton Mifflin, 1906; New York: Dover, 1962. [Volumes indicated by roman numerals.]

Letters   Henry David Thoreau. *Letters to a Spiritual Seeker*. Ed. Bradley P. Dean. New York: Norton, 2004.

MW   Henry David Thoreau. *The Maine Woods*. Ed. Joseph J.
        Moldenhauer. Princeton, N.J.: Princeton University Press, 1972.

PJ   Henry David Thoreau. *Journal. The Writings of Henry D. Thoreau*.
        Ed. Elizabeth Hall Witherell et al. 8 vols. to date. Princeton, N.J.:
        Princeton University Press, 1981–. [Volumes indicated by arabic
        numerals.]

RP   Henry David Thoreau. *Reform Papers*. Ed. Wendell Glick.
        Princeton, N.J.: Princeton University Press, 1973.

W   Henry David Thoreau. *Walden*. Ed. J. Lyndon Shanley. Princeton,
        N.J.: Princeton University Press, 1971.

Wk   Henry David Thoreau. *A Week on the Concord and Merrimack
        Rivers*. Ed. Carl F. Hovde, William L. Howarth, and Elizabeth Hall
        Witherell. Princeton, N.J.: Princeton University Press, 1980.

WF   Henry David Thoreau. *Wild Fruits: Thoreau's Rediscovered Last
        Manuscript*. Ed. Bradley P. Dean. New York: Norton, 2000.

Thoreauvian Modernities

FRANÇOIS SPECQ AND LAURA DASSOW WALLS

Introduction

THE MANIFOLD MODERNITY OF
HENRY D. THOREAU

ALL THE ESSAYS GATHERED in this volume offer, to some degree, scholarly meditations inspired by thinking about Thoreau. Here—in the continuing relevance
of his writings to our time, as they were once relevant to his time—resides
his essential modernity. His writings mean something different to us now, of
course, but what remains central is their capacity to stimulate thought and to
address pressing issues in a renewed way. As Laura Dassow Walls emphasizes
in her essay in this volume, "Walking West, Gazing East," "The text we read, if
we are to read it at all, let alone read it together in concert, must find a way to
stay alive. It must generate and sustain a living network all along the lengths
from its creation to our translation." This idea of a network is supported by her
notion of "vascularity," with its suggestion of nurture and circulation of energy,
irrigation, development, relationality, and the way a work is alive by what she
calls its "vibration" for us. Laura also insists that "Thoreau means something
risky, endangering, like the 'sweet edge' of the scimitar." It is this "edginess," the
fact that his works continue to unsettle rather than "inspire" in a loose sense,
that defines his modernity, or continuing relevance.

This volume pursues three distinct but parallel lines. First, it fundamentally
offers a series of "dialogues": it asks how Thoreau himself entered into various
forms of dialogue with his time (in its historical, social, and economic dimensions; in its philosophical and religious situation; and in its scientific and epistemological concerns); it asks how we, as readers situated in a very different
context (often identified as "postmodernity"), also enter into various forms of
dialogue with Thoreau's work as his writings speak to us, interrogate us, challenge us to consider alternative modes of thinking about economics, science, or

the environment. Of course, our approach to Thoreau's dialogue with his own time (a dialogue that may variously be described as critical, exhortative, embittered, or humorous) is filtered through our own historically situated concerns as well as our own personal preferences and references. It is precisely this "double articulation" of literary and cultural criticism that makes Thoreau's writings so lively—open to so many reorientations.

Second, this volume suggests that Thoreau himself constantly sought to articulate the *timeless* and the *timely*, convinced as he was that it was not only possible or profitable but necessary to widen our views of the universe in ways that were inevitably proper to our historical situation but that simultaneously spoke to our common, eternal condition as human beings, a condition that he viewed as universal. In other words, Thoreau offered a *literary anthropology* that attended to our inhabiting "a common dwelling," one not only physical or geographical but also intellectual and "metaphysical" in a broad sense. The ideal that he opposes to what he perceived as "degenerate times" is thus less a nostalgic image of the past than a utopian image of the eternal, from which the present should draw the resources for a better future—thus intrinsically connecting the timeless and the timely.

Third, this volume is faithful to the spirit of Thoreau's intellectual search in its commitment to an exploration that knows no frontiers, one that is decidedly "without bounds" precisely because it is timeless and universal. More specifically, since the starting point for this volume was the first conference ever devoted to Thoreau held on European soil, it can be said that all the contributors, in various ways, articulate their reflections in ways that are *transatlantic*. Thoreau, like the rest of his fellow Transcendentalists, imbibed and responded to European literatures and philosophies, both ancient and contemporary; thus we, in turn, can explore his works in the light of current intellectual developments on both sides of the Atlantic. The authors of these essays have found useful a variety of contemporary philosophical approaches, including those of John Dewey, Richard Rorty, Hans Georg Gadamer, Gayatri Spivak, Jacques Derrida, and Bruno Latour. Thoreau certainly helps us think more broadly, and it is the germinating power of his thought as well as its persistent challenge to our own thinking that this volume seeks to explore through his connections to philosophy, environmental studies, and political science.

As a result, our approach to the question of "Thoreau's modernity" has deliberately been left as broad as possible. Rather than attempt to pinpoint specifically or grasp in the abstract the meaning of that most notoriously elusive term, we have preferred to let each essay address the question of what is modern/pre-modern/postmodern/antimodern in Thoreau in its own terms and with its own methods. Rather than reach a final definition of Thoreau's modernity, we seek to put on display the question's various dimensions. Let it be emphasized also that this is the reason "modernity" has been pluralized. In skirting definition and devoting ourselves to openness, we show ourselves to be worthy children of the postmodern age, which has taught us that reaching synthesis and consensus often comes at too high a price. There have been not one but multiple moder-nities, not only across the world's societies but among various communities in the same society. Hence these essays offer approaches that are intellectually very different, even incompatible, although it is notable that most of the authors emphasize *relationality* as a central feature of Thoreau's writings.

Just a few preliminary remarks, then, follow so as to provide some further reference points. It is essential to distinguish between modernity as a historical moment associated with modernization (as addressed by David Robinson, for instance) and the question of *Thoreau's* modernity, which is a different matter. This distinction points to the double meaning of "modern": until the eighteenth century, the meaning of modern as "of one's time" prevailed, as the notori-ous quarrel between the ancients and the moderns reminds us. But "of one's time" is not a monolithic concept; instead, it is made of contradictory elements, some looking backward and some forward. The latter came to prevail during romanticism, when to be "modern" was to be *ahead* of one's time; fundamen-tally, modernity may be defined today as the critical conscience of the historical process of modernization. In this sense, Thoreau's critical consciousness offers reflections on modern culture that seem to be heir to both cultural pessimism à la Rousseau and intellectual optimism à la Kant.

"Modern," as the *OED* reminds us, comes from the Latin word *hodiernus*, which means "that is of today." At heart, then, this is the basic sense in which we also understand the term in this volume: "modern" refers primarily not to the historical moment known as "modernity," a moment that has now passed, but to the various ways Thoreau's works can be regarded as of their day as well as of our own. And indeed, *Le Grand Robert*, the French-language equivalent of the *OED*, gives as its most fundamental definition "that which is of the time of the person speaking." In these essays, it is both the author and the scholar who speak, and the intersection of their two voices creates the "dialogical"

dimension of our scholarly practice. It is only because it is dialogical that scholarly work can, hopefully, be alive in the best sense and, concomitantly, allow
the original works themselves to stay alive in their turn. Scholars would not
exist without the works on which they comment, but the works themselves
would not long survive if there were no scholars to hand them down to posterity, to make them accessible to new readers. This may be described as the work
of *translation*, work that seeks not to abolish but to explore the linguistic and
historical distance that separates us from works of the past while also showing their continued relevance to today's new readers. Our greatest hope is that
this volume, rather than offering any grand theoretical claims about modernity
as such or definitive pronouncements about Thoreau, will further our goal of
keeping this dialogue open and alive. These new essays from across Europe and
the United States are designed to support that dialogue by crossing national and
linguistic boundaries.

Thus the transatlantic, exploratory features of the original conference have
been retained and enhanced. Charles Capper has recently argued that if, as
the postmoderns tell us, modernity means "a self-reflexive engagement in a
world seemingly without fixed 'foundations,' the leading Transcendentalists . . .
pushed closer to that leap than did any other intellectual circle before the twentieth century" (30). We agree, and would add that although Emerson has been
deeply explored in this vein, Thoreau is still awaiting his due. This volume puts
on display a variety of conclusions, some in tension and challenging each other,
some in resonance and strengthening each other. It is in this variance that, we
maintain, Thoreau most reveals his relevance to us today as an "American" icon
who speaks beyond the shores of the United States and as a "modern" whose
stance, at odds with modernism, evokes today, perhaps more than ever, the
dimensions, contradictions, and plurality of Thoreauvian modernities.

The first of our three parts, "Thoreau and (Non)Modernity," brings together essays that consider Thoreau as a social thinker who set himself against the "modern" currents of his day but who also contributed to the emergence of a new
era through his understanding of the epistemological and (post)metaphysical
stakes of modernity. By questioning humanity's place in the social, economic,
natural, and metaphysical order of things, Thoreau thus ushered in a rethink-

ing of humanity's role in the natural world, which nurtured the environmental movement. Laura Dassow Walls, in "Walking West, Gazing East: Planetarity on the Shores of Cape Cod," reads Thoreau's essay "Walking" and his book *Cape Cod* alongside each other, reminding us that these two writings were composed together during the same span of years: they thus present themselves as a pairing of opposed possibilities—West and East, America and Europe, future and past—in a dialogic relationship. Whereas "Walking" promotes a more univocal sense of space and history, foregrounding a teleology that was aligned with the catchwords of historical modernity, *Cape Cod*, she argues, offers a more complex and "pluralized" understanding that points toward the openness of postmodern thinking—or, more accurately, "nonmodern" thinking—understood not as an ironical game depriving the world of any real significance but as an enlargement of the literary, social, and natural fields across four fundamental temporal and spatial dimensions, which she calls "mobility, planetarity, vascularity, transjectivity." The setting for her proposal is a planetary, or cosmopolitan, perspective rather than a narrow sense of national purpose. Thoreau's work is thus "modern" in the larger sense of an awareness of one's belonging to the same small world, a sense that in turn grounds environmental awareness insofar as it points to the multiple, unstable relationality (the underlying notion that links her four concepts) between the different parts of the world and between human beings. Walls necessarily downplays the notion of a distinct or bounded modernity, since for her what matters is connection between past and present, which she sees as layered and deeply interactive, hence inseparable. For her, Thoreau inaugurated the perception of an emerging world of instability, complexity, multipolarity, and "multiscalarity," offering "a transcendence of modernity itself." Thoreau's "modernity" lies precisely in the idea that he looked through the beginning of the modern moment all the way to its end in a prophecy that anticipated "postmodernity": in his capacity to reach from his time to our own, he lives on through his provocations to us.

Michel Granger, in "Antimodern Thoreau," draws on Antoine Compagnon's notion of "antimodern" to analyze what he regards as Thoreau's multiple antimodern stances, that is, the various ways the disgruntled New England writer objects, rather than adapts, to the United States of his time, battling against modernity. Granger reviews Thoreau's opposition to materialism, urbanization, capitalism, democracy, and the scientific revolution, showing how in each case Thoreau voiced his elitist distrust of prevailing views, animated by "values [that] are not those of the time." Although this may seem to offer a one-sided approach to Thoreau, Granger suggests that, on the contrary, "his criticism allowed him to free himself from the prevailing conventional notions of his time and to develop a fascinating mode of thinking well in advance of his age," thus closely linking modernity and antimodernity. Granger explains that some of Thoreau's most "modern" ideas, such as his call for nature preservation, are rooted in a fundamentally antimodern distrust, thus to some extent conjoining (and skirting the divide between) modernism and antimodernism. While Walls sees Thoreau's environmental awareness as grounded in his nonmodern intellectual stance, Granger sees it as a consequence of his antimodern stance. To be sure, Thoreau devised a mode of writing meant to "wake his neighbors up," and in this respect he too was modern in the sense of addressing a contemporary audience and thus very much of his own time. In the final analysis, if Thoreau's criticism is not irremediably outdated (which is what ultimately defines his modernity), it is because, first, we today are still fundamentally heir to the same modernity he was opposing, and, second, as Thoreau believed in the transhistorical value of universal principles, his way of addressing his audience remains relevant today, testifying to his desire to improve humanity as a whole. Finally, Granger suggests that Thoreau's antimodernism, far from being outdated, is redeemed by a literary experimentalism that makes him, in literary terms, a premodernist.

William Rossi, in "Thoreau's Multiple Modernities," does not rest satisfied with the idea that Thoreau rejected modernity in any simple sense and considers instead Thoreau's adherence to a complex temporal layering that offers not a diluting but a recapturing of modernity on a higher plane. Rossi is wary of the pitfall of defining modernity "monolithically," arguing instead for a "pluralized" sense of Thoreau's relation to modernity and describing the enterprise of Thoreau's Journal through Bruno Latour's notions of "inscription" and the "circulation" of reference. However, Rossi's main purpose is to analyze "Autumnal Tints," which he suggests "is not a simple romantic nature essay," for it deeply engages Latourian questions of how nature is transcribed or translated for an audience. Attentive as he is to Thoreau's desire to fulfill ideals rather than merely critique what exists (thus laying an emphasis different from that of Granger), Rossi underlines the way Thoreau literally embodied what attention to the natural world was, meant, and involved, thus offering a model not in the simple sense of arrogant superiority but of a heuristic dimension as defined by Latour, that is, as an effort to combat both "inattention" and "single vision." As

Walls also emphasizes, Thoreau is eager to bring complexity to the fore, and in this respect what may be taken as an antimodern stance is actually a rejection of commonly accepted, simplistic conceptions of the world. Rossi also shows that Thoreau's gesture, in drawing his reader's attention to scientific, social, and literary complexity, was essentially, intrinsically ecological. The second point Rossi emphasizes is Thoreau's eagerness to "demonstrate"—in the etymological sense of manifesting—how, as opposed to modernity's "linearizing" of time (what François Specq has elsewhere called "vectorizing"), time itself should be pluralized. In the end, Rossi's essay amounts to an advocacy of neither a "postmodern condition" nor a "modern" one but a recovery of an "ontological condition" that absorbs and transcends both.

David M. Robinson, in "Thoreau, Modernity, and Nature's Seasons," offers his own take on Thoreau's literary tackling of seasonality. Robinson describes "two Thoreaus," the first one (like Granger's) decidedly antimodern in his resolute opposition to the social and economic transformations associated with historical "modernity" and the Industrial Revolution: see Thoreau's rantings against "degenerate times." But Robinson also emphasizes that "modernity" is characterized by "crucial shifts of consciousness," which Thoreau confronts and examines just as resolutely. In other words, if Thoreau was socially antimodern (as his writings seem to suggest), he was intellectually alert and attuned to the more advanced thinking of his time. As an intellectual, he chose not to adhere blindly to the standard wisdom or ideology of his time (the myth of progress, for one) but to envisage it critically. In this critique, the role of the intellectual is not to stand in systematic opposition to everything, but to create distance, or to distance oneself, from commonly accepted knowledge. Robinson emphasizes that knowledge, for Thoreau, was centrally *scientific* knowledge: although Thoreau lived and wrote mostly before Darwin published his *Origin of Species* in 1859, a crucial landmark in the scientific revolution, he participated fully in elaborating a mode of thinking whose decisive embodiment was Darwin's career. In this respect, as Robinson makes clear, Thoreau fully addressed the newer sense of humanity's embeddedness within natural cycles (a consequence of the current scientific revolution), which powerfully shattered human beings' centrality and primacy. Thus Thoreau was decidedly "modern"—ahead of his time—insofar as he contributed decisively to the emergence of environmental awareness, which he did by supporting a less anthropocentric worldview and countering the excesses of modernity. As Granger suggested as well,

antimodernity and modernity would thus be linked, and Robinson subtly identifies the ambivalent nexus of classic, genteel observation, and forward-looking
thinking. Furthermore, as Robinson emphasizes, far from being triumphant,
modernity was riddled with a sense of loss and even trauma in the face of a col-
lapsing worldview, a collapse that amounted to the end of metaphysics. In this
new, decentered world, while the place of humans was less secure, the need for
ethical responsibility was even more essential.

Randall Conrad, in "An Infinite Road to the Golden Age," offers a close
reading of a passage from the Journal in which Thoreau evokes the old Carlisle
road. Conrad's close reading deciphers and disentangles the various threads
and allusions that create the richly textured layering typical of Thoreau's prose.
He suggests that the old Carlisle road stands as an image of the antimodern refusal of commodification and Manifest Destiny, of the flight or escape from the
modern world, and of the desire for timelessness, all of which make Thoreau "an
antimodern social thinker." Conrad thus echoes Granger and Robinson, but,
even more deeply, Conrad simultaneously celebrates the power of the imagination and of poetic freedom in a "vivid prose poem" that is meant not so much as
a desperate celebration of escapism as an urge to maintain "mobility" (as Walls
argues in her essay) in a nonexploitative way. Imagination is what keeps us going and is thus essential fuel for life. The old Carlisle road is less an expression of
disgruntled pessimism and reaction than a metaphor for intellectual and poetic
alertness, crucial aspects of the way we situate ourselves in the world.

In part 2, "Thoreau and Philosophy," Thoreau's writings are addressed
through a variety of approaches, all linked to the philosophy of his time and to
current philosophical debates.

Joseph Urbas, in "'Being Is the Great Explainer': Thoreau and the Ontological Turn in American Thought," recovers an overlooked dimension of Transcendentalism, namely, its consistent turn away from epistemological skepticism and toward a metaphysics of ontological realism. Urbas seeks to displace,
or at least to qualify, the now predominant notion that Thoreau's modernity lies
in his interest in science and in his emphasis on epistemology; in Urbas's analysis, this focus has led Thoreau scholars to overemphasize Thoreau's anticipation
of postmodern epistemology (especially a conception of science as an activity
embedded in processes of social relations) at the expense of recognizing ontology, or the "science of being," as his primary concern. Accordingly, Urbas traces
the insistent presence in Transcendentalism of the themes of being, foundation,

ground, reality, or substance—a turn that may hardly seem "modern," but, as Urbas suggests, this stance, focusing as it does on life and living, prefigures the neopragmatist emphasis on experience as directly linked to being. Thoreau's return to a philosophical tradition predating Descartes (whose philosophy is commonly regarded as key to the emergence of modernity) does not, however, make him philosophically antimodern or nostalgically premodern. Instead, by emphasizing a metaphysical realism grounded in experience, Urbas seeks to reconcile ontology and epistemology: knowledge, in his reading, is not self-contained or self-referential but "knowledge of *what is*" in the fullest sense; it is *relational* (an insight approached, from different premises, by Walls) in the sense of relating the individual to "what is": knowledge "relates our being to Being."

Urbas's essay brings to the fore a craving for "contact" with reality (in Thoreau's word) that leaves aside any need for discursive analysis or, put differently, in which being subsumes knowing. The central role is then played by a rock-bottom, "permanent" reality that knowledge will never know and that may only be approached through discarding the pretensions of knowledge. Urbas's essay thus accounts for Thoreau's diffidence toward knowledge and celebration of "useful ignorance" and in so doing points, like Robinson, but, again, from different premises, to one of the roots of our modern environmental awareness. In his abiding sense of the world's ontological aloofness, Thoreau, like the other Transcendentalists, affirmed a sense of humanity's periphery to nature—thus recovering a different source for antianthropocentrism, one diametrically distinct from postmodernism's emphasis on language. Thus Urbas suggests that, although Thoreau's adherence to ontology would seem to be rather antimodern, it actually anticipates our own contemporary ontological turn in philosophy via a neopragmatist approach based on the idea that "truth here is contact with reality." It is this desire for being that accounts for the Transcendentalists' "search for a prose style consubstantial with being" and their preference for literary works that are as "vascular and alive" as their authors.

Henrik Otterberg, in "Character and Nature: Toward an Aristotelian Understanding of Thoreau's Literary Portraits and Environmental Poetics," complements Urbas's insistence on "the search for a prose style consubstantial with being" by suggesting how this notion bears on Thoreau's Journal. However, although they both share a wariness toward postmodern modes of thought, Otterberg leans toward the epistemological side—in a nutshell, if Urbas was on the side of Plato, Otterberg is on that of Aristotle. Indeed, in considering the Aristotelian dimension of Thoreau's thought, Otterberg paves the way for a reconsideration not only of the early Journal (seen as explicitly adhering to an Aristotelian fusion of art and character) but also of the late Journal (seen as oriented toward a recognition and representation of the laws of nature). Otterberg thus offers a way out of what he perceives as the misleading postmodern emphasis on discontinuities for their own sake: in accordance with the Aristotelian search for law through the aggregate of phenomena, the late Journal was geared to the elaboration of the "Kalendar" (which Kristen Case analyzes at length). According to Otterberg, Thoreau brings an Aristotelian sense of consistency and law to his understanding of both human and physical nature. As a consequence, the late Journal should be regarded not as a mere collection of discontinuous observations in which chance plays the leading part but as a deliberate enterprise geared toward the winnowing of discrete observations to produce and establish "facts" whose ultimate "representation" (a key term in Otterberg's analysis) is embodied in the Kalendar. The Kalendar amounts to a careful distillation of discrete events, just as individual character, as embodied by style, is a distillation of ordinary events: thus what Otterberg calls the "portrayal of nature" closely parallels the portrayal of human character in the writer's style. He thus emphasizes the programmatic dimension of the Journal, its control and deliberateness, rather than its spontaneity, which he regards as fundamentally illusory. In this perspective, Otterberg not only refuses to endorse the views of postmodern aesthetics but even hints that the postmodern emphasis on the discrete and the provisional is *the* antimodern stance. Far from contradicting Walls's emphasis on Humboldt's and Thoreau's search for empirical wholes, then, Otterberg adduces another philosophical tradition that supported and inspired Thoreau's quest for stable laws amidst the flux of phenomena. What relates Otterberg's analysis to ecocritical concerns is his suggestion that the elaboration of laws is more conducive to environmental awareness than the personal, individual, aesthetic enjoyment of discrete observations, thus turning his back on a romantic understanding of nature writing toward the Aristotelian tradition instead.

Bruno Monfort, in "Thoreau's Work on Myth: The Modern and the Primitive," analyzes the complex links existing between modernity and Thoreau's use of mythology, especially what is at stake in the modern use of ancient mythology. Modernity itself can become the object of a mythologizing process, as in Thoreau's analogy between the locomotive and the "winged horse" in *Walden*.

But Monfort also considers the way ancient mythology itself is used by Thoreau, in a situation of "belatedness" and "self-consciousness," to suggest that mythology embodies a form of "interconnectedness of the natural world with humanity's invention of it." He thus shows that mythological references point not to an antiquarian or antimodern stance but, on the contrary, to the "permanence" or timelessness of "the mostly anthropological function of mythopoeia." By this Monfort means that "myths are ultimately mere social-historical constructs that contribute to the emergence of what we call reality, which is not limited to the materiality of the world."

Christian Maul, in "'A Sort of Hybrid Product': Thoreau's Individualism between Liberalism and Communitarianism," draws on contemporary political and social theory to show how the "communitarian approach," as developed especially by Michael Walzer (and exemplified by his notion of the "connected critic"), can revive the Transcendentalist argument that individualist self-reliance and the collective demands of a harmonious society are not mutually exclusive but rather reinforce each other. Maul uses current debates over communitarianism to shed light on Thoreau's stance in relation to the historical and political context he lived in but also to show that Thoreau's searching approach, preoccupied as it was with toeing a line between two equally destructive options (absolute individualism vs. dissolution of the individual within society), anticipated modern developments in political science. Furthermore, Thoreau's "liberal communitarian" stance also had a literary counterpart, for his writing offered practical examples of how to counterbalance the evils of economic and social modernity, restoring the possibility of a healthy, harmonious society. Maul's Thoreau, who favors synthesis over division, is thus very different from Granger's detached, elitist critic; to Maul, Thoreau's deep wish was to serve democratic and communal ideals.

The essays that constitute our third and final part, "Thoreau, Language, and the Wild," all center on Thoreau's relationship to wild nature in its philosophical, scientific, and literary dimensions.

Dieter Schulz, in "Nature, Knowledge, and the Method of Thoreau's Excursions," draws a parallel between Thoreau's daily and literary practice of the excursion (arguably the central genre in his writings) and Hans Georg Gadamer's notion of "method," which literally refers to the idea of "following or accompanying something on its way." Like Walls, Schulz emphasizes relationality and the construction of wholes, but, instead of pointing to Humboldt, he traces and emphasizes the long line of thinkers, from the pre-Socratics to Heidegger and Gadamer, who all point to nature as a "cosmos" or "living whole." According to Schulz, "Thoreau's walks illustrate a notion of method that moves us back to the beginnings of Western thought." In that sense, Schulz considers a Thoreau who had nothing to do with Baconian scientific method (a separational practice characteristic of modern science) but instead favored a form of knowledge that is essentially relational. Schulz thus lays stress on Thoreau's participation in a pre- or antimodern tradition that runs from the ancient Greeks to the twentieth century. His Thoreau emphasizes "walking" as a connective practice, one conducive to a form of relational knowledge that has more to do with poetry than with science in a strict sense: walking, a kind of relational knowing, opens us to the world and enables us to eschew scientific dogmatism. Offering his own version of Thoreau's "vascularity," Schulz draws many parallels with current developments in science and the humanities: Jakobson and Waugh's "phonosemantics," Peirce's "iconicity," the antimechanistic and antideterministic brands of biology associated with the notions of "biosemiotics" and "autopoiesis." According to Schulz, if the openness of experience—perceived as essentially "dialogical"—is central to both the sciences and the humanities, the separation between these "two cultures" is also transcended.

Kristen Case, in "Thoreau's Radical Empiricism: The Kalendar, Pragmatism, and Science," focuses on a long-neglected aspect of Thoreau's career, his "Kalendar" project, which, building on Walls's pioneering exploration of Thoreau's relation to science, Case connects to the "empirical holism" of Alexander von Humboldt. Case also argues that the Kalendar anticipates major trends in contemporary science and philosophy, including pragmatism (which conceives of knowledge as "a mode of participation" [Dewey]) and Bruno Latour's science studies. Her emphasis on relational knowledge and on method and process corroborates Schulz's approach, although her focus is more decidedly epistemological, whereas Schulz connects Thoreau to a post-Heideggerian ontology. For instance, Case points to the way Thoreau's observations have contributed to the contemporary study of global warming, and she emphasizes ways that the Kalendar project foregrounds Thoreau's wide-ranging reconception of the human as part of nature (as also analyzed by Robinson). In this respect, her analysis connects particularly well to ecocriticism: Thoreau's practice fundamentally moves the lines, displaces the separation between human beings and nature, as "the entire project reflect[s] a desire to recontextualize the human."

She further argues that "Thoreau's late work enacts . . . a new conception of the human," one that no longer relies on the dichotomy of object/subject, as opposed to the earlier humanism associated with historical modernity. Case also considers the challenges that face literary scholars who study works such as the Kalendar and the Journal and calls for "a new attention to the various functions of writing and a particular engagement with writing as a way of tracing, recording, and strengthening relations." This is, she affirms, a fundamentally ecocritical project, a convergence that offers a way out of the notorious "two cultures" split—thus corroborating Schulz from different premises.

Michael Jonik, in "'The Maze of Phenomena': Perception and Particular Knowledge in Thoreau's Journal," complements Schulz and Case in his analysis of Thoreau's Journal. Like them, he focuses on Thoreau's sense of relation to the world, but Jonik sheds a sensibly different light on the subject. In the first place, he departs from Schulz in seeing Thoreau's relationality as a heritage of Kant's philosophy rather than as a departure from Enlightenment epistemology, thus reinforcing Walls's emphasis on Thoreau's continuity with the Humboldtian tradition and exemplifying Walls's notion of the "transjective." But he also offers a different approach from that of Case, who focuses on the way the Kalendar foregrounds "law," or at least generalization, a sense of the typical: Jonik, focusing on the Journal, brings to the fore Thoreau's passion for particularity and instancing, his ardent acknowledgment of "the resistant thingness of objects," which fuels his constantly renewed appetite for perception. Insofar as things resist being grasped, they also resist being captured by "universal laws," yielding a perception that is essentially poetic—even, in Jonik's words, "the rarest poetry." In this respect, Jonik comes close to Schulz's emphasis on truth at the expense of (scientific) method. While he thus regards Thoreau primarily as a poet (an aspect further analyzed by Specq), Jonik strikes a balance, describing Thoreau's work as "an attempt to see from both [the scientific and the poetic] points of view" and reaching "a point where the two intersect and mutually intensify yet remain unresolved." As a consequence, where others in this volume emphasize integration, Jonik insists on tension instead, a tension that is not productive of wholes but is nevertheless creative, as it keeps the perceiver forever active. Jonik also worries that critics tend to overemphasize visual perception and suggests that Thoreau adheres to an "ecological perception" that "takes into account the multiform richness and particularity of sensation presented to us by our mobile world," thus qualifying H. Daniel Peck's seminal analysis of Thoreau's Journal as premised on a search for "symmetry" through a primarily visual mode of knowledge and organization (see *Thoreau's Morning Work*). According to Jonik, "ecological perception is another way of describing [Thoreau's] poetic dwelling *with* particulars." While he is close to Schulz in his stress on Thoreau's relation to the ineffable, Jonik shows a greater sensitivity to the poetry and the poetics of Thoreau's writings, which are regarded not only as embodied philosophy but as supremely poetic creations.

François Specq, in "Poetics of Thoreau's Journal and Postmodern Aesthetics," complements both Case's and Jonik's approaches by focusing on the more writerly aspect of Thoreau's reconception of humanity's place in the physical world. Indeed, Case argues that the Kalendar and the Journal should be seen as partners rather than as competing projects and that both are "the richer for Thoreau's choice to let the traces of process remain." She also points to "a life still very much devoted to the uniquely human practice of writing." Specq echoes this statement and develops the idea that writing was ultimately Thoreau's primary activity, the one that connects his various interests and concerns. Specq's essay also answers Case's call for revising our way of reading when we are faced with "atypical" literary texts, those often associated with the phrase "nature writing." What, asks Specq, are the implications of Thoreau's sense that his Journal pioneered a new aesthetics? And of the conviction that, as historically situated readers, our reading of Thoreau's Journal today cannot but be impacted by our postmodern inheritance? Specq ultimately claims that, although our awareness of postmodern aesthetics opens up our literary appreciation of the Journal—and actually made possible its reemergence as an object for literary study—it would nevertheless be misleading to postmodernize this work. While Thoreau's Journal of the 1850s displays some of the central features of postmodern aesthetics, insofar as it is a work both adamantly nonhierarchical and nonteleological in which perception and representation are constantly destabilized, it nevertheless conveys to us the absoluteness of a world whose presence emerges or surges at the exact meeting point between its existence out there and human consciousness within.

David Dowling, in "Fraught Ecstasy: Contemporary Encounters with Thoreau's Postpristine Nature," brings out a different dimension of Thoreau's relation to historical modernity as he considers how Thoreau's denunciation of the environmental degradation resulting from crass materialism, and the accompanying demise of the divine, anticipates contemporary ecowriting as exemplified by Canadian novelist Douglas Coupland. Dowling suggests that both writers exemplify what Jordan Fisher Smith has called "nature noir." From this perspective, Thoreau displays a "protopostmodern sensibility," one that prefigures Coupland's environmentalist aesthetics. For both authors, nature appears as the locus of a search for spiritual regeneration, a search that inevitably stumbles upon the dramatic, disturbing impact of capitalist exploitation on the natural environment. Rather than skepticism or irony, however, what Dowling emphasizes in his reading of Thoreau is an unfailing faith in the possibility, even for human beings living in sweepingly abused environments, to nevertheless harbor hope and a sense of future regeneration. Dowling thus connects Thoreau to current debates on environmental justice even as he links him to the postmodern search for an alternative economy.

Thomas Pughe, in "Brute Neighbors: The Modernity of a Metaphor," focuses on the import and implications of Thoreau's metaphor of "neighborhood" with animals in *Walden*. He argues that Thoreau was aware of the ambiguous potential of anthropomorphic tropes with reference to animals, as they can amount either to symbolic appropriation or to critical distancing. However, his analysis of key passages from *Walden*, especially from the chapter "Brute Neighbors," suggests that for Thoreau animal tropes had a subversive dimension insofar as they questioned the separation between human and nonhuman beings. In this respect, Pughe's analysis complements Case's argument that Thoreau radically "recontextualizes" the human in accordance with a biocentric conception of the world, one that emphasizes nonanthropocentric interconnectedness. Like Case, Pughe thus explicitly connects his understanding of Thoreau to ecocriticism. Their theoretical backgrounds, however, are significantly different, as Pughe sees Thoreau as anticipating contemporary animal studies in their various guises (ethological studies and Derridian philosophy, in particular). Pughe describes Thoreau as consistently and decidedly trying to "reach beyond" the narrow limits of what makes humans human, a critical effort seen in his trope of "brute neighbors." Pughe's essay thus squarely situates itself within the pale of posthumanism. Compared with Case, his conviction that humans and animals share a "common dwelling" is not only physical but ontological, reflecting their respective situations within the pragmatist and the post-Heideggerian philosophical traditions.

Michel Imbert, in "'Tawny Grammar': Words in the Wild," also chooses, like Pughe, to interrogate Thoreau's use of animal tropes; but Imbert focuses more specifically on the darker undertones of the neighborhood trope, which Pughe only briefly considers. Whereas Pughe, building upon Elisabeth de Fontenay, foregrounds the possibility of "translating the language of beasts" as a way of conveying the sense of neighborliness of human beings and "nonhuman persons," Imbert, although he pursues similar modes of analysis, instead resolutely emphasizes the inexpressible, the unutterable, the untranslatable—in other words, the unassimilable—and in this sense, he echoes Jonik's emphasis on "the resistance of things." Imbert thus points to the "intractable otherness" of the animal, which he argues Thoreau regarded as a mirror image of the ungraspable nature within the human. Imbert relates this to a form of third language, situated outside, or rather prior to, both mother tongue and father tongue, which Thoreau calls "tawny grammar." Imbert accordingly explores what he perceives as a parallel between Thoreau's chasing of the loon and his description of the thawing sandbank, in which the attempt at capturing the wildness of language amounts to a desire for "the aboriginal language of the body," or wild language. Imbert concludes that the thawing sandbank passage "subtly adumbrates the modern eagerness to recapture and give utterance to some suppressed animality and the unspeakable otherness it figures," thus emphasizing an even more radical form of posthumanism than the one analyzed by Pughe, one that lays emphasis less on interconnectedness between the human and the nonhuman than on the humans' surrender of their all-mastering *logos* to the wildness of a nonhuman "tawny grammar."

ભ ભ ભ

Thoreau's writings, like crystals or water drops, refract the light of meaning according to how that light is given. The light of his own time is not the same as ours, but in both our historical moment and his, the unified language of the page breaks and fractures into a multiplicity of possible meanings. No one of our authors sees quite the same Thoreau; but every one of us sees a Thoreau who draws our attention across the old poles of humans and nature, epistemology and ontology, relational knowledge and absolute being, the social community and the self-reliant individual—the old poles that have constructed our philosophy as well as his. Yet Thoreau does not inscribe himself within these old and familiar polarities, which is why we each come to such different Thoreaus, even as we converge in so many ways. Instead, he points us to somewhere beyond, using knowledge that can be uttered to lead us to the brink of knowledge that cannot—at least, not yet. At this brink, we stop and gaze into the mist, trying to see farther. Thoreau's answer was to write that knowledge was like the lighting up of the mist by the sun, a phrase meant not to put an end to knowledge or to poetry or to philosophy but to point beyond what Derrida called "betrayals of repressed human possibilities" (*The Animal* 105) to other powers of reason, more comprehensive logics, more demanding responsibilities. We each of us, in our dialogues with each other, have come thus far: we hope that our conversations will enable you, our reader, to see still farther.

Part One

THOREAU AND
(NON)MODERNITY

LAURA DASSOW WALLS

Walking West, Gazing East

PLANETARITY ON THE SHORES
OF CAPE COD

THOREAU'S ESSAY "WALKING" has become one of his most canonical texts, and its ringing declaration, "in Wildness is the preservation of the world" (*Exc* 202), is the founding motto of the American environmental movement. *Cape Cod* is much less well known, perhaps because where "Walking" rings with triumphal declarations, *Cape Cod* is uneasy and disquieting. One enters Thoreau's last book through the scene of a shipwreck, and its pages are haunted by his morbid and graphic descriptions of dead bodies and living "wreckers" who see in corpses nothing beyond commodities. Yet these two works do not represent stages in a writer's evolution; they are exact contemporaries, written during the 1850s and published shortly after Thoreau's death. Nevertheless, taken together, they seem to inscribe, like pole and antipole, the antipodes of his thought. The same America that one erects and celebrates is in the other undermined and deconstructed, so thoroughly that the book's final sentence becomes its culmination and justification: "A man may stand there and put all America behind him" (*CC* 215).

Putting these two texts in relationship with each other asks for a set of tools different from those usually available to the literary critic. They share an excursive shape; or, to be more precise, one, *Cape Cod*, is an excursion, literally a long walk, while the other, "Walking," is a meditation that offers a theory of long walks and so seems to explain and justify the first. Their respective formats and topics suggest they be read not only together but in the "context" of travel literature or, more exactly, the literature of scientific exploration; that is, Thoreau modeled his travel repertoire not on the middle-class leisure activity of tourism but, putting on what he called his "bad-weather clothes" (*Exc* 101), on the rough-and-ready explorers who sought not self-cultivation but knowledge of the exterior unknown that, upon their returns from their various errands to various wildernesses, they could share with the world. Thoreau deliberately extends the genre of the scientific expedition to compel an *inner* exploration in tandem with the outer: as he asked in *Walden* (after reading the five large volumes narrating the Wilkes Expedition of 1838–42), "What does Africa,—what does the West stand for? Is not our own interior white on the chart?" (*W* 321). In the genre Thoreau is crafting, travel is a condition for thinking; that is, one *must* travel in the world in order to travel in the mind. In his classic study of Thoreau and travel writing, John Aldrich Christie noted that, for Thoreau, "geographic exploration became his most consistently used symbol for philosophic search" (265). True, except that for Thoreau exploration was more than just a "symbol," even as he insisted all nature must *be* as well as *mean*: as Thoreau asked in his first book (also a travel narrative), "Is not nature, rightly read, that of which she is commonly taken to be the symbol merely?" (*Wk* 382). So one must actually, really *move*. And movement, mobility, does not merely give access to a tourist's refined aesthetic sensibility. Thoreau means something risky, endangering, like the "sweet edge" of the scimitar when sun glimmers off both its sides (*W* 99), like the scimitar edge of a windswept beach, that sweet edge between life and death where one must face the fact of one's own mortal body cast up by the waves and reigning over the shore.[1]

The bulk of Thoreau's work takes the form of the excursion, but the genre is not limited to Thoreau or even to writings generally bracketed as travel literature, such as Lewis and Clark's westward adventures and Alexander von Humboldt's *Personal Narrative* of explorations through those other, more southern Americas. Melville is constantly inscribing excursions, for instance, to Typee or up the coast of Chile or down the Mississippi or around the world; Margaret Fuller's breakthrough occurred during, and by way of, her excursion to the Great Lakes; Poe's longest and greatest work, *The Narrative of Arthur Gordon Pym*, projects Thoreau's "white" interiors from the blank charts of scientific explorers to an Antarctic landscape that literalizes the nightmares of imperial conquest. Much of Washington Irving's writing is excursive, from "Rip van Winkle" (who travels in time as well as space) to *Tour on the Prairies* and *Astoria*, and Mark Twain took his readers down the Mississippi, through the Far West, and thence abroad. William Hickling Prescott wrote epic works of history tracing the military excursions of Spanish conquistadors across Mexico and

Peru; Hawthorne's eerie novel *The Marble Faun* could be set against *Cape Cod* as an excursion that puts all Europe behind him (and it's worth remembering that Hawthorne lobbied to go along on the Wilkes Expedition as its official historian); Louisa May Alcott made a Thoreauvian river excursion the crux of her novel *Moods*; and so on. The tension between worlds outer and inner, nature and language, wild and convention, the mortal challenge of real exploration and the prepackaged satisfactions of tourism runs through all these works. Each in its way proposes that in this voyage something quite large is at stake: the self, to be sure, but also that collective called "America," its shape and history and future, perhaps even the future (if there is to be one) of all humanity.

One could even venture that Thoreau's era was defined by the expedition, starting with Columbus; accelerating with the Spanish conquests; continuing with the Spanish explorations up the Pacific Coast from Tierra del Fuego to Alaska, the French traders and missionaries across Canada and scientific explorers across the South Pacific and Egypt, the British measuring India, the journeys to North America to discover, and claim, a continent. In these voyages, nature, discourse, and nation were fused, and the resulting empires reached just as far as (and no farther than) the collections and archives of scientific explorers. Nation and transnation form another uneasy tension: as Paul Giles has recently observed, "Antebellum American authors do not so much ground their work upon native soil as situate it on a highly charged and fraught boundary between past and present, circumference and displacement, and the challenge each individual writer faces is in mapping out a discrete location, in finding a space from which to speak" (107). Adding the excursive dimension to American literature reminds us how writing indeed becomes mapping, a discursive cartography driven by the urgent need to establish some stance among vectors that keep shifting and sliding into new permutations. Complex interrelations among peoples and cultures, nations and natures were unfolding all around Thoreau, as he and his neighbors, like everyone everywhere, were being forced to scale up their lives from local to global on the emerging networks of commerce, and knowledge, and power.

Works in this large and restless genre respond to questions set in four dimensions: mobility, planetarity, vascularity, transjectivity. These four intertwined strands can be teased apart for analysis only with some violence. Yet doing so provides two benefits. First, such an analysis sidesteps the dead-end dualisms that arrest understanding, as, for instance, between text and context, or nature and culture, or subject and object. Second, such an analysis puts "nature" and the various modes of traversal across, and habitations in, nature not at the periphery of "culture," as do virtually all other modes of literary analysis; instead, it works on the assumption that "nature" is no more separable from "culture" than oxygen is from life. This is a fundamentally ecological approach to reading that takes seriously the proposals made by philosophers, anthropologists, and cognitive scientists (starting with Humboldt in the early 1800s) that ideas as much as objects compose, or constitute, the material world and that objects as much as ideas manifest, or realize, thought.[2] Thus ideas are material and materiality is ideal, and the distinction between matter and idea is yet another dichotomy that must be recognized and bracketed. So, for instance, even as I struggle to articulate these "ideas," I work on a computer keyboard made warm by electricity that comes from a coal-burning power station; I print them out on paper that once grew as trees. My very thoughts have a carbon footprint, and in articulating them, I hope they will justify the resources I use by affecting the intertwined worlds of thought and matter, changing how others think and therefore how they materialize their thoughts in this world whose fate we share in common. It's all any writer hopes for, Thoreau included.

First, then, *it must be mobile.* In this literature, the narrator—and perhaps also the author herself—*moves*, and the world around the narrator/author also moves. Margaret Fuller, having removed herself to Niagara Falls, is there overwhelmed by "an incessant, an indefatigable motion," a "weight of perpetual creation" so overbearing and so inescapable that her nerves suffer and fray (*Summer* 3). Mobility may be fast, like Thoreau on the train to Montreal or Chicago watching the landscape blur into unsuspected patterns of change, or slow, like an afternoon's long saunter into a kairotic eternity. It may be global, like Hawthorne's excursion to Rome, or local, like Thoreau's excursion to Walden Pond. It may be physical, as when Thoreau shakes sand out of his shoes on the beach of Cape Cod, or mental, as when he reads the 170-plus books of travel documented by Christie—or when we read one book, *Walden*. It may be closed, held within the radius of a day's walking or the political boundaries of that entity we may name America, or it may be open ended, as when Thoreau gets lost returning to Walden from town after dark—"not till we have lost the world, do we begin to find ourselves, and realize where we are and the infinite extent of our relations" (*W* 171) — or when Whitman imagines a passage to India that ends in the infinitude of boundless cosmic space.

Second, *it must be planetary*. Mobility takes the traveler from one local place to the next. As I write I hear the street traffic in Lyon, France, which sounds exactly as it did awhile before in Columbia, South Carolina, and as I remember it sounding longer ago from my apartment in urban Seattle. The global is always local at every point; there is nowhere that is not somewhere in particular. Travel across the globe means not moving "up" to some privileged vantage that transcends place but through, crossing many places, a movement across the solid breadth of the earth's surface that is lost in the word "global." As Gayatri Spivak observes, "The globe is on our computers. No one lives there." By contrast, "the planet is in the species of alterity, belonging to another system; and yet we inhabit it, on loan" (72). Hence Spivak proposes the word "planetarity" to name this planetary other that we, strangely, inhabit.[3] Movement that engages with such planet-thought induces the need for *comparison*: while in France, I am constantly comparing it with the United States, from the sounds of sirens (in one a bimodal song, in the other a wobbling wail), to the look of the houses, to birds familiar and unfamiliar, and to the sounds of languages. I grasp for navigational markers: even as my plane landed in Paris, it dropped through clouds that bore the very look of French impressionism.

For in such strangeness I easily get lost, and thus I must constantly face the problem of *navigation*, how to orient myself. To do so, I must scale up. To find my way around the neighborhood, I reach for a map of the city; to seek the lost cathedral of Cluny, I reach for a map of the region; to understand why twilight in Lyon lingers so late into the evening, I reach for a map of the planet. Alterity has forced me to become a planetary thinker, moving up and down across scale levels. If I make such reorienting gestures of comparison a habit of thought, soon every object in my field of vision accumulates its cognates all around the world, and nothing comes singly or simply. Everything comes bearing traces of something somewhere else, rather as Thoreau's New England neighbors come to him bearing traces of the Brahmins in India who, according to British reports, inflict upon themselves unspeakable penances. By following this trajectory, Thoreau soon is scaling up from his one individual life, to his neighbors' many lives, to the general dilemmas of an intellectual living and thinking in a capitalist economy, and finally to the abstracted entity of "Economy" (the title

of the first chapter in *Walden*), the highest scale level of all. Even while Thoreau
hoes his beans, he reminds himself that the star that lights his labor "illumines
at once a system of earths like ours" (*W* 10)—planetary thinking gone stellar.
As he leans out the window one night, he experiences "something invigorat-
ing in this air which I am peculiarly sensible is a real wind blowing from over
the surface of a planet" (*PJ* 7: 309). Planetarity means never losing sight of the
sometimes surprising extent of your relations.

Scale levels are temporal as well as spatial, and, indeed, one of the fascina-
tions of nineteenth-century science was the way geology had learned to loop
together space and time, such that natural objects assemble temporal layers.
Things become legible as timescapes: as Humboldt said of mountains, "Their
form is their history" (*Cosmos* 1: 72). Thoreau learns to read the form of the forest as a stratigraphic history extending back for hundreds of years; Humboldt
moves at ease across temporal scale levels from the immediate lived instant, to
the span of a lifetime, to the historical, to the geological, to the cosmic, jumping
among them so as to destabilize linear flow and dizzy the uninitiated reader.
With practice, Thoreau becomes equally adept: "Time is but the stream I go
a-fishing in," he says in *Walden* (98). At Walden, one can dip up here an Indian
arrowhead, there a locomotive, elsewhere the cellar of a freed slave. Even so,
a few miles from Lyon, one can stand by the chapel of the monks of Berzé-la-
Ville, built in the twelfth century, and watch the high-speed TGV train to Paris
arrow by: with one eye trace a delicate fresco manufactured here in this village
a millennium ago, with the other track the sleek streak of railroad cars manufactured yesterday in the nearby town of Belfort. Time is laminar, it never displaces, it only adds more layers, more folds. In Canada, Thoreau discovered medieval feudalism alive and well; today we can fly to East Africa and admire the
allegedly Paleolithic lifestyle of tribal Masai, then, should our car break down,
borrow from one of those same young Masai a mobile phone. Planet-thought
asks us never to reduce all levels to one level. There are great and important
differences between the Romanesque chapel and the TGV train. One used to be
an important supply station on the medieval network of European Catholicism,
and from its enduring walls you can ponder the formation and maintenance of
modern global networks of capital. The other will transmit you to the ends of
the earth at a speed that makes connection almost instantaneous but that makes
the chapel itself almost invisible: look fast!—and it's already gone. New proper-
ties emerge across different speeds and scale levels, as Henry Adams recognized

when he meditated on the Virgin and the Dynamo. Thoreau learned this too: he might have wanted the ocean to be nothing but a larger Walden, but when he put this notion to the test, he allowed the ocean to teach him difference.

Third, *it must be vascular*. It must, that is, find a means to connect across such distances in space and time, such differences in scale levels. The text we read, if we are to read it at all, let alone read it together in concert, must find a way to stay alive. It must generate and sustain a living network all along the lengths from its creation to our translation, or it will die. A canonized text such as *Walden* has thrived by creating, with a great deal of help across several generations, a strong and vital network in bookstores and universities and academic presses and conferences worldwide; at the heart of that vascular network is the book Thoreau wrote, beating life and energy into it.[4] Curiously, because Thoreau succeeded so well in linking his book with his place, Walden Pond, the pond itself also functions as the heart of its own living vascular network, as a busy state park, as a pilgrimage site, as a symbolic center for a certain sort of cultural work. Its form is its history indeed: writing as cartography loops together temporal sequence and spatial simultaneity. The map Thoreau created for "The Pond in Winter" is the nexus for this looping, for in this cartographic gesture, Thoreau entwined physical space and historical place together with his brief moment in the pond's timescape by means of a discursive "space" in a text, a book that, thanks to its superb portability, can weave all of us together in imagination and, on occasion, in actuality. The surface of the pond, the surface of all nature, becomes a hieroglyph composed of folded layers of time and scale.

Finally, *it must be transjective*. This is an ugly word, but we need a way to designate what Thoreau called the space "*between*" the separating poles of "objective" and "subjective." As he said in his Journal, "I think that the man of science makes this mistake, and the mass of mankind along with him: that you should coolly give your chief attention to the phenomenon which excites you as something independent on you, and not as it is related to you. The important fact is its effect on me. . . . With regard to such objects, I find that it is not they themselves (with which the men of science deal) that concern me; the point of interest is somewhere *between* me and them (*i.e.* the objects)" (*J* X: 164–65). Pointing to that space "somewhere *between*" allowed Thoreau to conceive of knowledge as relational, that is, as existing only in the mutual relationship between knower and known; in effect, subject and object become mobile, capable of switching places, each swerving to know the other—like Thoreau vowing,

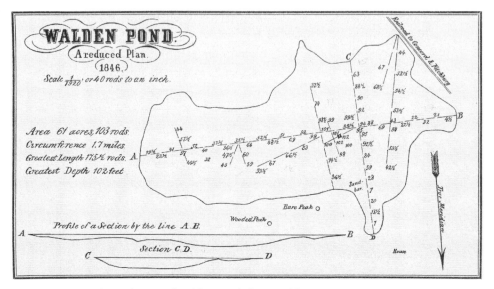

FIGURE 1. Thoreau's Map of Walden Pond, from *Walden*.

at Walden, to "know beans" and learning that in the iterations of knowing, the boundaries between object and subject collapse: "It was no longer beans that I hoed, nor I that hoed beans" (*W* 159). Or in the Maine woods, setting out to know his Indian guide Joe Polis and discovering that it is instead Polis who knows Thoreau, rather too well. The journey can get on only when the two agree to a reciprocal exchange of knowledge, on equal terms. Relational knowledge destabilizes the most basic modern dualism of all, that separating subject from object, putting epistemology itself into question.

In *Walden*'s most iconic moment, Thoreau, canoeing on the pond, comes across a loon. He pursues, the loon dives, he pursues again, the loon rises, laughs, dives, and the two engage for an hour in "a pretty game, played on the smooth surface of the pond, a man against a loon." Thoreau's language insists on the reciprocity of the game that is being played: man and loon gaming each other, each thinking to outwit the other, each engaging the other, the loon laughing all the while. It is not the man but the loon who finally chooses to end the game, uttering one of his "long-drawn unearthly howl[s]" as if "calling on the god of loons to aid him," and it is the loon's god who responds, not the human's, raising the wind and the rain that drive Thoreau off the pond, leaving the loon "disappearing far away on the tumultuous surface" (*W* 233–36). This small episode is paradigmatic: first, it displays both man and loon, subject and object, in motion, mobilized in a way that confuses which is which. As Thoreau becomes object to the loon's scrutiny, the two describe a system unfolding on the smooth surface of the pond, turning the pond into a text on which a certain game is inscribed, a certain kind of *poiesis*, or making: not a hunt to the death but an interspecies aesthetic play. Second, the fact of the pond introduces the problem of scale level: here is a microcosm. By contrast, Thoreau's source text, *Moby-Dick*, is a macrocosm: Thoreau's hour on a pond, Ahab's lifetime on an ocean. A loon, a white whale. An episode, an epic. How are these two scales related? What interconnections ring them together?

Third, the fact that the loon is an actual bird, not merely an actual *species* of bird but a single, real, physical, living bird, is insisted upon.[5] There is here one singular bird (*that* loon), one historical pond (*that* one, Walden), one biographical human (*that* man, Henry D. Thoreau). These three entities knot together a material ecology whose reality is necessary to the meaning: take away any part of the material ontology of any one of the three, and the poetic system collapses. But the system is not limited to the pond, the hour, or the page. The three in movement form a node in a larger vascular system that depends, for meaning to circulate, on the specific reality of each element of that system and their specific interactions. There exists here no break between the "real" and the "ideal," "particular" and "general," "textual" and "material," "knowing" and "being." Each pole is seamlessly intergraded and interwrapped with the other, all along the scale: neither term can leave the other behind. It becomes clear that the apparent dualism they describe—let's call it "man" and "animal"—is produced by a certain set of operations performed in view of various interests. Depending on our own interests, we may amplify the objectivity of the loon (go to Peterson's bird guide to examine typical plumage patterns, locate a recording of loon calls, investigate the migratory and nesting patterns of loons across New England), or of the man, or of the pond; or we may amplify the essential ideality of the encounter (after all, it is a text, not a pond, that we hold in our hands) and emphasize that this symbolic encounter takes place wholly in the subjectivity of the mind, first Thoreau's, then our own; his confession to us reifies his own subjectivity, our deliberations affirm our own. But on neither end, not that of object nor that of subject, can the opposing term be wholly ignored. Thus to begin, in Cartesian fashion, by defining the opposition, the essential duality, and then seeking the terms that complete it is to close out Thoreau's space between, the middle ground—the pond, the page—on which this scene is unfolding. We have here not an opposition but a concatenation, which is why we must bracket the antique and failing division between "objective" and "subjective," together with all the ways it inscribes modernity into our thinking, before we even begin to think. These mirroring terms, so freighted with the angst of the nineteenth century, carry far too heavy an ideological load to be useful in the twenty-first. Thoreau's play of gazes and minds, human to nonhuman and back, demands that we think transjectively, throw our attention beyond the mirror, or, better, smash the mirror and try to imagine a system in which man, loon, canoe, pond, wind, rain, railroad are all gathered, a temporal knot, a fact that knots together the whole world for just that one instant, poised in the tumult.

What I would like to claim here is a new sort of "green machine," a heuristic for reading productively at least a certain range of literature. "Mobility" brings to our reading the physical constraints of *passage*, that is, transport from one place to some other place, always through some material medium, on the ground, in the water, by air; and the accompanying changes of "scene" that are always much more than scenery, for they are as much natural as cultural, as much lin-guistic as material, and not background or silent channels or intermediaries but active and demanding mediators. A planetary perspective emplaces literature in the midst of ecologic relations, which function not as an outside "context" within which we read the "text" (I'm afraid I can no longer believe in "text" and "context") but as a field in which multiple interacting elements bear an integral relationship with each other. Literature becomes a mode of mobility, of moving around among worlds, speaking for or "articulating" within a complex ecological matrix of varying scale levels, from local through global to cosmic, or from personal and limited (say, a writer's notebook) to a network of publishers, libraries, bookstores, and readers. The vascular dimension might pay particular attention to the material circulations of writer, reader, and book in the way of, for instance, the recent work of David Dowling and Leon Jackson; Jackson's resituating of literary professionalism to what he calls "authorial economies" represents an important paradigm shift here.[6] This shift toward tracing social/material/textual economies is very much in concert with Thoreau's insistence, in *Walden*, on the intimate interplay among mental, moral, and physical econo-mies in the most literal and material of ways: food, clothing, shelter, fuel. Finally, and perhaps most important of all, transjectivity returns to nature its voice, restoring it from silent backdrop to active and noisy agent, like the screeching jays and barking squirrels in Thoreau's essay "The Succession of Forest Trees,"[7] or the trails and arrowheads of Walden's woods that give voice to those "un-chronicled," hence otherwise voiceless, nations of Indians who once lived and hunted there. Or if one wants to move to other authors, consider Melville's silent but extremely articulate White Whale, James Fenimore Cooper's vast and brooding forest, or—to switch genres—the natural scientists who bespeak the glacial history of Walden Pond, or who have recently, and shockingly, translated to the rest of us what Thoreau's plants have to say about climate change: a third of the species Thoreau chronicled at Walden have disappeared from the pond, with another third about to vanish.[8]

This proposed heuristic helps elucidate the range of Thoreau's writings, the bulk of which—his Journal, his Indian notebooks, his maps and drawings and surveys, his Kalendar or phenological charts—are not literary "works" and so resist being read by more conventional literary tools. Yet these writings show themselves to be highly mobile, gleefully planetary, unusually useful in reveal-ing the working machinery of vascularity, and dizzyingly transjective; they play energetic and important roles across all four of my dimensions. I believe my heuristic brings them back to visibility, even centrality, in Thoreau's canon. But here I will instead use my four dimensions to address the puzzle presented by the more literary works with which I opened, "Walking" and *Cape Cod*. How can we understand their radically different premises and outcomes, especially given that they came into existence together?

Both are, of course, texts about mobility. "Walking" is a manifesto on the transformational power of walking when practiced not as a mere means of trans-portation or exercise but as "the enterprise and adventure of the day" (*Exc* 189). *Cape Cod* gives us an extended instance of that transformational power. Both essays move ostentatiously across scale levels, although in different manners: "Walking" via a moral absolutism that declares the triumph of the American master-narrative, turning a day's walk into an epic reenactment of America's westward manifest destiny; *Cape Cod* by a peculiar particularism that desta-bilizes all such reckoning and concludes by exploding epic destinies entirely. Both create vascular networks, "Walking" via the tracery of material acts on the landscape and by contributing its thesis ("in Wildness is the preservation of the world" [*Exc* 202]) to American environmental ideology, which, through the agency of the Wilderness Society and the Sierra Club, turned it into a defining motto: this is a text with long legs indeed. But there is one telling difference. Only *Cape Cod* is transjective. That is, "Walking" is characterized by a blithe, even smug, celebration of the American star of empire; for all the beauty of its language about the wild, by containing this language within a nationalist frame, it turns back any viewpoint beyond its own.[9] By contrast, *Cape Cod* is riddled throughout with multiple viewpoints, myriad perspectives and moods that pluralize, carnivalize even, any singularity of perspective. If "Walking" affirms America as Nature's Nation, *Cape Cod* systematically undermines and undercuts every certainty. In the one, the Wild is mapped onto the West, America's cardinal direction; in the other, the planetary ocean, that "wilderness reaching round the globe," mocks our cardinal directions and nibbles at the base of all our foundations, from piers and ports to history and knowledge.

"Walking" begins by advertising the moral courage of the heroic "Knight" or "Walker Errant" who spends four hours at least, daily, in touch with his "senses" via a dispensation from heaven that entitles him to become a "Saunterer," or "*Sainte-terrer*," in quest to reconquer the "holy land" from the hands of the "Infidels," or those who do not, like Thoreau, believe in nature, "in the forest, and in the meadow, and in the night in which the corn grows" (*Exc* 185, 202). Who do not, that is, believe in "the Wild" as "the preservation of the world," a wild that Thoreau associates with both the great civilizing movement to the American West and, confusingly, with swamps and deserts and oceans, bleak and dreary places "whose glance no civilization can endure" (*Exc* 202). Such places can be found even in the Atlantic-facing neighborhood of Concord, and Thoreau is pleased that the ten-mile radius of a day's walking should coincide so perfectly with the precise extent of land he needs, narrow enough to know well but also wide enough to surprise. Yet some places are better than others: famously, Thoreau directs his walks, when left to his own devices, to the west-southwest, for "the future lies that way to me, and the earth seems more unexhausted and richer on that side. . . . Eastward I go only by force; but westward I go free" (*Exc* 195–96). In a flagrantly universalizing gesture, he declares, without any apparent irony, that "something like this is the prevailing tendency of my countrymen. I must walk toward Oregon, and not toward Europe. And that way the nation is moving, and I may say that mankind progress from east to west" (*Exc* 196). Thus, although earlier in the essay he asserts that where he walks has no name, let alone no national name ("You may name it America, but it is not America" [*Exc* 192–93]), here he trumpets the superiority of America as the direction of progress, where the moon is larger, the heavens higher, the stars brighter. The West becomes the locus of the American mission to civilize the wild with "the bush-whack—the turf-cutter, the spade, and the bog-hoe," weapons by which the farmer "displaces the Indian" and "redeems the meadow," earning land by a right denied to the poor and feeble Indians, who lack the wit and skill to follow the European's westward star of empire (*Exc* 206–7).

In *Cape Cod*, Thoreau moves from nation to planet. First, he violates his principle of the ten-mile radius by taking the train to a new site—one that he accessed, notably, via modern technology and that he chose by looking, also notably, at a map; via this upward shift in scale level, Thoreau was able to judge that there must be a good thirty miles of "uninterrupted" beach on the outside of the cape north of Eastham. This move allows him to make a further dramatic shift in scale level, from the quiet shore of a cozy neighborhood lake to the noisy beach of a world ocean. Thoreau registers this shift in several ways. At one point he suggests, rather hopefully, that "the ocean is but a larger lake" (*CC* 98), involving him in no very great transformation; but this hope is shattered in the opening chapter, "The Shipwreck," which lands him on a strand littered with the remains of the brig *St. John*, which had wrecked in a storm two mornings before. Thoreau arrived in time to watch the collected bodies, "twenty-seven or eight in all"—about a quarter of the lives lost—being nailed into coffins while other bodies were still washing ashore. Many were never found. He notes that he witnessed "no signs of grief, but there was a sober dispatch of business which was affecting." He, however, seems little affected; his own emotional state is sober, businesslike, even clinical and detached: he notes rather coldly that "I saw many marble feet and matted heads . . . and one livid, swollen and mangled body of a drowned girl" (*CC* 5). Yet colder still appear the actions of the "wreckers," professionals who claimed everything of value in the jetsam washed ashore, and the seaweed collectors, who untangled their harvest from dead bodies and bits of torn clothing: "Drown who might, they did not forget that this weed was a valuable manure. This shipwreck had not produced a visible vibration in the fabric of society" (*CC* 7). Thoreau implicates himself here, for he, too, is a wrecker, gathering up the spectacle for profit (he even playfully claims a few trivial objects by crossing sticks over them [*CC* 91–92]), registering his own lack of feeling before going on with, like the rest, no visible vibration in the fabric of his society.

But this is, as the reader soon realizes, untrue. The "vibration" resonates more and more, strengthening until it shakes the text entirely apart. The Atlantic is not, after all, merely a larger lake. The differences that emerge as Thoreau scales upward are profound and startling on many levels. The first is sensual and immediate: the "incessant" "dash and roar of the waves" unnerves Thoreau just as Niagara's huge voice unnerved Fuller, with such a "tumult" as to drown out his own voice (*CC* 100, 51). The inhumanity of a nature that would kill so casually evokes emotion too deep to register in any superficial way, as when Thoreau remarks that "a man can attend but one funeral in the course of his life, can behold but one corpse" (*CC* 9). His tone seems dismissive, but readers aware of Thoreau's biography will recognize his cryptic signal: this book, too, like *A Week*, memorializes the death of his brother John in Henry's arms, another "St. John," another shipwreck that, undermining at their outset the two brothers' great hopes and plans together, shadowed Henry's remaining career. Biographically informed readers will also be aware that almost exactly a year after his survey of the wreck of the *St. John*, Thoreau was dispatched to locate, unsuccessfully, the body of Margaret Fuller, shipwrecked with her family in a hurricane off New York's Fire Island. All he found was a rag from the coat of her husband, the marquis d'Ossoli, from which Thoreau cut a button. Hence his conclusion, in the face of these multiplied corpses, casts himself in the proleptic role he seems to imagine for another: "I saw that the beauty of the shore itself was wrecked for many a lonely walker there, until he could perceive, at last, how its beauty was enhanced by wrecks like this, and it acquired thus a rarer and sublime beauty still" (*CC* 10). This insight, that nature forces the survivor to wrest from death an existential beauty, could be applied to all his work after the death of his brother, including *Walden*; but articulating this terrible truth required the tremendous scale shift from kettle pond to world ocean. From its shores alone Thoreau can feel himself on "the highway of nations," watching "the sea nibbling voraciously at the continent" (*CC* 12).

Other differences from Walden Pond emerge as Thoreau walks the sands of the cape itself: scale levels literally shift and collide, and he loses the ability to gauge distance and size. When he first strikes the beach and looks out at the water, he is amused by the fact that "the smallest objects floating on it appeared indefinitely large" (*CC* 52). When he returns to the beach, the same observation recurs, now joined with the book's opening imagery to deepen the ominous vibrations: "Objects on the beach, whether men or inanimate things, look not only exceedingly grotesque, but much larger and more wonderful than they actually are." Heaps of rags appear like "bold and rugged cliffs," and the relics of one lone human body "had taken possession of the shore, and reigned over it as no living one could, in the name of a certain majesty which belonged to it" (*CC* 84–85). Amidst all this death there is also life on the cape—this scimitar blade of land edging the continent—although this life too confuses, is anomalous and monstrous. The voices of birds sound not sweet and earthly but, gull voices, like "some vibrating metal . . . as if one had rudely touched the strings of the lyre, which ever lies on the shore; a ragged shred of ocean music tossed aloft on the spray" (*CC* 55). The sea clam he eats tastes savory but makes him sick to his stomach. He reaches to take up bizarre anomalous creatures such as the "beautiful sea jellies," but they cannot be held without slithering away "like quicksilver" (a nice allusion to Emerson's "lubricity of objects" in "Experience"). What right, wonders Thoreau, "has the sea to bear in its bosom such tender things as sea-jellies and mosses, when it has such a boisterous shore, that the stoutest fabrics are wrecked against it? Strange that it should undertake to dandle such delicate children in its arms" (*CC* 54). No Walden Pond this: one day placid, on the next this same ocean will play with the vessels of ships and commerce "like sea-weed, distend them like dead frogs, and carry them about, now high, now low, to show to the fishes, giving them a nibble. This gentle Ocean will toss and tear the rag of a man's body like the father of mad bulls, and his relatives may be seen seeking the remnants for weeks along the strand" (*CC* 98).

What can we do with texts at such apparent odds with each other? One reeks of satisfaction in the face of providential progress, the other breathes peril and confusion in the face of anarchic energies. Paired, these two texts face each other like two opposite compass points: walking west from Walden points to the Future, Oregon, Nature, the land, myth; gazing east from Cape Cod points to the Past, Europe, Culture, the ocean, history. In one direction, a unified teleology underwrites the narrative of America; in the other, a pluralized teleology undermines the very existence of America. Given these two cardinal directions, West and East, one could fill in the rest of Thoreau's compass rose: to the north, "Ktaadn" and the Maine woods, with their own wild, anarchic energies, thence to Canada, land of Frederick Douglass's North Star and the more truly free,[10] which paradoxically also houses medieval feudalism and a militarized nation-state whose soldiers have had all the self-culture drilled out of them. To the south, slavery, the land of cotton and whips, whose commercial economy does not stay anchored in the South but penetrates Massachusetts itself and undermines the freedoms for which England had supposedly founded *New* England. That is, complexly, "West" orients "*South*west" as it becomes contaminated by southern expansionist manifest destiny; "East" orients "*North*east" as it is braced by the wild energy that will scour a corrupting America clean as the rocks on which the *St. John* foundered.[11] In "Walking," the national teleology is compulsively reiterated. In *Cape Cod*, it is deconstructed from the Puritan founding fathers onward: Thoreau acidly remarks that the Pilgrims, when told by the Indians that "there was not any who owned" the land, "appear to have regarded themselves as Not Any's representatives" and henceforth made good their claim. As he adds, presciently, Indians may yet knock on the door of the White House someday to assert their claim; "At any rate, I know that if you hold a thing unjustly, there will surely be the devil to pay at last" (*CC* 33).

That is, not only does wild nature nibble at human certainties; so do the records of history itself. Thoreau's antiquarian research into the cape turns up an unsuspected French prehistory, one that predates the English and that the English have overwritten. As he writes, "the Englishman's history of *New* England commences, only when it ceases to be, *New* France" (*CC* 183).[12] A long discursion into this French history, so effectively silenced by the English, encourages Thoreau (himself of French descent) to "consider what stuff history is made of,—that for the most part it is merely a story agreed on by posterity" (*CC* 197)—that is, of course, by *American* posterity, in this land so riddled with contestation and so repeatedly bisected by victory and defeat. One is myth, the other history: where the mythic certainty of "Walking" celebrates the triumph of the West, the historical narratives of *Cape Cod* destabilize not just one particular narrative but narrativity itself, calling into question the very act of writing history. Literally so: Thoreau's contemporary, the nationalist historian George Bancroft, turns out to be mistaken, which means, as Bradley Ray King says, that the Puritan "errand into the wilderness" is really *multiple* "errands," each one resting on its own past and projecting its own future. Pluralizing the "myth" of America in this way suggests that Thoreau can, standing on Cape Cod, envision multiple Americas—perhaps even one that would, in less than 150 years, elect a black president with an African name and Muslim ancestors.[13]

How important was it, on Cape Cod, to be facing eastward toward Europe? That it was *Irish* laborers who washed ashore in such numbers may suggest an American continent actively weeding out foreigners, like a border patrol policing its boundaries, but it is also true that the American continent weeded out its own native daughter Margaret Fuller in the same way as she was returning from Europe, having, indeed, "put all America behind her." For Fuller's republican partisanship in the Italian Revolution of 1848 led her to envision a future led not by young *America*, which to her dismay had stood resolutely on the sidelines rooting for the forces of oppression rather than freedom, but by young *Europe*, a revolutionary movement whose energies still vibrate across the planet today. Cardinality is, again, confused. And more, by facing eastward, Thoreau also faces, as in *Walden*, an Asia across the Pacific Ocean as well, a trajectory that paradoxically lands him on the far Pacific shore, the strange mirror of the Atlantic. As Thoreau remarks in his conclusion (once again using maps to scale up), no doubt "good walking" could also be found in present-day Washington State, from the Columbia River's mouth to Cape Flattery at the opening of the Strait of Juan de Fuca—a beach that is still, as Thoreau puns, "a wild, rank place, and there is no *flattery* in it" (*CC* 213, 147).[14] I have walked this wild, rank beach and can testify that its wrecks and brutal beauty, and the Pacific Northwest's pluralized and confusing histories, are, as Thoreau suspected, a precise analogue of his fierce Atlantic. Recall Thoreau's planetary meditation: "The ocean is a wilderness reaching round the globe, wilder than a Bengal jungle, and fuller of monsters, washing the very wharves of our cities and the gardens of our seaside residences" (*CC* 148–49). Even, it turns out, the wharves of Walden Pond, which he had once judged to be "a good port and a good foundation" for his own business enterprises (*W* 21).

So the "wild" both separates these two texts and brings them together. The dismal and quaking swamp of "Walking" escapes the bounds of this text's nationalism to become the dismal and shifting sands of Cape Cod. Swamps and sands make for uneasy ground, a "littoral" zone that is, as Thoreau noted, the seat of life, of generation, "the laboratory of continents" (*CC* 100). Thoreau's language here links swamp and beach to the rocks of Mount Katahdin, where amidst "the hostile ranks of clouds" he found himself in "a cloud-factory,— these were the cloud-works, and the wind turned them off done from the cool, bare rocks" (*MW* 64). In these landscapes, swamp and ocean and mountaintop, he is—we are—in over our heads, dealing with what in "Ktaadn" he calls "Titanic" forces that look upon humans with contempt and threaten to drain "some part of the beholder, even some vital part," through the "loose grating of his ribs as he ascends. . . . Vast, titanic, inhuman Nature has got him at disadvantage, caught him alone, and pilfers him of some of his divine faculty" (*MW* 64). Or as he says of Cape Cod, that "vast *morgue*" in this "wild, rank place": "There is naked Nature,—inhumanly sincere, wasting no thought on man, nibbling at the cliffy shore where gulls wheel amid the spray" (*CC* 147). Or, finally, in "Walking": "Here is this vast, savage, howling Mother of ours, Nature lying all around, with such beauty, and such affection for her children, as the leopard" (*Exc* 213). Nature the leopard mother, the loving predator, the animal other that subtends and deconstructs all our human polarities. Here beyond all reckoning lies hope in "the wild and dusky knowledge—*Gramática parda*—tawny grammar—a kind of mother wit derived from that same leopard" (*Exc* 214); and here also lies despair. In bitter summation, Thoreau offers, in *Cape Cod*, the spectacle of the so-called charity houses that dot the strand and pretend to offer shelter to the shipwrecked. Thoreau and his walking companion, Ellery Channing, shivering in the cold wind, really could use some shelter, but the charity house they find is, of course, nailed shut. In a scene worthy of Stephen Crane, Thoreau squints through a knothole in the door and sees nothing within but some stones, wads of wool, and an empty fireplace. Looking into "the very bowels of mercy," he finds "not bread but a stone"; in that "night without a star," there is no planetary view, no humanity, no cosmos but "Night or Chaos" and "the wreck of all cosmical beauty there within" (*CC* 60). Thoreau does not make the parallel explicit, but the man who wrote a book about building a house was asking a difficult question of his own work: was his house at Walden Pond like this charity house on Cape Cod? Full of humanitarian promise but finally empty and heartless, no shelter, no food, no fuel or matches, no light, the cosmical wreck of humanity?

Of course, he hoped for better for his own charity house. As he tells us, there was no lock on the door of his Walden shelter, and the shelter he built in prose, too, is hardly nailed, shuttered, and dark but is thrown open to all—so open that it literally turns inside out, its furniture resting on the open ground, plants twining around the legs of his desk, a "beautiful housekeeping" that erases the polarities between indoors and out (*W* 38). In "Walking," Thoreau imagines a still more open house, one deep in the pines and oaks, belonging to a family who recline on sunbeams and whose coat of arms is a lichen (*Exc* 218). In Montreal, he praises the Catholic cathedrals that seem to him a forest turned outside in, leading him to propose that "our forests are such a church, far grander and more sacred" (*Exc* 89). In *Cape Cod*, the grim, dark house on the beach is lost and abandoned, the vascular network that supplied it broken, the earnest instruction book that offers to guide us to it a parody of his own *Walden*—but our *Walden*, far from abandoned, is in good repair to this day, well supplied and abundantly furnished with readers and scholarship such as this, open to all, with doorways on every continent, translated into a plurality of languages, sitting right on those railroad tracks (as his map of the pond documents) that encircle the globe. But this is not the work of one lone individualist writer but of thousands who labored to build the tracks that lead still more readers to Walden's house, where the quietly desperate may seek shelter for a season and, repaired themselves, perhaps join the ranks of track repairers working everywhere and at all hours to keep the lines open, the doors flung wide to all.

The answer to the puzzle of how, finally, one might link such disparate and contradictory yet simultaneous works as "Walking" and *Cape Cod* lies in Thoreau's suggestion in "Walking" about the nature of his movement. "The outline which would bound my walks, would be, not a circle, but a parabola, or rather like one of those cometary orbits, which have been thought to be non-returning curves, in this case opening westward, in which my house occupies the place of the sun" (*Exc* 195–96).[15] If one adds Cape Cod to Thoreau's parabolic figure as the *other* case opening *east*ward, one might arrive at an ellipse, that is, an orbiting ovoid figure with *two* foci, one the snug harbor of his house, one the wild beach fronting the world ocean. This moves Thoreau's philosophy of knowledge in the direction of Michel Serres, who notes that Kepler "describes the planets as circulating in an elliptical orbit with two centers—the sun, brilliant and fiery, and a second, dark one that is never spoken about. Indeed, knowledge has two centers; by its gigantic movement the Earth shows us the double pole." Thoreau, like Serres, senses that sunlight is not enough. The Kantian/Copernican revolution that placed the human mind as the sun at the center of knowledge is not enough. We need a second revolution; "we need another beacon" (Serres and Latour 178). Objects and subjects, being and knowing, describe a kind of double star. Thoreau's orbit is an elliptical one around that double star, a double center, a double beacon, humanity and nature, the neighborly and the wild, West and East, Walden and Cape Cod.

The problem with Thoreau's parabolic figure is that it still bespeaks a Newtonian mathematical regularity, the periodic return of the orbiting planets and now, we know, even those wandering comets. But Thoreau's language is reaching for something else, a mathematical figure that did not yet exist, the chaotic patterning that centers not on mathematical exactness but on fuzzy patterns, not on Keplerian foci but on strange attractors, where periodic systems are not stable and predictable but dynamic and mobile and resilient (or not). As I argued years ago, Thoreau set out to explore a Newtonian universe and, while carefully documenting the periodic returns of nature's seasons, found himself living in a *post*-Newtonian universe of chaos and complexity, very much a "postmodern" or "posthuman" universe that we still struggle to incorporate into modern modes of thought and behavior (Walls, *Seeing* 238).[16] Thus Thoreau's writing articulates not a mathematically describable orbit but a poetically describable pathway, one composed of multiple, continual passes or "loops" in his walking and reading, loops that form an ever-enlarging vascular system of connections, tracks, and passages. What Thoreau was responding to was not the world of the past but the world that was even then emerging: destabilized, multiscalar, planetary in scope, characterized not by areas and boundaries but by littoral zones full of anomalies and hybrids. To describe this world he needed to invent a new means of discourse, and his movements around that paradigmatic modern dualism, nature and culture, ended by inscribing a figure that moves, in cometary fashion, restlessly around and beyond them—a transcendence of modernity itself, straining to see a horizon that we, even yet, cannot see beyond.

NOTES

1. "If you stand right fronting and face to face to a fact, you will see the sun glimmer on both its surfaces, as if it were a cimeter, and feel its sweet edge dividing you through the heart and marrow, and so you will happily conclude your mortal career" (*W* 98).

2. I have detailed this genealogy at length in *Passage to Cosmos*.

3. In *Through Other Continents*, Wai Chee Dimock extends Spivak's concept, which she renames "planetary," by rethinking American literature "against the history and habitat of the human species, against the 'deep time' of the planet earth" as described by geology and astronomy. As she demonstrates, situating literature in the shared ecology of the planet helps us think beyond the civil bounds of the nation-state to "*another place*" (quoting Michael Walzer), one "not territorial but associative, and extending as far as those associations extend" (6–7). I hope my own essay will contribute to this project.

4. My line of thought owes greatly to Bruno Latour, whose essays in *Pandora's Hope* are, as I have elsewhere detailed, particularly useful for thinking about Thoreau's practices of inscription. (See my early essays "Textbooks and Texts from the Brooks: Invent-

ing Scientific Authority in America" and "Romancing the Real: Thoreau's Technology of Inscription," and, more recently, "From the Modern to the Ecological: Latour on Walden Pond.") In particular, Latour's concept of "circulating reference" opens up Thoreau's practices of walking and journal writing, as I show in "Romancing the Real"; for Walden Pond as a "quasi object" and a brief exploration of the way "a text acts as the beating heart that holds together a circulatory system of social/natural networks" (108), see "From the Modern to the Ecological." For further work in this vein, productively applied to "Autumnal Tints," see William Rossi's essay in this volume.

5. I have in view here Derrida's insistence, in the opening of *The Animal That Therefore I Am*, that the cat who instigates his inquiry is "a real cat, truly, believe me, *a little cat*. It isn't the figure of a cat. It doesn't silently enter the bedroom as an allegory for all the cats on the earth" (6, emphasis in original). This, he explains, is what differentiates philosophy from poetry, for only poetry can think concerning the animal; thinking concerning the animal is precisely "what philosophy has, essentially, had to deprive itself of" (7).

6. See Jackson; Dowling.

7. For Thoreau's use of rhetorical "noise" to construct a literary form of serious science that grants agency to both subjects and objects, see my *Seeing New Worlds* (199–211).

8. See Willis et al.; see also Kristen Case's essay in this volume.

9. Joseph J. Moldenhauer notes that the unified text we have as "Walking, or the Wild" was originally two separate lectures that were eventually merged into a single essay (*Exc* 561–62). This textual history helps account for the structural contradiction noted here.

10. The reference is to the *North Star*, an antislavery weekly journal Frederick Douglass published in Rochester, New York, from 1847 to 1864; Thoreau and Douglass were acquainted, and the Thoreau family home was a station on the Underground Railroad, whose members helped escaping slaves reach Canada, where they were legally free.

11. Note that Thoreau's map of Walden Pond (*W* 286; figure 1), placed as it is amidst his continued self-conscious play with cardinal directions as embodied in his own daily walks, the sun's daily cycle, and the planet's seasonal circle, creates a *cosmogram*. Art historians and historical archaeologists have uncovered widespread use of cosmograms among diasporic Africans in the New World; while the resemblance may be coincidental, it's possible Thoreau encountered evidence of this folk tradition either directly, perhaps among Concord's freed slave population (most of whom had lived near Walden Pond, as Thoreau himself documents), or through his extensive ethnographic reading. Further research is needed to resolve this question.

12. The surprising extent of Thoreau's research into the explorers and cartographers who preceded the English to the northeastern region of the New World has recently been documented by Hessler.

13. Personal communication of 7 May 2009; see King's essay "Thoreau's Rhetoric of Estrangement in Cape Cod."

14. Deleuze and Guattari remark that where European books are arboreal, American books are rhizomatic; and further, that while in the American East occurs "the search for arborescence and the return to the Old World . . . there is the rhizomatic West, with its Indians without ancestry, its ever-receding limit, its shifting and displaced frontiers. . . . America reversed the directions; it put its Orient in the West, as if it were precisely in America that the earth came full circle; its West is the edge of the East." As they add, "Every great American author creates a cartography. . . . Each makes a map that is directly connected to the real social movements crossing America" (19, 520n18). Something like their sense that America thus becomes a "pivot point" for cardinality, and thus for the modernity released by global exploration, lies behind my own sense of Thoreau's deliberate play, both lived and linguistic, with mapping, walking, exploration, and solar/planetary movements.

15. Emerson used a related figure in "Poetry and Imagination," although he drew on non-Euclidean geometry to do so: "All is symbolized. Facts are not foreign, as they seem, but related. Wait a little and we see the return of the remote hyperbolic curve" (*CW* 8:40).

16. Neither term seems to me adequate, although this is not the place to propose alternatives. Our difficulties arise when we hold onto a nostalgic belief in "modern" as the culmination of history rather than encompassing it as a historical moment, always fractured and multiple, contested, unevenly distributed, and today in many places superseded. This nostalgic narrative projects "postmodern" not as the twin sibling of "modern," born in the same gesture, but rather as something that comes, absurdly, apocalyptically, "after" history, "after" the human. My own perspective, reflected in this essay, takes, with Latour, the "modern" to be a historical ideology that is now visible as such; that is, "we have," as Latour told us two decades ago in a moment now itself slipping into history, "never been modern."

Antimodern Thoreau

> We should be as good as the worthies of antiquity,
> but partly by first knowing how good they were.
> We are a race of tit-men, and soar but little higher in our
> intellectual flights than the columns of the daily paper.
>
> *Walden* 107

UNDOUBTEDLY, IN ANY DISCUSSION of "Thoreauvian modernities," it is somewhat provocative to call Thoreau an "antimodern," but provocation is not out of keeping with this eccentric writer.[1] The quotations to be discussed will reveal more than a simple opposition to what was modern in his time: Thoreau was a keen observer of the changes taking place in his society and a most perceptive critical thinker of antebellum America as the country became increasingly industrialized and urbanized. He was well aware of the new forces at work, and his criticism allowed him to free himself from the prevailing conventional notions of his time and to develop a fascinating mode of thinking well in advance of his age.

Like so many romantics, Thoreau was a misfit in his century and did not even try to adapt. The choice of a literary life gave him the opportunity to maintain a distance from the "confused *tintinnabulum*" of his contemporaries (*W* 329), to analyze the changes, and to urge his readers to be aware of what was wrong with the new society.[2] He said that he would have preferred "not to live in this restless, nervous, bustling, trivial Nineteenth Century," but he never intended to go West among the Indians or to live in complete isolation. He added that he just wanted to "stand or sit thoughtfully while it goes by" (*W* 329–30), that is, to be a witness, a close observer of the century he disliked, though at times it did fascinate him. His Journal and essays sift and qualify his many contradictory reactions toward this new mode of life.

Thoreau's distrust of progress and of what he termed "so-called improvements" led him to the assessment of what had become received ideas or prevailing dogma. It made him view his age from a distinctive angle, according to an antimodern mode focused on the negative new forces that shaped society, in particular the current insistence on an economic approach to human questions. He became an observant, critical thinker who did not share the major assumptions of the period and did not generally adhere to the ideology that propelled American society. He was thus in a position not only to see through the prevailing discourse that blinded the majority but also to perceive the failures and inhuman errors.

Thoreau's Ambivalent Jeremiad on Modernity

Antimodern Thoreau, however, explicitly perceived himself as modern in an 1852 remark that served to define his point of view; when he was mistaken for a pacifist Quaker in Quebec, he replied: "I thought, if there was any difference between us, it might be that I was born in modern times" (*PJ* 4: 379–80). After his return from Harvard, he had been under Emerson's mentorship and had been intellectually shaped by Transcendentalism, an intellectual avant-garde movement dedicated to undermining those traditions that the Transcendentalists felt were weighing too much on contemporary America; Thoreau accordingly rejected the burden of the past, the authority of previous generations, and the opinions of Philistines.

His critical attitude toward the past did not mean that he blindly followed contemporary trends, adopted the cult of progress, or believed in the positivism of science. On the contrary, Thoreau raised many objections to the forces that were transforming American society. His resistance required qualifications, reversals, and reticence as he expressed his disgruntlement over the dominant ideology of the mid-nineteenth century. Thoreau's ambivalence is nowhere more obvious than in his combination of pessimism and optimism. Most often, he expected negative consequences from the materialistic, technological, scientific evolution, just as he severely criticized political institutions and leaders who were incapable of distinguishing between good and evil. He belonged to the rural world, a setting which in his view was conducive to conscience and the capacity to criticize the decadence of modern times. He placed moral value in this opposition to society and the government of the majority, having scant hope that society might improve, since he had a very low opinion of "the mass of men" (*W* 8).

When he vents his pessimistic criticism of modern society, Thoreau has a polemical, provocative, even insulting way of degrading those he opposes because he considers them as victims of modernity.[3] In the early pages of "Economy," his style becomes hyperbolic to the point of grotesque exaggeration when he ridicules the American success story that to him is nothing more than torture, which in turn is destructive of the individual. Or he uses the rhetoric of inversion in which commonly accepted ideas or values are inverted into their opposite.[4] Thoreau supports views contrary to what people usually believe: his values are not those of the time; he refuses to belong to the majority, and from his eccentric position he enjoys pillorying the errors of the era.

In this original role, he employs language that may initially sound meaningless to people of common sense in order to awaken the consciousness of a few open-minded readers. His argumentation does not seem to be planned but moves along by fits of aggressive, paradoxical assertions meant to startle readers out of an easy acceptance of modern trends, to shock them so that they will question the validity of what they ordinarily take for granted.

In his denunciation of modern times, Thoreau uses a characteristically American rhetorical form, the jeremiad. It is two-sided, that is, both critical of the degeneracy of society and optimistic about the possibility of regeneration for the individual who practices moral uprightness.[5] It therefore is not merely negative but proposes an alternative way of life. This duality is precisely at the very core of Thoreau's ambivalence: opposing the criticism of a hopeless society and offering an optimistic opportunity of improvement when the individual is concerned. Through self-discipline and reliance on one's conscience, one may hope to achieve true progress, that is, to live according to one's principles, to resist public opinion, and to disobey unjust laws. His denunciation of modernity leads to both the practice of self-culture and the attempt to convince the audiences of his lectures or the readers of his essays that there exists a significant way of thinking differently. Though Thoreau was aware that he could only reach a limited number of readers, literature remained his preferred mode of action, based on the belief that ideas can be shared and that this will ultimately result in greater critical awareness and moral regeneration for a few. In his essays he voiced his dissent from the major cultural assumptions of antebellum America, but always in a literary form that preserved the complexity of his original thought.

The Deleterious New Economy

Throughout his works, Thoreau frequently condemns the modern market economy, such as in *Walden* where he expresses his hostility to trade, which "curses everything it handles" (70), or in the radical expostulation of "Life without Principle": "This world is a place of business. What an infinite bustle! . . . It is nothing but work, work, work. . . . I think that there is nothing, not even crime, more opposed to poetry, to philosophy, ay, to life itself, than this incessant business" (*RP* 156). The new economic dispensation leaves no room for the development of humanity, for culture and literacy, that is, for all that is susceptible to improve the quality of human life. Thoreau goes against the grain of the American business society: "We are warped and narrowed by an exclusive devotion to trade and commerce and manufactures and agriculture and the like, which are but means, and not the end" (*RP* 175). He also objects to the conception of it held by leaders and intellectuals, or "those who style themselves statesmen and philosophers who are so blind as to think that progress and civilization depend on precisely this kind of interchange and activity" (*RP* 176). In opposition to the mainstream, he limits progress to moral and spiritual refinement.

With even more precise insight, he analyzed the new industrial system that was developing in the middle of the century: "I cannot believe that our factory system is the best mode by which men may get clothing. The condition of the operatives is becoming every day more like that of the English; . . . the principal object is, not that mankind may be well and honestly clad, but, unquestionably, that the corporations may be enriched" (*W* 26–27). He understood that the ultimate goal was to maximize profits for some, not to improve the human condition: the horrors of the English Industrial Revolution had reached the United States. Workers were exploited, the division of labor resulted in meaningless work (*W* 50), and the new economy encouraged "artificial wants" (*RP* 177). Thoreau had a fairly clear idea of the forces that shaped American society before the Civil War: he was aware of the social cost of industrial capitalism. In particular, he realized the toll on the rural population, the end of a meaningful, moral way of life that he encapsulated in a few words: "the fall from the farmer to the operative" (*W* 64). Thoreau questioned the cult of progress based on technical improvements, refusing to adopt them blindly. Were they really improvements for humanity? What did the telegraph really allow one to say? What was the point of traveling fast with the railroad (*W* 93)? What was this new necessity to hurry? As an antimodern, Thoreau took his time to think about the dehumanizing disorientation brought about by this modernity.

In his assessment of the changes introduced by railroads, which he ironically called "that last improvement in civilization" (*W* 35), Thoreau acknowledged positive elements: "regularity and precision," "punctuality," an "electrifying" quality that "refreshed and expanded" him (*W* 117–19). He was enthusiastic about the possibilities of exchanging, of importing such a variety of products, and he enjoyed writing a long catalog of exotic goods. The railroads provided an opening on the world, and for once, the chauvinistic New Englander that he was felt "more like a citizen of the world" (*W* 119). He then stopped his praise and concluded negatively, realizing that this was the end of the pastoral world of Concord: "So is your pastoral life whirled past and away." Thoreau finally rejected this symbol of the modern world, which to him was irremediably "restless": "I will not have my eyes put out and my ears spoiled by its smoke and steam and hissing" (*W* 122). In a later comment on the fact that some huckleberry fields had become private property, excluding children from contact with nature, Thoreau generalized on the effects of "civilization and division of labor": "This is one of the taxes which we pay for having a railroad. All our improvements, so called, tend to convert the country into the town" (*WF* 58–59). Obviously for him, there was no positive compensation for this loss of freedom, no redemption for this change.

Undemocratic Thoreau

In the years that followed the establishment of Jacksonian democracy and its intended politics of egalitarianism, Thoreau was at odds with the prevailing democratic ideology. Not only did he consider politics as something "superficial and inhuman" (*RP* 177–78), but he also condemned the fundamental text of the United States: "Its very Constitution is the evil" (*RP* 74). He deemed that politicians acted out of expediency, not principle: in contradiction to the proclaimed American ideal of liberty, they supported slavery. Nothing was to be expected from the political approach to solving the problems of society.

In his more political essays, Thoreau repeatedly sounded undemocratic. He expressed his preference for an elite of individuals who are superior in terms of culture, intelligence, aesthetic awareness, and moral distinction. This implied a conception of society where some are superior to others and legitimately should be granted the responsibility to make decisions because they know best. He regretted that the dominant ideology made this ideal politically incorrect: "It is thought Utopian to propose spending money for things which more intelligent men know to be of far more worth," he said in *Walden* about culture and education (109). His vocabulary provides further proof of his inegalitarian views: his exemplar was "the nobleman of cultivated taste," and he called the noteworthy authors of classics "a natural and irresistible aristocracy" (*W* 109, 103).

At the core of this elite was the man of genius who stands in opposition to "the mass of men," precisely those that the modern political system tried to empower.[6] In his nature writings too, he opposed the majority, the "rest of mankind," "most men" who "do not care for Nature" (*WF* 237), to the "only one in a hundred" (*WF* 13) who knows about it. Thoreau even went so far as to say bluntly that if there were town commons for the poor, "why not a forest and huckleberry field for the town's rich?" (*WF* 238). Apart from the provocation of the formulation, it suggests that the few who care for nature, know about it, and have a spiritual and aesthetic appreciation of it should have a special place for themselves apart from "the mass of men." Thoreau was antimodern in his opposition to democracy and equality, preferring instead a special status according to culture, intelligence, or superior needs. He hated the tyrannical rule of the "underbred and low-lived and illiterate" and explicitly said so in *Walden* (107).

Reservations about Science

Modernity in the middle of the nineteenth century had much to do with the development of science, its specialization and professionalization. Thoreau was well aware of the new trend and realized the social incentive to acquire the identity and prestige of a professional, positivist scientist. He was attracted by the scientific method, by the precision of its measurements and its classification of facts. He was in contact with Boston and Harvard naturalists, and yet he refused to join the Association for the Advancement of Science in 1853 (*PJ* 5: 469–70). Once again he was unable to adapt to the age. He could not fit, because he realized he was an old-time "mystic, a transcendentalist and a natural philosopher."

He refused to get bogged down in the study of details and to lose sight of the purpose of life: he needed a minute description of the natural phenomena he witnessed, but then he had to go beyond facts for meaning and for what they revealed of human experience.[7] His perspective remained holistic, including the observer's emotion in his perception of the quality of nature's beauty. He did not want to relinquish intuition, imagination, and the personal life of the observer, the experience derived from the daily contact with Nature, which was to him a sort of divinity, with a will and a plan. That was why he gave his preference to older generations of naturalists who had not renounced a metaphysical approach; like them, he called himself "a natural philosopher"—a label that had already gone out of fashion.

Thoreau had an ambivalent, divided attitude toward science throughout the 1850s, even when his study of nature became more systematic. His reservations, however, did not prevent him from being a precursor to many contemporary scientists, as when he rejected spontaneous generation and the notion of "special creation": he accepted the determinism of the laws of nature and welcomed evolution. Though antimodern, he revealed his capacity to eschew traditional modes of thinking.

His rejection of a reductive, specialized science coincided with his dismay at the disappearance of a truly all-inclusive culture. He exclaimed: "Have we no culture, no refinement,—but skill only to live coarsely and serve the Devil?" (*RP* 173). Intellectuals, he said, did not think deeply, and there were "so few moral teachers" (*RP* 166). The result of this absence of mentors was that people believed in "shams and delusions" (*W* 95). He repeatedly blamed the press for this negative evolution: "The newspapers are the ruling power" (*RP* 178). They shaped public opinion, imposed a superficial and stereotypical way of thinking, lending too much importance to politics, to "mere gossip" (*RP* 169). Even worse, they profaned the mind with what is trivial (*RP* 173). Society was thus governed by irrational fashions unrelated to what people need in order to lead better human lives.

Thoreau challenged the antebellum concept of progress: to him, the criteria should not be "money or fame" (*RP* 159), neither more goods nor more machines, and certainly not vapid scientific knowledge. Progress had to be judged on moral criteria, on individual culture, the ultimate goal being "a high and earnest purpose" (*RP* 177). His perspective leading away from what is materialistic had little to do with the prevailing ideas of his time.

The Choice of Nature

With such a litany of arguments against contemporary society, Thoreau might have wasted his life in constant opposition and might have become a militant conservative, but he remarked that "the attitude of resistance is one of weakness, inasmuch as it only faces an enemy; it has its back to all that is truly attractive" (*WF* 165). Consequently, rather than "tinkering, mending the old worn-out teapot of society" (*WF* 166) or becoming involved in politics, he chose instead to focus on the beauty and the complexity of nature: he adopted a "natural life," an alternative mode of life centered on the observation of nature, on the perception of its aesthetic, sensual, and moral uses.

His antimodern mode of living was regressive: a return to nature intended to compensate for the fact that in modernizing itself urban society had lost sight of the importance of having an awareness of nature. Thoreau expressed a nostalgic defense of the rural way of life, identified with the "country people" (*WF* 105), and said, "I trust that we dwellers in the huckleberry pastures . . . shall be slow to adopt the notions of large towns and cities" (*WF* 55). He resisted any form of change that did not seem favorable to humanity.

His underlying assumption was the romantic valuation of regenerative nature in opposition to "urbaphobia," the perception of the city as decadent because it exaggerates the changes of the nineteenth century out of proportion and thereby symbolizes the "restless" world.[8] To this sterile agitation, Thoreau's art of life opposes the slow "drenching of the reality which surrounds us" (*W* 97): "It requires more than a day's devotion to know and to possess the wealth of a day" (*RP* 169). The spectacle of the vigor of nature provides a "tonic" or an antidote to resist the pernicious effects of the modern world: "We require just so much acid as the cranberries afford in the spring. . . . They cut the winter's phlegm, and now you can swallow another year of this world without other sauce" (*WF* 106).

Yet, if he could say in *Walden* that "from the desperate city you go into the desperate country, and have to console yourself with the bravery of minks and muskrats" (8), Thoreau was able to transcend this attitude of despair, to think of the future and propose ideas to the next generations. In the late 1850s, he realized the absolute necessity of preserving wild nature, which was a prophetic idea revealing an awareness of what would be necessary for the survival of humanity. In this new attitude, he relinquished his individualistic approach and adopted a more collective perspective. He opposed private property, the cornerstone of the American ideological and economic system. He considered that towns, not individuals, should own beautiful natural sites: they "should belong to the public" and be placed under the supervision of "a committee appointed to see that the beauty of the town received no detriment" (*WF* 236). Whole areas of wilderness should be put aside and left without any commercial use; primitive forests should be preserved "for higher uses—a common possession forever, for instruction and recreation" (*WF* 238).[9] In his late manuscripts, Thoreau, therefore, formulated the essential ideas for the creation of national parks. In advance of his age, he reached the conclusion that natural resources are not inexhaustible and considered that the environment is not just to be exploited for its resources but that its wild state is valuable in and of itself and must be preserved unimpaired for future generations.

In his resistance to the Industrial Revolution, Thoreau envisioned an improved way of life that would be related to nature. Natural spaces close to towns and cities should be preserved for pleasure and instruction, for contemplation, for breathing, for observing the change of seasons, for the realization that "all Nature is doing her best each moment to make us well" (*WF* 239). In his funeral service eulogy, Emerson was definitely wrong when he regretted Thoreau's lack of ambition and ridiculed the fact that he had merely become "the captain of a huckleberry party" (*Emerson's Prose* 409), when Thoreau in fact had realized early on that urban, industrial modernity requires a natural antidote. He stressed the necessity of a temporary periodical *rewilding* of the individual, of the possibility of educating some people by suggesting that they should occasionally live without thinking about money, without going to the market to sell or buy. He described his own life as that of an aesthete, sensitive to a beauty that no wealth can buy, his relation to nature thus appearing as a deliberate course to "take a position outside the street and daily life of men . . . out of the usual course" (*WF* 165).

From Antimodern to Premodernist in Literature

The failure to fit into the modern world with a respectable job expected of a former Harvard student led Thoreau to adopt literature as the central activity of

his life. In "Life without Principle," he explained that he did not read newspapers, for they devoted too much attention to politics: "As I love literature, and, to
some extent, the truth also, I never read those columns at any rate. I do not wish
to blunt my sense of right so much. I have not got to answer for having read a
single President's Message" (*RP* 177). Literature provided a refuge from the danger of corruption of the mind by politics and the affairs of the world. Therefore,
more than in the village, he found his literary inspiration in the leisurely but
minute observation of nature, in the cultivation of the bean-field "for the sake of
tropes and expression" (*W* 162), and in the writing of "excursions": this enabled
him to express his views on the ideal of a "natural life." His solution was not to
live fully in the modern world but to live apart, in the New England countryside.

Thoreau devoted a major chapter of *Walden* to reading and to his "theory"
of literature: there he adopted an openly antimodern posture, praising high-
minded literature, the "classics," a literature that had gone out of fashion but that
he wanted to redeem because it recorded the noblest thoughts of humanity. This
choice was made in opposition to contemporary, superficial serialized fiction
and popular travel narratives. To this "easy reading" (*W* 104), "for feeble intel-
lects" (*W* 107), he preferred philosophical literature, which discussed the crucial
questions that have to do with the human condition.

An essential aspect of Thoreau's antimodern stance resides in his special
interest in a select language, like the study of some "words of an ancient language, which are raised out of the trivialness of the street, to be perpetual suggestions and provocations" (*W* 100). He recovered the original meanings of
words, which enabled him to resist common sense, what "They," his neighbors,
said without thinking. By adopting the idiom of the ancients, Greek or Latin,
or that of seventeenth-century English, he identified with that exclusive group
of intellectuals and thinkers of the past. It gave him new possibilities of expression to convey a vision that was impossible to impart with simple stock
phrases. Thoreau made a significant remark about this: "It is a ridiculous demand which England and America make, that you shall speak so that they can
understand you" (*W* 324). He refused the conventional expectations of society,
which wanted a univocal communication only fit for carrying out business; he
preferred a more expressive, polysemic language. Paradoxically, his rejection
of the simplicity of daily language led him to a premodernist position. In his
formal act of resistance to the language of the majority, Thoreau accepted the

risk of obscurity (*W* 325), entailed in the private quest for the unutterable. He was aware of it in one of his key literary statements: "Perhaps the facts most astounding and most real are never communicated by man to man. The true harvest of my daily life is somewhat as intangible and indescribable as the tints of morning or evening" (*W* 216–17). And yet he tried to reach the "intangible."

Thoreau put forward his own divided consciousness as the origin of the text, knowing that he was "the scene, so to speak, of thoughts and affections; and [was] sensible of a certain doubleness" that made his voice complex and uncertain.[10] With a sort of pre-Freudian intuition he realized that there was an alien part in him, "no more I than it is you" (*W* 135). His commitment to sincere and authentic writing was such that he admitted that he did not fully control his choice of words, as when he described the sound of a hooting owl "made more awful by a certain gurgling melodiousness," then paused and added, "I find myself beginning with the letters gl when I try to imitate it" (*W* 125). These two enigmatic letters reappeared in the episode of the thawing railroad sandbank about the word "globe" (*W* 306), suggesting that they mysteriously stand for something essential to him. His writing became experimental in this paragraph as Thoreau tried to evoke how he felt about the sound and shape of letters.

These disconcerting occurrences of resistance to the social demand for comprehensibility and legibility, his remarks on the practice of "*extra-vagance*," did not result in a hermetic modernist text.[11] *Walden* is predicated on the belief that there is meaning and that it will be found: "the at present unutterable things we may find somewhere uttered" (108). Thoreau did not expect all "John[s] or Jonathan[s]" to "realize all this" (*W* 333), to care or to understand, but he had no doubt that he could make sense of his eccentric perception of the world, of his unique vision of life, and could communicate it with his "true expression" (*W* 324).

Thoreau's essays draw their modernity from the antimodern protest that set him apart from a society obsessed by trade, consumerist materialism, and technological advances. Writing was his chosen way of resisting the attraction of the forces shaping antebellum America, to contradict the tyranny of public opinion. His antimodern tastes and opinions led him to value language as an idiosyncratic weapon and to adopt a premodernist literary posture in *Walden*; similarly, his rejection of positivist science enabled him to develop his own approach and, consequently, to become a forerunner in preserving the environment. The symbiotic relationship of the modern and the antimodern in Thoreau's worldview is such that modernity and antimodernity frequently overlap, even to the point of being, at times, interchangeable.

NOTES

1. For "antimodern," I am indebted to Antoine Compagnon's *Les antimodernes*, a typology of nineteenth- and twentieth-century French writers (including Baudelaire, Chateaubriand, Péguy) characterized by "a reaction, a resistance to modernism, to the modern world, to the cult of progress" (9, my translation). These writers reacted to a specific historical context, notably, the French Revolution and the place of the Catholic religion in postrevolutionary French society, all of which makes a detailed comparison with Thoreau impossible within the limits of this essay. Compagnon's work is, however, a thought-provoking study that underlines the fact that there are considerable differences between the antimoderns and the traditionalists or reactionaries. The antimoderns he discusses had a close but ambivalent relation to modernity, and, paradoxically, their resistance to an overconfident reverence for progress contributed to the ultimate definition of modernity; their opposition often led them to take refuge in literature (10). The use of "antimodern" applied to Thoreau thus suggests a watchful awareness of and a critical attitude toward modernity.

2. Later in life he admitted, "My work is writing" (*J* 9:121, 18 Oct. 1856).

3. See, for example, his reference to dyspepsia in the discussion of politics, in "Life without Principle" (*RP* 178–79).

4. For example, good/bad (*W* 10), unfortunate/successful (*RP* 165).

5. This duality is explored by Harold K. Bush Jr. in his introduction to *American Declarations* (1–11).

6. This conception of an elite is perceived negatively today when the reference to elitism implies a disapproving judgment, as when Alfred Tauber writes, "There is a dark streak of elitism in Thoreau's confidence in knowing the Right, in his disdain of the democratic process, and in his lofty self-righteousness" (191). Philip Cafaro writes about the end of the chapter "Reading": "Note how odd it strikes our ears, this talk of 'magnanimous' or 'refined' villages. It likely sounds precious, pretentious, or elitist" (*Thoreau's Living Ethics* 195)—as if being unrefined and uneducated were preferable.

7. David Robinson remarks about Thoreau's nature observations: "They display not only an arresting sense of detail, but a concomitant desire to reach for a more comprehensive category of explanation for the particular phenomenon. Thoreau consistently

tries to see a particular fact or event not as a random or unique occurrence but as indicative of a more comprehensive idea or law" ("Thoreau and Idealism" 41).

8. For a discussion of this opposition to the city, see Baubérot and Bourillon.

9. See also *J* 12:387, 15 Oct. 1859.

10. "However intense my experience, I am conscious of the presence and criticism of a part of me, which, as it were, is not a part of me, but spectator, sharing no experience, but taking note of it" (*W* 135).

11. See Gilmore; his argument stresses a belief in openness, a desire for visibility and legibility that leads American culture to ferret out what is hidden. This ideological bias produced the contrary impulse in American literature.

WILLIAM ROSSI

Thoreau's Multiple Modernities

A PARADOX ATTENDS the very timeliness of *Walden*, for, in a certain sense, the question of Thoreau and modernity is nothing new. If only implicitly, critics of every era since Thoreau began to publish have addressed his relation to what he described as "this restless, nervous, bustling . . . Nineteenth Century" and to ours (*W* 329). If there has been little consensus, this is in part because in our equally restless era of professional literary and cultural criticism, "one generation abandons the enterprises of another like stranded vessels" (*W* 11).

But another reason, of course, is that Thoreau's own opinions on the subject were hardly settled or even uniform. Sometimes he seems to pose a simple choice. Employing the railroad, the agent of technological modernization, as a potent symbol of our socially "constructed . . . fate, an *Atropos*, that never turns aside," he echoes the voice of a station manager, warning his readers "sincerely by any power to get off its track." Yet a few sentences farther along in the same paragraph, he commends the instrumental rationality of "railroad time": "We live the steadier for it." By the paragraph's end, this model has become the metaphorical template for readers to form parallel routes of their own: "Every path but your own is the path of fate. Keep on your own track, then" (*W* 118). Apparently, rejecting modernity *tout court* is not an option.

Yet dwelling thus within modernity does not prevent Thoreau from taking up a position "in the angle of a leaden wall" (*W* 329) or on the shore of Walden Pond, nor from claiming conviction that "my genius dates from an older era than the agricultural" (*Wk* 54). He can be located in any one of several positions about what he liked to call our "present condition" precisely because he was both ambivalent about and preternaturally attentive to its unstable potential.

The very multiplicity of his positions marks him as a self-conscious inhabitant of a nervous, bustling modernity, however much for the same reason he sometimes treasured a stance apart from it. Determined "to stand . . . precisely [in] the present moment; to toe that line" between past and future eternities, he was modern sometimes in spite of himself, both prophet and product of our modern condition (*W* 17).

Despite these shifting positions, in Thoreau's writing on the subject as well as in much critical commentary, the process of modernization is usually characterized monolithically. Exclusively Western in its origin and agency, in this version modernization is inevitable and uniform, a force, like the locomotive, that drives history and that disrupts while reconstituting social, environmental, even metaphysical relations. This monolithic conception of modernity is apparent in predictions of inevitable secularization and industrialization associated with Western influence and its forms of liberal democracy. In the Enlightenment version dominant in Thoreau's day and still widely taken for granted, Western modernization is thus assumed to represent the sole model against which all other societies are measured and the only path to be taken toward their own modern futures. Yet just as the secularization hypothesis predicted a privatization and political impotence of religion that have dramatically failed to materialize, so the Enlightenment notion of modernization as "a single, culture-neutral model in which complexity and reflexivity replace simplicity and tradition" has given way to one of "multiple" or "alternative modernities" (Jager 27; Eisenstadt). As the title of this book suggests, it is time to pluralize Thoreau's relation to modernity as well.

One way to do so is to follow closely Thoreau's own strategies for negotiating modernity as both monolithic ideology and actual project. Accordingly, this essay will argue that Thoreau's determination to dwell deeply and differently in the full modernity of his moment is expressed not only as a theme in his writing. For him it was also a discipline, a distinctive, self-conscious *practice* of writing that informed not only the Journal but especially the Kalendar and the late natural history writings produced from the Journal. Where Kristen Case recovers crucial dimensions of Thoreau's science in the Kalendar, I hope to shed light on that project from another direction. After examining Thoreau's efforts to acquire, translate, and represent natural knowledge in the Journal, I will then show how the seasonal narrative of "Autumnal Tints," as informed by this practice, presents a complex intervention into normative modern temporality.

That the poetics of Thoreau's practice were sometimes expressed in romantic terms might seem to disqualify him from the modernity I am claiming. In common parlance and for many commentators, "romanticism" and "romantic," especially when coupled with "reform," have long been virtually synonymous with a naïveté or false consciousness respecting modernity. The most recent exponent of this skeptical heritage, as now applied to environmental writing and literary ecocriticism, is Timothy Morton's *Ecology without Nature: Rethinking Environmental Aesthetics*. Morton argues that, as descended from romanticism, both nature writing and contemporary ecocriticism are caught up in an illusory literary project of "ecomimesis." Desiring to merge his or her identity with nature, the romantic writer or contemporary ecocritic, Morton argues, creates a self-image of the "beautiful soul."[1] "The landscape on the other side of the chasm between subject and object," however, "turns out to be the beautiful soul in inverted form . . . beautiful nature." Like the soul, this nature is "opaque, exclusionary, absolutely right and proper" even while being at the same time reified as a glittering romantic object, an "ambient world" (119).[2] In thrall to this illusion, the romantic writer or contemporary ecocritic forfeits critical distance. Forgetting that "'nature' is an arbitrary rhetorical construct, empty of independent, genuine existence behind or beyond the texts we create about it," allows him or her to maintain "a critical position about everything except [his or her] own position" (121). But this position amounts to little more than a consumerist "window-shopping . . . subjectivity," one that, among other things, disables thoughtful environmental action (111).

Unfortunately, with the exception of Wordsworth, Coleridge, and Thoreau, Morton provides no extensive analyses of specific "nature writers." But for Thoreau his claim is at best problematic. Nature was for Thoreau, as writer and naturalist, neither simply a mirror nor, as positivist promoters of science were beginning to insist, absolutely independent of the inquiring subject. Indeed, rather oddly for a critic of "nature writing," Morton takes no account whatever of the role of empirical natural history or natural science. Although, as others have argued, the term "nature writing" inadequately captures the variable mixture of modes that characterize this body of literary nonfiction, it nonetheless correctly denotes a dependence on empiricism for establishing and engaging environmental otherness.[3] When combined with first-person narration, from the mid-nineteenth century onward and especially in the hands of gifted empirical observers like Thoreau, Mary Austin, Richard Jefferies, Barry Lopez, and Terry Tempest Williams, this mode often registers a resistance or a complement to the elimination of the scientific subject, as Lorraine Daston and Peter Galison have argued, in professional scientific writing (191–251; see also Daston).

That Thoreau was quite aware of his descriptive practice as both writing and resistance to a new epistemic regime is evident in the following Journal passage, written in May 1854, when *Walden* was in press:

> There is no such thing as pure *objective* observation— You[r] observation—to be interesting, *i.e.*, to be significant, must be *subjective* The sum of what the writer of whatever class has to report is simply some human experience—whether he be poet or philosopher or man of science— The man of most science is the man most alive—whose life is the greatest event—senses that take cognizance of outward things merely are of no avail. . . . If it is possible to conceive of an event outside to humanity—it is not of the slightest significance—though it were the explosion of a planet— Every important worker will report what life there is in him—(*PJ* 8: 98)

Note that natural knowledge here is not described as the product of any kind of mystical "merging." Because the most qualified "worker[s]" are those "most alive," that is, most psychophysically alert and responsive, their "report[s]" will be, in Lawrence Buell's terms, "doubly accountable": faithful both to the physical environment and to "discursive mentation" (*Environmental Imagination* 92). Unlike the skepticism of some romantic authors, Thoreau's is not directed at science per se but rather at the possibility or desirability of expunging intentionality.[4] In Thoreau's case, what Morton regards too simplistically as "ecomimeticism" is more accurately described as "empirical holism" (Walls, *Seeing* 84–93).[5]

The writerly self-consciousness exhibited in this passage is not unusual in the Journal, which contains numerous such reflections.[6] Indeed, Thoreau deliberately fashioned the Journal project itself as a vehicle for inscribing the experience of a "man of most science," "most alive" in this sense. By "project" I refer not only to the thirty manuscript journal volumes he filled from the spring of 1850 to the summer of 1861 (an average of about eight hundred pages per year) but rather to the whole lived and cumulative process, including the regular routine or method that grounded it, one that encompassed his daily excursions into the surrounding woods, hills, ponds, and rivers and back to his study; the field notes he took on these walks; the quasi-daily indoor composition of what Princeton Journal editors call "current journal," frequently in the form of present-tense narratives that experientially re-create the excursions; and the uses he afterward made of it as a naturalist, including lists of plant, bird, and animal species observed, phenological charts, and the Kalendar that Kristen Case examines in fine detail.[7]

At first glance, the relation between these functions and levels of the Journal may seem one of progressive distancing from the experience of nature as such, an increasing reduction of experience to categories. Yet from the early 1850s, when he began the practice of alternating walking and writing, Thoreau seems to have taken that distance—the epistemological gap between experience and knowledge—into account. In July 1851 he counsels himself, in his field note taking, not to "tread on the heels of your experience   Be impressed without making a minute [i.e., a note] of it. Poetry puts an interval between the impression & the expression—waits till the seed germinates naturally" (*PJ* 3: 331).[8] Then in early September, having apparently further refined the dynamic between writing and walking, he reports: "I succeed best when I *re*cur to my experience not too late, but within a day or two when there is some distance but enough of freshness" (*PJ* 4: 28). This will suffice to indicate how self-consciously and pragmatically Thoreau worked to construct a vitality of experiential reference in the Journal. As emphasized here, that practice hinged on the imaginatively "*recur*sive" and cumulative act of inscribing the events and phenomena encountered on his excursions, including what William James would call the "affectional facts" as integral to experiential events, rather than erased as if such events were "outside to humanity" (*PJ* 8: 98). The Journal's many present-tense narratives of these excursions, which, beginning in the early 1850s, dramatize this practice, may also be considered its first fruits.

By locating the Journal project within "humanity," Thoreau also locates it in culture as much as in nature. In this respect, his practice mingles two ontological domains that, according to Bruno Latour, have been falsely separated in the monolithic discourse of "modernity" (a theory he details in *We Have Never Been Modern*). Indeed, Latour's anthropological account of a scientific excursion in the Amazon, and the constructivist theory of reference he develops there, can further clarify not only the epistemology of Thoreau's practice but also the complex narrative temporality in one of the late essays derived or, more accurately, translated from the Journal: "Autumnal Tints."[9]

One of Latour's primary purposes in accompanying the team of Brazilian and French scientists—a botanist, a soil scientist, and a geomorphologist—is to make visible the enormous intellectual, social, technological, and material labor involved in constructing natural knowledge. For Latour, the process conventionally described in terms of data gathering, analysis, and hypothesis testing is more fully understood as a delicate, laborious effort to articulate real relations to nonhuman nature, where "articulate" carries the double meaning of making material and intellectual links and giving distinct expression to "an ontological property of the universe" (*Pandora's Hope* 303). In this collaborative effort, language (or, more generally, the sign) plays a crucial role. Latour rejects the correspondence model of reference because "in actual practice one never travels directly from objects to words, from the referent to the sign, but always back and forth through risky intermediary pathway[s]" from the field to the lab and back (42). Instead, to emphasize both the constructive labor involved and also the workers' immersion in the rich, nonhuman context, Latour speaks of "inscriptions" or "translations" to describe the various mediations by which material nonhuman nature is made legible and available for analysis or representation.

Notably, each stage in this process represents both a loss and a gain. On the one hand, the sampling and classifying process involves the reduction or loss of particularity, materiality, and multiplicity as specimens are necessarily categorized, standardized, and abstracted from their living, concrete context. On the other, each new inscription along the chain of investigation provides a "new handle." As each reduction discloses new patterns, new features that were previously invisible, the reference of notations is enriched and amplified. By means of them, the observer in a sense sees more than when he was submerged in a forest of phenomena. "Thanks to inscriptions," Latour writes, "we are able to oversee and control a situation in which we are submerged, we become [provisionally] superior to that which is greater than us, and we are able to gather together synoptically all the actions that occurred over many days and that we have since forgotten" (*Pandora's Hope* 65).

In this process, the expedition logbook, like the lab protocol book, is essential. Without it, the collective labor of building the relevant understanding through each information-producing step in the chain would be lost. The logbook "allow[s] us to return to each data point in order to reconstitute its history" (Latour, *Pandora's Hope* 46). In order for reference to accumulate and thicken, these steps must "be traceable, allowing for travel in both directions": from the text back down to the materiality and particularity, the original totality of which has been displaced piecemeal as word or sign replaced a particular feature "while conserving a trait that defines it" (63). It is from such labor, "such *movements* that knowledge derives" (39). Hence, the quality and vitality of insight gained in the process of investigation, the truth of reference, lies not in correspondence between theory and physical phenomenon, as if in some meeting or "contact" point between subject and object. Rather, reference "*circulates* all along the reversible chain of transformations" or translations (71).

The parallels between this process and the Journal project should be apparent.[10] Not only does Thoreau's meticulously indexed Journal serve a function similar to the logbook in Latour's account, but his compositional method itself, together with the narrative re-creation of daily excursions, serves to mediate the repeated immersion in phenomena and reflective distance through which natural knowledge is articulated: as Thoreau writes, "I succeed best when I *recur* to my experience not too late, but within a day or two when there is some distance but enough of freshness." As H. Daniel Peck puts it, this process not only "made [Thoreau] systematically alert to what the next day's observations might reveal. But it also drew his attention to . . . the perceptions of yesterday and the day before, which, when brought forward into the act of composition, established their relation to the present." Combined with his habit of continually cross-referencing his observations, this writing practice built the Journal into a kind of "material memory," in Peck's phrase (45).[11] It is, then, from the *narrative* as well as descriptive tracking of seasonal phenomena that the higher-level inscriptions—the lists, charts, and above all the calendars—were generated, further amplifying and further circulating reference up and down the chain: from field notations and the rich particularity of seasonal phenomena re-created in the Journal, to the calendar categories, and back.

"Autumnal Tints" makes an interesting test case for these claims, since of almost all the late environmental writing, this essay is the least "scientific" in any conventionally accepted sense. Indeed, without knowing anything about the Journal project or the Kalendars, "Autumnal Tints" could be read as an excellent example of precisely the "consumerist window-shopping subjectivity"

Morton critiques—a literary work that pictorially packages New England fall foliage to serve a future generation of carbon-spewing spectacle seekers, tooling around and tuning into the beauty of nature. As Buell points out, in creating this extended seasonal sketch, Thoreau took advantage of a fashionable market (*Environmental Imagination* 231). Like other popular nature essays appearing in such midcentury magazines as *Harper's*, *Putnam's Monthly Magazine*, and the *Atlantic*, "Autumnal Tints" exhibits an engaging, mostly genial tone, combining naturalistic with picturesque, even painterly description (as its title advertises), full of whimsical similes and fanciful reflections that occasionally edge into broad satire.[12]

But this is not a simple romantic nature essay, displaying the author's fantasy of merging with the beauty of nature. While not devoid of lyrical moments, the main narrative work of the essay is not simply to celebrate the season but to exhibit the process of seasonal ripening, from late August through late October, through a precise, richly embodied description of symptomatic New England plant and tree species. Most importantly for my purposes, "Autumnal Tints" represents a further translation of the Journal's "material memory." Indeed, as Peck astutely observes, the essay partakes in the "same conceptual endeavor as Thoreau's chart of November," a "counterpart" document that "emerge[d] out of a long process of [perceptual] category-formation" (96). Resisting the new positivist standards of objectivity I noted earlier, the essay's core autumnal narrative presents the phenomenon of fall as mediated through the narrator's consciousness, slowed down and savored. Yet while eccentric and whimsical at times, Thoreau is obviously also a careful naturalist, a botanist. Finally, if, as I have argued, the Journal project provided the place where Thoreau's natural knowledge was made, it is in "Autumnal Tints" and other late natural history writings that this knowledge is made *public*.[13]

More specifically, this knowledge and the narrative Journal practice integral to it are mobilized to engage two features of modern lived experience. The first of these is a paradoxical combination, among Thoreau's contemporaries and ours, of inattention to the complexity and richness of environment, on the one hand, and a specialist or single vision concerning it, on the other. One intention of the narrator is clearly to model an embodied attentiveness and environmental memory, not merely to critique an ingrained public inattention. Not coincidentally, several characters sketched in the essay appear to have been rendered inattentive by their participation in market capitalism. These include,

for instance, "the market-man" whom the narrator spies "driving into the village" and whose consciousness, he imagines, is composed "chiefly [of] husks
and little thought," just "blasted pig-corn, fit only for cob-meal" (*Exc* 236); or
the farmer whose eye for "meadow-hay and the more nutritious grasses which
grow next to" it does not detect the fine "purplish mist" made by the spreading
flowers of the purple grass that tremble all around him, a glory that is literally and figuratively "beneath his notice." Perhaps "because it is so beautiful he
does not know that it exists; for the same eye does not see this and timothy"
(*Exc* 226). Nor, importantly, is the narrator himself immune to fits of inattention or to single vision, a problem to which the essay returns in the end but
leaves unresolved. Thus, at one point, while he haggles "with this man and that"
over "the cost of carting" soil amendments, the beautiful "parti-colored leaves"
decompose around him, adding fertile depth to the soil and making us "all the
richer for their decay" (*Exc* 240).

Yet a deeper reason for inattention stems from the fragmentation not only
of modern awareness but of memory. This, the second feature of modernity the
essay counters, describes a condition in which the depth of being has been forgotten and, with it, the depth and multidimensional temporalities of lived experience. Here it is important to note that Thoreau frames the essay as an exercise
in remembering as well as representing the fall, a phenomenon that "is scarcely
remembered from year to year" even by "the majority" who have witnessed it
(*Exc* 223). If specimen leaves could be outlined or preserved "unchanged" in a
book, the narrator imagines, "what a memento such a book would be!" (*Exc*
225). Yet, no more than the objectivist report Thoreau earlier characterized as
"outside to humanity" could such a book of specimens ever reawaken seasonal
memory in a way that "speaks to our blood," as this essay attempts to do (*Exc* 227).
If, as the narrator claims, "by the twentieth of August, everywhere in woods and
swamps we are reminded of the fall" (*Exc* 225), then we—author, narrator, and
audience—are not so much learning something new as being awakened to what
at some level we have always known: our own mortality (Milder 186–91). Yet,
far from expressing melancholy or loss, the narrator represents such awareness
as an attainment of full maturity. If the maturation of leaves could "teach us how
to die," we would "glow" even now "in the midst of [our] decay" (*Exc* 241, 228).

This fall into time, the transient recovery of being and mortality carried by
the autumnal narrative's richly embodied seasonality, is set against the normative modern temporality associated with specialization, market capitalism, and

other forms of tunnel vision. This is the "empty, homogenous," linear temporality famously described by Walter Benjamin (*Illuminations* 261), an ontological
condition that, beginning in the early modern era, according to Charles Taylor,
gradually displaced a multidimensional temporality, in which events were more
commonly experienced as ritually "gathered, . . . reordered, and punctuated"
by transcendent or "higher time," a displacement Taylor calls the "Great Dis-
embedding" (*Secular Age* 748n45, 195). But while Thoreau's glowing celebration of mortality as part and parcel of autumnal experience brings the audience face-to-face with the contemporaneity of their own decay, the essay seeks
neither simply to protest modern temporality nor to replace it with some lost
premodern mode of life. Instead, by intercalating other temporal modalities of
experience, "Autumnal Tints" represents modernity as temporally dimensional
rather than monolithic.

To this end, Thoreau employs several narrative strategies while also incorporating the audience into the essay's central consciousness.[14] David Robinson
has noted the "brief but memorable" embedded narratives interspersed through
the essay, wherein the narrator "enact[s] moments . . . of profound sympathy
and openness" (*Natural Life* 189). These, I would add, serve not only an autobiographical function, representing Thoreau's extraordinary openness to autumnal phenomena. They also foster sympathetic identification, modeling the
narrator's attentive immersion on behalf of the contemporary bioregional audience whose embodied memory of "the fall" he seeks to reawaken. The effect
is to recover in collective regional memory a multidimensional, alternatively
modern temporality. Thus each subsection of the essay marks a moment in the
core autumnal narrative, frequently signaled with the temporal adverb "now,"
that serves both to locate the audience in the unfolding seasonal narrative and
to mark out the seasonal curve or Kalendar. While "Autumnal Tints" is full of
humorous, reflective digressions, this adverb repeatedly pulls the audience back
into the intensifying present of the unfolding season.[15] At the same time, within
each section the audience is situated bodily, incorporated into the present-tense
narratives that Thoreau had originally constructed in the Journal, creating a
series of moments embedded within the ongoing temporal arc.[16] The result is a
representation of "our" time that is neither one dimensional nor empty but full.

In the final chapter of *A Week on the Concord and Merrimack Rivers*, as
the narrative moves into fall, Thoreau returns to a distinction made earlier in
the chapter between knowledge that is truly "cumulative" and knowledge that

merely accumulates—acquired information, as we might say, contrasted with knowledge borne through lived experience and brought into the fullness of the present: "Much is said about the progress of science in these centuries. I should say that the useful results of science had accumulated, but that there had been no accumulation of knowledge, strictly speaking, for posterity; for knowledge is to be acquired only by a corresponding experience. How can we *know* what we are *told* merely? Each man can interpret another's experience only by his own" (*Wk* 364–65). Similarly, through what I have called its core seasonal narrative, "Autumnal Tints" represents a cumulative temporality in the embodied richness of the narrator's sharp seasonal sensibility—a felt fullness culminating in the unfolding present, contrasted with the comparative emptiness and fragmentation he has associated with normative modern temporality. As registered in "Autumnal Tints," this cumulative temporality is demonstrably the product of the Journal practice I have described and thus a kind of personal harvest. But, to the extent that the narrator not only acknowledges his own distractions, his own implication in normative modern time, but also seeks to reawaken richer awareness of a corresponding seasonal experience in his audience, "Autumnal Tints" also makes this alternative modern temporality available to the regional, and now wider collective, community.

NOTES

1. Morton takes this phrase, which encapsulates "the single most important notion in [his] book" (7), from Hegel's account in *The Phenomenology of Spirit* (383–409).

2. "On the whole, nature writing, and its precursors and family members mostly in phenomenological and/or Romantic writing, has tended to favor a substantialist view of nature—it is palpable and *there*—despite the explicit politics of the author" (Morton 16). The "ambient poetics" fostered by such writing "shuttles subject and object back and forth so that we may think they have dissolved into each other" (15).

3. For an anatomy of genres amalgamated in Thoreauvian environmental nonfiction, including natural history and travel narrative, see Buell, *Environmental Imagination* 397–423.

4. Although often depicted as a quixotic rearguard action against the rising tide of scientific modernity, Thoreau's position is more accurately seen as part of a recurring debate, continuing down to our day, between constructivist, on the one hand, and realist,

rationalist, or positivist accounts of scientific practice, on the other. See Barbara Herrn-stein Smith 1–17.

5. Walls contrasts what she calls "rational holism," which conceives the whole "as a divine or transcendent unity fully comprehended only through thought," with an emergent alternative, "empirical holism," which "stressed that the whole could be understood only by studying the interconnections of its constituent and individual parts" (*Seeing* 4, see also 84–93).

6. Walls has compiled a useful collection of Thoreau's commentary on science and writing in *Material Faith*.

7. For the evolution of Thoreau's Journal, including the method of composition described here, see the historical introductions to the Princeton edition of Thoreau's Journal, particularly 1: 592–93, 2: 446–47, 3: 480–81, 488–90; see also Howarth. For two rare specimens of Thoreau's field notes, see the third illustration following *PJ* 5: 598. On the relationship between Thoreau's Journal project and the composition of *Walden*, see Rossi, "The Journal and *Walden*."

8. While this passage is conventionally romantic in its aesthetic aim of "expressing nature," in using the language of empiricism it notably does not mystify *whose* "impressions," *whose* experience mediates the expression or *whose* hands shape it.

9. Here I am indebted to Laura Dassow Walls's suggestive efforts to show "how Thoreau's [scientific] endeavors can be read through Bruno Latour's account of the process of science" in "Textbooks and Texts from the Brooks" (17) and to her essay "Romancing the Real."

10. The parallels between Latour's Amazon fieldwork and Thoreau's journal method are explored by some detail in Walls ("Romancing" 140–48).

11. Compare also Peck's observation regarding the form created by Thoreau's compositional practice. Not only did the Journal's "open form" create the daily product or "record of the complex reciprocity between relation and category, fact and idea, observation and generalization." It also enabled the Journal to serve "as the instrument through which that reciprocity was perceived, understood, and enacted" (87).

12. As, for instance, when he comments sarcastically that, instead of having "only a single tree or 2 for suicides," a little more tree planting in villages might improve the worldviews as well as the temperaments of villagers (*Exc* 247).

13. Because, before its publication in the *Atlantic* in October 1862, "Autumnal Tints" was delivered several times as a lecture, in what follows I refer to its audience more or less interchangeably as auditors and readers. For a chronology of lecture deliveries together with contemporary reviews and responses, see Dean and Hoag.

14. As John Hildebidle notes regarding the late natural history essays, this consciousness is not the "I" common in Thoreau's earlier writings "but 'you' or 'we.' Certainly the

first-person pronoun is infrequent, relatively speaking, and often tied directly to the second and third person. 'I' occurs . . . only three times in the first six paragraphs of 'Autumnal Tints' and then is swept aside by a flood of 'we' and 'our'" (88).

15. Two examples of this embedding in the "Scarlet Oak" section: "Now too, the first of October, or later, the elms are at the height of their autumnal beauty" (*Exc* 235); "The smallest Sugar Maples in our streets make a great show as early as the fifth of October. . . . As I look up the Main Street they appear like painted screens standing before the houses, yet many are green. But now, or generally by the 17th of October, . . . the large Sugar Maples also are in their glory" (*Exc* 242).

16. "Stand under this tree [scarlet oak] and see how finely its leaves are cut against the sky, as it were, only a few sharp points extending from a midrib. They look like double, treble or quadruple crosses" (*Exc* 249). "This very perfect and vigorous [scarlet oak], about forty feet high, standing in an open pasture, which was quite glossy green on the 12th, is now, the 26th, completely changed to bright dark scarlet, every leaf, between you and the sun as if it had been dipped into a scarlet dye" (*Exc* 252–53).

DAVID M. ROBINSON

Thoreau, Modernity, and Nature's Seasons

The Antimodern Thoreau

Although Thoreau was known to the larger public of his own day as a disciple and imitator of Emerson and a hermitlike writer on natural history, his stature has grown steadily over the past century and a half. He is now recognized as an environmental prophet and an early critic of the mania of excessive consumption in the emerging American market economy, and his place in the international pantheon of influential modern authors seems secure. A wisdom source for Gandhi and Martin Luther King Jr. as well as for the Sierra Club and green sensibility generally, Thoreau appears to be the most "modern" author among the founders of a distinctive American literature, a thinker whose precepts speak as if directly to the maladies of the twenty-first century, both spiritual and political.

Thoreau was, of course, as skeptical of popularity and fame as he was of new clothes. Were he to consider his present status as among the first of the "moderns," our own contemporary, how would he react? Would he feel comfortable with the label "modern"? All indications point decidedly to the negative. "Modern" was the last thing that Thoreau aspired to be, and he held in frank contempt those who pursued the most "up-to-date" trends in the culture. If anything, Thoreau was antimodern, bristling with resistance to much of the rapidly changing nineteenth-century world in which he found himself. He was fascinated instead by the old and so-called outdated and drawn to those who were in one way or another throwbacks to some lost better world or adept at some forgotten way of doing things. Modernity was, for Thoreau, the problem. His works are, in many respects, attempts to answer that problem.

This contempt for the modern is crucial in understanding Thoreau's temperament and his sense of himself, and I will describe it first in addressing Thoreau's relationship to modernity. But his resistance to the modernity of his age was selective and did not blind him to important trends of thought that were reshaping his era's sense of the human place in the universe. For it was Thoreau's age that began an unsettling interrogation into the reigning assumptions about the place of the human in the natural world. This revision of the hierarchy of nature is central to the concept of modernity. Despite his protestations to the contrary, Thoreau is in some key respects a cutting-edge modern thinker who anticipated and commented trenchantly on a set of issues that would engage his culture for decades. Thoreau was not a divided man, but modernity is a capacious term. So I will give you two Thoreaus, one in a pitched battle with the "modern" and the other who steps ahead of his contemporaries in confronting one of the crucial shifts of consciousness that defines "modernity."

We first find in Thoreau the delightfully abrasive critic of all things new. This is the caustically ironic voice we encounter in the opening pages of *Walden*, in the essays "Walking" and "Life without Principle," and throughout his voluminous Journal. Thoreau's account of his two-year life-experiment at Walden Pond provides some of the most persuasive evidence for his antimodern stance. The experiment was arguably an attempt to escape from the modern world, to shed its values, its desires, and its accoutrements, to cleanse himself completely from the pollution of the modern. We typically consider *Walden* the account of a return to nature; it is equally a return to the past, or an attempt to make such a return. "I kept Homer's Iliad on my table through the summer," Thoreau wrote, "though I looked at his page only now and then" (*W* 99). Thwarted in his planned course of reading by "incessant labor with my hands"—the building of his house and the cultivation of his enormous bean-field—Thoreau nevertheless kept the book in view. It stood for him as a reminder of his higher aspirations, which had been postponed because of the more immediate necessities of house building and cultivating his bean-field. Nevertheless, he continued to see himself as a student and to regard his ultimate purpose as reading and writing rather than farming. "My residence was more favorable, not only to thought, but to serious reading, than a university" (*W* 99), a remark that we can take not only as praise for his lakeside surroundings but as a subtle cut at collegiate pretensions.

Thoreau's hand labor was, in large part, for the sake of Homer and the other ancient authors that he extols in his chapter on "Reading." He hoped to live simply, by the work of his hands, in order to read them with the proper attention and discernment. He praised "the oldest Egyptian or Hindoo philosopher" for revelatory insights that still had not been bested, maintaining that "no time has elapsed since that divinity was revealed" (*W* 99). Such reading was of itself an act of self-strengthening, as refreshing as a bath in the pure waters of Walden Pond. Thoreau's proviso about such elevating reading, however, was that it must be done in the original languages of the ancients, not in a modern translation. "The student may read Homer or Æschylus in the Greek without danger of dissipation or luxuriousness, for it implies that he in some measure emulate their heroes, and consecrate morning hours to their pages" (*W* 100). The past here represents heroic discipline and consecration to a great task, qualities that Thoreau finds missing from the world of modernity. "The heroic books, even if printed in the character of our mother tongue, will always be in a language dead to degenerate times; and we must laboriously seek the meaning of each word and line, conjecturing a larger sense than common use permits out of what wisdom and valor and generosity we have" (*W* 100). Such reading is a challenge, but an edifying one, bringing out capabilities and virtues that were never tapped by what Thoreau calls, dismissively, "the modern cheap and fertile press" (*W* 100). Modernity, in this representation, is a steady, or perhaps accelerating, flight away from wisdom. Thoreau lives, he feels, in "degenerate times."

The attack on degenerate times is, in fact, the argument with which Thoreau initially confronts his readers in *Walden*, where he portrays economy as a virtue somehow lost in the modern world. "Most of the luxuries, and many of the so called comforts of life, are not only not indispensable, but positive hinderances to the elevation of mankind" (*W* 14), Thoreau argues, mounting his famous attack on the unacknowledged modern slavery of money, work, and the consumption of goods. It is not simply that men and women have lost their capacity for frugality and simplicity but that in losing those capacities, they have also lost their moral compass and their awareness of the spiritual. Thoreau recognizes how the pursuit of material goods, an endless one in which temporarily satisfied hungers only awaken new ones, destroys both the judgment and the capacity we need to maintain our independence as moral beings. Moral independence, he would argue, is the only condition that constitutes a durable sense of self-worth, without which all other pleasures are hollow.

He thus moves through the categories of necessities—food, clothing, and shelter—with a ruthless eye toward eliminating the superfluous, less because these extras are luxurious than because their attainment distracts us, and distracts us critically, from our ultimate fulfillment. "My purpose in going to Walden Pond was not to live cheaply nor to live dearly there, but to transact some private business with the fewest obstacles" (*W* 19–20). We all, Thoreau implies, have such business to transact. The retreat to the cabin at Walden was in this sense a fundamentally antimodern experiment. Thoreau was a farmer, at least in his first summer when he raised a large crop of beans, but a farmer who used methods that were largely regarded as uninformed and primitive by the farmers around him. With ironic self-deprecation, he referred to himself as "merely a squatter" (*W* 54). He cited the practices of early settlers and of the Indians as guides, believing that they represented an antithesis to the modern world of 1840s Concord. And he explicitly framed his experiment as a return, an attempt to recapture something lost to his world. A Journal entry written during his first summer at Walden, inspired in part by his admiration of Wordsworth, captures the mood of wistful backward looking that explains his motivations. "To live to a good old age such as the ancients reached—serene and contented—dignifying the life of man—Leading a simple epic country life—in these days of confusion and turmoil" (*PJ* 2: 200–201). Serenity rather than turmoil; contentment rather than confusion—these characterizations of the superiority of the past were woven into *Walden* and remained a defining part of Thoreau's sensibility.

Mortality and Modernity

The antimodern Thoreau that I describe here was, however, strikingly modern in a very significant way. Thoreau confronted the religious implications of what we have come to call the Darwinian revolution quite early and offered an honest and thoughtful response to it that has a continuing relevance. Most significantly, Thoreau understood that the central lesson of the unfolding scientific work of his day was that humans were, in fact, part of natural history. As natural creatures, men and women shared the planet with many other creatures, partaking in their vitality but also in their vulnerability and mortality. I would hasten to add, of course, that this in itself was no new idea, as a glance at Ecclesiastes 3.19 suggests: "For that which befalleth the sons of men befalleth beasts; even one thing befalleth them: as the one dieth, so dieth the other; yea, they have all one breath; so that a man hath no preeminence above a beast: for all is vanity."

However ancient this idea may have been, it was threatening to mainstream thinking in the nineteenth century and remains so today. Thoreau's was an age that held to hard lines of demarcation between human and the "lower" animals and regarded humans as exceptional through the religious doctrine of the immortal individual soul that promised to negate death entirely. Thoreau, through his studies as a naturalist, came to see the difficult truth of mortality with clarity and also with an acceptance that was both direct and surprisingly positive.

"One abstains from writing or printing on the immortality of the soul," Emerson remarked in "Immortality," "because, when he comes to the end of his statement, the hungry eyes that run through it will close disappointed; the listeners say, That is not here which we desire" (*Complete Works* 8: 345). As Emerson explained to his disappointed hearers in lectures on the subject of everlasting life, "Nature never spares the individual." No individual can, or should, expect immortal life as a particular individual. "We have our indemnity only in the moral or intellectual reality to which we aspire. That is immortal, and we only through that. The soul stipulates for no private good" (8: 343). Emerson's observation about the difficulty of addressing the question of immortality to a nineteenth-century audience has, I think, a direct connection to Thoreau's striking frankness on this subject. The anxiety and resistance generated by evolutionary theory, and particularly by Darwin's articulation of the concept of natural selection, was intricately interwoven with a larger spiritual crisis about the possibility of an afterlife. The more closely that human origins and human behavior were connected with the natural world, the deeper the anxieties, generating the war between science and religion that defines what we mean by "modernity" in many crucial respects. Thoreau can accurately be described as both a naturalist and a religious thinker, and his consideration of this central question thus stands as one of his most important intellectual achievements.

In the "Spring" chapter of *Walden*, Thoreau told of walking back to his Walden cabin in the dark of night and encountering the stench of a dead horse, which decayed "in the hollow by the path to my house" and "compelled me sometimes to go out of my way, especially in the night when the air was heavy." Nevertheless, he found the odor of the horse's decay a reassurance of "the strong appetite and inviolable health of Nature" (*W* 318), a power that is at work in both the new life springing up everywhere around the pond and the continuing death that, as he recognizes, makes that new life possible. Thoreau thus turns the decaying carcass of the horse into an emblem of nature's inevitable processes and opens a larger meditation on the expendable quality of particular creatures or, more bluntly, the cheapness of life, an unexpected turn of thought for a writer so wholly identified with the recognition of the beauty and intrinsic value of the natural world. But as a close observer of nature, Thoreau could not have missed its essential violence. As he wrote in "Spring," "I love to see that Nature is so rife with life that myriads can be afforded to be sacrificed and suffered to prey on one another; that tender organizations can be so serenely squashed out of existence like pulp,—tadpoles which herons gobble up, and tortoises and toads run over in the road; and that sometimes it has rained flesh and blood!" (*W* 318). Thoreau describes events familiar to anyone who has closely observed the natural world. Starvation, accident, the preying of one animal upon another—this is the "brutal," as we call it, natural world. It is a world of which human beings, their social organizations, and their wars are also a part, as Thoreau signals in his subtly ironic remark that "sometimes it has rained flesh and blood!"

But Thoreau is by no means horrified with what he sees. Or perhaps it is better to say that he resists the conventional response of horrified denial of the bloody facts of nature and attempts to see natural processes from a larger perspective, one that necessarily discounts the needs and desires of human beings. What, from a limited standpoint, may appear to be cruelty or ruthlessness Thoreau tries to understand instead as the process or mechanism that serves as a guarantor of nature's power and richness. While he does not speak the emerging language of natural selection or the modern language of biocentrism, he is clearly beginning to conceptualize both these perspectives and consider their implications. Enormous loss, measured on a human scale, becomes less significant when seen from a higher and more comprehensive perspective. Such losses, however terrible they seem, leave nature's fundamental vigor untouched.

Published in 1854, some five years before Darwin's *On the Origin of Species* would appear, Thoreau's discussion of the fecundity and ferocity of natural processes offers an instructive example of the ways that philosophical and ethical discourse merged with early scientific observation in the mid-nineteenth century. "Spring" was a relatively late addition to the long-evolving manuscript of *Walden*, which reflected not only Thoreau's experiment of life at the pond but the beginnings of his projects in natural history and plant cataloging after his return from the pond.[1] These studies not only had generated a clearer understanding of the processes of natural change and evolution but had challenged Thoreau to consider its philosophical and religious implications.

Modernity and the Seasons

Scholars have long recognized, although with differing reactions, Thoreau's turn toward the factual and the empirical in his later career. His Journal gradually evolves from a tool for speculative thought, introspection, and the drafting of passages for publication into a place in which he records his almost daily excursions into the woods, with numerous listings of plant and animal observations, notes on seasonal changes, descriptions of the landscape under dusk, dawn, or moonlight conditions, and so forth. For many years the consensus of literary scholars, enthralled by the structural and metaphorical achievement of *Walden*, was that this change marked a declension, a loss of imaginative and artistic power. Thoreau himself reinforced this idea in passages in which he berates himself for what he feels is a narrowing of intellectual range. In 1851, some four years after he had returned to life in Concord from his Walden cabin, he lamented in his Journal: "I fear that the character of my knowledge is from year to year becoming more distinct & scientific—That in exchange for views as wide as heaven's cope I am being narrowed down to the field of a microscope—I see details not wholes nor the shadow of the whole" (*PJ* 3: 380). Recent scholars who have approached Thoreau from the context of environmental ethics or science studies or, more broadly, as a capacious philosophical thinker have found that his later years were enormously expansive ones and that his observations as a naturalist are part of a larger philosophical effort to synthesize a theory of nature's processes of change and renewal.[2] The difficulty was to reconcile these observations about the phenomena of the natural world with human self-conceptions and aspirations.

It was through his deeper recognition and understanding of the seasonal cycles of the natural world that Thoreau would begin to develop a response to his era's eroding confidence in the immortality of the individual human soul. This was, for him, a great intellectual task, but it was also a work grounded in emotion and loss. His descriptions and meditations on seasonality, which placed humans within a natural cycle, were in part grief-driven; they also reflect his own struggles with vulnerability, aging, and mortality. We are not ordinarily accustomed to seeing Thoreau through the lens of emotional pain. He cultivated stoicism in his personal life, a quality that he magnified in the personae of his published work and even of his Journal. He was a man with edges, even to his closest friends, and his abruptness, impatience, and tendency toward judgment

of others cost him companionship that he craved. During their long friendship, Emerson accused him of intellectual coldness (Richardson, *Life* 266), a
charge that wounded Thoreau deeply; in his eulogy for his friend, Emerson
commented on Thoreau's bald frankness in dealing with others, remembering
his "accusing silences," "searching" comments, and, most of all, "terrible eyes"
from which no fault of his companions "seemed concealed" (*Complete Works*
10: 465–66). But this impatience and gruffness should not be taken as a sign
that Thoreau was exempt from his era's qualms, including its angst over death
and immortality. His growing sense of the remorselessly evolutionary qualities
of nature and its disregard for individual survival was more than theoretical.
He sustained deep emotional injuries from his brother John's death, and the
ensuing grief, guilt, and anxiety eventually led him to Walden Pond, where he
withdrew, hoping to write a memorial to his brother.

Both *A Week* and *Walden* are thus conditioned emotionally in Thoreau's
grieving for John, emotions that generated in turn an existential crisis over his
own mortality.[3] With his innately sympathetic and symbolic consciousness,
Thoreau saw himself in the dead horse on the path to the pond, just as he had
seen himself in the other creatures and events surrounding the pond—the wild,
untameable loon, the outlaw woodchuck, the quiet fish swimming under the
ice, even the pond itself. He saw that he had to come to terms with these living
creatures but with their inevitable deaths as well. His growing appreciation of
the cycle of death and rebirth enacted in the seasonal year thus became central
to his later work. Always aware of and sensitive to the seasons, it was in the years
after he returned from the pond that Thoreau made himself into a systematic
recorder and perceptive theorist of seasonality and natural cycles, a celebrator
in particular of the transitional seasons of spring and fall. Scholars have identified the spring of 1852 as a key moment in this turn, a period in which we see
the Journal emerging as a calendar of Concord natural life.[4] Of particular note is
Thoreau's entry of 18 April, in which he writes, "For the first time I perceive this
spring that the year is a circle," and goes on to ask, "Why should just these sights
& sounds accompany our life?" (*PJ* 4: 468). The circular, and thus endless, year
takes us into itself as part of an unending cycle that is both stable and infinitely
various. This recognition grew over the next decade through Thoreau's extensive observation and recording of natural phenomena in his Journal, the task
that evolved into his life's work. While it was "scientific" work in the sense that
it required close scrutiny of natural phenomena, detailed records, and a certain

systematic goal, it was a science that remained deeply imbued with Thoreau's semispiritual conception of the seasonal cycle as an experience as well as an observable fact.

At the center of these observations was an intense interest in plant regeneration and seed dispersal. Thoreau's late essay "The Succession of Forest Trees"—which was part of a vastly larger unfinished work, the drafts of which were edited and published as *Faith in a Seed* by Bradley P. Dean in 1993—explains the capacity of pine forests to succeed hardwood and vice versa.[5] Thoreau describes the vast numbers of acorns that he found in evergreen stands around Concord, evidence that squirrels and birds had transported seeds over a wide area. These were the source of the hardwood forest that replaced the evergreens when they were logged or burned. The essay is in the first place an empirical refutation of the folkloric ideas, still held by many farmers, that trees spontaneously generated themselves. But, more importantly, it is an illustration of the way plants and animals regenerate themselves through a kind of profligate reproduction, wastefully but powerfully efficient. As he wrote in *Faith in a Seed*, while "a great pine wood may drop many millions of seeds in one year," perhaps "only half a dozen of them are conveyed a quarter of a mile and lodge against some fence, and only one of these comes up and grows up there" (36). Over time, though, that single tree will itself sow a new group of seedlings, and the pine wood will have begun to extend itself. This process suggests "how persevering Nature is and how much time she has to work in," a method that seems inconceivable to the limited human conception of time. "In this haphazard manner Nature surely creates you a forest at last, though as if it were the last thing she were thinking of. By seemingly feeble and stealthy steps—by a geologic pace—she gets over the greatest distances and accomplishes her greatest results" (*Faith* 36).

It is evident that in such passages Thoreau is walking a very thin line between two ways of describing nature. The first is a conception of nature, conventional for this era, in which a Creator, working in recognizable intentional terms, advances the process of creation. The second, more modern theory, one that we associate with Darwin, sees a process in which the continuation and regeneration of life is a question of chance and adaptation, dependent on a vast production of seeds to guarantee the survival of a few of them. Thoreau's language is mixed: he personifies nature as an intentional creative power ("how persevering Nature is"), but he also uses phrases that seem to deny intent and emphasize chance (Nature's "haphazard manner" and her "seemingly feeble and stealthy steps"). But the thrust of the essay is to revise the way that the process of plant regeneration is thought of by expanding the time frame in which one considers the process. This is clearly liminal discourse, moving from one philosophical frame of reference to another and carrying two opposed conceptions of natural processes simultaneously.

As Robert Sattelmeyer has explained, Thoreau had been exposed to several forms of evolutionary theory in the 1840s and 1850s before his projects on seed dispersion began (*Thoreau's Reading* 78–92). Robert Chambers's *Vestiges of the Natural History of Creation* (1844), which described the present natural world as the result of a long process of organic evolution, had caused great consternation and stirred vigorous debate in the middle and late 1840s and was opposed by America's leading scientific voice, Louis Agassiz. Thoreau knew both Chambers's theory and Agassiz's countertheory of special creation, which resisted the idea that earlier species evolved into later ones, holding that each was a particular and special creation of God. Although Thoreau knew Agassiz and had even supplied him with specimens of animal life for his cataloging and research, he could not accept the special creation theory because, as Sattelmeyer has argued, it seemed to rob nature of a sense of ongoing creative vitality. Thoreau instead held "the notion of a universe in a continual state of becoming, where nature was dynamic and evolving" (*Thoreau's Reading* 88).[6] As Thoreau's Journal entries in the late 1840s and early 1850s demonstrate, he was keen to observe the signs of perpetual creativity and undeniable living force in nature, celebrating it both in Journal entries and in his chapter "Spring" in *Walden*. Thoreau's intense interest in seasonal change reflected this conception of the perpetual energy and dynamism of nature. By early 1860, when Thoreau read *On the Origin of Species*, he was already deeply engaged in his "Kalendar" of natural life in the Concord woods and his studies of seasonality and seed dispersion that were the basis of his later essays.[7] Thoreau folded Darwin's theories into his own more limited investigations of plant propagation and seed dispersal, and it seems clear that Darwin's depiction of the development of the forms of natural life tallied well with Thoreau's sense of nature's inexorable process of change, death, and renewal.

The Vital Natural World

As the reaction to Darwin, both immediate and ongoing, has suggested, the process of evolutionary change raises difficult questions about our conceptions of our individual lives as humans and about the life, and significance, of the human species as a whole. The general intellectual reorientation of which Darwin's work was perhaps the most prominent element called into question biblical accounts of the earth's origins and linked humans with an animal ancestry. Of greater concern to many, it also called into question the "soul" and its link with an eternal life after death, which had been assumed a unique aspect of human existence. Moreover, by recognizing man as a "species" among many others, it linked humanity with the long history of development, change, and extinction that the fossil record had revealed. As Darwin wrote and as naturalists had known for many years from the fossil record, "species and groups of species gradually disappear, one after another, first from one spot, then from another, and finally from the world" (*On the Origin* 317–18). In a variety of ways, therefore, evolutionary theory challenged the stability of the assumptions that had shaped the concept of human identity in Western culture.

Yet it was precisely this revelation of a changing, and therefore vital, natural world that Thoreau craved. The rotting corpse of the horse did not mean stench and decay to him but an unconquerable vitality—it was not a symbol of death but of life itself. The paragraph in which the rotting horse appears begins with a comment about the dangerous inertia of ordinary life in Concord, with Concord representing, as always for Thoreau, typical American middle-class experience. "Our village life would stagnate if it were not for the unexplored forests and meadows which surround it," he asserts (*W* 317). While he finds that life amidst his neighbors can become stifling, the "forests and meadows" around Concord are the places in which new and vital experience can still be obtained: "We need the tonic of wildness,—to wade sometimes in marshes where the bittern and the meadow-hen lurk, and hear the booming of the snipe; to smell the whispering sedge where only some wilder and more solitary fowl builds her nest, and the mink crawls with its belly close to the ground" (*W* 317). The sentence barrages us with images of living things, birds and reclusive animals that few persons ever encounter but that indicate the unbounded variety of natural life and energy in places where most people never go.

To seek out and encounter such life is to begin to be a part of it, Thoreau believes, because it demands a kind of open receptivity, a state of being fully awake, that is the best insurance against inertia and stagnation. The paradox inherent in this recognition is that the acquisition of such knowledge is never-ending. We can never finally "know" nature in any complete sense, and that, for Thoreau, is a crucially important, and positive, recognition. "At the same time that we are earnest to explore and learn all things," he writes, "we require that all things be mysterious and unexplorable" (*W* 317). Knowledge generates the need for new knowledge, and our learning must always lead to new mysteries. We must believe, therefore, that "land and sea be infinitely wild, unsurveyed and unfathomed by us because unfathomable" (*W* 317–18). Thoreau acknowledges that the growth of human knowledge inevitably suggests the limits of the human capacity to know. To survive intellectually and spiritually we must condemn ourselves to a condition of perpetual inadequacy and dissatisfaction.

Thoreau's meditations on nature's vastness and on its cycles of death and rebirth led him to welcome any experience as valuable that reminded men and women of their somewhat inconsequential roles in the larger drama of which they were a part, providing a necessary philosophical humility largely absent from the predominant religions and philosophies of the day. "We need to witness our own limits transgressed, and some life pasturing freely where we never wander" (*W* 318), he observed. Given the inevitable cruelty of nature's cycles, the fact that they entailed death as well as new life, he argued that "compassion is a very untenable ground" (*W* 318) as a philosophy of nature. It was of course the assumption of a human-centered and compassionate universe that Darwinian evolution challenged directly and that was the basis for much of the cultural resistance to it. Adaptability and survival were the fundamentals of the Darwinian conception of evolutionary change. While there were direct religious challenges to Darwinian evolutionary theory, perhaps as important was the general cultural angst that Darwin's *Origin* generated, largely by displacing humanity from the center of nature and by suggesting that a dark struggle for survival was nature's fundamental engine. But as he came to understand through his own researches a natural world that changed and thereby extended itself, a nature that could be described in terms of metamorphosis but not of compassion, Thoreau found innocence rather than cruelty as the best term through which to comprehend nature. "The impression made on a wise man is that of universal innocence" (*W* 318), he concluded. He meant an innocence so complete that the individual self loses primacy and consequence in the larger workings of nature's cycles. As Emerson had written, "Nature never spares the individual" (*Complete Works* 8: 343). It is a stoic wisdom, reinforced no doubt by Thoreau's affinity for classical philosophy. But in its immediate cultural context, it is also a strikingly modern stance, incorporating aspects of Darwin's vision of natural evolution even before it was fully articulated and anticipating how profoundly disconcerting evolutionary nature would be to the nineteenth-century religious sensibility. Thoreau's thinking about nature's cycles of life and death and the human place in them stands in contrast to much of the cultural response to Darwin largely because its central premise was that men and women must rethink their assumption of their centrality in the natural world; they "must witness [their] own limits transgressed" (*W* 318).

NOTES

1. On the development of the *Walden* manuscript, see Shanley; Sattelmeyer, "Remaking"; and Milder 118–64.

2. Important contributions to the recovery of the later Thoreau include Howarth, Buell, Milder, Richardson, Walls, Berger, Robinson, and Dean's editions of *Faith in a Seed* and *Wild Fruits*.

3. For further detail, see Robinson, *Natural Life* 29–76.

4. See Lebeaux 151–64; Milder 120–21; and Richardson, *Life* 256–72. As Richardson explains, this was also the period in which Thoreau first read William Gilpin's work on the process of nature description, which had a profound impact on both his observational practices and his prose style.

5. Also of importance is Dean's edition of *Wild Fruits*, a project connected with Thoreau's studies of seed dispersion. For discussion of Thoreau's work in seed dispersion, see Walls, *Seeing* 179–99; Berger; and Robinson, *Natural Life* 176–201.

6. See also the discussion of Thoreau's problematic relationship with Agassiz by Walls, *Seeing* 113–16, 144–47.

7. Thoreau gained access to Darwin's *On the Origin of Species* (1859) at the Concord Library and copied passages from it in his "Commonplace Book, 1856–1861." See Sattelmeyer, *Thoreau's Reading* 163, 89–92; and Walls, *Seeing* 194–99.

RANDALL CONRAD

An Infinite Road to the Golden Age

A CLOSE READING OF THOREAU'S
"ROAD—THAT OLD CARLISLE ONE"
IN THE LATE JOURNAL
(24 SEPTEMBER 1859)

In memoriam: STEPHEN F. ELLS (1935–2008)
conservationist, Thoreauvian, old Carlisle road saunterer

THOREAU'S JOURNAL ENTRY for 24 September 1859 runs to eight and a half pages in the Torrey-Allen edition—pages and pages of natural history observations interspersed with a few passages of a much more eccentric construction. The "old Carlisle road" is the subject of these eccentric passages, particularly the baffling 330-word sequence we are examining in this essay.[1]

Thoreau's homage to the old Carlisle road is one of the most difficult passages to be found in the Journal, but I hope to show that we can decipher it with the help of science, mythology, theology, psychology, folklore, and women's fashion notes—and when we do, we will realize some ways in which it addresses Thoreau's modernity.

Here is the passage:

> Road—that old Carlisle one—that leaves towns behind; where you put off
> worldly thoughts; where you do not carry a watch, nor remember the proprietor;
> where the proprietor is the only trespasser,—looking after *his* apples!—the only
> one who mistakes his calling there, whose title is not good; where fifty may be
> a-barberrying and you do not see one. It is an endless succession of glades where
> the barberries grow thickest, successive yards amid the barberry bushes where

you do not see out. There I see Melvin and the robins, and many a nut-brown maid *sashé*-ing to the barberry bushes in hoops and crinoline, and none of them see me. The world-surrounding hoop! faery rings! Oh, the jolly cooper's trade it is the best of any! Carried to the furthest isles where civilized man penetrates. This the girdle they've put round the world! Saturn or Satan set the example. Large and small hogsheads, barrels, kegs, worn by the misses that go to that lone schoolhouse in the Pinkham Notch. The lonely horse in its pasture is glad to see company, comes forward to be noticed and takes an apple from your hand. Others are called great roads, but this is greater than they all. The road is only laid out, offered to walkers, not *accepted* by the town and the traveling world. To be represented by a dotted line on charts, or drawn in lime-juice, undiscoverable to the uninitiated, to be held to a warm imagination. No guide-boards indicate it. No odometer would indicate the miles a wagon had run there. Rocks which the druids *might* have raised—if they could. There I go searching for malic acid of the right quality, with my tests. The process is simple. Place the fruit between your jaws and then endeavor to make your teeth meet. The very earth contains it. The Easterbrooks Country contains malic acid. (*J* XII: 348–49, 24 Sept. 1859)[2]

I see this passage as an effort to elevate the old Carlisle road metaphysically to serve as a pathway for the imagination and a stimulus to it. It is a vivid prose poem that has, in parts, a satirical ring. It is cryptic in parts, owing to a cascade of images and themes in the middle. These apparently disconnected tropes occupy about five lines of print, seemingly a wild cascade of images and rhetoric linked by idiosyncratic associations.

Spinning Thoughts, Flying Ideas

I know of only two Thoreauvians who have commented at all on this passage. One was the late Steve Ells, who wrote extensively about Thoreau's lifelong relationship to Estabrook Country and the old Carlisle road. The second, Dr. Michael Sperber, is a neuropsychiatrist and the author of a study of Thoreau from a clinical as well as a humanist perspective.

Ells writes: "His detachment permits him to hear his thoughts, even when they spin" (95). Sperber cites Thoreau's Journal passage as evidence of hypergraphia, or overwriting, a behavior associated with the manic-depressive disorder known as bipolar depression, stating, "the flight of ideas and stream of associations, characteristic of mania, are so extensive that they obscure the meaning of Thoreau's prose."[3]

Obscure? Not entirely. When Thoreau was writing for his Journal (as Bill Rossi reminds us in his essay in this volume), he always carried a pencil and notepaper in the field. He would jot down enough notes and details to remind him of the whole observation. Later in the day or the week, he would make the time to copy out a full and more polished version in his Journal pages.

Clearly, when this "manic" flight of associations suddenly demanded expression, Thoreau simply jotted down the disjointed images as each arose. Later, he copied these essentials, perhaps with a bit of elaboration, into the entry for 24 September.[4] Possibly he intended to make more of it at another time, or possibly he liked it the way it was. Certainly this passage, in fact, the entire Journal entry, exemplifies that nontraditional structure (or even nonstructure) of Thoreauvian journal writing that François Specq illuminates for us in his essay in this volume.

Textual Explication

From its ungrammatical opening, through its metaphysicalization of a physical landscape, through its delirium of associated tropes at midpoint, to its concluding Yankee drollery about a pseudoscientific test for malic acid, this passage is idiosyncratic . . . protomodern . . . and, to be sure, private. It was written entirely in one sitting and perhaps lightly enhanced later, yet with no intention of polish for publication. Nevertheless, like any intriguing verbal construct, it calls for explication.

"Road—that old Carlisle one . . ." This is an odd English usage to introduce a specific road in the real world. It is as ungrammatical as if I were to begin in French, *Parvis—celui, ancien, de René Descartes à Lyon*, and so on. But what a great Neoplatonist exclamation it makes! First the essence—"road," then the actual or accidental—"that old Carlisle one."

We are taking an excursion on a path that promises to idealize our experience, to make us see independently of the everyday world. On this road, Thoreau says, we leave "worldly thoughts" behind—we become open to higher perceptions. (Thoreau uses "worldly"—a key word—not in our contemporary sense of "sophisticated" but in a traditional religious sense, referring to the ma-

terial world, the realm of all things profane, as opposed to the spiritual realm.)
We do not carry a watch, that is, we are also leaving behind the idea of measured
time and therefore the everyday criterion of punctuality, and so on. Further, we
ignore the landowner, whoever he may be; in fact, we deny him any ownership
rights. The apples in the orchards are not *his*, Thoreau declares.

The play of vision is reciprocal between the saunterer on the road and the
people in a succession of "glades" and "yards." Either we are on the road and
cannot see fifty berry-gatherers behind the thick shrubs, or else we are among
the berry-gatherers and do not see out to the road. In either direction, we are
sightless, or else objects are invisible. Thoreau thus establishes a theme of sight,
vision, and sightlessness while at the same time laying out a topography for the
landscape. The "glades" are the large berry-bushes that bound the "yards," which
are the spaces that can be occupied by people. Finally, since this succession is
"endless," we are invited to visualize the landscape as if infinitely reflected.

In spite of all this invisibility, Thoreau sees one acquaintance (his friend
George Melvin), some wildlife (the robins), and "many a nut-brown maid." We
recognize that Thoreau is borrowing an old cliché in literature and folk culture
("nut-brown" connotes the fullness of nature),[5] but who are the actual maids
picking the berries? Are the young women of Estabrook really brown? They
may be tanned after months of summer sunshine, yet the more likely meaning
is that these maids are ripe, as when a nut turns fully brown, ready to seed the
earth. The adjective "nut-brown" associates the maids with health, the seasons,
and the earth—with nature, reproduction, regeneration.

In contrast to so much naturalness, their apparel gives them an unnatural
gait—sashaying (strutting)—and it also binds them to the world of ladies' fashion, the world of hoops and crinoline (i.e., ladies' wear), hence returning us to
"worldly thoughts." Around this period, an issue of *Notes and Queries*, a journal
for ladies (written by men), spoke of the present age as "these days of crinoline
and hoop-petticoats."[6] Hoopskirts, in which the hoops, a succession of increasingly wide circles, were sewn into the crinoline, causing the skirt to bell out,
were ubiquitous in Thoreau's time. His mother and sisters wore them.

The lines beginning with "The world-surrounding hoop" and concluding
with "the Pinkham Notch" comprise the delirious midpoint of our passage.
What sounds like disconnected exclamations is actually a chain of tropes linked
by the theme of circularity: hoops and crinoline; world-surrounding hoop; fairy
rings; the jolly cooper (makes hoops); the furthest isles (i.e., the outer rim of

the world); girdle round the world; Saturn (the ringed planet); barrels worn by schoolgirls.

Each expresses the "circle" metaphor that is such a determining archetype in Thoreau's prose, especially in *Walden*. The effect of disjointed association lends Thoreau's writing the density of a prose poem or a stream-of-consciousness narrative, if there had been such a thing in the nineteenth century. Each trope comes into its own only when it has resonated with the others. This is the case, for example, with the image of a world encircled by a hoop and also encircled by commerce, as we will see below.

"Hoops," as in "hoops and crinoline," introduces the first circle image and gives rise to the next two associations, also circular—"The world-surrounding hoop! faery rings!" The world-surrounding hoop suggests Saturn, sixth planet from the sun. Saturn is girdled by a ring—certainly a unique model of a "world-surrounding hoop." What is Saturn doing in Estabrook? Thoreau had a real-life association between the old Carlisle road and Saturn on account of his acquaintanceship with a farmer named Perez Blood, who lived pretty far up the road, near the Carlisle town boundary. As the owner of a 30-power telescope, Blood doubled as an amateur astronomer. In 1847 and again in 1851, Thoreau and Emerson had gone along the old Carlisle road to visit Blood, and they used his telescope to get a close look at the ring around Saturn.

What about "faery rings," the richest of these circle tropes? Fairy rings are one thing in nature, another in folklore. In nature, an actual fairy ring refers to a circle of unusually lush grass-growth in a field, caused by a fungus.[7] In folklore, fairy rings (also known as pixie circles and *ronds de sorcière*) were held to be the miniature dance-floors of fairies. Inside the charmed circle, the little sprites would gather to make merry, dance, and play enchanting music. What does this have to do with vision? Quite a lot: in some parts of Europe, superstition held that the passing mortal who stepped inside a fairy ring would be punished with the loss of an eye or be struck blind. In some legends, a mortal who stepped inside the fairies' perimeter would become invisible to ordinary people outside and might remain a captive of the fairies.[8] With these two words "faery rings," Thoreau's circles acquire more connotations: magic, punishment, blindness. We remember that along the old Carlisle road, the successive "yards" are bounded by barberry bushes. *Those* are the fairy rings. We are the people who can't see out—or the ones who can't see in.

Interrupting Thoreau's prose cadences while continuing the hoop theme, we have the line about the "jolly cooper's trade."[9] The cooper's trade, of course, is the fabrication of barrels—both the staves and the hoops that hold them tightly together. If the cooper's trade is glorified as "the best of any," we have certainly left real life behind, so that this jolly cooper is not only an idealized stereotype but practically a supernatural figure—almost a symbol for the divine Creator who has set bounds to our globe with *his* hoops.

This theme of the circumferential limit of the world is continued in the next sentence fragment, which creates a further break in rhythm and tone: "Carried to the furthest isles where civilized man penetrates." I hear this grandiloquent conceit as sarcasm—Thoreau's spoof of the typical boast of American commerce as it began to go global by rail and ocean. This idea and these very expressions were commonplaces of the time, as we will see shortly.

In the exclamation "This the girdle they've put round the world!" Thoreau continues his sarcasm. "Girdle put round the world" reminds us of Shakespeare's character Puck, who declares: "I'll put a girdle round the earth in forty minutes."[10] By conjuring up Shakespeare's world of shape-shifting and delirium, Thoreau lends a supernatural aura to the Estabrook lands—just as he gives Estabrook a prehistoric and ceremonial atmosphere by associating the boulders with the Druids.

Yet this echo of Shakespeare's magic has a dark side, because "girdle," a double-edged metaphor, also connotes the diabolical operations of commerce. "This the girdle *they*'ve put round the world." Who are *they*? Surely this refers to the proprietors of this world, namely, the businessmen who are always fencing parts of it off for worldly gain.[11] Thoreau in many writings abundantly expresses his loathing of the diabolical role of commerce,[12] and perhaps this is what furnishes a link to Satan in the next sentence.

Notice how Thoreau, having interrupted his own cadence with other people's jingles and slogans, reestablishes a strong rhythm for his own voice by using this ten-syllable line propelled by the vigorous repetition of a compact, regular dactylic foot: "Sáturn or Sátan sét the exámple."[13] In one of the few actual puns in this paragraph, "Saturn" phonetically summons "Satan." This invocation of God's opponent, in turn, invites us to consider Saturn itself not as a planet but as a divinity. And Satan, God's opponent and fallen angel, in turn reflects Saturn, who in Greek myth was the ruler of the gods until he was overthrown. It isn't far-fetched to suggest that "set the example" could mean "has provided the model for a girdled world," the world that belongs to all of us but has been enclosed for the gain of a few. Also, remember, we do not wear a watch—but Saturn sometimes is Father Time.[14] Under Saturn, we risk falling back into the world of measured time and businesslike punctuality—indeed, mortality itself, the human condition—just as we were escaping from it along the old Carlisle road. "Large and small hogsheads, barrels, kegs, worn by the misses that go to that lone schoolhouse in the Pinkham Notch." Since these barrels are held together by hoops, Thoreau is continuing the circular "hoop" motif. However, notice the oneiric symbolism in this fantastic conceit of girls wearing barrels for clothing. Thoreau remembers the actual experience of seeing nut-brown maids gathering berries while wearing "hoops and crinoline," and now, in the manner of dream-work, he reproduces the same theme, but this time with literalness— schoolgirls wearing not just hoops but entire barrels.[15]

Invisible Ink and Malic Acid

With this, Thoreau's delirium of associations abates as he continues the meta-physicalization of Estabrook, playing further upon the theme of sight and invisibility. Evidently not afflicted with the humans' invisibility problem, the "lonely horse comes forward to be noticed," placing itself in our field of vision. The apple we feed to it fulfills *nature's* intended purpose, not that of "the proprietor." Often in Thoreau, apples grown for the market symbolize the evils of commodification, and it is not surprising that Thoreau denies the proprietor any right to *his* apples.[16]

By its central position in the paragraph, this apple in our hand serves to link the apples at the beginning of this passage with the malic acid quest of the conclusion. The Estabrook apple, the bloom still fresh on it, is both a fruit and a token. It affords spiritual nourishment to those who saunter along the old Carlisle road, at least for those whom Thoreau now calls "the initiated"—those who obey a higher law than that of commerce and "worldly thoughts." It restores a person's balance.[17] "Others are called *great* roads." Indeed, Great Road was a ubiquitous highway name in Thoreau's era, as common as today's Main Street. But the old Carlisle one, Thoreau declares, is greater than any of them. This superlative serves to elevate the road beyond any worldly roads of commerce and everyday life.

In a new series of tropes, Thoreau now presents the road itself as invisible. In the first place, it is not a finished road. It is only "laid out," and thus would be represented by a mere dotted line on a map. Thoreau specifies that the old Carlisle road is "offered to walkers" beyond any jurisdiction or commercial concern. In fact, any wagon (whether for business or pleasure) is excluded because the road is too rocky, and the distance anyone travels goes unmeasured ("no odometer"). Also, as noted earlier, Thoreau imparts a prehistoric aura to the boulder-strewn Estabrook landscape when he interjects, "Rocks which the druids *might* have raised—if they could."[18]

Even for walkers, the road is hard to locate ("no guide-boards indicate it"). We can keep it invisible (and therefore keep it secret) on the map if, instead of ink, we use citrus juice to trace the dotted line. Using lemon juice to write with, as generations of schoolchildren have discovered, results in an "invisible ink" message that becomes legible only after you hold it close to a source of heat.

Very significantly, Thoreau designates "a warm imagination" rather than a physical fire as the heat source. Imagination allows us to see—and read—what is invisible. Our experience on the old Carlisle road requires imagination, which gives the road its true value. Concluding our Journal passage, Thoreau seems to indulge his Yankee humor, directly addressing you and me and teasing us with a quasi-scientific reference to his "tests" for malic acid, a chemical compound found naturally in fruits, including apples. (It is what makes apples tart.)

Thoreau couches his instructions in a mock language of mechanical operation, as if our jaws were a cider press. In plain English, he is telling us to take a bite of the apple—or, rather, he dares us to do so. It may prove too bitter to swallow, for Estabrook Country apples ran to extreme tartness.[19] Ralph Waldo Emerson, in a lecture of 1858, referred jocularly to several varieties, naming two of them "Bite-me-if-you-dare" and "Beware-of-this" (Ells 96).[20] Ingesting the apple identifies us strongly with the earth itself and especially with the magical land of Estabrook Country, as Thoreau suggests in the concluding words of this passage. From the realms of the supernatural or spiritual, we are brought back down to earth, as it were, by sampling an Estabrook apple while remaining free, high minded, and balanced.

Biographical Context

Before proposing some more connections from literature, science, folklore, and fashion, I want to step back from the text, discuss Thoreau's powerful attraction to Estabrook Country, and speculate on Thoreau's psychological state in the autumn of his forty-third year. When he visited Estabrook Country throughout the 1850s, Thoreau pursued the same botanizing and natural-history investigations that preoccupied him in Walden Woods. It was in these fields, as much as in any other locale, that Thoreau found "remarkable proof" of the continual dispersion of seeds by animals, wind, and water (*J* XIV: 187; Ells 109ff., 145). Estabrook thus furnished a good deal of the evidence Thoreau used to support his final burst of creativity as a naturalist.

Thoreau had important personal ties to this land and its road. Estabrook was where his father had built a mill to cut cedar wood for pencil making in the first years of the family business. Thoreau apparently remembered the site; he referenced "the old mill" in some of his field notes.[21] Still more significantly, a spot near the southern end of the old Carlisle road had become the resting place of Thoreau's own Walden house. It had been hauled over to Estabrook in 1849, and since then a farm family had been using it (symbolically enough!) as a place to store seeds.[22] Thoreau remains tight lipped about his feelings whenever passing his old house in its latter-day location. Among the handful of entries mentioning the house in the late Journal, he only once uses an expression that could be read as poignant—"my house that was" (*J* VII: 235, 7 Mar. 1855). Yet common sense would tell us that Henry felt deep emotion whenever he passed by that former residence so rich in spiritual discovery. After all, at the outset of his intensified natural-history pursuits around 1851, he had worried that he was moving too far away from the poetic inspiration of his younger, creative years.

What sort of community lived in Estabrook Country? The area was underpopulated, yet at this time there were still perhaps a score of residences along the old Carlisle road, the Lowell road, and other ways through Estabrook.[23] Thoreau seems to have progressed from an aloof characterization of the local rustics as a race of "groveling coarse & low-lived men" (*PJ* 4: 101, 26 Sept. 1851, qtd. in Ells 85) to a more sympathetic understanding, at least, that many of these families were driven by "haggard poverty and harassing debt" (*J* XII: 367, 3 Oct. 1859). In summer and especially fall, the Estabrook fields were quite popular with Concord's saunterers, berry-gathering parties, poets, and picnickers, including Waldo's daughter Ellen Emerson and her friends. The residents of Estabrook whom Thoreau especially favored included his friend the poet Ellery Channing, who lived on Punkatasset Hill; Minott Pratt and his family, who lived *sans façons* on their farm and always made Thoreau welcome as a visitor; the hunter George Melvin, often encountered in the pages of the Journal,[24] and the astronomer-farmer Perez Blood, mentioned above.

From the evidence, Thoreau's overall mood or state of mind at the age of forty-two in the autumn of 1859 was, I daresay, saturnine. The year had begun with the death of Henry's father in February at age seventy-one. The grieving process, to judge from Journal entries (especially *J* XI: 435–39), preoccupied Thoreau. According to biographer Richard Lebeaux, the parental death stirred multiple anxieties, and Thoreau struggled as intimations of mortality divided his spirit (and Journal entries) between heavy depression and self-exhortations toward productivity.[25]

Apollo: Revolt from Worldly Service

With the passing of his father, Thoreau, the only surviving male in the family, legally became head of the household and personally assumed responsibility for managing the graphite business. Thoreau shouldered responsibility for improving his earnings in other ways too, taking on surveying jobs and increased public lecturing. While this productive work brought him a measure of what some psychologists call generativity, the jobs rankled him. He believed they dragged him down from imaginative contemplation and botanizing, his true callings. As he did frequently in the past, he now likened himself to the sun god Apollo toiling for Admetus (Lebeaux 321).[26]

Estabrook Country held one highly negative association for Thoreau in this context that undoubtedly helped to determine his image of the circle as a circumference (girdle or boundary). In those days, municipal officials were required annually to perambulate the town line in order to reaffirm the town's legal boundaries, often in the company of a surveyor. Thoreau's profession had placed him in the company of several Concord selectmen as they traipsed across lots and wilderness for several days in September 1851. By the time they had walked the Carlisle boundary in Estabrook Country, Thoreau in his Journal declared that he felt "inexpressibly begrimed" after a week spent with "the most common place and worldly minded men. . . . A fatal coarseness is the result of mixing in the trivial affairs of men." (The old Carlisle road, we recall, should be a place "where you put off worldly thoughts.") "Fatal" is a strong term, yet I am sure Thoreau means it quite literally. Remaining free is a struggle against the death of the spirit, a struggle for life. Striving to reclaim his "tone and sanity," Thoreau at that time invoked the poet's duty to remain pure and aloof. "Let him perambulate the bounds of Imagination's provinces[,] the realms of faery, and not the insignificant boundaries of towns" (*PJ* 4: 84–85, 20 Sept. 1851, qtd. in Ells 84).

Perambulating the realms of faery—isn't this exactly what Thoreau seeks to accomplish in the passage we are analyzing?

The Primordial Apple, the Stimulating Scent of Decay, and Edenic Tropes

We may now take a closer look at various contexts from literature, science, popular culture, and folklore that help to illuminate Thoreau's old Carlisle road paragraph.

Consider once again Thoreau's repeated references to apples. If the proprietor has no right to them, Thoreau implies, they belong to everyone—human and horse alike. Yet in the beginning, apples were forbidden to humans on the highest authority. As most of us know, in Christian tradition the apple symbolizes the fruit of the tree of the knowledge of good and evil that was offered by the beguiling serpent. Eating it against God's commandment got the first humans banished from paradise so that they would not eat next from the tree of eternal life. "In Adam's fall, we sinned all," as the old schoolbook rhyme puts it. Wryly superimposing Genesis and paleontology, Thoreau in the same Journal entry infuses Estabrook's fields with "the scent the earth yielded in the saurian period, before man was created and fell" (*J* XII: 346). Is it the theme of the Fall that accounts for Thoreau's invocation of Satan, next to Saturn? The example set by Satan that we know from the Christian myth of the Fall is, precisely, the primordial lure of "worldly thoughts."

The first man and woman had attained godly wisdom—had "become as one of us, to know good and evil," according to God (Genesis 3.22). As a consequence, they were doomed to know shame, experience mortality, and be dragged down to merely human existence—to the level of "groveling coarse & low-lived men," Thoreau might have said. Expelled from Eden, the primal couple were condemned to "worldly" life.

It is evident that Thoreau experienced a powerful rush of imagination during this 24th of September in the field, when he jotted down this sequence of tropes and exclamations. Was there some external stimulus for Edenic imaginings? Possibly there was, for olfactory stimulation is one thing that can bring on transient pathognomic mania (i.e., a momentary flight of ideas, stream of associations, or altered consciousness).[27] The passage we are analyzing is flanked by musings on a type of tree fern known as dicksonia. Thoreau's highly sensitive nose prompted him to write extensively about "the sweet smell of decay" given off by these plants: "The very scent of it, if you have a decayed frond in your chamber, will take you far up country in a twinkling. You would think you had gone after the cows there, or were lost on the mountains. It will make you as cool and well as a frog,—a wood frog, *Rana sylvatica*" (*J* XII: 345–46, 24 Sept. 1859). It certainly sounds as if Thoreau really, as we say, got off on the sweet smell of the dicksonia, which possibly helped trigger his rush of associations.

As he saunters along the old Carlisle road, it seems Thoreau is seeking to reverse the negative postlapsarian narrative, to bring humanity back to Eden and away from worldly life. The new Eden is none other than magical, misty, prehistoric Estabrook Country, which brings forth its abundance of apples and berries every autumn for the nourishment and use of an innocent humanity. Its gates are not marked, but we can find our way into it if we make our chart visible using our "warm imagination."

More about the Hoopskirt

As already remarked, Thoreau's circle imagery includes hoops, as in "hoops and crinoline," an idiom for ladies' wear. Thoreau (along with many working and farming women, to be sure) considered hoops and crinoline to be ill suited for field excursions such as berry-picking. Only a week prior to the paragraph we are studying, Thoreau composed this wry passage in the Journal, referring to his sister Sophia:

> Grasshoppers have been very abundant in dry fields for two or three weeks. Sophia walked through the Depot Field a fortnight ago, and when she got home picked fifty or sixty from her skirts,—for she wore hoops and crinoline. Would not this be a good way to clear a field of them,—to send a bevy of fashionably dressed ladies across a field and leave them to clean their skirts when they get home? It would supplant anything at the patent office, and the motive power is cheap. (*J* XII: 332, 16 Sept. 1859)

This jibe against human superficiality and the pursuit of fashion is related to a brief Journal entry made two years earlier: "I heard some ladies the other day laughing about some one of their help who had helped herself to a real hoop from off a hogshead for her gown. I laughed too, but which party do you think I laughed at? Isn't hogshead as good a word as crinoline?" (*J* X: 7, 10 Aug. 1857). But wait a minute—here is Thoreau, in 1857, writing about a young woman wearing a barrel—or at least a barrel hoop! This brief entry is clear evidence of a mental association that, forming over the course of two years, gave rise to the image in our 1859 passage of the barrel-clad girls.[28] (It should be pointed out that the maid in Thoreau's anecdote helped herself to a barrel hoop that was made not of iron but of the pliable sapling wood commonly used for household storage barrels.)

Finally, consider one last bit of popular culture that Thoreau is satirizing. I claimed earlier that Thoreau is mocking commercial commonplaces when he exclaims, "Carried to the furthest isles where civilized man penetrates. This the girdle they've put round the world!" I suggest we listen to a Fourth of July oration of the period in which we find both of these tropes, "the furthest isles" (a cliché equivalent to "the ends of the earth") and a world-surrounding girdle (in the form of the "belted" American continent). Narrating the progress of American independence, our speaker declaims thus:

> With successive strides of progress, it has crossed the Alleghenies, the Ohio, the Mississippi, and the Missouri . . . has belted the continent with rising states; has unlocked the golden treasuries of the Sierra Madre; and flung out the banners of the Republic to the gentle breezes of the peaceful sea. Not confined to the continent, the power of the Union has convoyed our commerce over the broadest oceans to the furthest isles; has opened the gates of the morning to our friendly intercourse. (Everett, "Oration" 296)[29]

And so on for another couple of hours one hot Fourth of July in Boston. This grandiloquence depicting the globalization of Manifest Destiny was produced by one of the great orators of Thoreau's day, Edward Everett. In spite of the man's lifetime of accomplishments—he was a president of Harvard and much more—Everett is remembered today for giving the *three-hour* cornerstone speech just *before* Abraham Lincoln's three-minute Gettysburg address in 1863. When you listen to the fulsome public rhetoric of nineteenth-century America, you realize with gratitude just how modern an author Thoreau really is.

Aids to Vision: Wider Journal Contexts

The old Carlisle road passage is not as isolated in the Journal as this close analysis may have made it appear. For full context, it is helpful to consider several related passages in the same entry of 24 September. The following passage about vision and blindness, written the same day, functions as a parable:

> Some eyes cannot see, even through a spy-glass. I showed my spy-glass to a man whom I met this afternoon, who said that he wanted to see if he could look through it. I tried it carefully on him, but he failed. He said that he tried a lot lately on the muster-field but he never could see through them, somehow or other everything was all a blur. I asked him if he considered his eyes good. He answered that they were good to see far. They looked like two old-fashioned china saucers.... This is the case with a great many, I suspect. Everything is in a blur to them.... Seeing is not in them. No focus will suit them. You wonder how the world looks to them,—if those are eyes which they have got, or bits of old china, familiar with soap-suds. (*J* XII: 347–48)

According to Thoreau, the man with the blurry vision represents the mass of humanity ("a great many"). Thoreau considers this sort of blindness either constitutional ("seeing is not in them") or perhaps willful ("no focus will suit them"). Although the man considers his eyes "good to see far," he must be counted among the "uninitiated" who are mentioned in the old Carlisle road paragraph in connection with invisible ink, and so on.

In an often-remarked Journal entry at the outset of his scientific pursuits, Thoreau wrote: "I fear that the character of my knowledge is from year to year becoming more distinct and scientific—That in exchange for views as wide as heaven's cope I am being narrowed down to the field of the microscope—I see details not wholes nor the shadow of the whole. I count some parts, & say 'I know'" (*PJ* 3: 380, 19 Aug. 1851). On many levels, Thoreau's accounts of Estabrook Country and the old Carlisle road are intended to free him from merely counting some parts of the whole. He intends here to recapture his soaring creative vision, which sees and unifies everything in nature—in the world.

The topic of heightened, specialized, or oblique vision provides a powerful connection to another famous Journal entry, written about "intentions of the eye": "It requires a different intention of the eye in the same locality to see different plants, as, for example, *Juncaeae* and *Gramineae* even; i.e., I find that when

I am looking for the former, I do not see the latter in their midst. How much more, then, it requires different intentions of the eye and of the mind to attend to different departments of knowledge! How differently the poet and the naturalist look at objects!" (*J* XI: 153, 9 Sept. 1858). And it is the naturalist, the man of science, who has the edge. His realistic vision, abetted by his imagination, is elevated above the poet's fine frenzy.

Heaven's Gate

Only six paragraphs preceding our passage, Thoreau composed *another* homage to the old Carlisle road that in some respects could be called an alternative or complementary draft of the passage we have explicated, echoing the same ambulatory and evocative cadence:

> Going along this old Carlisle road,—road for walkers, for berry-pickers, and no more worldly travellers; road for Melvin and Clark; not for the sheriff nor butcher nor the baker's jingling cart; road where all wild things and fruits abound, where there are countless rocks to jar those who venture there in wagons; which no jockey, no wheelwright in his right mind, drives over, no little spidery gigs and Flying Childers; road which leads to and through a great but not famous garden, zoölogical and botanical garden, at whose *gate* you never arrive. . . . When I wade through by narrow cow-paths, it is as if I had strayed into an ancient and decayed herb-garden. (*J* XII: 345–46)

Once again, the uneven, rock-strewn road does not admit the minions of law or commerce—or anyone's vehicles ("jingling cart," "little spidery gigs") drawn by their commercialized horses. (Flying Childers, also mentioned in *Walden* [53], was the fastest race horse of his time in England.) The circles in this passage are the wheels of the vehicles themselves ("no wheelwright in his right mind").

The road takes walkers and berry-pickers into a not-quite garden of Eden ("great but not famous," "ancient and decayed"). As the Torrey-Allen edition of the Journal notes, this gate at which we never arrive anticipates Thoreau's famous metaphor only one page later, "you may have sauntered near to heaven's gate" (*J* XII: 347). Heaven's gate continues to recede, urging us forward.

I need not add that sauntering near to heaven's gate anticipates, in turn, the paradisiacal or golden age landscape affectingly depicted at the end of Thoreau's "Walking" (1862), the essay that Laura Dassow Walls insightfully dissects in her essay in this volume. The concluding paragraph reads: "So we saunter toward the Holy Land; till one day the sun shall shine more brightly than ever he has done, shall perchance shine into our minds and hearts, and light up our whole lives with a great awakening light, so warm and serene and golden as on a bank-side in Autumn" (*Exc* 222). As noted earlier, Thoreau once expressed fear that his botanizing would mean the death of his poetic side. The old Carlisle road passage and others related to it are proof that Thoreau's imagination can spring to life, responding to the golden sunshine. It bursts forth right in the midst of Thoreau's pages of botanical note-taking like a gushing stream that will not be repressed. Thoreau's creative mind blossoms whenever he finds his way to magical Estabrook as botanist *and* poet in a perennial season of fertility.

In one Roman legend, banished from the skies by Jupiter, Saturn escaped to Rome, where he presided over a golden age, a reign of unbroken peace and harmony on earth. Thus another example is set by Saturn, one that has nothing to do with his morbid role as Time and Mortality.

Modernity and the Old Carlisle Road

Our reading of the old Carlisle road paragraph, in itself and in context, helps to answer a number of questions about Thoreau and modernity. Is Thoreau constructing a modernity in this passage? I believe he has constructed an anti-modernity. After all, the old Carlisle road passage is Thoreau's journey to salvation, to which he selflessly invites fellow saunterers—at least if they can read the secret signs, swallow the Estabrook apple of knowledge, master the paradox of invisibility, and approach heaven (and unity with nature) by living in the moment. Thoreau's poetic language resists rationalism, and it registers deep-seated instabilities and discrepancies. Thoreau is a literary modernist—at least in those five lines in the middle of this passage! At the same time, I concur with Bill Rossi and other authors in this volume that Thoreau decidedly must be grouped as an antimodern social thinker.

The key is Thoreau's consistently negative application of the word "worldly." For Thoreau, at least in this passage, what is worldly is modernity. And modernity, he asserts, is the way of the world—the bounded, real world. Modernity is the gravity that pulls him and us away from our quest for transcendence. If not resisted by alert natures, it invariably brings disaster by dragging us down from paradise.

As most often, Thoreau's critique of market economy is highly subjective in the present passage—a generalized phobia, in fact.[30] Commodification is satanic, evil, against nature; it blinds us. To say the very least, Thoreau's universal dread of the marketplace serves as a vital counterweight to the all-encompassing rationalization of society. Writing about the old Carlisle road and Estabrook Country in the late Journal, Thoreau has created a primordial and supernatural land as a refuge from modernization and the expansion of commerce. The real world, and Estabrook Country itself, may be bounded at the perimeter by "worldly" imperatives, yet we are free to saunter into Estabrook on the pathway of invisibility—that old Carlisle one. It is the road of imagination that leads through a land where we can see things that the mass of men cannot, and where we never reach our ethereal destination (heaven's gate) because our heaven is our presence in the moment.

At the Thoreau Society's 2008 annual gathering in Concord, I listened to Laura Dassow Walls speaking about Thoreau's "last explosion of creativity" in his final years of excitement over his insights into natural regeneration and growth.[31] In the old Carlisle road passage, I think we find another form of that creative explosion. It is Thoreau's promise that we can always free ourselves from material servitude by finding our way to that familiar pathway of the mind, protected by his "house that was," the wellspring of Thoreau's imagination and creativity.

NOTES

1. The sequence is a single paragraph as edited by Torrey and Allen; Thoreau's manuscript shows an additional paragraph break (Online Journal Transcripts, 30: 11–12). This second paragraph begins at the words "There I go searching for malic acid."

2. This is the text as edited in Torrey-Allen, with one exception. I have preferred the manuscript's "This the girdle they've put round the world!"—a more indignant exclamation—to the editors' interpolation of a verb—"This is the girdle" (Online Journal Transcripts).

3. Sperber 30–31. Hypergraphia is described in Flaherty.

4. Thoreau's manuscript shows five phrases inserted with carets, two of which are in pencil rather than ink (Online Journal Transcripts).

5. "The Nut-Brown Maid" is the heroine of an old ballad published by Thomas Percy in his popular and influential *Reliques of Ancient English Poetry* (1765), which Thoreau read as a student.

6. "Hoop Petticoats and Crinoline" 256.

7. A long-standing belief held that fairy rings were watered by none other than Puck, the mythic nature-spirit invoked by classic authors, notably Shakespeare. Shakespeare's Puck declares, "And I serve the fairy queen, / To dew her orbs upon the green" (*A Midsummer Night's Dream*, 2.1).

8. See, among other sources, Morgan 13; Sikes 103 ff. (and the illustration "Plucked from the Fairy Circle" [76]).

9. Cf: "O the gallant Fisher's life, / It is the best of any: / 'Tis full of pleasure, void of strife, / and 'tis beloved of many . . . ," the first lines of a song in the sixteenth chapter of Izaak Walton's *Compleat Angler*, a work well known to Thoreau. I am indebted to Brent Renalli for identifying this probable source.

10. Shakespeare, *A Midsummer Night's Dream*, 2.1. Cf. Sperber 32.

11. Thoreau had complained of fruit orchards fenced in by commerce when traveling twelve miles north of Boston: "Consider Nahant, the resort of all the fashion of Boston . . . the visitor comes away with a vision of Mr. Tudor's ugly fences a rod high, designed to protect a few pear-shrubs" (*MW* 153–54). Though these were privately owned fruit orchards, they belong to the world of commerce all the same, for the proprietor was none other than Boston's "ice king," Frederic Tudor, who made his fortune shipping ice (including Walden Pond ice) to the farthest isles (Martinique, Cuba, and eventually India).

12. That is, with the exception of his ambivalent mythologizing of the iron horse in the "Sounds" chapter of *Walden*, wherein he declares, "What recommends commerce to me is its enterprise and bravery." In a sense, Thoreau in the present Journal passage could almost be spoofing this earlier praise of commerce, which is essentially romantic although seasoned with hints as to the dark side of enterprise ("If the enterprise were as innocent as it is early!," etc. [*W* 117]).

13. This line is unified by the assonance of the broad "a" (Sáturn, exámple) and the alliteration of unvoiced sibilants—all those esses leading off the stressed syllables (Saturn, Satan, set, -sample) might remind us of the subtle serpent Satan speaking. The rhythm is continued through the next phrase, "Lárge and small hógshéads."

14. The myth of time devouring its children was a factor in the evolution of Cronos/Saturn (initially a god of agriculture) into *Chronos*—Time itself. Even as Father Time, Saturn held on to his agricultural implement, the sickle, giving rise to the commonplace of the Grim Reaper.

15. I am not sure what to make of "lone schoolhouse" (see note 28). The theme of solitude or isolation seems to be prolonged in the next section with "lonely horse."

16. "Remarking to old Mr. B—— the other day on the abundance of apples, 'Yes,' says he, 'and fair as dollars too.' That's the kind of beauty they see in apples" (*J* XIV: 103, 7 Oct. 1860).

17. "I fill my pockets on each side," Thoreau remarks comically, "and as I retrace my steps, I eat one first from this side, and then from that, in order to preserve my balance" (*J* XI: 292, 7 Nov. 1858, qtd. in Ells 97).

18. Why couldn't they? No doubt nature and geologic evolution are stronger than the druids' power. Thoreau's allusion is to Stonehenge. (In Thoreau's time, it was believed that Stonehenge had been raised by order of these priests of ancient Britain, who flourished ca. 800 BCE, though we now know that it antedates the druidic era by far, dating from around 2500 BCE.)

19. Today's consumers, accustomed to only a few types of commercially grown apples, will be surprised to learn that "the number of distinct varieties grown by Americans in the 19th century was somewhere around 14,000" (Hensley). I am indebted to Steve Spratt for calling my attention to this reference.

20. Emerson, "Country Life," *Atlantic Monthly* Nov. 1904, qtd. in Ells 92.

21. Today the exact site in Estabrook Country is somewhat disputed (Ells 76, 122–23).

22. The house's afterlife is recounted in Harding 224. In the late Journal, Thoreau makes relatively indifferent mention of "my old house" in its final location only about four times (Ells 110, 145–48).

23. Cf. the map by Herbert Gleason (1906) at Ells 77.

24. Cf. *J* IX: 148, 1 Dec. 1856; *J* IX: 151, 3 Dec. 1856.

25. For an absorbing analysis, see Lebeaux 300–306, 314–21. It would be rewarding, but beyond the scope of this essay, to interpret the old Carlisle road passage in light of the "shift in emotional climate" that the loss of his father would bring upon Thoreau, who sensed his own mortality and did "not feel entirely in tune with the season" during the years 1858–59 (300, 306).

26. Thoreau would compare his subjection to commerce to that of Apollo, the sunny god of prophecy, music, and all things high minded, who in legend was obliged to live one year on earth in service to Admetus, king of Thessaly (as when he notably complains that "trade curses everything it handles" [*W* 70]). See also Ells 131, and Thoreau's letter to H. G. O. Blake only two days after this journal entry (*Letters* No. 44, 174–76). I am indebted to Michael Sperber for calling my attention to the last-mentioned reference.

27. Dr. Michael Sperber, pers. comm., 18 Aug. 2008.

28. Thoreau's recollection of this maid's barrel hoop may have combined with some memory of or reading about "that lone schoolhouse" in New Hampshire. Thoreau passed through Pinkham Notch, a pass in the White Mountains, on 7 July 1858, just before ascending Mount Washington (*J* XI: 14), but none of his accounts of ascending this peak mentions any schoolhouse, let alone schoolgirls. Thoreau's excursions to Mount Washington did involve numerous stop-overs in local hamlets, and he may well have observed a schoolhouse somewhere around Pinkham Notch, but this cannot be confirmed from his writing or from such sources as Borst's *Thoreau Log*.

29. While the United States' westward expansion to the Pacific and then to Japan was achieved largely by "Old Rough and Ready" Zachary Taylor's aggressive defeat of Mexico in 1848 and by Commodore Matthew Perry's black gunboats anchored in Japan's Tokyo Bay in 1853–54, our speechmaker presents this globalization of Manifest Destiny as a tranquil unfolding to the Pacific.

30. See, in this volume, "Antimodern Thoreau," in which Michel Granger thoroughly characterizes the Thoreauvian hatred of commercialism and commodification.

31. Walls, "Constant."

Part Two

THOREAU AND PHILOSOPHY

JOSEPH URBAS

"Being Is the Great Explainer"

THOREAU AND THE ONTOLOGICAL
TURN IN AMERICAN THOUGHT

I BORROW MY TITLE from Thoreau's Journal for 26 February 1841 (*PJ* 1: 273). The bold assertion of the explanatory power of being would itself seem to require a bit of explanation, for—strictly speaking—how can being *explain* anything? Isn't explanation, after all, a properly *discursive* activity, performed by a human subject? Isn't Thoreau confusing two distinct orders of reality (or kinds of relations)—the natural, on the one hand, and the linguistic, rational, or intellectual, on the other?

To try to make sense of the assertion, I shall adopt an approach that combines the perspectives of then and now, that sees Thoreau's position as consistent with the metaphysics of the period—from the age of "Coleridgeism" (Murdock 156) and Transcendentalism in New England to the emergence of Hegelian circles in the West—but also as very much relevant to recent debates over the dominance of "epistemology-centered philosophy" and its possible "evasion" (C. West 4–5) or "overcoming" (Taylor, "Overcoming Epistemology"). Not only does Thoreau's abiding interest in ontology mark him as a man of his times, it also provides us with one of the keys to his enduring modernity. Still more, it poses a peculiar problem to us as historians of Transcendentalism and products of our own intellectual moment. Could it be that our view of the movement is colored by a widespread conception of philosophy that privileges epistemological questions above all else—that makes Emerson's philosophy Emerson's *epistemology* (Van Leer) or Thoreau's ethics a "moral agency of *knowing*" (Tauber)? In our representations of the period and its thinkers, is our paradigm that of "philosophy-as-epistemology," to borrow Richard Rorty's formulation (136)? The conceptual challenge posed by Rorty's powerful critique of the epistemological tradition and its "self-certainty" has yet to be adequately addressed by specialists of the movement, and the impressive wave of recent scholarship on Thoreau and science only makes a proper response to the challenge all the more urgent.[1] On Rorty's account of the history of philosophy from Descartes to Kant and beyond, "science, *rather than living*, became philosophy's subject, and epistemology its center" (61, emphasis added). Wasn't Thoreau, in a crucial sense, resisting such a radical redefinition of philosophy and the destructive opposition behind it? Despite his growing passion for science, wasn't he often skeptical of its pretensions and of our individual claims to knowledge?[2] Indeed he was, and what the resistance and the skepticism suggest, in my view, is where the final emphasis should fall. For Thoreau, knowledge was not an end in itself. Science underlabors for life, for being.

I shall be arguing, then, that Thoreau's writings and those of the Transcendentalist movement as a whole should be seen as part of an *ontological turn* in American thought.[3] With this broad intellectual background in place, I shall examine a few specific examples of a distinct ontologizing tendency in Thoreau. This tendency may be seen, in positive historical and metaphysical terms, as characteristic of the ontological turn in contemporary thought. But the same ontologizing impulse may also be seen, negatively and in neopragmatist terms, as a classic example of the "foundationalism" that typifies the tradition of epistemology as handed down to us from Descartes, Locke, Hume, and Kant. It is, in particular, Thoreau's tendency, at certain crucial moments, to collapse knowledge into being that provides a perfect illustration of Rorty's thesis that the epistemological tradition is driven by "the desire for confrontation and constraint" and based on a model of truth as "contact with reality" (315, 176).[4] On this model, being itself becomes, to borrow Thoreau's own words, "the great explainer." At these moments, "explanation" is no longer the product of a discursive subject but the result of a sudden encounter with a brute fact that imposes its reality and truth upon us.

I begin with a double historical claim: first, that there was an ontological turn in American thought in the early to mid-nineteenth century; second, that the Transcendentalist movement was part of this turn and furthermore saw itself as such. These are not claims I make lightly. The evidence for them is quite simply overwhelming.

But before I turn to specifics, a brief acknowledgment is in order. What I call the ontological turn, as applied to writers like Thoreau, Emerson, and their peers, is a variation on what Herbert Schneider once called, in a brilliant aperçu left largely undeveloped, Transcendentalism's "escape from phenomenology." I would like to shift Schneider's emphasis and present the movement in more positive terms— less as an escape *from* than as a search *for*—a quest for what Thoreau called in *Walden* a "solid bottom" (330), a quest for metaphysical foundations. Thoreau's was an age much preoccupied, not to say obsessed, with "permanence" and the grounds of being, selfhood and religious faith. In their metaphysics, the Transcendentalists may be described as realists—that is to say, they embraced metaphysical realism, which, to borrow Roy Bhaskar's useful definition, supposes "an *ontology*, as distinct from epistemology." The distinction is crucial, if we would avoid the "epistemic fallacy"—an exclusively epistemological definition of being, or the belief that "ontological questions can always be reparsed in epistemological form: that is, that statements about being can always be analysed in terms of statements about our knowledge (of being)" (*Reclaiming* 13). Transcendentalism had a strong ontology, which was one of the things that made its philosophy "new." And Thoreau's own philosophy, as Bill Rossi observes, has a clear ontological dimension ("Thoreau's Transcendental Ecocentrism" 29, 37, 38, 39). Thus, to put Thoreau's thought in proper historical perspective, we must avoid construing it in the exclusive terms of philosophy-as-epistemology, all the while refusing to indulge our own postmodern aversion to metaphysics—an aversion that Rorty, of course, wholeheartedly shares.

Which is not to say that epistemology—or, to take a well-known example, the distinction between the Understanding and Reason—was not important, indeed crucial.[5] What I am claiming, rather, is that epistemological questions were, in the broader scheme of things—and here I include the all-important question of religion—secondary; they were the means or the starting point but not the end of inquiry. The distinction between Reason and the Understanding is less important, in and of itself, than what the distinction provides and what Lockean philosophy notoriously excluded—namely, an ontology of spiritual things. Reason, to put it simply, is being (Barfield 113). Emerson, for one, saw this very clearly and—even when most carried away with enthusiasm for Coleridge's terminology—correctly identified this higher faculty with the "real," with "permanent attributes," with "the soul itself" (*Letters* 1: 412). Another example that suggests that epistemology should not be given the final word is Frederic Henry Hedge's poem "Questionings" (1841), which begins thus, in a skeptical quandary:

Hath this world, without me wrought,
Other substance than my thought?
Lives it by my sense alone,
Or by essence of its own?

Though Perry Miller was certainly right to see in this poem an illustration of "the basic epistemological problem with which Transcendental philosophy commenced" (*Transcendentalists* 383), that is where neither the poem nor the movement's philosophy left off. Significantly, Hedge's perplexed and "bounded self" ultimately finds a secure external ground in "boundless Mind" (384), just as Emerson's response to the "representative skeptic" closes on a confident evocation of "the eternal Cause" ("Montaigne," *CW* 4: 105).

Thus when Thoreau's friend Orestes Brownson called ontology the "great," "unsolved" problem of philosophy and "the true metaphysical question" of the age ("Eclectic Philosophy" 52, 53), he was right. And, furthermore, he was not the only one to say so. C. S. Henry, in his introduction to a translation of the French philosopher Victor Cousin, declared ontology to be "the grand problem of philosophy" that Kantianism had failed to solve (*Elements* xxiv). And if Kant, in Cousin's words, had "almost entirely rescinded ontology from philosophy" (*Introduction* 397), Lockeanism was seen as far worse, eventuating in "the destruction of being." With Lockeanism, Cousin claimed, "nothing exists in itself, neither God, nor the world, neither you, nor myself" (*Elements* 78). Following Cousin's lead, Theodore Parker complained that with Lockean sensationalism it was impossible to "pass from ideas to things, from psychology to ontology." The end result of such a doctrine, Parker exclaimed, is that there is "no ontology, but [only] phenomenology" and that soul and body alike are "philosophically hurled out of existence!" ("Transcendentalism" 8, 9). In the search for an alternative to Lockeanism's destruction of being, George Ripley, like Parker, Brownson, Thoreau, and many of their contemporaries, turned not only to Coleridge but also to Cousin, who put the skeptical impasse of contemporary philosophy into broad historical perspective and proposed, as a way out, a new metaphysics that would open up a "bridge" or "passage from psychology to ontology" (*Elements* 143; Ripley, *Philosophical Miscellanies* 1: 68–100).[6] The contemporary obsession with ontology did not escape the keen eye of Mary Moody Emerson, who subtly mocked the fashionable Cousin and his "bridges" to ontology in an 1837 letter to her nephew Ralph Waldo Emerson (*Selected Letters* 379). This was a vogue that Mary had herself in many ways anticipated. The "new" ontology was hardly new to her. Not for nothing had Waldo called her "Plato" in a philosophical dialogue cowritten by them in 1824.[7] Nor is it an accident, I would submit, that Waldo, despite his undeniable lifelong fascination with psychology and epistemological questions, should later define the object of philosophy as, above all, metaphysical—that is to say, as "the account which the human mind gives to itself of the constitution of the world" ("Plato," *CW* 4: 27).

In light of such examples as these, we can see why Cyrus Bartol, a member in good standing of the Transcendental Club, saw fit to draw a parallel between the Transcendentalist and the "ontologist" (318); or why James Murdock, in the first major philosophical study of the movement, insisted that "to understand more fully the metaphysics of the Transcendental writers, we must not overlook their *ontological* doctrines." Indeed we mustn't. Murdock's emphasis is correctly placed. He saw quite clearly, too, that it was the Transcendentalist conception of Reason that provided a ground for ontology: "If Reason acquaints us with the true and essential nature of all things, then the field of ontology is open fully to our inspection, and we may form there a perfectly solid and safe science" (183).

Lest I be suspected, in making the case for an ontological turn, of cherry-picking my examples and operating too narrowly or exclusively on the margins of the period, I shall now cite a few examples that represent recognized landmarks in the history—or immediate prehistory—of Transcendentalism.

I begin with Samuel Taylor Coleridge and James Marsh's "Preliminary Essay" to Coleridge's *Aids to Reflection* (1829). Marsh's "Essay" follows Coleridge closely in grounding religion in an ontology of spiritual things. Which is why *being*—understood as the spiritual principle that grounds existence—is one of the most frequently repeated words in the "Essay." Being is, furthermore, a term that Marsh develops and emphasizes well before any discussion of the distinction between Reason and the Understanding. The purpose of the "reflection" that Coleridge would foster in his readers is, as Marsh presents it, essentially ontological: "to aid reflection on the principles and grounds of truth in our own being," for it is "by reflecting upon the mysterious grounds of our own being, that we can alone arrive at any rational knowledge of the central and absolute ground of all being" (495–96, 492–93). *Aids to Reflection* is of course also, as Marsh acknowledges, a vindication of the Christian religion. But here too the emphasis is ultimately ontological for Marsh and Coleridge alike, since Christianity is at bottom "a faith in the reality of agencies and modes of being essentially spiritual or supernatural." As Marsh explains in a crucial gloss on one of Coleridge's "Aphorisms on Spiritual Religion," Christianity "is not, therefore, so properly a species of knowledge, as a form of being" (496, 504). Marsh's conclusion here is perfectly consistent not only with *Aids to Reflection* but with Coleridge's earlier works, such as *The Statesman's Manual* (1816) and *The Friend* (1818), also well-known favorites among the Transcendentalists. If Christianity is the one true rational religion for Coleridge, that is because it is ultimately an ontology: "But let it not be supposed, that it is a sort of *knowledge*: No! it is a form of BEING, or indeed it is the only knowledge that truly *is*" (*Friend* 1: 524). Christianity's truth, in other words, is its correlation to Being. It is "that one only true religion, which elevateth Knowing into Being, which is at once the Science of Being, the Being and the Life of all genuine Science." Coleridge insisted that "the Bible alone contains a Science of *Realities*" (*Statesman's Manual* 93, 49).

Frederick Henry Hedge's epoch-making article "Coleridge's Literary Character" exemplifies this resolutely ontologizing spirit in the following description of "one of the characteristics of the present age": "There are certain periods in the history of society, when, passing from a state of spontaneous production to a state of reflection, mankind are particularly disposed to inquire concerning themselves and their destination, the nature of their *being*, the *evidence* of their knowledge, and the *grounds* of their faith" (120, emphasis added). Hedge's specific reference is to Germany and "German Metaphysics"—his topic in the second half of the essay—but it is difficult not to read these lines as an explicit commentary on his own intellectual milieu. Terms such as *being, evidence,* and *grounds* mark the discourse of the times and its "ethos of deference to the object" (Buell, *Environmental Imagination* 104), which Thoreau shared. They express a new preoccupation with ontology on the western side of the Atlantic as well. And perhaps most significant of all in Hedge's survey of recent German philosophy is his personal ranking of the major post-Kantian philosophers. Hedge rejects Fichte as "altogether too subjective" ("Coleridge's Literary Character," 124). Schelling, on the other hand, is declared "the most satisfactory" because the most "substantial." Hedge prefers the thinker he identifies explicitly as "the ontologist of the Kantian school," a thinker who in fact "begins a new period, and may be considered as the founder of a new school" (125). As Hedge would later point out in his anthology *Prose Writers of Germany*, Schelling represents a break with the Kantian legacy because of the "objective or realistic direction of his thought" (509, 57). It is worth pointing out, too, that the two major interpreters of German metaphysics for an American audience in this period—Coleridge and Cousin—were both heavily influenced by Schelling and by the ontological turn he had initiated in German philosophy. And as we know, Hedge's anthology helped to continue the chain of ontologizing influences well into the 1860s and beyond through its decisive impact on one of the founders of the Saint Louis Hegelian school (Goetzmann 5).

With Hedge's landmark article, we see an ontological commitment that is consciously assumed and that would become very much a part of the self-image of the age. Hedge's marked preference for Schelling reflects the movement's interpretation of recent developments in European philosophy as a salutary shift toward metaphysical realism and the science of being. But we should note again that the goal of the new philosophy is ultimately religious: "to establish and to extend the spiritual in man" (Hedge, "Coleridge's Literary Character" 126). The new metaphysics is underlaboring for the kind of spiritual religion that Lockeanism had rendered impossible. Another example that confirms this new ontological and spiritual commitment as a form of historical consciousness in the movement is William Henry Channing's preface to Théodore Jouffroy (one of Victor Cousin's pupils and followers):

> The original thinkers, who have succeeded Kant, have turned their attention almost exclusively to logical and ontological questions. A later age may pronounce the methods they have pursued delusive, and distrust the results at which they have arrived; but it will also probably acknowledge, with respect, that these eloquent writers have awakened a new reverence for the human spirit, and communicated to the minds of their own and other lands, fresh vigor, by the freedom of thought, and depth of sentiment, with which their works are inspired. (Translator's Preface xiv)

Emerson's writings may also be included among the manifestations of an ontological turn in American thought. The essay *Nature* is, among other things, an inquiry into the ultimate causal ground of being—Spirit. *Nature* is a properly metaphysical inquiry "respecting the laws of the world and the frame of things" (*CW* 1: 39), and these terms prefigure his ontologizing definition of philosophy—"the account which the human mind gives to itself of the constitution of the world"—in the lecture on Plato in *Representative Men*. The year following the publication of *Nature*, and just three weeks after receiving his aunt's "ontology" letter mocking the vogue for Victor Cousin's metaphysics, Emerson described his own immediate intuition of the ground of all being: "A certain wandering light comes to me which I instantly perceive to be the Cause of Causes. It transcends all proving. It is itself the ground of being; and I see that it is not one & I another, but this is the life of my life" (*Journals* 5: 337). Emerson's essay "Self-Reliance" may be seen as another metaphysical inquiry. Self-reliance, to be sure, designates an "epistemological attitude" (Goodman 51), but the essay itself may also be seen as an inquiry into the ground of autonomous selfhood and ethical action, an inquiry into the ground of "universal reliance," which is found outside the mind, in the cause: "We first share the *life* by which things exist, and afterwards see them as appearances in nature, and forget that we have shared their cause. Here is the fountain of action and of thought" (*CW* 2: 37; emphasis added). Life, it should be noted also, often carries an explicit metaphysical or ontological import in the period, which we have seen in Coleridge and Emerson and which is conspicuous elsewhere in writers such as Marsh, Brownson, Ripley, Parker, and Thoreau. Life, to put it simply, is *being* and above all *religious faith*.[8] Seen from this perspective, the contemporary obsession with ontology is hardly to be wondered at. Could the stakes have possibly been higher?

To wrap up this overview, I shall indicate some of the other manifestations of an ontological turn in the period. To be ranked high among these is the popularity of Victor Cousin, whose philosophical project, as I have already mentioned, proposed a way out of the skeptical impasses of eighteenth-century philosophy by opening up a "bridge" or "passage" from psychology to ontology. George Ripley claimed that Cousin had more readers in the United States than any other living philosopher (*Philosophical Miscellanies* 1: 29). Arch-Lockean Francis Bowen was compelled to acknowledge in the pages of the *North American Review* that "the writings of Cousin form the popular philosophy of the day" (1). Cousin was the Jacques Derrida of the time, and the vogue for his philosophy in America in the 1830s and 1840s might be seen as the first invasion of "French Theory" (though of a quite different philosophical orientation, of course). But if Cousin's philosophy became popular, it was because it spoke to the deep metaphysical needs of an age earnestly seeking to "reclaim reality," to borrow a phrase from Bhaskar. Emerson described this longing in "New England Reformers": "We are weary of gliding ghostlike through the world, which is itself so slight and unreal. We crave a sense of reality, though it come in strokes of pain" (*CW* 3: 161). Thoreau's search for "some sure foundation" ("To a marsh hawk in Spring—" [*PJ* 2: 92]), for what *Walden* calls a *"point d'appui*," or "hard bottom," is an expression of the same yearning: "Be it life or death, we crave only reality" (98). Bronson Alcott, for his part, declared in less dramatic terms that Thoreau, Emerson, Margaret Fuller, and himself were "each working distinct veins of the same mine of Being" (*Journals* 180).

As I have already suggested, patterns of usage also suggest an ontological turn in the period, with the widespread occurrence of terms such as *being, foundation, ground, reality, existence, substance,* and *object.* The topic of an 1834 sermon by *Christian Examiner* editor James Walker—"Foundations of Faith," which quotes Cousin (14)—is typical of the period. Orestes Brownson, never one for half-measures, pushes the ontologizing discourse of the times to the point of caricature in this description of the Transcendentalist position:

> The *real* aim of the Transcendentalist is to ascertain a *solid ground* for faith in the *reality* of the spiritual world. Their speculations have reference in the main to the *grounds* of human knowledge. Can we know anything? If so, how and what? Here is the *real* question with which they are laboring. Some of them ask this question without any ulterior views, merely for the sake of satisfying their own minds; others ask it for the purpose of legitimating their religious beliefs; others still, that they may obtain a *firm foundation* for political freedom. This question is, as every philosopher knows, *fundamental*, and must be answered before we can proceed scientifically in the construction of any system of religion, morals, or politics. ("Two Articles" 272, emphasis added)

Permanence is another of the salient ontologizing concepts of the day. The craving for reality that Emerson and Thoreau expressed was, at its deepest metaphysical level, a craving for permanence, for a ground beyond the vicissitudes of experience, of empirical reality—"below freshet and frost and fire," as Thoreau puts it at the end of "Where I Lived, and What I Lived For" (*W* 98). Or as his friend Brownson wrote: "In a world where so much is mutable and fleeting, nothing is more earnestly craved than that which shall not change nor pass away" ("Two Articles" 266). Not the least of the paradoxes of the "movement" is that it was also very much a quest for a principle of permanence. Looking back on the period in 1870, Brownson saw the search for a "permanent principle" as characteristic of the times ("Emerson's Prose Works" 211), and he was right there too. He was of course alluding, first and foremost, to Theodore Parker's *A Discourse on the Transient and Permanent in Christianity*; and Parker's argument for a principle of permanence, it should be noted, is a perfect specimen of metaphysical realism, appealing as it does to an objective order of facts existing independently of our theories:

> Now the true system of Nature which exists in the outward facts, *whether discovered or not*, is always the same thing, though the philosophy of Nature, which men invent, change every month, and be one thing at London and the opposite at Berlin. Thus there is but one system of Nature as it exists in fact, though many theories of Nature, which exist in our imperfect notions of that system, and by which we may approximate and at length reach it. Now there can be but one Religion which is absolutely true, existing in the facts of human nature, and the ideas of Infinite God. That, *whether acknowledged or not*, is always the same thing and never changes. (*Discourse* 13–14, emphasis added)[9]

Emerson too, at the close of his lecture on Montaigne in *Representative Men*, urges his listeners to look for "the permanent in the mutable and fleeting" (*CW* 4: 105). George Ripley's *Discourses on the Philosophy of Religion* seeks the "primal source of reality" or "original fountain of Being" in Saint Paul's ontology of spiritual things, in "things unseen," which possess "the only permanent existence" (25).

The ontological turn reflected not only a deep metaphysical and spiritual need but also a high literary ideal. In Emerson and Thoreau, in particular, we frequently encounter the ideal of a prose that bodies forth thought, of writing that is grounded in or consubstantial with being. Style is—or should be—a reality, a "conversing with real being," as in Plato (*CW* 4: 36). Writing should provide a ground to stand on, as Emerson says in his notebook on rhetoric: "Always plant your foot upon a stone. The strength of writing is to have ever a fact under you." In a passage from Thoreau's Journal that Emerson copied into this same notebook a few pages earlier, we see that the Thoreauvian quest for a point d'appui, or "hard bottom," is pursued in literary expression as well, making it ideally one with philosophical content and lived experience: "'If the writer would interest readers, he must report so much life, using a certain satisfaction always as a *point d'appui*. However mean & limited, it must be a genuine & contented life that he speaks out of. They must have the essence & oil of himself tried out of the fat of his experience.' H. D. *Thoreau*. MSS. 1856 Dec. 23." (Emerson, *Topical Notebooks* 2: 180, 172). For Emerson, Montaigne's writing is the best model of this solidity, this consubstantiality with the writer's whole being: "The sincerity and marrow of the man reaches to his sentences. . . . Cut these words, and they would bleed; they are vascular and alive" (*CW* 4: 95). Alcott agreed, praising Montaigne's writing as "marrowy": "Writing of life, he omits nothing of its substance" (*Concord Days* 135). The year after the publication of Emerson's lecture on Montaigne, Thoreau would defend in the Journal the same ideal of "vascular" expression as a manifestation of individual being in its entirety, as "the act of the whole man": "The intellect is powerless to express thought without the aid of the heart & liver and of every member" (*PJ* 4: 28).

It is especially significant too that Schelling—the thinker who had initiated the ontological turn in German philosophy, as Hedge pointed out to his contemporaries—should also have provided Emerson with a crucial distinction on writing for his boldly realist 1838 lecture "Being and Seeming": "'Some minds,' said Schelling, 'speak about things; some minds speak the things themselves'" (*Early Lectures* 2: 307). Recopying the same quotation in 1850 (the year of the publication of the "Montaigne" lecture in *Representative Men*), Emerson listed the writers who had given him "things," including among others Plato, Bacon, Montaigne, Shakespeare, and Henry More (*Journals* 11: 273). "The old writers" such as these, says Emerson, "when they had put down their thoughts, jumped into their book bodily themselves" (*Topical Notebooks* 2: 174). Transcendentalist admiration for the sixteenth- and seventeenth-century writers—writers of the Platonizing period that preceded the psychological and epistemological turn of the eighteenth century—is of course well known. Thoreau, for his part, singled out for special consideration Sir Walter Raleigh, a writer endowed "so richly with the substance of life and experience," whose prose brings us "upon a greener ground and greater depth and strength of soil," whose sentences "are rooted in fact and experience" (*EEM* 212, 211).

I should add three final elements in this overview of manifestations of an ontological turn in the period. I have already alluded to the spread of Hegelian ideas to the west (where Cousin's thought migrated as well), with the emergence in the late 1840s of an Ohio Hegelian school and, after the Civil War, a second Hegelian school in Saint Louis with well-known ties to the Transcendentalist movement. I should also mention the resurgence of interest in Plato and Cambridge Platonism. The very fact that Theodore Parker published three articles on these two subjects in the *Christian Examiner*—all within the space of one year—appears to me symptomatic. Cousin's edition of Plato is part of this same phenomenon. Finally, I would cite the massive tutelary presence of Saint Paul—"the philosophic Apostle," as Coleridge called him (*Friend* 1: 97)—and his ontology of spiritual things. I consider Acts 17.28 ("In Him we live and move and have our being")—a verse constantly echoed throughout the period—to be something like the "text" of the ontological turn. Jones Very turned the verse into a sonnet ("In Him We Live"), which Emerson included in his edition of Very's writings. Margaret Fuller did a variation on it to describe Emerson, in her review of *Essays: First Series*, as "a man whose only aim is the discernment and interpretation of the spiritual laws by which we live and move and have our being, all whose objects are permanent, and whose every word stands for a fact" ("Emerson's Essays" 2). It is perhaps also significant of the ontologizing spirit of the age that James Freeman Clarke should first have come up with the idea of writing a book on Saint Paul (*Autobiography* 101–2) in the same year that saw the publication of Hedge's article on Coleridge.

In sum, then: whether we are talking about writers such as Schelling, Coleridge, Cousin, Marsh, Hedge, Emerson, Thoreau, Parker, Ripley, Clarke, and Alcott or about phenomena such as the enthusiasm for Platonism and Saint Paul, the search for a prose style consubstantial with being, or the corresponding admiration for the "marrowy" style of the early modern writers—all of these fit the common ontologizing pattern of the period.

This is a period that, to borrow an idea present in both Coleridge and William Ellery Channing, made "truth correlative to being" and "knowledge, to reality" (*Biographia Literaria* 1: 142, 264; *Dr. Channing's Notebook* 62). The Transcendentalists developed the ontologizing, realist tendency of these precursors. As Emerson put it in a late lecture, "the substance with which we deal is real. Knowledge is perceiving of what is" (*Later Lectures* 2: 242). Here is the key to Transcendentalism's critique of the epistemological tradition—a critique conducted from a metaphysical realist position. The Transcendentalists were often skeptical about the claims of epistemology. I quote here by way of illustration a few passages from Thoreau's journal for February 1851, a period that saw him much concerned to deflate the pretensions of epistemology when compared to the magnificence of being as a whole: "I do not know that knowledge amounts to anything more definite than a novel & grand surprise on a sudden revelation of the insufficiency of all that we had called knowledge before. An indefinite sence [*sic*] of the grandeur & glory of the Universe." Stigmatizing our claims to knowledge as mere boasting or "conceit," dismissing knowledge itself as "often-times worse than useless beside being ugly," Thoreau pleads, in characteristically contrarian fashion, on behalf of ignorance—even to the point of calling for the creation of a "society for the diffusion of useful Ignorance" (*PJ* 3: 198, 184; see also "Walking," *Exc* 214).

As Bhaskar points out, "to be a fallibilist about knowledge, it is necessary to be a realist about things. Conversely, to be a sceptic about things is to be a dogmatist about knowledge" (*Realist* 43). The Transcendentalists—Thoreau included—were not "dogmatists about knowledge." Like Theodore Parker, they were, rather, exponents of the doctrine that James Freeman Clarke would later embrace, in his book on Saint Paul, as the doctrine of the transience or "relativity" of knowledge in contradistinction to the permanent metaphysical ground of reality and being (*Ideas* 117). The poet Jones Very, similarly, in a Pauline sonnet entitled "Knowledge and Truth," emphasized the transience and partiality of the first term—which is "but in part and done away"—and privileges the second term, Truth, as of "heavenly birth" and equated with permanence and the ultimate ground of our being. "To know the Truth" is "man's rest and highest goal" (Very 252); it is, as Coleridge put it, to elevate Knowing into Being.[10] Or to quote a well-known verse from Saint Paul: "For now we see through a glass, darkly; but then face to face: now I know in part; but then shall I know even as also I am known" (1 Cor. 13.12).

Knowledge is knowledge of *what is*. Science is not an end in itself; it is not classification for its own sake. Ideally, science grounds us, makes us at home in the universe. It relates our being to Being, the cause of the object to "the Cause of Me," as Emerson put it in an early lecture entitled, appropriately, "Home": "To what end else is the learned classification of botany, of natural history, to what end except as an aid to bring the object to me in its place and connexion so that I may clearer see its relation to me and to the Cause of Me? I do not wish to know that what I have been content to call a shell is by you called a strombus or a buccinum nor that what I have been contented to call a butterfly is a Vanessa, but I wish *to unite the shell and the moth to my being*" (*Early Lectures* 3: 30, emphasis added). Thoreau expressed a similar desire to elevate knowing into being in another February 1851 passage of his journal. Quoting Cudworth, Plato, and particularly Aristotle, Thoreau asserts that there is "something better than reason & knowledge, which is the principle and original of all"—something that constitutes a form of *methexis* or participation in the ground of all being: "My desire for knowledge is intermittent but my desire to commune with the spirit of the universe—to be intoxicated even with the fumes, call it, of that divine nectar—to bear my head through atmospheres and over heights unknown to my feet—is perennial & constant" (*PJ* 3: 185).

Perhaps the best illustration of Thoreau's notion that being is "the great explainer" is to be found in *Cape Cod*. Here we see the same craving for reality referred to in *Walden* momentarily "satisfied,"[11] in Thoreau's first real, direct encounter with the "thing itself," innocent of all mediating representations: "I was comparatively satisfied. There I had got the Cape under me, as much as if I were riding it bare-backed. It was not as on the map, or seen from the stage-coach; but there I found it all out of doors, huge and real, Cape Cod! as it cannot be represented on a map, color it as you will; the thing itself, than which there is nothing more like it, no truer picture or account; which you cannot go farther and see" (*CC* 50; *PJ* 3: 33). The question *What is Cape Cod?* is what Emerson calls, in "The Over-Soul," a "question of things"—a question that cannot be answered in words but only by an encounter with the "thing itself." The "tide of being" and life finally acquaints his friend Thoreau with the true reality of Cape Cod, and thus, as Emerson would say, "the question and the answer are one" (*CW* 2: 168). Maps or descriptions of this destination cannot yield true knowledge of it. What is needed is the unrepresentable "thing itself." Truth here is contact with reality, a reality that Thoreau is now riding "bare-backed." All distance between subject and object is abolished. Thoreau has found his point d'appui. The cape is "under" him. Being itself is "the great explainer." Reality here, to quote Rorty, is "unveiled to us, not as in a glass darkly, but with some unimaginable sort of immediacy [that] make[s] discourse and description superfluous." It is the conversion of knowledge "from something discursive, something attained by continual adjustments of ideas or words, into something as ineluctable as being shoved about" (375–76). Thus epistemology's quest for certainty and its model of truth as "contact with reality"—*"Contact! Contact!"* as Thoreau exclaims in *The Maine Woods* (71)—lead to collapse of knowledge into being, or its determination by being, in what Bhaskar calls the "ontic fallacy" (*Reclaiming* 157).[12] Truth is then grounded, not in accuracy of representation, not in the correspondence of idea to reality, but in immediate contact, in ontological participation, resemblance, or identity.

Implicit in Thoreau's strange assertion that being is "the great explainer" is the idea that "like can only be known by like." Here is the full quotation in Thoreau's

Journal: "My prickles or smoothness are as much a quality of your hand as of myself—I cannot tell you what I am more than a ray of the summer's sun— What I am—I am—& say not. Being is the great explainer. In the attempt to explain shall I plane away all the spines, till it is no thistle but a cornstalk" (*PJ* 1: 273). Or as Thoreau wrote a year and a half earlier: "That virtue we appreciate is as much ours as another's. We see so much only as we possess" (*PJ* 1: 74). I should note that the Heraclitean maxim "like can only be known by like," one Emerson liked to repeat (*CW* 4: 7; *Journals* 3: 213, 16: 261, 262), became something of a commonplace in the period—in large part thanks to Coleridge (*Lay Sermons* 78) and Baron Joseph-Marie de Gérando (1: 486, 2: 30), for whom it was also a favorite. Emerson's assertion that "as I am, so I see" (*CW* 3: 46) is a variation on the idea. Or in Alcott's words: "Each sees only that which his own being displays to him" (*Journals* 75). This preconditioning of knowledge by being holds true for our knowledge of God as well. To quote James Freeman Clarke: "We not only know God, but we probably know him more certainly than anything else in the universe, since 'in him we live and move and have our being'" (*Ideas* 63). What Clarke is giving here, in effect, is a reformulation over fifty years later of William Ellery Channing's conception of man's "likeness to God" (*Works* 293). Channing's colleague James Walker would insist, similarly, in his sermon devoted to Pauline "spiritual discernment," that our knowledge of God is preconditioned on our "participation in divine things," our "partak[ing] of the Divine nature" ("Spiritual" 215, 220).

For Thoreau, the Heraclitean maxim also applies to our possible knowledge of history: "Critical acumen is exerted in vain to uncover the past; the *past* cannot be *presented*; we cannot know what we are not. But one veil hangs over past, present, and future, and it is the province of the historian to find out not what was, but what is" ("Dark Ages," *EEM* 144; *PJ* 1: 318). As with science, true knowledge of history would thus seem to consist in an abolition of the alterity or spatiotemporal distance that separates the inquirer from the fact. In the quest for historical truth, too, knowledge ultimately collapses into identity of being. Emerson would appear to agree with Thoreau here: "Belzoni digs and measures in the mummy-pits and pyramids of Thebes, until he can see the end of the difference between the monstrous work and himself." The two "run into one," as when Emerson communes across time and space with Plato or Pindar ("History," *CW* 2: 7, 15). Thoreau speaks of the Persian poet Saadi in similar terms: "I know for instance that Sadi entertained once identically the same thought that I do—and thereafter I can find no essential difference between Sadi and myself.

He is not Persian—he is not ancient—he is not strange to me. By the identity of his thought with mine he still survives. It makes no odds what atoms serve us" (*PJ* 5: 289). What is required is Immediate Presence, the Here and Now, not the There and Then. As Thoreau says, "Time hides no treasures; we want not its *then* but its *now*" ("Dark Ages," *EEM* 143). The historical fact or figure is either immediately present to our being, or it has no real claim to existence.

I have emphasized Thoreau's drive to objectivity,[13] which appears to be especially strong in 1851–52 (*PJ* 4: 158, 174–75, 418–20)—the same period in which, as we have seen, he conducts his own critique of epistemology. But out of respect for the "varied tendencies of his mind" (McIntosh 301), for its oft-noted "inconsistency" (Garber 102), "contradictions" (McIntosh 213), and "conflicting" or "dissonant" motives (134), I should not omit the strong countervailing current in his thought: "Who shall say what *is*? He can only say *how* he *sees*" (*PJ* 2: 355). I should not omit his insistence that "it is always the first person that is speaking" (*W* 3). To quote the Journal:

> There is no such thing as pure *objective* observation—You[r] observation—to be interesting i.e. to be significant must be *subjective*[.] The sum of what the writer of whatever class has to report is simply some human experience—whether he be poet or philosopher or man of science—The man of most science is the man most alive—whose life is the greatest event—senses that take cognizance of outward things merely are of no avail. It matters not where or how far you travel—the farther commonly the worse—but how much alive you are. If it is possible to conceive of an event outside to humanity—it is not of the slightest significance— though it were the explosion of a planet—Every important worker will report what life there is in him. (*PJ* 8: 98)

True science is verified by life, by our individual being, which it in turn expands and empowers ("the man of most science is the man most alive" or "the healthiest" [*Exc* 28]), in what Cameron has called "exhilaration" or transfiguration (153) and Hildebidle the "blessed condition" of sainthood (106). Here we are dealing not with a narrow, isolated subjectivity, with a perceiving mind cut off from the world, but with knowledge grounded in individual being and experience as they mesh with and are enlarged by the whole of existence, as they find their place and power in the ontological continuum. The cause of the object, however distant, is united with the Cause of me, for my own enlargement or "ontological upgrade" (Rossi, "Following" 90). Individual being is a "conduit" for the same life force that science investigates and confirms.[14] The true scientist does not report a phenomenon purely external to him but only "what life there is in him." Like can only be known by like.

I would like to close my own inquiry on another Thoreauvian image of the solid bottom or point d'appui—the cornerstone, which is, interestingly, a recurrent image in Jones Very's poetry as well (108, 115, 221). The image comes from Thoreau's March 1848 letter to his friend Harrison Blake: "That faint glimmer of reality which sometimes illuminates the darkness of daylight for all men, reveals something more solid and enduring than adamant, which is in fact the corner-stone of the world." Here stands revealed the ultimate fact, the absolute metaphysical ground of existence, which once again deflates the pretensions of our epistemology, which shows our common-sense world of appearances and institutions to be "the baseless fabric of a vision" (*Letters* 215). Thoreau's cornerstone is the reality that throws into sharp relief the relative insignificance of our claims to knowledge. In Very's words, it "brings to naught / The creeds and systems formed by erring men" (221).

Admittedly, such revelations of "divine reality" (Hodder 97, 98), such "faint revelations of the Real" (*Wk* 385), such glimpses of "the corner-stone of the world"— of Being, of the Cause of all causes, the Life of all life—are rare (Hildebidle 106),[15] but we should not therefore conclude that our ordinary condition is one of groundlessness. That would be to abandon the world to skepticism, to make the ground of existence somehow dependent on our experience. That would make us dogmatists about knowledge and skeptics about things. But as Emerson replies to the skeptic who would cast doubt on the universality of the causal nexus ("the cement of the universe," in Hume's famous phrase), "seen or unseen, we believe the tie exists." Natural laws "do not stop where our eyes lose them." Our natural belief in their constancy is well founded: "The good globe is faithful" (*CW* 4: 96, 6: 117, 3: 166). As Theodore Parker put it, the true system of nature does indeed exist in the outward facts, *whether discovered or not*. And here is the metaphysical realist lesson of *Walden*, as it is of "Self-Reliance" and of so many other writings that mark the ontological turn in American thought: the point d'appui is always there. Though we become distracted, move among appearances, and forget that we "share the life by which things exist," the ground of "universal reliance" remains securely in place. "There is a solid bottom every where" (*W* 330). Thoreau is thus, as Peck puts it so well, "this most grounded of writers" (6).

Earlier in the same March 1848 letter to Harrison Blake, Thoreau urged his friend (and presumably himself): "So simplify the problem of life, distinguish the necessary and the real. Probe the earth to see where your main roots run. I would stand upon facts" (*Letters* 215). Another friend—Emerson—cited among Thoreau's "higher gifts" his "insight of the real or from the real" (*Journals* 13: 54).[16] It is not hard to see why.

NOTES

1. See Robinson, *Natural Life* 213n8 for a useful overview of contributions to the theme of Thoreau and science.

2. Thoreau's criticisms of or reservations about science have often been noted by commentators. See, for example, Paul 262–63; Baym 233–34; Hildebidle 108; Cameron 136–37; Peck 63–64; Buell, *Environmental Imagination* 117; Milder 179–80; Hodder 279; and Robinson, *Natural Life* 115–16.

3. Tempting as it may be to read Thoreau's later career as a decisive shift from metaphysics to science (McGregor 33–86), I would submit that the opposition itself—a legacy of positivism—needs to be set aside. The metaphysical realism of the "ontological turn" was not incompatible with a properly scientific worldview. On the contrary, in its Emersonian version, it arguably formed a ready foundation for Thoreau's later empirical endeavors (Robinson, *Natural Life* 111–15), just as it enabled the late Emerson, in what is surely one of the most extraordinary moments in his philosophical career, to entertain the possibility of an evolutionary emergence of spirit from matter—despite a lifelong commitment to the "sovereignty of mind" (*Later Lectures* 2: 97–98). As for Thoreau, even if the explicit appeals to Being or "Realometer[s]" (*W* 98) do tend to disappear with his increasing devotion to field studies, there is no particular reason to suppose on his part an abandonment of metaphysical realism and its principle of permanence for a thoroughgoing empiricism that would in fact have provided him with a *less* adequate conceptual framework for scientific activity, as he saw quite clearly in *Walden* (see note 9). What made the scientist did not unmake the ontologist.

4. Walls has emphasized Thoreau's "epistemology of contact" (*Seeing* 126, 228, 245).

5. Two remarks, by way of preliminary clarification, lest my argument for an ontological turn be deemed a mere repetition of the standard view that Transcendentalism moves from Locke to Kant or from the Understanding to Reason. On the one hand, it cannot be said that Kant was generally perceived as an ontologist, either by Transcendentalists with firsthand knowledge of his writings or with some sense of the recent history of German

philosophy (Frederic Henry Hedge, the later Orestes Brownson, W. H. Channing), or by those who understood him largely through the writings of Victor Cousin (the early Brownson, George Ripley, C. S. Henry). The second group considered, with Cousin, that Kant's doctrine collapsed into "ontological skepticism" (Ripley, *Philosophical Miscellanies* 1: 128); the former pointed out to their readers that the ontological turn in German philosophy occurred *after* Kant. I would observe, too, that this perception of Kant was fixed early on by two highly influential 1829 reviews of Cousin published just three months apart—the first by Alexander Everett, who criticized Kant for "abandon[ing] the external world to the skeptics" ("History" 104); the second by Sir William Hamilton, who concluded, similarly, that Kant's philosophy was "restricted to the observation and analysis of the phenomena of consciousness" and "leads to absolute skepticism" (205, 206). Fifteen years later, Brownson, in a long essay on the *Critique of Pure Reason* published after his break with Cousin, would confirm his rejection of Kant's teaching on the same grounds—that it had "no foundation in ontology" ("Kant's Critic" 447). On the other hand, it is undeniable that the Coleridge-inspired misconstrual of Kantian "Reason" appealed strongly to writers such as Emerson and Theodore Parker, as René Wellek noted long ago ("Emerson" 44–48, "Minor Transcendentalists" 669). But what is especially noteworthy in Coleridge's departure from the Kantian definition is of course the ontologizing, intuitionist direction it takes (see the crucial passage in *The Friend* [1: 155–56], where Coleridge cites not Kant but Jacobi and extends the latter's definition, making Reason "an organ identical with its appropriate objects": "Thus, God the Soul, eternal Truth, &c. are the objects of Reason; but they are themselves *reason*"). Reason is now the faculty synonymous with—or enabling a direct intuition of—Being. If Kant is a salient figure in the period, then, it is from our present perspective for largely *negative* reasons—as an object either of criticism or of misappropriation. Either way, however, the reception of Kantianism serves as a symptom of the strong ontologizing tendency of the times.

6. For Thoreau's readings in and on Cousin, see Sattelmeyer, *Thoreau's Reading* 20–23.

7. See Mary Moody Emerson, *Selected Letters* 185–88; and Ralph Waldo Emerson, *Journals* 2: 246–49, 250–52.

8. Orestes Brownson, for example, in the long, three-part essay on Kant referred to above (note 5), distinguishes at the outset "Doctrines of Life" (i.e., ontologies) from "Doctrines of Science" (which "concern [themselves] mainly with the principle, the genesis, and the validity of our cognitions") and concludes that only the first can be considered "philosophy properly so called" ("History" 145, "Kant's *Critic*" 449). And if true philosophy stands for life, even more so does religion. I take two further examples, from James Marsh and Charles Emerson. Working up to his conclusion that Christianity is not

"a species of knowledge" but "a form of being," Marsh quotes Coleridge: "Christianity is not a *theory* or a *speculation*; but a *life*. Not a *philosophy* of life, but a life and a living process" (504). Charles Emerson may possibly be echoing this passage in an 1834 letter to Elizabeth Hoar: "For me Lizzie, how am I a-weary of philosophy, & find a world of odds between that & religion. The one is a laborious effort against the senses—a raised & refined view of life which we are capable of so long as we are calm & strong, but from which we fall down so soon as the mind is distracted or tired out & the grasp of its faculties is relaxed. Religion is itself a life—it is the regenerate soul, not estranging itself from what is about it, but welcoming it all, the very meanest relations to the material, its bondage to pains & weakness,—& piercing through the dusky rind of things into the divine love that is their centre & cause" (Bosco and Myerson 298).

9. *Walden* provides an interesting parallel here, showing that a *metaphysical* realism—as opposed to a narrow empiricist version that epistemologizes being, in the concept of the "empirical world" (Bhaskar, *Realist* 16, 28, 35, 37, 58)—is the basis of Thoreau's science: "Our notions of law and harmony are commonly confined to those instances which we detect; but the harmony which results from a far greater number of seemingly conflicting, but really concurring, laws, *which we have not detected*, is still more wonderful. The particular laws are as our points of view, as, to the traveller, a mountain outline varies with every step, and it has an infinite number of profiles, *though absolutely but one form*" (290–91, emphasis added; see also "Autumnal Tints" on the reality of the scarlet oak as opposed to its far brighter appearance: "You see a redder tree than exists" [*Exc* 254]). Thoreau has, in other words, a category of "the real but non-empirical" that supposes "the transfactual operation of causal laws prior to, outside and independently of human experience" (Bhaskar, *Reclaiming* 155). His realism draws a clear distinction between causal laws, on the one hand, and their empirical grounds or manifestations in "particular" facts or events (those instances that we detect), on the other.

10. Peck applies a similar distinction to Thoreau. While insisting that the Journal is "the record of a lifelong epistemological search," he acknowledges that Thoreau's quest also has a "deeper," "metaphysical" dimension: "This quest is not only for knowledge but for Truth—for an all-encompassing understanding of 'cosmos'" (64).

11. *Satisfaction*, here and in the Journal entry that Emerson copied into his notebook on rhetoric, is synonymous with ontological plenitude, or solid grounding in reality. Emerson used the word in the same sense in "History" to describe the historian's ideal oneness of being with his object (*CW* 2: 7) in a passage I shall return to below.

12. In an extension and completion of Rorty's critique, Bhaskar argues that it is paradoxically epistemology's foundationalism and its tendency to reduce everything to itself (the "epistemic fallacy") that pave the way for the collapse of knowledge into being (the "ontic fallacy"): "The drive to certainty, powered by epistemology's sceptical foil, sets

up a dialectic in which correspondence must give way to, or be philosophically under-pinned by, identity. Similarly, accuracy of representation must pass over into immediacy of content." Bhaskar concludes with the intriguing suggestion—borne out, it would seem, by the Transcendentalists—that "perhaps the real meaning of the epistemological project is not epistemological at all, but ontological" (*Reclaiming* 158).

13. The refusal of anthropomorphism that Cameron has noted in the Journal may be seen as an instance of this (11, 147), though she would probably object to my characterization (since she also claims that "seeing nature outside the self does not objectify it" [153]).

14. I borrow the term *conduit* from David Robinson and note its consistency both with Laura Dassow Walls's theme of *vascularity* and with the imagery of the period, which emphasized the "in" and the "through" rather than the "on" of empiricist sense-impressions. Emerson, for example, extends to man the Coleridgean conception of nature as "*conductor* of the causative influence" (*Aids* 267). See "Spiritual Laws," where he describes successful men as "visible conductors" whose "virtue" is—like that of a "pipe"—to be "smooth and hollow"; or the poem "Pan": "O what are heroes, prophets, men, / But pipes through which the breath of Pan doth blow / A momentary music" (*CW* 2: 79; *CompW* 9: 360; cf. *Journals* 2: 221, 402, and especially 5: 96, where the editors trace the image back to George Bancroft's sermon on temperance). Orestes Brownson singled out the "pipe" imagery for particular scorn in a later attack on Transcendentalism ("Protestantism" 411–12).

15. I thank Laura Dassow Walls for pressing me for further clarification on this point in her response to the spoken version of my essay.

16. Thoreau's realist commitment, his strong ontology and cautious epistemology, his oft-noted respect for the independence of nature (Paul 360–62; Garber 102; Buell, *Environmental Imagination* 125; Peck 67), and his recognition of the relativity of our knowledge of it should make us leery of any attempt to enlist him on the side of post-modern fact-constructivism. Here I part ways, among the philosophers, with Rorty and, among the Thoreauvians, with Walls (*Seeing* 86, 248–50, and especially her insistence that "facts are fashioned"). For a trenchant critique of constructivism, see Boghossian (especially chap. 3).

Character and Nature

TOWARD AN ARISTOTELIAN UNDERSTANDING
OF THOREAU'S LITERARY PORTRAITS
AND ENVIRONMENTAL POETICS

REPRESENTATION IS A RICH concept when it comes to Thoreau, regarding both his own work as a writer and his judgments of others. It not only pertains naturally to political and communal matters but also touches on fundamental rhetorical and aesthetic concepts of ethos and mimesis. My basic contention, which I will flesh out in the following, is that a comprehensive reading of Thoreau suggests that he can be characterized as a reader and environmental writer of Aristotelian bent. In his abiding emphasis on consistency and probability and in his search for law rather than stochastic variation in literature as in nature, Thoreau evinces an Aristotelian mode of perception and analysis as the latter has been received and understood in the West.[1]

Beginning with his opinions as a reader, it is true that Thoreau neither worked as a formal critic nor announced a literary canon of his own. This said, it is interesting to note that the fiction and travelogues he read often veered toward the epic (see, e.g., Christie). Even the natural history works Thoreau perused tended to portray feats and challenges of various sorts—difficult climbs and chartings of terrain, risky soundings, and long, arduous hikes in inclement weather.

Here is how Thoreau describes the Swedish naturalist Linnaeus, apparently without irony, in an early Journal entry of November 1839: "Linnaeus setting out for Lapland, surveys his 'comb' and 'spare shirt,' 'leathern breeches' and 'gauze cap to keep off gnats,' with as much complacency as Bonaparte would a park of artillery to be used in the Russian campaign. . . . The quiet bravery of the man is admirable" (*PJ* 1: 86). Somewhat later, in his review-essay "Natural History of Massachusetts" of 1842, Thoreau adds the following to his earlier portrait:

"Science is always brave, for to know, is to know good; doubt and danger quail before her eye. What the coward overlooks in his hurry, she calmly scrutinizes, breaking ground like a pioneer for the array of arts that follow in her train. But cowardice is unscientific; for there cannot be a science of ignorance. There may be a science of bravery, for that advances; but a retreat is rarely well conducted; if it is, then it is an orderly advance in the face of circumstances" (*Exc* 6–7).

What emerges from these lines is a martial disposition, youthfully and rather breathlessly praising courage and action. But Thoreau's stylistic ideals also stress practical experience and a lack of artifice. He would in time come to laud other journeying naturalists such as Humboldt and Darwin, whose respective literary styles benefited from their authors' outdoor lifestyles and field studies, remaining skeptical toward what he saw as purely desk-bound products. A Journal entry of August 1851 erupts: "How vain it is to sit down to write when you have not stood up to live! . . . The writing which consists with habitual sitting is mechanical wooden dull to read" (*PJ* 3: 378–79).

To these Thoreauvian elevations of bravery and energy one could add that he did not consider them evanescent phenomena. They instead adhered, as it were by necessity, to select and admirable characters whose dynamic ethoses imbued all they put down in pen and ink. A Journal entry of February 1841 explains as much: "Nothing goes by luck in composition—it allows of no trick. The best you can write will be the best you are. Every sentence is the result of a long probation.—The author's character is read from title page to end—of this he never corrects the proofs—we read it as the essential character of a handwriting without regard to the flourishes" (*PJ* 1: 276). Thus a writer's style is comprehended as akin to an inner essence, distilled from the massive log of quotidian events, trivial as well as memorable: "How we eat, drink, sleep, and use our desultory hours now in these indifferent days, with no eye to observe, and no occasion excite us—determines, determines our authority and capacity for the time to come" (*PJ* 1: 276). This relation also applies in a degenerative sense, of course, which Thoreau made clear in an 1840 *Dial* essay on the Roman satirist and stoic Aulus Persius Flaccus. In his summation Thoreau lifts his attention from Flaccus's works, which he has found both disharmonic and depraved, to conclude that "the artist and his work are not to be separated. The most willfully foolish man cannot stand aloof from his folly, but the deed and the doer together make ever one sober fact" (*EEM* 127).

Looking back to the *Poetics* of Aristotle, these saliently emphasize that the character "should be consistent and the same throughout; even if inconsistency be part of the man before one for imitation, as presenting *that* form of character, he should still be consistently inconsistent" (*Poetics* [1454a] 2327).[2] In his discussion of the plot, or what he calls the "combination of incidents," Aristotle adds that "the poet's function is to describe, not the thing that has happened, but a kind of thing that *might* happen, i.e. what is . . . probable or necessary." He reveals a vestige of Platonism in concluding that poetry is thus "something more philosophic and of graver import than history, since its statements are of the nature rather of universals, whereas those of history are singulars" (*Poetics* [1451b] 2322f). Nevertheless, Aristotle maintains that the work of art should be based on "an imitation not of persons but of action and life" — not, then, of psychologies per se but of their emanation from a sequence of actions.

A couple of lengthy literary portraits Thoreau wrote in the 1840s display how his view of character shared crucial elements with that of Aristotle. In a manuscript from around 1843 (delivered before the Concord Lyceum but rejected by the *Dial*), he presents the spectacular British explorer, court member, and amateur historian Sir Walter Raleigh, of whom he asserts: "Perhaps no one in English history better represents the heroic character" (*EEM* 178). True, he finds fault in Raleigh's occasional vindictiveness, his taking bribes and engaging in piracy. But surmounting these defects were, in turn, Raleigh's unwavering loyalty toward Queen Elizabeth; his successful voyages (he brought potatoes and, perhaps more ominously, tobacco from the New World); and his stoic death after fifteen years of incarceration in the Tower of London on what seem to have been spurious charges of treason. Courage and energy run like glowing threads through all of Raleigh's actions, according to Thoreau's profile, and one notes that these traits are also said to fire his speech and writing.

Admittedly, Thoreau begins his panegyric on Raleigh's literary merits in purely quantitative terms: "As he was heroic with the sword, so was he with the pen. The History of the World, the task which he selected for his prison hours, was heroic in the undertaking and heroic in the achievement" (*EEM* 197). Still, it is not for insights regarding global history that one should read Raleigh's tome, Thoreau argues, but primarily as a worthwhile imprint of the English writer's own history. This turn toward the personal also ushers in a qualitative assessment of Raleigh, where he is made to incarnate at once an ideal character and a much-desired literary style: "There is a natural emphasis in [it]," Thoreau writes, "like a man's tread, and a breathing space between the sentences, which the best of more modern writing does not furnish. His chapters are like English parks or rather like a Western forest, where the larger growth keeps down the underwood, and one may ride on horse back through the openings" (*EEM* 198).

When Thoreau toward his conclusion returns to the subject of Raleigh's stylistics, he portrays them as representative not only of the man himself but of his age and milieu. The Elizabethan authors had greater vigor and more naturalness to their style than the writers of today, Thoreau maintains. And so he adds a life of action as a positive factor to his stylistic equation: "You have constantly, [when enjoying the Elizabethans,] the warrant of life & experience in what you read. The little that is said is supplied by implication of the much that was done. The sentences are verdurous and blooming as evergreen and flowers, because they are rooted in fact and experience, but our false and florid sentences have only the tints of flowers without their sap or roots" (*EEM* 211).

If Raleigh was a hero above most all other men to the young Thoreau, the Scottish historian and political philosopher Thomas Carlyle corresponded to Raleigh among more intellectual questers—"the hero, as a literary man" (*EEM* 243). In Thoreau's portrait of 1847, Carlyle is also described as peerless in his class: "Perhaps, no living English writer evinces an equal literary talent" (*EEM* 234). Thoreau sees Carlyle as a writer whose character, like Raleigh's, is truly integrated with his texts: "We have not attempted to discriminate between his works," he writes, "but have rather regarded them all as one work, as is the man himself" (*EEM* 258). Thoreau's Carlyle is a seminal stylistic liberator, severing "the fetters which a merely conservative, aimless, and pedantic literary class had imposed upon it, and setting an example of greater freedom and naturalness" (*EEM* 232–33).

Despite the fact that Carlyle could not credibly be portrayed as a conventional man of action, Thoreau still chose to describe his deeds in corporeal terms, as a laborer diligently earning his own and others' keep by the sweat of his brow (*EEM* 244). Thoreau emphasizes Carlyle's strong community engagements and his role as an early spokesman for a laboring class that still had a year or so to wait for Marx and Engels's *Communist Manifesto*. But the laborer metaphor also mirrors Thoreau's increasingly pragmatic view of literary style, according to which Carlyle formed an ideal. "Who cares what a man's style is," Thoreau writes, "so [long as] it is intelligible—as intelligible as his thought.

Literally and really, the style is no more than the *stylus*, the pen he writes with—and it is not worth scraping and polishing, and gilding, unless it will write his thoughts the better for it. It is something for use, and not to look at" (*EEM* 232).

A few comments toward the end of his "Sir Walter Raleigh" essay make clear how far Thoreau was prepared, by the mid-1840s, to venture with his thoughts on good writing—and this was shockingly far by contemporary standards. In a telling passage, Thoreau negatively contrasts what he sees as the scholar's ephemeral and tedious rhetorical flourishes with the woodchopper's and the farmer's concise, unadorned, even flinty speech and urges all pen-wielding in-tellectuals literally to earn calluses on their palms, as these would work favor-ably on their modes of exposition. "We are often astonished," Thoreau writes, "by the force and precision of style to which hard working men, unpractised in writing, easily attain, when required to make the effort," adding that "the sentences written by such rude hands are nervous and tough, like hardened thongs, the sinews of the deer, or the roots of the pine" (*EEM* 212, 213). Sum-ming up, Thoreau maintains that "a sentence should read as if its author, had he held a plough instead of a pen, could have drawn a furrow deep and straight to the end" (*EEM* 213). Beyond the time-bound sexual undertones, one notes Thoreau's desire for a style that would literally do the famous Emersonian plea justice by rejecting foreign and "rotten" diction while garnering its strength directly from the local, fertile soil.

We see, then, how character and style are intertwined in Thoreau's poet-ics—and this to such a degree that one may legitimately suggest that he saw *all* writing, regardless of genre, as autobiographical in the final analysis. With his conviction of human consistency of character and in his imperative toward a life of energy and action, he can be seen as Aristotelian in his own, shadow poetics.

In the following, I wish to discuss some fundamentals of what Lawrence Buell has called Thoreau's environmental imagination, which I see as bearing on his poetics—and, of course, the other way round. I understand Thoreau's view of character as essentially parallel to his view of outward nature. Where he com-prehends literature—whether poetry or prose, of whatever genre—as perme-ated and directed by its author's ethos, he correspondingly tends to see nature as fundamentally law-bound, this core trait sanctioned either by a deity akin to the Christian God, as hinted in early Thoreauvian texts, or by a more self-sufficient and protoecological regime of interaction, cooperation, and development, as presented in later ones.

How does one write nature, then, according to Thoreau? A few rudimentary distinctions regarding his writing practice seem warranted here. Almost all of Thoreau's published works—lengthier as well as shorter—had their precursors in shorter essays and/or lecture notes. The latter in turn are almost without exception based on Journal entries relevant to the subject at hand. Thoreau thus at regular intervals systematized his notes, then grouped and revised them to form the basis of more voluminous texts—a veritable "winnowing" technique, as it has been well described.[3]

Hence, when it comes to Thoreau's nature depictions, the literary scholar has an early warning to heed regarding the level of the investigation at hand. If one, for instance, chooses to concentrate on Journal entries, these very easily give the impression of a realm of total spontaneity, where mere personal whim and the harvests of chance vie for attention. In particular, scholars who have conducted close readings of the mature Thoreau Journal from around 1850 on have been predisposed to fall into this trap of appearances. What may be said without controversy—at least in sweeping and relative terms—about the later Journal is that it tends to avoid abstract, idealistic digressions on stock themes (love, friendship, duty, and so forth) in favor of a more pragmatic empiricism and solid rootedness in natural phenomena actually observed by the writer. Thoreau's youthful, platonic-romantic obsession with the pure and unsullied wanes, as does his questing for absolute truth. He becomes more recognizably scientific in outlook and more careful in noting his facts.

But does it necessarily follow from this, as the influential deconstructionist Sharon Cameron has claimed, that a diagnosis of Thoreau's mature Journal will reveal a recurrent antisocial impulse, pointing, as she does, to its relative lack of vivifying figurative language, its amorphousness, and seeming endlessness? The answer must arguably be both yes and no. That Thoreau's stylistic economy eventually becomes frugal with metaphorical and metonymical anthropocentrisms, to instead lavish itself with empirical observation, is true enough.

Yet the apparent formlessness of his later Journal conceals a crucial aspect of its larger rationale, one that is easy to forget. Thoreau had as his explicit, if admittedly long-term, goal to compile a comprehensive phenological "Kalendar" of the natural events taking place in Concord and its environs. In the summer of 1851, Thoreau began reading works of natural history in earnest and compiled the first of what would become several hundred lists and charts on every conceivable local seasonal phenomenon, such as the migration cycles of birds and the leafing, flowering, fruiting, and seeding of plants. The Smithsonian Institute had in the same year called for what it termed a "Registry of Periodical Phenomena" and invited all interested and able persons to record such observations; the Smithsonian list, as Brad Dean has observed, bears striking resemblance to the phenological lists Thoreau began assembling at precisely this time. These latter are almost certainly the foundation for the gargantuan project that eventually included his texts in progress posthumously edited by Dean and published by him as *Faith in a Seed* (1993) and *Wild Fruits* (2000).

Having become inspired by the proto-Enlightenment Englishman John Evelyn's *Kalendarium Hortense, or Gardener's Almanack* of 1664 — this was during the spring of 1852 — Thoreau would now and then refer to his Journal as tending toward a similar calendar — "*my* New Testament," as he eventually referred to it in 1859 (*J* XII: 389). In the end, then, the sum of his field observations would contribute to the construction of an "archetypical" year for the inclined reader to await and follow. When his health failed him in early middle age, Thoreau naturally had to abandon his monumental project. But the manifold strengths of its technique are on display already in *Walden* (1854), a book Thoreau had considerable time to revise and polish. As is well known, *Walden* integrates more than two years of residence at the pond, and several years of journal entries, into the general structure of an annual cycle.

It can be illuminating to consider Thoreau's environmental aesthetics also from a ground-level, rather than a bird's-eye, perspective, taking — as he would say — an "insect view of the plain." Thoreau's cherished micro-to-macro analogies, which he often employed in his political tropology, found frequent use also in his nature-oriented writings. A fact ascertained, Thoreau held in "Natural History of Massachusetts," would in time "flower in a truth" if only the observer by implication were patient and diligent enough (*Exc* 27).

One could muster from this that Thoreau wished to load every discrete nature observation with spiritual connotations, akin to the philosopher and theologian Swedenborg a century and a half earlier. But such a conclusion would be too hasty. It would also open Thoreau's nature depictions to a criticism similar to that dealt out by Emerson to Swedenborg in the former's *Representative Men* of 1850. The Swede, Emerson felt with some justification, in time became so intricate and dense in his ecstatic thread-binding and allegorizing that his texts became useless as spiritual exegesis, effectively losing their pedagogical value.

But how did Thoreau come to understand what he called a "fact" in 1842? He arguably gives us his clearest definition in a late Journal entry of February 1859: "It is only when many observations of different periods have been brought together that [the writer] begins to grasp his subject and can make one pertinent and just observation" (*J* XI: 439). A fact, then, to this view springs from a series of discrete observations over time, ultimately forming a sort of normal distribution in a statistical sense. This is of course far from the popular image of the romantic artist, guided by his or her spontaneous inspiration and pathos, which has long been applied to Western nature writers—Thoreau included. Such writers were supposedly spurred by their search for the evanescent, fleeting, and ever-unique aspects of discrete natural phenomena, all the while disdaining organization, of whatever sort, in their quest for the sublime.

With these aspects in mind, we may favorably consider a controversial passage in the "Sounds" chapter of *Walden*. Thoreau's narrator has just sat down to rest by the sunny side of his little pondside house: "As I sit at my window this summer afternoon, hawks are circling about my clearing; the tantivy of wild pigeons, flying by twos and threes athwart my view, or perching restless on the white-pine boughs behind my house, gives a voice to the air; a fishhawk dimples the glassy surface of the pond and brings up a fish; a mink steals out of the marsh before my door and seizes a frog by the shore" (*W* 114). There is a closely corresponding Journal entry of August 1845, but, interestingly enough—and to the consternation of a number of Thoreauvians—this makes no mention of a mink. And there is more. Yet another textual variant extant in the first draft of *Walden*, written in 1846–47, reads as follows: "A muskrat steals out of the marsh before my door" (Shanley 158).

This leaves us with a plethora of interpretive options. Taking a purely skeptical view, Thoreau may simply be seen as having embellished in the quiet upon his original notes. Alternately, he could be understood as having failed to recall the irksome circumstance that he probably couldn't see the marsh from this particular vantage, thus rendering the grafting of the mink (or muskrat, or indeed *any* creature he may have previously seen there) erroneous in the immediate context. Thoreau's mentioned line of sight should reasonably have been toward the frequently waterlogged Wyman's Meadow to the southwest of his dwelling, almost abutting the shore of his swimming cove more immediately south. But a rise in the land between the house and marsh, as a number of annotators have pointed out, seems to preclude this possibility.

Yet there is also the *third* interpretative possibility, amounting to an Alexandrian stroke against the perceived Gordian knot. Read carefully, Thoreau's inaugural phrase of the passage in question comes across as noncommittal as to whether or not the narrator is experiencing his reported sights and sounds in *real time*. "As I sit by my window this summer afternoon," Thoreau begins, and this could just as well be an Aristotelian marker of the likely—based on an aggregate of similar experiences—as the actual regarding what immediately follows. At any rate, all of the above glosses (including my own) rather naively assume that Thoreau was consistently intent on conveying only such optic and audio impressions as he may have experienced at any one interval and from any one vantage.

In fact, the *Walden* paragraph in which the mink phrase was eventually included is remarkable for its panoramic frog's-eye perspective and panacoustic attentiveness, arguably signaling more of seasoned awareness than singular perception. Are we sure, in short, that Thoreau wished to describe a *particular* summer evening by the pondside? Or did he perhaps rather wish to convey a *typical* one? The range of observations given is at any rate extraordinary and establishes Thoreau's narrator as near omniscient within the confines of his book.

Thoreau's mode of nature portrayal, from the miniature in "Sounds" to the expansive Kalendar project—which I have called Aristotelian in tendency—is not, at least to my mind, to be seen as antiquarian or antimodern. Instead, it poses a provocative and perennial question, perhaps especially relevant to adherents of postmodern aesthetics in their emphases on gaps, lacunae, and indeterminacies as central to understandings of character and nature. Namely, do only discrete impressions and singularities matter? If not, a more ecocritical outlook would seem called for in consistently embracing processual and composite environmental depictions, which strive to give insight into deeper structures than spontaneously grasped and momentary phenomena—even if the latter of course are important to the whole. Guided by such lights, one will inevitably move toward the aggregate, statistically relevant, and probable in one's view and portrayal of nature.

Underlying the normativity of Aristotle was his will to discern laws, preferably natural ones, and this in turn explained his extraordinary thirst for empirical fact. Thoreau, admittedly active much later, nevertheless shared Aristotle's enthusiasm over and curiosity of the world around him, and his study of nature (as indeed his judgments of human character) were also goal oriented toward grasping process and law.

Witness here, to call up a final example, Thoreau's diligent and careful botanical essay, "An Address on the Succession of Forest Trees," given as a lecture in 1860, which sets out to systematically explain how pine and oak forests naturally replace each other. Readers of Thoreau's Journal will recognize observations made during the full run of the 1850s, and they may also recall, of course, the conclusion of Thoreau's "Natural History of Massachusetts" essay almost twenty years earlier, where the writer maintained that "we do not learn by inference and deduction, and the application of mathematics to philosophy, but by direct intercourse and sympathy. It is with science as with ethics, we cannot know truth by contrivance and method; the Baconian is as false as any other" (*Exc* 28). To arrive at the conclusions presented in "Succession of Forest Trees," however, Thoreau had precisely to lean on method and (admittedly simple) mathematics: covering the same ground over and over, patiently counting nuts and seeds and seedlings, hoping to discern patterns of growth and spread. And while he does not discuss Bacon further in his extant writings, he may have come to understand that the rationale underlying Bacon's stringent methodology was based on the conviction that the biblical Fall had caused a momentous diminution of human power. The sacred role of science, as Bacon consequently—and quite radically—saw it, was to restore man's position by furthering his knowledge of the natural world and its laws.

Taking its cue from a number of early and seldom-discussed writings by Thoreau, in particular his essays of the 1840s on Sir Walter Raleigh and Thomas Carlyle, this essay initially argued that Thoreau harbored an Aristotelian view of human character and poetic style. A writer's welter of worldly actions, from the mundane to the heroic, all, to Thoreau's view, serve to influence the writer's character, which in turn ultimately determines the style emanating from his or her pen. From this at once all-encompassing and deterministic premise regarding human psychology and artistic endeavor, I proceeded to suggest that a similar epistemological tendency seems to underpin Thoreau's vast cataloging of his local landscape during his mature years. Thoreau was ever on the lookout for lawbound process in nature, diligently logging his various field sightings, soundings, and other impressions over the years and often synthesizing them into expected patterns or predictions. He recognized early on that we tend to notice only what we look for in nature, and he made it his task—one might venture—to guide his readers toward a deeper understanding both of themselves and of their natural environments.

NOTES

1. Comments on and quotes from Aristotle appear early on in Thoreau's Journal. The Greek was an important source for students during Thoreau's 1833–37 Harvard years. Thoreau did not personally own a volume by Aristotle but borrowed his *Historia Animalium* from the Harvard University library during the late 1850s (Seybold 81ff.; Sattelmeyer, *Thoreau's Reading* 123).

2. Here and henceforth, I extrapolate from what Aristotle, strictly speaking, deems necessary only to characters of dramatic tragedy, his poetics regarding other genres having been lost. In view of his treatise's reception history, however, I trust such a broader inference regarding character as literary manifestation may be motivated, even though fidelity to Aristotle's ultimate intent cannot be ascertained.

3. See Dean and Hoag, "Thoreau's Lectures before *Walden*," 130, 147, 161.

Thoreau's Work on Myth

THE MODERN AND THE PRIMITIVE

THIS ESSAY IS NOT a systematic study of mythological references in Thoreau's works, though I will discuss quite a number of them; instead, the point I wish to make is that, in handling the thorny question of the relevance of ancient myths and mythology for modern times, Thoreau was taking his cue from a number of prior texts at a time when the notion of myth as vehicle of access to transcendence was becoming increasingly reified in middle-class culture and literary circles. The first and longest of these texts is likely to have been the discussion of the origins of Greek myths in the latter sections of book 4 of Wordsworth's *The Excursion*. These sections of Wordsworth's most philosophical poem are known to have contributed to the popularity of Greek mythology in England and America later in the century along with a much shorter text, Wordsworth's sonnet of 1806, "The world is too much with us":

> The world is too much with us; late and soon,
>
> Getting and spending, we lay waste our powers:
>
> Little we see in Nature that is ours;
>
> We have given our hearts away, a sordid boon!
>
> The Sea that bares her bosom to the moon;
>
> The winds that will be howling at all hours,
>
> And are up-gathered now like sleeping flowers;
>
> For this, for everything, we are out of tune;
>
> It moves us not.—Great God! I'd rather be
>
> A Pagan suckled in a creed outworn;
>
> So might I, standing on this pleasant lea,
>
> Have glimpses that would make me less forlorn;

> Have sight of Proteus rising from the sea;
> Or hear old Triton blow his wreathed horn.

Wordsworth's poem is exemplary; it echoes German thought in its celebration of the Greek mode of mythopoeia, positively asserting the visionary power that still lies in the matrix from which all mythologies emerge, the interaction between the mind and its natural environment. Wordsworth was indebted to the Schlegel brothers, Friedrich Schlegel in particular in his "Talk on Mythology" ("Rede über die Mythologie"). The "talk" is section 2 of his *Dialogue on Poetry* (1800): distressed by the materialism, philosophic and economic, that followed the loss of religious faith and the rise of empiricism, Schlegel called for the making of new mythologies that could speak for transcendent truth, tracing the steps of the ancient mysteries, showing their relevance to modern life and their function in modern literature. Modern poets must create "magic," but in doing so they all have to start from scratch, for they lack the shared mythology that all the ancients had. The ancient mythology came from the imagination, but it also "imitated" what was "most immediate and vital in the sensuous world." Modern mythology, on the other hand, was the conscious re-creation of the world-weary poet. Mythology appealed to the poetic mind, promising to effect not perhaps a breakthrough into transcendent truth but at least a move away from the world that "is too much with us." The poet's latter-day wish for a reemergence of mythology is thus tainted with ambiguity: instead of empowering the poet to base his claim for authority on an effective visionary power that was up to the task, the poet's aspiration or desire for *new* myths might fail to provide a new mythology, except of the reflexive, self-conscious sort that consists in celebrating the power of the imagination to produce a new mythology. Wordsworth's programmatic sonnet may not be so much a blueprint for moments of unqualified visionary power enacted as poems as an anticipation of poems that thematize and examine their capacity, or incapacity, to do so.

At a time when, as Margot K. Louis explains, emphasis shifted from myths (increasingly regarded as inessential even for the Greeks) to mysteries (considered as the true mystic core of ancient religion), the notion of myth as vehicle of access to transcendence is thus hardly challenged in Wordsworth's sonnet; it is virtually left alone and untouched. Wordsworth's sonnet contains seeds of the notion of myth, which, as we move into the Victorian period, becomes increasingly reified in middle-class culture and literary circles. Strange to say, the word "mythology" was not to be found in the *Oxford English Dictionary* before the 1831 edition. The word "myth" was not used in English at that time; in *Sartor Resartus* (completed in 1831, published in 1836), Thomas Carlyle introduced the word "mythus" for the concept of myth into the English language. Thoreau himself used the word "mythus" in the "Sunday" chapter of *A Week on the Concord and Merrimack Rivers*, borrowing it from Carlyle, who had himself borrowed it from German usage. Carlyle is here a key figure mediating between England and Germany. Inspired by notions exemplified in Friedrich Creuzer's *Symbolik und Mythologie der alten Völker besonders der Griechen* (1810), he emphasizes the role of mythus as a symbolic tool with which mankind fabricates its cultural environment in a world where man "everywhere finds himself encompassed with symbols, recognized or not recognized," moving on to a very Thoreauvian statement: "Not a hut he builds but is the visible embodiment of a thought, but bears visible record of invisible things; but is, in the transcendental sense, symbolical as well as real" (*Sartor Resartus* 163 [bk. 3, pt. 3, "Symbols"]).

At the beginning of the period with which Burton Feldman and Robert D. Richardson deal in their classic anthology and study *The Rise of Modern Mythology* (around 1700), the word "myth" still generally referred to Greek and Roman mythology—tales about gods and semidivine heroes. The study of these stories was decidedly ancillary to the study of classical languages and literatures—the major subject in secondary school and college. Mythology was not considered a subject in its own right. By 1860, however, Western intellectuals and scholars had ceased to regard myths as fables; they had grown interested in mythology for its own sake and in myths from many cultures—India, China, Germany, Africa, and the New World. Myths as narratives were out. Mythology was fashionable, with myths no longer a body of knowledge recorded in old stories but a mode of thought common to all cultures. By the 1860s myths could still be interpreted individually as interesting though inconsequential little narratives, but by then they were an object of interest for the newly emerging "human sciences" as they accrued into mythology, becoming a field of study unto itself that could illuminate other fields, including the comparative study of religions.

Simultaneously, myths were disappearing from school curricula. Classical learning had been in decline for some time, in contrast to its respected role during the eighteenth century. Meyer Reinhold in *Classica Americana*, a classic study of the problematics of "Classical America," calls the period 1790–1830 a "Silver Age" for classics, during which classical learning was seen as pedantic, elitist, impractical, and even detrimental to the new American nationalism. Rote teaching methods for classical languages, which produced only superficial learning, were partly to blame, as was the paucity of classical scholarship in the United States. This view of the problem has had its influence but is not entirely sustainable, as we shall see presently.

It has indeed been argued that interest in classical mythology may well have declined with the interest in classics in schools and colleges, but the picture is not so clear—far from it. Mostly, it may be safer to say that the study of classics in America was transformed over time and put to different and sometimes much broader social uses. As Caroline Winterer convincingly explains, interest in the classics shifted from the teaching of grammar (the drilling of pupils in the memorization of grammatical rules) to more politically oriented uses, especially during the antebellum era, and it became gradually desirable (mainly though not exclusively in Whig-oriented circles) to scan classical texts, more the Greek than the Roman sort, for models of oratory and civic virtue and for patterns of self-transformation and self-improvement. In such circumstances, classics were indeed brought to life in the imaginations of students, yet one may wonder what relevance mythology may have had in that context. We may speculate that, if knowledge of mythology did not prosper in schools and colleges because it was hardly yet considered a legitimate academic subject, it simultaneously became more and more part of that modicum of bourgeois culture of which any well-bred member of society was expected to be in possession, if only because novelists and poets (mostly British) had sprinkled their productions with classical and mythological allusions. Myths became parlor tales. Myths were not revelation. At best they were poetry. Such a concern went hand in hand with the rise of the middle class and its mode of life: to put it briefly, myths left the schoolroom and took up residence in the parlor.

One book was a major agent in this transformation of the cultural landscape of mythology: *The Age of Fable*, aka the first book of *Bulfinch's Mythology* (Cleary). What remains to this day the most popular handbook of classical mythology ever published in the United States (or, for that matter, in the English language) was itself designed with a view to its relevance for parlor usage: in his preface to *The Age of Fable* (first published in 1855), Bulfinch makes a statement of his intentions that is quite explicit about this. He indicates that he has tailored his book to out-of-school audiences; it is not for the classroom but for "the parlor." His audience was not to be schoolchildren but "the reader of English literature, of either sex," and others "more advanced" who may require mythological knowledge when they visit museums or "mingle in cultivated society" (Bulfinch 5, 6). That he did not write the book for school use but for the parlor and family circle is made clear repeatedly: Bulfinch calls his work, with its mixture of instruction and entertainment, "a classical dictionary for the parlor." It was thus conceived as, among other things, a practical guide "to teach mythology not as a study but as relaxation from study" (4) and to help readers detect and identify classical allusions and quotations in the works of modern authors.

Such words are programmatic: they reveal something about the uses to which, for some time past, mythology had been destined. The parlor in itself was a salient example of the behavior, typical of the period, that attempts to strike a balance between aristocratic or elitist pretensions and republican values. The parlor is the place in the house where such a compromise may best be worked out. Americans tried, as Richard L. Bushman puts it in *The Refinement of America*, to "reconcile their commitment to aristocratic gentility with their devotion to republican equality" (xvi). Parlors were smaller-scale imitations of the rooms of royalty and the aristocracy transferred to ordinary homes. They were conceived of as rooms for light refreshment, music, games of cards, and, most of all, conversation. In the nineteenth century, says Bushman, the presence of such a room "was a testament of the family's refinement, proof that they understood how to be polite, that . . . they could appear as polished beings, capable of grace, dignity, and propriety." By the middle of the nineteenth century, although not all homes had parlors, almost all architectural books included them in home design. Decoration could be elaborate. The furnishings, Bushman tells us, "stood for repose, polish, economically useless knowledge, beauty, and decorative activity." The spread of the parlor was "one of the great democratic movements of the nineteenth century." By creating parlors, people "implicitly claimed the right to live like rulers" (Bushman 273).

If Marie Cleary's various and sometimes overly simple summaries of the situation of mythology prior to the publication of *The Age of Fable* are something to go by, it is hardly surprising that Bulfinch's book, composed along such lines, was, from a scholarly point of view, a much tamer and far less complete compendium than the prior school handbook it displaced and replaced. Though never designed to be a schoolbook, it gradually replaced Andrew Tooke's *Pantheon*, which had been the more current and widespread standard reference work for American teachers in the field for a century and a half. Andrew Tooke, master of the Charterhouse (a famous London public school), had translated into English in 1698 the Latin work *Pantheum Mysticum*, written by a French Jesuit, François Pomey, for the dauphin and first published in 1659. Tooke's book remained in use throughout the eighteenth century and was still widespread in the early nineteenth century; an American edition was published in 1825, but imported volumes must have been far more numerous in American schoolrooms and school libraries, as Cleary explains. Tooke's book was radically different from Bulfinch's. The English author clearly labels his book on its title page "for the use of schools," meaning grammar schools like his own Charterhouse, where the classical languages were the main curriculum. That this was a schoolbook is also apparent in the abundant quotations (frequently from Ovid's *Metamorphoses*, a major source) in both the original languages and translations; there are footnotes throughout to identify the passages quoted. The book is written, according to the long version of its title, "in a short, plain and familiar method, by way of dialogue" between two youths. One is named Paleophilus, a young "lover of things past" and an inveterate questioner; the older, wiser one who answers the questions is named Mystagogus—in other words, "initiator into the mysteries." The English schoolmaster thereby created what was, according to Feldman and Richardson, the standard English mythology reference for his time.

Contrary to what Cleary indicates, then, *Bulfinch's Mythology* may not have ushered in a "new age" for myths when it superseded Tooke's handbook. But Bulfinch's book certainly did introduce mythology as an acceptable ornament into the realm of gentility. Mythology became a cultural commodity that could be openly marketed. What with the anti-intellectualism of the Jacksonian period, it seems almost certain that mythology as such had become unpopular school material by the 1830s and 1840s. Up to that time, its mysteries and recondite or elaborate meanings may have been regarded by scholars as objects of both reverence and textual elucidation; the school tradition had retained a sense of the awful mysteries mythology harbored. To say that, with the advent of the "new" conception of mythology, myths became the printed equivalent of the gewgaw or trinket would probably overstate the case. A professional American classicist of the magnitude of Charles Anthon (1797–1867) at Columbia College (whose writings Hawthorne, in pre-Bulfinch days, ransacked for borrowings) could make a fortune with the publication of his many scholarly books and weighty dictionaries, which contained whole sections devoted to ancient myths and mythology. Certain it is nonetheless that myths became safer, more innocuous affairs when it became broadly conceivable to dismember the corpus of mythological narrative into collections of tales suitable for parlor use, and this in turn helped make myths one of the essential ingredients in a very Victorian genre: children's literature.

Hundreds of volumes appeared that retold the original myths with a youthful audience in mind: moral complexities were exposed in mythological form; alongside Greco-Roman tales, Norse, Germanic, and Celtic mythology could be quarried for mythological patterns; the tales of the Grimm brothers were being translated into English; and elves, fairies, and leprechauns started to proliferate and run about in the pages of countless children's books, illustrated or otherwise. Few could still read mythological stories in the original languages, and in any case reading some of the most notorious, whether in translations from Ovid or in convenient summaries, would have been tough going for the more sensitive readers, such as children and women: stories of rape, revenge, and cannibalism abound in classical myths, and that kind of material (however present in the original stories) was partially or wholly, but wisely, left out of Bulfinch's duly sanitized versions of the myths, or presented in much attenuated form.

Once myths had been expurgated of all that would be offensive, their growing acceptability as auxiliaries in the tasks of family education (as opposed to mere school instruction) conferred upon mythology a familiar yet problematic status: myths could hardly be taken seriously in themselves, except when they carried with them a disposition to respectability, which trails morality behind it. American writers of the period, such as Hawthorne, were thus faced with a dilemma: as is well known, Hawthorne published a number of collections of mythological tales carefully rearranged and retold for young readers (*A Wonder-Book for Girls and Boys* [1852], *Tanglewood Tales, for Girls and Boys* [1853]), and he was in contact with educators and circles of educational reformers such as Horace Mann (who had married Hawthorne's wife's sister Mary Peabody). But when it came to telling stories about the historical past of New England, his capacities as a storyteller were clearly challenged by the powers of mythical tales. In "Edward Randolph's Portrait," Lieutenant-Governor Hutchinson considers Cotton Mather's narratives about New England in an unfavorable light and compares them to mythological tales, which are treated in a rather disparaging manner: "[He] has filled our history with old women's tales as fanciful and extravagant as those of Greece and Rome" (Hawthorne 645). Alice Vane, his favorite niece, is well aware of the nature of her uncle's denigration, "and yet . . . may not such fables have a moral?" (645). Alice Vane is then characterized by the captain of Castle William as a quasi-mythological character: "[He] fancied that the girl's air and mien were such as might have belonged to one of those spirits of fable— fairies or creatures of a more antique mythology, who sometimes mingled their agency with mortal affairs, half in caprice yet with a sensibility to human weal or woe" (646). Part of the power that resides in the story of the mysterious portrait of Randolph, an enemy of the people, and in the telling of such stories may owe to the very fact that they cannot be believed because they bear only a tangential relationship to any definable reality. They enable the teller to preserve New England history against the certainties of positive knowledge. Hawthorne may thus have been of two minds about the mythical character of his own stories, which could not be openly claimed. The kind of relevance that his character Alice Vane submits to the reader is of a highly moral and allegorical kind and thus subservient to the historical circumstances that the mythical or quasi-mythical story serves to clarify in moral-political terms; but it is worth noting that in the story, this clarification is only momentary, and the significance of the portrait is a precarious interval in a continued history of moral-historical obscurity. The myth makes sense only within a limited range of political circumstances and serves a serious purpose, though it is probably characteristic that the moral message it conveys is not heeded by Lieutenant-Governor Hutchinson, and the Boston Massacre does indeed take place.

As it turns out, the concluding sections of Hawthorne's tale fail to fully corroborate the moral-political import of the historical fable by calling the reader's attention to what it stages—namely, the precariousness of its own status as an object of belief. That it might be imaginary is not relevant here: as myth is mostly concerned with the collective fate of a community, it was never designed to be believed in as reality but derives whatever authority it may hold for an audience from the fact that it may not, even as it is disbelieved, be regarded as merely a figment of the individual mind. Unless a fable or "legend" reflects the concerns of the community or the nation as a whole, it runs the risk of being received as a tale, frivolous or charming, rather than as a myth that calls for a different, more earnest kind of attention. Even then, as a narrative pleasurable in itself (and made even more so by the circumstances in which it is told and received), the mythical potential of any tale may incur the charge of being mere fabulation unless it becomes moralized or allegorized—but then it is likely to lose its power of attraction for the audience. Then its moral substratum will not receive the attention it deserves, and it may even be dismissed as too much of an artifice precisely for being displayed as the true contents for which the fable is merely the occasion.

That Hawthorne was aware of the perplexing nature of mythical fables did not deter him from catering to the market of children's books, nor was he shy of attending to the middle-class tastes of his prospective audiences, a field where he predates Bulfinch, however much he occasionally shows himself troubled (or maybe amused) by the difficulties involved. In this respect, pending further discussion of the nature of his commitment to that line of publication (which would be somewhat irrelevant to the present essay), we might propose that, regarding the problematics of mythology, Hawthorne probably shared with Bulfinch a broader variety of concerns typical of middle-class culture than Thoreau ever did. This is both ironic and symptomatic in view of the fact that during the six years prior to the book's appearance, Bulfinch had served as the secretary of the Boston Society of Natural History, of which Thoreau had become a corresponding member in 1850. Yet the relationship between myth and nature evaded Bulfinch completely. He was to treat myth as a purely literary device that poets resort to in good taste for their readers' enjoyment. Thoreau's interest in and work on myth strikes deeper roots in a different context, one that conferred higher cultural value to myths and made them a controversial, highly debated problem in the intellectual circles of New England. Thoreau, when he uses mythology to make the link with nature, displays affinities to the notion that myths were not merely old tales from the ancient world nor parts of that age-old cultural heritage the urban bourgeoisie prided themselves on duly appreciating and preserving, even as they domesticated ancient mythical tales to suit modern times—which meant mostly their own newfangled cultural needs.

We may assume, then, for the sake of our argument, that whatever shaped Thoreau's culture of myth probably dates back to a period when that process of domestication had not been complete. To be sure, his thorough knowledge of classics (studied long ago by Ethel Seybold) should have made him relatively immune to the temptation of ever "modernizing" myths to the extent of considering them as independent fragments rescued from a dead past, to be used freely for such modern-day purposes as the total demise of their original contexts, historical and otherwise, made them available. But mostly, it must have been a different cultural environment, one in which myths were construed as neither tale nor mere fable, that led Thoreau to consider that, beyond their narrative aspect, myths had a potential for renewed significance. Margaret Fuller before him had not wanted to miss this potential: in 1841 she initiated a series of ten "conversations" on mythology, in which Emerson and other Transcendentalists had taken part. Unfortunately, we do not have a written transcription, only a summary published in the late nineteenth century (1895) by Caroline Healey, the only extant source to document these sessions. The discussions conducted by Fuller about myths attempted to make human sense of these stories about gods and theogonies by reading them as allegories of the various qualities in the human mind. Roughly speaking, the spiritual power of myth is claimed by Fuller, but it always verges on the allegorical. In the first conversation, she is challenged by Emerson's assertive and masculine euhemerism: myths are not stories about gods; they are stories about heroic mortals who have undergone apotheosis, and anyway, heroes are the true myth-bringers through their heroic deeds. This approach to myth is generally associated with Euhemerus, a fourth-century BC Greek who claimed that Greek myths sprang from actual historical events and personages.

Thoreau's own approach to myth and mythology thus occurred in the context created both by the typically Victorian emphasis on treating myth as a literary device and by the equally typical insistence of mainstream Transcendentalism (with Emerson as its leading man) on regarding myths as means of making the material world everywhere an emblematic embodiment of "spirit," with an emphasis on the concrete manifestation and attainability thus permitted. We take little risk in assuming that Thoreau was unlikely to have had any inclination for the mythology turned parlor game approach to myth, but it may also be doubted that he could have agreed with Emerson's rather casual, offhand manner of treating mythology, which he took for granted as one item in a long list of unacknowledged expressions of the heroically transcendent in humanity. Certainly Fuller did consider myths with far more earnestness, but turning them into allegories of the mind, as she most certainly did, tended to drain them of their more substantial claim to relevance as stories and narratives that after centuries still carried with them a peculiar form of significance. What I would like to emphasize by contrast is that Thoreau's handling of myth is, roughly speaking, nonconceptual and to a certain extent might be called pragmatic: myth is only accidentally an idea carrier, but as it has been continuously rooted in linguistic usage and the practice of discourse, as a series of forms that may accommodate any range of "modern" contents, myth has managed to survive and has mostly resisted change and transformation for that very same reason.

To make this point, a close reading of a well-known passage in *Walden* is in order, along with a revision of what has come to be regarded as one of its standard interpretations:

> When I hear the iron horse make the hills echo with his snort like thunder, shaking the earth with his feet, and breathing fire and smoke from his nostrils, (what kind of winged horse or fiery dragon they will put into the new Mythology I don't know,) it seems as if the earth had got a race now worthy to inhabit it. If all were as it seems, and men made the elements their servants for noble ends! If the cloud that hangs over the engine were the perspiration of heroic deeds, or as beneficent to men as that which floats over the farmer's fields, then the elements and Nature herself would cheerfully accompany men on their errands and be their escort. (*W* 116)

"If all were as it seems," Thoreau exclaims. "What happens instead," writes Stanley Cavell in a classic commentary on this passage, underscoring what he sees as Thoreau's crucial point, "is that men will mythologize their forces, as they always have, project them into demigods, and then serve their projections" (*Senses* 97). The Calvinist doctrine of election by God for purposes of salvation had displaced former myths about men's powerlessness to regulate their own lives. It had now been superseded by "the new mythology [which] will make the railroad engine (their technology, their inventions) their fate." It thus revealed "their inability to trust themselves to determine their lives; or rather, to their inability to see that they are determining them." "We have determined," Cavell continues, "that we shall be governed by fate—by something that denies for us the incessant exercise of our control" (97). Thoreau declares: "We have constructed a fate, an *Atropos*, that never turns aside" (*W* 118).

A concentration on historical and social process could help us avoid the analytical trap that more or less pictures the railroad materializing out of thin air and transforming everything in its path. Thoreau challenges the deification of technology in the "Sounds" chapter of *Walden*. He engages the concept of determinism by employing the image of railroad tracks in a way that subverts its meaning; he thereby proceeds to unmask, in what might pass for virtually Marxian/Barthesian terms, human self-alienation in what spuriously appears as a sacred form: the technologies themselves are cast as primary agents of historical change. A mythology of the so-called iron horse is a factor in the domination of men by their own creation, which returns to them in an alienated form as an object of fascination and admiration and builds up a mental-ideological construct that goes largely unrecognized and therefore uncontrolled. The new modern mythology that has risen in the wake of material improvement in transportation started right away to elicit worship of the "technological sublime"; but then it is actually a secularized variant of the "opium of the people," a minor branch of the religion of progress by which Thoreau's contemporaries are wholly mystified.

Such a reading of the passage seems to me very one-sided. It leaves the mythological element out of the picture. Thoreau does criticize the lack of "deliberation" that betrays itself in the modern confusion between a material production that results from human technical ingenuity and imaginary creatures like dragons and winged horses. If examined at closer range, however, Thoreau's point may be more complex than a perfunctory exercise in cultural criticism. Such an exercise might end up accommodating the machine in the garden. As Thoreau makes clear, however, he is wary of gardens and gardeners:

> Gardening is civil and social, but it wants the vigor and freedom of the forest and the outlaw. There may be an excess of cultivation as well as of any thing else, until civilization becomes pathetic. A highly cultivated man,—all whose bones can be bent! whose heaven-born virtues are but good manners! The young pines springing up in the corn-fields from year to year are to me a refreshing fact. We talk of civilizing the Indian, but that is not the name for his improvement. By the wary independence and aloofness of his dim forest life he preserves his intercourse with his native gods, and is admitted from time to time to a rare and peculiar society with nature. He has glances of starry recognition to which our saloons are strangers. The steady illumination of his genius, dim only because distant, is like the faint but satisfying light of the stars compared with the dazzling but ineffectual and short-lived blaze of candles. The Society Islanders had their day-born gods, but they were not supposed to be "of equal antiquity with the *atua fauau po*, or night-born gods." It is true, there are the innocent pleasures of country life, and it is sometimes pleasant to make the earth yield her increase, and gather the fruits in their season, but the heroic spirit will not fail to dream of remoter retirements and more rugged paths. It will have its garden plots and its parterres elsewhere than on the earth, and gather nuts and berries by the way for its subsistence, or orchard fruits with such heedlessness as berries. We would not always be soothing and taming nature, breaking the horse and the ox, but sometimes ride the horse wild and chase the buffalo. The Indian's intercourse with Nature is at least such

as admits of the greatest independence of each. If he is somewhat of a stranger in her midst, the gardener is too much of a familiar. There is something vulgar and foul in the latter's closeness to his mistress, something noble and cleanly in the former's distance. In civilization, as in a southern latitude, man degenerates at length, and yields to the incursion of more northern tribes. (*Wk* 55–56)

The machine and the garden therefore belong in the same category; both are outcomes of the process of civilization, although at different historical stages. Both are highly civilized, then, but belong in a different type and season of Western civilization, which, lately, has empowered itself for conquest as simultaneously "new" and "wild" through a rather devious use of the mythmaking capacity of language and discourse to make the machine far more unfamiliar to white men than it really is. The (pseudo-)Indian naming of the machine paradoxically confers upon it a local habitation and a name on the wild side of the settlement, as it were. Being vaguely reminiscent of the Indians' way of referring to the railroad locomotive, which would serve to assert their own alienation from the white man's civilization and its technologies, such naming in the white man's tongue gains for the machine the status of a legendary animal that, in this capacity, may be an impressive addition to the time-honored lineup of our very own legendary or mythological creatures as only the latest, oddest, and most fantastic of its denizens.

Speaking of the mobile steam engine as we assume the Indians do, we do not merely do the same as they do: by imitating them, we position ourselves to produce in their stead a kind of mythological discourse not theirs but very similar to theirs, patterned after theirs, thus colonizing their discourse as well as their lands; but in this linguistic annexation by imitation there is hardly anything preserved that is truly Indian. The "Indian" naming of the locomotive reinvents Indian mythology as the white man's rhetorical ploy to effect the transfer from inanimate to animate, and simultaneously from mobility to animation, within the precinct of his own culture as he makes that culture partake of the wildness it seeks to obliterate: the mechanical object, that already familiar alien, merely becomes more organic and "natural" as it turns "horse," but it has been cultural from the outset. Only the culture has evolved, it has modernized itself and needs to see itself as renewing its bonds with the primitiveness of the natural world and the "wilderness" and the wild men who used to live there precisely because it proves so destructive of anything wild. As, with characteristic astuteness, Thoreau deeply observes, true wild men will not play up their links to nature; they will try to assert that man and nature are mutually independent. Therefore, "iron horse" is Indian language used by white men largely for their own purposes. We are not listening to what Thoreau a little bit farther on calls "the Indian muse":

> Homer and Ossian even can never revive in London or Boston. And yet behold how these cities are refreshed by the mere tradition, or the imperfectly transmitted fragrance and flavor of these wild fruits. If we could listen but for an instant to the chaunt of the Indian muse, we should understand why he will not exchange his savageness for civilization. Nations are not whimsical. Steel and blankets are strong temptations; but the Indian does well to continue Indian. (*Wk* 56)

After listing the mythological potential and merits of men's new invention, he concludes: "It seems as if the earth had got a race now worthy to inhabit it" (*W* 116). This may sound ironic, but not necessarily so, or at least it may not be merely ironic. If we read on, moving along to the next sentence, we are surprised and destabilized by what may sound as a less optimistic estimate of the situation: "If all were as it seems . . . ," meaning here, "Would that this were true!" and not simply "Only in case this should come true." Nature then would be the escort of men on their technological errands. This is the destabilizing element: the difference between these two acceptations of "if" is between mere distanced analytic hypothesis and commitment to a defense of the validity of mythology.

In his first phrase, Thoreau thus might imply that the mythopoeic process (the invention of a new mythology) is not in itself illegitimate and may even be the inevitable outcome of man's estate as an imaginative being. It may signify the race's redemption from the contingency of its material and historical situatedness by its own power of mythogenesis. We find a confirmation of this positive appreciation of myth when we come to the part beginning with "If all were . . . ," the first section of the next sentence. "If" is not hypothetical here; it is the precative "if" that we find in wishes and prayers; it expresses the desirability of the state of affairs that the prior sentence presents as "seeming." Implicitly, however, saying "if" does amount to a recognition that what one wishes seems all the more desirable if it is not available at the moment. Hence God is, or the gods are, called upon to facilitate its advent. What amounts to a wish or a prayer in turn calls our attention back to the approximate way in which the iron horse is referred to by the writer, who dutifully conveys his uncertainty about the kind of winged horse or dragon that will be put into the new mythology. The implication is that what we have right now by way of a mythology is at best a vague, inchoate, indeterminate form, a still undetermined object that deserves attention, but only for what it is. And what is it if not a manner of speaking in which the process of mythologizing is incipient and eventually abortive? It does not evolve beyond the stage of approximation, and the writer's uncertain language is mimetically commensurate to the incapacity of ordinary speakers. What happens at this stage, then, is that men are deluded about mythology and the degree of completion of the mythopoeic process that their habitual handling of the language may achieve: what they, through the way they refer to it in the language, take for mythological creatures are not full-fledged constituents of a genuine mythology but poor impermanent substitutes, ideological-metaphorical surrogates to the real thing, and their significance evolves into the kind of misguided reverence toward things technological that would mistake vague similarities for true identities.

Hence, the emergence of the iron horse as a huge mythological beast is treated as a mere analogy, but the writer (as can be easily seen) allows himself to be carried away by the analogy and seems to communicate to the reader the extent to which he is enjoying himself in the process. He does not simply deconstruct the game; he plays it all along, at least to some extent and not without gusto. He rides the iron horse, indulging the activity as he goes. There is indeed a degree of irony involved in the fact that the speaker is rather uncertain about how to position himself toward the "mythological" terms of his own discourse, or, rather, he does position himself in an implicit, roundabout way by handling the analogy he develops in an ambiguous manner. The writer is at no time truly assertive: what he builds up is an analogy, and he performs the job in a casual manner for which he does not really accept responsibility. To a degree, he agrees to share in the practice if not in the values of the putative audience he addresses, and part of this audience is probably made up of the "they" in "they will put into the new mythology." Part of the audience is also the agent, so that "they" should at least half recognize (only half) themselves in what the writer writes: their typically carefree or casual mythologizing is a funny exaggeration, even a ludicrous habit. So he plays up the mythological aspect, and the iron horse takes life as a horse and metaphorically or really is shod with snowshoes. Rhetorically speaking, the speaker overstates his case, and the language (and the notion) of the new mythology is bound to appear hyperbolic. But he is not the one who actually commits the more or less comic hyperbole. He communicates to the audience in passing that *he* does not do the putting and the exaggerating, "they" do it. Therefore, he need not endorse or approve what he is content to describe analogically for their sake and in terms he did not devise, though he chooses to take them up in his discourse. However much it may be, sound, or seem true to them, such truth as lies in their mythologizing of the iron horse is still a distortion of the nature of true mythology, especially of true Indian mythology.

Where does he stand, then? If we leave out the idea that the word "mythology" is used here with simple or single derogatory or ironic intent, we may look at this passage in a slightly different light, especially if we relate it to another passage in "Walking":

> You will perceive that I demand something which no Augustan nor Elizabethan age—which no *culture* in short can give. Mythology comes nearer to it than anything. How much more fertile a nature at least has Grecian mythology its root in than English literature! Mythology is the crop which the Old World bore before its soil was exhausted, before the fancy and imagination were affected with blight;—and which it still bears wherever its pristine vigor is unabated. All other literatures endure only as the elms which overshadow our houses, but this is like the great Dragon tree of the Western isles, as old as mankind, and whether that does or not, will endure as long; for the decay of other literatures makes the soil in which it thrives. (*Exc* 209)

And Thoreau, clearly and openly an admirer of mythology here, moves on to proclaim that an American mythology is bound to rise:

> The West is preparing to add its fables to those of the east. The valleys of the Ganges, the Nile, and the Rhine, having yielded their crop, it remains to be seen what the valleys of the Amazon, the Plate, the Orinoco—the St Lawrence and the Mississippi will produce. Perchance, when in the course of ages, American Liberty has become a fiction of the past,—as it is to some extent a fiction of the present,—the poets of the world will be inspired by American Mythology. (*Exc* 209)

The two passages are not contradictory but converge toward a shared conception of what mythology is, which in no way implies that Thoreau conceives of mythology as a unified concept. The marked difference between the passage from *Walden* and that from "Walking" is that the latter is more explicit and may not be or sound as critical as the former, but it is still marked by some irony, though of a different kind. What Thoreau implies in the "Walking" passage is that an American mythology will inevitably rise, that it may be seen as a necessary outcome of the growth and progress of the republic, but its rise is bound to be, or threatens to be, impossibly slow to the point of being almost indefinitely postponed due to the effective lack of historical progress toward the ideal of liberty for which the American republic stands. Such progress may even take so much time that, at some future date, it will be thought to have been purely fictive and imaginary. Due to what appears as the perspective of a perpetual deferral, the true past will be re-created from the future as the fruit of a present yet to come that took so long in coming that it might as well never have existed. Thus it may be immaterial for the future whether it existed or not, because the republican ideal of liberty will be mythologized anyway (the emergence of mythology is not dependent on history but on discourse, and there is no shortage of that article), but its historical (non)existence as a continually deferred ideal does make a lot of difference for men at the present day and in the course of future history. *They* will not be content with discourse, nor will their aspirations be fulfilled by it or by any form of modern mythology. This is a pessimistic, even sinister paradox, a darkly ironic statement that inverts and denies all apocalyptic prophecies of the age and hopeful predictions to the contrary; it is marked and accompanied by what one imagines is a wry kind of smile, but still it is quite different from saying what, in the interpretation I started with, we might assume Thoreau declares in *Walden*: that modern mythology is a by-product of the intellectual and spiritual alienation of modern men when confronted with the marvelous achievements of modern technology, which entail a corresponding incapacity in said modern men to see themselves as dominated by or enslaved to their own mechanical inventions, which they mistake for degraded versions of mythological creatures.

In my view, the points that Thoreau makes in both passages show that there are two major constructions of mythology that, with different degrees of emphasis, underlie each of Thoreau's two statements on that subject, but he does not use them alternately, though they may well be potentially in conflict. He conflates them, either for purposes of his own that have yet to be determined or because he simply is not in a position to make the distinction between the two.

Let me try to clarify these implications. What is striking is that "mythology" seems to have a potential for serious meaning, being a sign of spiritual vigor, but then it can also be dismissed easily as a flimsy guise for the shallowest sort of admiring commitment to treating the latest thing in machinery as an allegory of progress, that comes as close as it possibly can to bypassing the necessities or requirements of realistic description. Mythologizing the machine as the "iron horse," or any kind of two-winged or four-footed mythological creature, is a way of making the world poetic, of re-creating it after age-old patterns that Thoreau recognizes elsewhere as "the most impressive proof of a common humanity":

> It is interesting to observe with what singular unanimity the furthest sundered nations and generations consent to give completeness and roundness to an ancient fable, of which they indistinctly appreciate the beauty or the truth. By a faint and dream-like effort, though it be only by the vote of a scientific body, the dullest posterity slowly add some trait to the mythus. As when astronomers call the lately discovered planet Neptune; or the asteroid Astræa, that the Virgin who was driven from earth to heaven at the end of the golden age, may have her local habitation in the heavens more distinctly assigned her, — for the slightest recognition of poetic worth is significant. By such slow aggregation has mythology grown from the first. The very nursery tales of this generation, were the nursery tales of primeval races. They migrate from east to west, and again from west to east; now expanded into the "tale divine" of bards, now shrunk into a popular rhyme. This is an approach to that universal language which men have sought in vain. This fond reiteration of the oldest expressions of truth by the latest posterity, content with slightly and religiously re-touching the old material, is the most impressive proof of a common humanity. (*Wk* 59)

We may conclude from Thoreau's statement that, after all, mythologizing is an easy job that may be and is conducted almost mechanically on a day-to-day basis and interpreted as an attempt to reenchant and poeticize the world through an ordinary use of poetic discourse. Everybody can do it, and "they" do it. As such mythological discourse is ubiquitous and has been updated to apply to the latest things in modernity, clearly mythology has fallen from grace. But this need not bother us. If mythology has emerged anew in common discourse, it may well be to find its best use in those everyday discursive activities from which, in substance and result, poetry may seem to differ but little: should we not regard the mythological names allotted to such objects as planets and asteroids as the ultimate proof that there is power in modern instances of the mythological? Here, the use of mythological forms will signify Nature's capacity to convey a glimpse of the divine, or the divinely natural, through its operations. The idea that the validity of mythology lies in its more serious, poetic import is thus permanently challenged by one form or another of ordinary usage that may ultimately materialize and even trivialize it. However much one might want to construe such persistence of mythology as the residual form of a cognitive enterprise that poetically and imaginatively unveils some genuine, perhaps esoteric, meaning of the universe, there is, in modern usage, little to distinguish it from mythologized forms of the ordinary mistakenly accessed as "poetic" by common wisdom.

Yet, Thoreau insists, myth retains, even in its modern, ordinary use, a capacity to align itself with other means of discovering and accessing truth; it still carries with it a distant echo of its having originated in such truth, and this echo, however muffled and distorted, is still heard. This corresponds to the view that human beings are active in making sense of their world and that they are free to make sense of the world in various ways. There is a distinctive paradox to mythology, then: whether or not it points to whatever abstracted truth may ultimately lie beyond human time and history, what men mostly experience in the "modern" use of mythological phrases, and as a result of such use, is not the truth of things out of this world but the persistence of our own "common humanity" contemplated from within its own confines. It may well be that the mythopoeic urge is widespread in common discursive usage and in the practice of language, but it is hardly current to see it described in such terms. Only rarely is the mostly anthropological function of mythopoeia focused upon and admitted. Truth may vary, but the language expressing whatever that truth may turn out to be is truly universal, if untrue in itself because it varies so much. This in turn is consonant with the fact that, most often, the ordinary sort of mythologizing is not carried out deliberately, and the common speaker is merely carried away by the common drift of discursive usage. Within certain limits and mostly for the purpose of exemplification, the Thoreauvian writer also allows himself to follow suit.

Thoreau the practical man and close observer of nature thus makes frequent references to what his contemporaries came to regard as the fantasies and unrealities of mythology. In *Walden*, for instance, he mentions the Greek myth of Deucalion and Pyrrha in "Economy" (they create men and women by throwing stones over their shoulders); in "Sounds," the Fitchburg Railway train becomes some huge mythological beast; "Brute Neighbors" contains further mythological references to the ants turned men (the Myrmidons) and, in the final section of the same chapter, to an unknown "god of the loons." In his late lecture about apples, Thoreau is not simply concerned with the scientific description of the apple and apple tree, he also tells about the meanings of the fruit and tree in history, poetry, religion, folklore, and myth. This is typical of the kind of approach one finds in Thoreau's texts: the evolution of man's relationship to the fruit as the object of study is thus to be made part of the natural history of the apple, to assert the interconnectedness of the natural world with humanity's invention of it (Sattelmeyer, Introduction xxxi–xxxii). To that extent, human knowledge of natural phenomena always already incorporates within itself the historical evolution of the human perception of such phenomena. Thoreau includes myths, mostly classical, into the accounts of his observations of nature as an object, the limits of which are in no way traced by the material coordinates of its empirical "reality."

Inevitably, however, when human beings freely imbue nature with meaning through a new kind of mythopoeia, problems arise from the belatedness inherent in such literary reenactments of ancient myths. Modern users do not do their mythmaking the way the Greeks did; they do it artificially or "deliberately," constantly bearing in mind, as they construct their new mythology, that the resulting vision owes its existence to the capacity inherent in humans to make their own social world. Mythopoeia (the deliberate, controlled creation of myths) is thus constitutive of the culture in which men live because any human culture expresses the built-in propensities of the race to mythmaking. The enthusiasm for the theogonic capability of myths might therefore be predicated on the knowledge that all myths are ultimately mere social-historical constructs that contribute to the emergence of what we call reality, which is not limited to the materiality of the world. Interacting between the creative mind and its natural environment, mythology will disallow an analysis of the world in merely material or purely historical terms. But then it also points to the limitations entailed by this sort of purely human construct. Thoreau's point, however, may not be half as disenchanted: whatever the degree of self-consciousness displayed in the calling upon ancient myths for modern purposes, whatever distortions they have undergone in the process, the mere fact that they could not but be reiterated points to their resilience as a humanly significant factor that has been permanently preserved through them. It is their humanity that men recognize in myths and in the environment they contribute to shape for themselves in their use of them.

CHRISTIAN MAUL

"A Sort of Hybrid Product"

THOREAU'S INDIVIDUALISM BETWEEN
LIBERALISM AND COMMUNITARIANISM

WHILE SPENDING TIME in Concord doing research at the Free Public Library, I entered a small bookshop owned by an elderly lady. As I was rummaging through the books, she asked me if I was looking for something specific. I answered that I was writing a thesis on Thoreau and that I was absorbing the atmosphere of the town to which he was so devoted. Her reply surprised me. "Oh," she said, "good old Henry. If every American owned a copy of *Walden* and read it carefully, our society would be a better one." Despite the fact that this Concordian woman may be favorably biased toward Ralph, Nathaniel, or Henry—as Concordians lovingly refer to Emerson, Hawthorne, and Thoreau— her statement seemingly testifies to the fact that some modern Americans still perceive a certain warmth radiating from Thoreau's writings; they seem to believe in the socially remedial effect that his works can have.

Thoreau was convinced that the ideal of individual autonomy that his mentor Emerson propagated as "self-reliance" had to be cultivated as the driving force of social reform. He believed that the autonomous self that persistently advances its spirituality, that explores its "private sea" (*W* 321) or its "inner ocean," to use George Kateb's phrase, could initiate social improvement, thus enhancing public morality and societal harmony. Not all of Thoreau's readers, however, shared his conviction of the preparatory function of self-culture in solitude for social reform. While Thoreau held that his detachment from community could protect him from the corrupting impact of civilization on his mind and soul and allow his self to undergo spiritual renewal, many of his early reviewers felt offended by his isolationist inclinations. They saw in them not only a threat to Thoreau's own physical and mental states but also a perversion of the social nature of man that endangered the internal coherence of society. In his article "The Hermit of Concord," William Rounseville Alger, a "neglected member of the Concord circle" (Scharnhorst), traces "a tone from the diseased and dispro- portioned side of the writer," adding that Thoreau "was unhealthy and unjust in all his thoughts on society; underrating the value, overrating the dangers, of intercourse with men" (Alger 383). Indeed, many of Thoreau's contemporaries perceived his withdrawal from social responsibilities as a corruption of the lib- erating and "useful" individualism embodied, for instance, by Benjamin Frank- lin. While the latter was committed to projects of public utility, Thoreau, in his quest for egocentric self-perfection, neglected his obligations toward commu- nity. Despite his admiration for Thoreau's works, Eugene Benson, who wrote under the pseudonym "Sordello" for the *New York Evening Post*, concluded in his review of *Cape Cod*: "With men like Thoreau society would be impossible" (1). Or, as Emerson himself says of his protégé: "If I knew only Thoreau I should think the cooperation of men impossible" (Porte, *Emerson in His Journals* 465).

However, Thoreau also had some apologists. In 1854, the year in which he published *Walden*, the *Boston Transcript* wrote that the thoughts expressed in the book are "already making a deep impression upon some souls" and that they "will reach far out into the tide of time" (Myerson, *Emerson and Thoreau* 395–96). And the *Lowell Daily Citizen and News* noted: "He has multitudes of readers all over the land, and, sooner or later, beneficial social results will appear as the fruits of his life and teachings" (9 December 1865). For modern Thoreau scholarship, the voices of his contemporaries are of great importance, particularly as they create a multifaceted picture of how Thoreau's (anti)social behavior was apprehended during his lifetime. We have to keep in mind, how- ever, that in one and a half centuries of Thoreau scholarship, assessments of the Transcendentalist's personality, his works, and his achievements on the part of both his admirers and his detractors have emerged from subjective judg- ments and individual literary taste, from either sympathies or antipathies. Crit- ics have predominantly based their appraisal of Thoreau and his concept of individualism on intuitive readings without applying objective interpretative criteria. Some shared Thoreau's moral beliefs; others did not. Some dismissed his idiosyncrasies as mere whimsicality; others admired them as likable uncon- ventionality. But whom shall the modern reader believe, Thoreau's detractors or his admirers?

The dispute between Thoreau's critics and his apologists echoes one of the most ardently led philosophical controversies of our time, the debate between liberalism, with its affirmation of self-determination, and communitarianism, with its demand for the individual's return into the social network. Just as Thoreau's detractors chastise him for his isolationism, escapism, and egocentrism, communitarian theorists such as Michael Sandel, Charles Taylor, and Michael Walzer claim that America's most prominent liberal political theorist of the twentieth century, John Rawls, erroneously conceives of the self as an isolated, decontextualized, atomistic subject unable to meaningfully relate to the values, habits, and customs of community. I argue that we can utilize this modern debate for our interpretation of Thoreauvian individualism to reveal that the Transcendentalist self is not a socially estranged and disaffected entity but a link between self-culture and militant intervention into the deplorable state of affairs in antebellum America. Thoreau was fully embedded in his society and prepared himself for social criticism and commitment by means of self-culture. Before we interpret Thoreauvian individualism from the perspective of the liberalism-communitarianism debate, however, let us briefly recapitulate the major claims of both camps and their impact on liberal and communitarian anthropology.

The Communitarian Self

Communitarianism is the philosophical expression of discontent with dwindling social cohesion and individual attachment to the social matrix. The theory opposes forms of radical, egocentric individualism and must be understood as an ontological, normative, and metaethical corrective to the theory of liberalism as proposed by Rawls.[1] A contemporary witness of milestone events of the human rights revolution such as the Universal Declaration of Rights and the student protests of the 1960s, Rawls, in his *Theory of Justice*, establishes the priority of justice over all competing values and the priority of individual rights over the common good. He states that "each person possesses an inviolability founded on justice that even the welfare of society as a whole cannot override" (3). Rawls finds that the range of state intrusion into individual lives and the dominance of community goals over self-determination must be constricted by a theory of justice that vindicates the priority of rights in accordance with individuals' intuition of justice. As the setting of his argument, Rawls creates his "original position," a fictitious normative framework that abstracts from the empirical world and creates ahistorical, hypothetical, and deindividualized selves that decide on principles of justice governing their coexistence. To establish moral objectivity and impartiality, Rawls installs what he calls "the veil of ignorance," a device that neutralizes the arbitrariness with which nature has endowed individuals with merits. The veil forces the members of the original position to decide on principles of justice regardless of the arbitrary and uneven distribution of assets. The results emerging from the original position, then, are the "liberty principle," which protects basic nonmaterial liberties such as freedom of speech, religion, and thought and the liberty of conscience, as well as the "difference principle," which defines the legitimacy of economic inequality, allowing for inequality if it serves all individuals.

The most powerful challenge to Rawls's work was formulated by Harvard professor of government Michael Sandel, who claims that privileging individual rights endangers democracy. Sandel opposes Rawls's postulate of the priority of justice and individual rights with his claim that their range can very well be limited by the claims of community and by a commonly shared understanding of the good. Essentially, Sandel attacks Rawls's ontology. He rejects Rawls's conception of the self as an entity that exists behind the "veil of ignorance" and outside social experience because this existence deprives it of the possibility of its identity being shaped and its ends being generated by society's norms and traditions. Indeed, Rawls's anthropology "rules out the possibility of any attachment . . . able to reach beyond our values and sentiments to engage our identity itself. It rules out the possibility of a public life in which, for good or ill, the identity as well as the interests of the participants could be at stake" (62). A self detached from the values it pursues will never be able to be fully constituted by them and to be described in the language of community. Sandel concludes that "Rawls's account rules out the possibility of what we might call 'intersubjective' . . . forms of self-understanding" (62). Sandel's alternative ontology suggests an encumbered self that fully exists in the social realm and that comprehends the habits and values of society as constituent elements of its identity.

Charles Taylor joins Sandel in promoting a nonatomistic individual; he proposes the image of the self as a self-interpreting animal that derives the tools for self-interpretation through dialogical relations with others and its situatedness in society as moral space. For Taylor, "living in a society is a necessary condition of the development of rationality, . . . or of becoming a moral agent in the full sense of the term, or of becoming a fully responsible, autonomous being. . . .

Outside society, or in some variants outside certain kinds of society, our distinctively human capacities could not develop" ("Atomism" 191). Taylor, however, extends the communitarian objection against liberalism into the realm of normativity. The self that maintains itself necessarily has to contribute to the maintenance of the social matrix and must willingly bear what Taylor calls "the obligation to belong" to a social framework.

Michael Walzer, in contrast, approaches Rawls from a metaethical perspective. He defends particularism against Rawlsian universalism and argues that a theory of distributive justice must always take into consideration the particular understanding of the good prevalent in a specific society. He is convinced that a decision on fair distributive principles cannot be made from behind the "veil of ignorance" but only on the basis of the social identity, aims, and desires of empiric selves. We must therefore consent to principles of justice not as deindividualized entities but as empiric individuals, as "ordinary people, with a firm sense of [our] own identity, with [our] own goods in [our] hands, caught up in everyday troubles" (*Spheres* 5). This firm sense is acquired in a particular society and shaped by a particular and commonly shared understanding of the good life.

Amalgamating the communitarian objections to Rawlsian liberalism, we can attribute the following characteristics to the role model of a prototypical communitarian self: first, the communitarian self is socially situated so that self-understanding is, as Nancy Rosenblum puts it, "oddly *un*self-absorbed and firmly world-oriented. Everything impinges on [the individual] and has constitutive potential" ("Strange Attractors" 578, emphasis in original). For this socially situated entity, the communitarians find diverse attributes: antiatomistic, encumbered, contextualized, embedded. These attributes denote an individual who embodies the classical understanding of the self as a *zoon politikon*, a self that exists in sociopolitical reality and that conceives of itself as an integral part of participatory democracy. Second, embedded in a narrative about a common history and culture, the communitarian self emerges as a socially responsible citizen who willingly accepts the obligation to belong. This obligation pledges the self to the renewal and stabilization of intersubjective relationships, its affirmed identification and solidarity with the community, and the maintenance of the commonly shared morality, habits, and norms that shape its identity and conscience. Third, its cultural embeddedness and willingness to bear the obligation to belong turn the self into a watchful observer of social processes and political institutions, an observer whom Walzer calls the "connected critic." The connected critic is neither alienated nor detached from the institutions and practices he criticizes (cf. Teichgraeber xii); he does not assess his community from a distant mountaintop but from within. He invokes his community's values and practices as objective standards for social criticism. Social criticism is thus relative to the social context within which it is formulated because it emerges from the perspective of the critic who is integrated in the dynamics of his community and who intervenes if social dynamics require intervention. The critic's intervention becomes inevitable whenever social dynamics produce victims of social or economic oppression, when a society's core values, its democratic norms and practices, are corrupted.

From Self-Culture to Connected Criticism

The communitarian qualms about the liberal conception of the self echo the criticism Thoreau had to face. Readers regarding Thoreau as a hermitic crank find substance in the claim that he was a determined liberal who egoistically sought self-fulfillment, that he defined justice as justice toward the rights of the individual. At the beginning of *Walden*, Thoreau admits that he gave in to the need to distance himself from the "false society of men" (*W* 33). He positions himself detached from social affairs and responsibilities, withdrawn into the world of subjective experience. In his most influential essay, "Resistance to Civil Government," he dramatizes the need of retirement by rejecting reliance on the state and emphasizing the necessity for the self to trust in its own life-creating potential: "You must live within yourself, and depend upon yourself, always tucked up and ready for a start, and not have many affairs" (*RP* 78). Like Rawls, Thoreau accepted laws only if they leave enough room for self-determination, self-exploration, and autonomy. He looked for "new, universal, and more liberal laws" (*W* 323); the self-reliant individual has to expand "the old laws" and interpret them "in his favor in a more liberal sense" (*W* 323–24).

If such remarks betray a decidedly liberal quest for individual rights and a concept of justice in terms of such rights, what does one make of Thoreau's repeated visits to the village, his lectures at the Concord lyceum, his activities in the Underground Railroad, and his intimate friendships with his brother John, William Ellery Channing, Emerson, and Hawthorne? How can we explain these "passionate ambivalences" (Moller xiii), his constant shuttling back and forth between Walden remoteness and Concord conviviality? Apparently, as Sherman Paul argues, in Thoreau "there was a need for love, a human hunger, that even the timeless spaces of nature never satisfied. . . . He wanted both an inviolable self and 'public influence'" (125). The former he found at Walden, the latter in society. Paul's reading, however, fails to do justice to the degree to which Thoreau's longing for solitude and his engagement in the public sphere depend on each other. Indeed, the liberal characteristics Thoreau embodied do not constitute a static and incontrovertible identity; instead, they support the self in constructing a socially viable identity that empowers it to exist contentedly and responsibly in the social matrix and to intervene if this matrix's stability is endangered. Solitude and social commitment, then, are not exclusive states of existence but mutually corrective instances that complement and require each other.

Thoreau, then, was not a genuine representative of Rawls's decontextualized self; instead, he epitomized the encumbered, nonatomistic self that Sandel's and Taylor's ontologies promote. He did not regard societal arrangements as mere instruments to advance his own goals; instead, he perceived himself as the embodiment of values and practices of the society in which he lived. He identified with society, for instance, by interpreting the sounds society generates. Although "there is in [his] nature . . . a singular yearning toward all wildness" (*Wk* 54), Thoreau rejoices in the sounds produced by civilization and translates them, by filtering them through the divinity and purity of wildness, into an aesthetic experience. During their first night on the shores of the Concord River, the brothers "saw the horizon blazing, and heard the distant alarm bells, as it were tinkling music borne to these woods" (*Wk* 41). "Even . . . a retired and uninhabited district like this" (*Wk* 41) is permeated by civilization and the sounds it produces, and Thoreau delights in these sounds even though they derive from "house dogs" as representatives of domesticated nature. Their barking "sounded as sweet and melodious as an instrument," Thoreau exclaims (*Wk* 41).

This "sufficiency of sound" (*Wk* 41), the acoustic manifestation of the commotion of civilization, is also wafted over to Walden Pond, often much to Thoreau's regret. "On gala days," Thoreau states, "the town fires its great guns, which echo like popguns to these woods, and some waifs of martial music occasionally penetrate thus far" (*W* 160). "As if a puff ball had burst," "as if somebody's bees had swarmed" (*W* 160), these sounds disturb Thoreau in his meditation, but after a moment of slight dejection during which he has to admit that he can never completely evade society, even if he wanted, during which he experiences the sound of the guns as "some sort of itching and disease in the horizon" (*W* 160), Thoreau turns this previously negative encounter into counterfeit patriotic sentiment and "mock vainglory" (Cavell, *Senses* 24). He states: "I felt proud to know that the liberties of Massachusetts and of our fatherland were in such safe keeping; and as I turned to my hoeing again I was filled with an inexpressible confidence, and pursued my labor cheerfully with a calm trust in the future" (*W* 160). Despite the fact that this is one of the most sarcastic passages in all of Thoreau's writings, it reveals that he is not indifferent toward the values that are celebrated on these "gala days," that he identifies with the ideas for which the military exercises stand: "the liberties of Massachusetts and of our fatherland." Although he does not share his contemporaries' enthusiasm for the festivities of these "gala days," he feels part of the nation that established individual freedom and happiness as incontrovertible values; he is willing to share this nation's remembrance of the struggle fought for the establishment of these values. Accepting them as constituents of his identity makes Thoreau an encumbered American self. As Emerson remarked, "No truer American existed than Thoreau. His preference of his country and condition was genuine" ("Thoreau" 429).

Due to his cultural embeddedness, Thoreau willingly bears his obligation to belong by criticizing social and political processes. This criticism, however, emerges from his situatedness within society, from his existence as a connected critic, and it testifies to Thoreau's genuine concern for his society and its moral integrity. When the temptations of modernity began to negatively affect intersubjective relationships, when the pluralization of values entailed the disintegration of traditional ties and the corruption of society's habits of the heart, when the republican ideal of society as a community of virtuous selves was unmasked as an illusion by the social reality of a mass of disembodied, deindividualized selves, Thoreau created literary works that raise the reader's awareness of the other, of intersubjective ties—works that, in essence, are all about taking care of the other: of neighbors, friends, nature. Thoreau was truly concerned about the disintegration of the ties that originally held his society together, and he aimed to redefine intersubjectivity on the basis of a revised understanding of Americans' common morality. He wanted to meet his contemporaries not in the framework of a political community but on the grounds of friendship and neighborhood; equal and sovereign selves were to meet on the basis of a mutual understanding of the good and a common affirmation of the values that the Founding Fathers had bequeathed them.

In the opening paragraph of his "Visitors" chapter, probably Thoreau's most convivial and intersubjective essay, the author says of himself, "I think that I love society as much as most, and am ready enough to fasten myself like a bloodsucker for the time to any full-blooded man that comes in my way. I am naturally no hermit" (*W* 140). And in a letter to his literary executor and editor, H. G. O. Blake, he writes that "as for the dispute about solitude & society any comparison is impertinent. . . . Of course you will be glad of all the society you can get to go up with. . . . I love society so much that I swallowed it all at a gulp—i.e. all that came in my way. It is not that we love to be alone, but that we love to soar, and when we do soar, the company grows thinner & thinner till there is none at all" (*Corr* 281). Despite his periods of solitary communion with nature, Thoreau did not conceive of himself as a decontextualized person. As Richard F. Teichgraeber has convincingly argued in his interpretation of Emerson and Thoreau as connected critics of the American market, "Thoreau's criticism of his world did not depend simply on detachment and enmity" (61). Rather, Thoreau acknowledged his embeddedness as a natural element of his identity. "Naturally," that is, by nature, he could not lead a hermitic existence, but he maintained the moral ties to his community and inescapably existed in the social realm. He understood that men need society and companionship; individuals may sometimes prefer to be solitary, but they never want to be alone. In solitude, the self can "soar," open the soul to the wild; "trivial business" is filtered out, and true society is "winnowed" (*W* 144). From the perspective of solitude, we view our existence and encumbrances in abstraction. By juxtaposing the chapters on "Solitude" and "Visitors," Thoreau points out that the company of genuine friends and true society does not disturb his introspection and self-exploration but that they empower his soul to stretch out and encompass the other. Via a vivid metaphor, Thoreau expresses how he literally incorporates true human society: he sucks out company and swallows it, thus making it a part of his physical and—on a more abstract level—spiritual constitution. The friendship of "full-blooded men" and the "finest [social] sediment" (*W* 144), then, enlarges the soul and entertains the self in the original sense of the word; true society holds the self together and maintains it.

Solitude and society coexist not as mutually exclusive realms but as complementary spheres whose intricate interaction enriches the individual's identity. Indeed, "periods of solitude and society can work together, drawing out our full human potential" (Cafaro, *Thoreau's Living Ethics* 117). Thoreau found company in the midst of nature and solitude among men. Thus, solitude never entails loneliness, and society never involves social determinism. Rather, this dynamic interaction granted Thoreau a full understanding of his Americanness. Despite his temporary detachment, he still moved in the moral space that provides the interpretative grid for self-interpretation, thus revealing that the indifference of the populace toward morally unjust legislation implies a more severe detachment from communal morality and a more anticommunitarian behavior than the merely physical distance Thoreau embodied. Although his project of self-culture accommodated the liberal claim for self-determination and for a reduction of state interference into his individual life, the communication of Thoreau's project, its aesthetic expression in lectures, letters, and books, bears the marks of the society within which Thoreau existed and with which he communicated. Via its literary acts, the sometimes solitary but constantly socially connected self interacts with the social framework that has generated its identity. The literary act, then, represents not a rejection but an integration of the social matrix into the self's life.

This integration can occur despite or precisely because of the individual's frustration with political and social processes. Reading in Thoreau's Journal that "we must have infinite faith in each other, if we have not we must never let it leak out that we have not" (*PJ* 4: 311), one is tempted to say that Thoreau belonged to these men who do not have this infinite faith in others, that in the face of the corruption of American morality he mistrusted others and detached himself from them. But he did not. Rather, he turned his disappointment about the world into the courage to disobey morally unjust laws and to call for a revision of the morality that was bound to cement his society. He engaged his community in a reassessment of its values and initiated that "shoring up of [American] moral foundations" (Etzioni 11) that communitarianism demands. Instead of detaching himself for good, Thoreau even felt drawn closer to the state by its immoral legislation because it forced him to reflect about what justice in a democracy means. The results of this reflection, then, encouraged his public attempt to restore the moral dimension of political action and the foundation of democratic functionality. Indeed, "his privatization is exhibitionistic, a public act calculated to engage others" (Rosenblum, *Another Liberalism* 104). In that sense, Thoreau was "inescapably implicated in the actions of his nation, responsible . . . for righting current wrongs and safeguarding the promise of America" (Cafaro, *Thoreau's Living Ethics* 199).

The dynamic interaction between solitude and society Thoreau embodied was part and parcel of his search for viable syntheses, for the reconciliation of the seemingly irreconcilable. These syntheses were first and foremost inspired by nature, for instance, by the sandbank of the Merrimack River or by the thawing sandbank near Walden Pond. In *A Week* he writes, "This sand seemed to us the connecting link between land and water. It was a kind of water on which you could walk" (199); in *Walden* he states that "innumerable little streams overlap and interlace one with another, exhibiting a sort of hybrid product, which obeys half way the law of currents, and half way that of vegetation" (305). The most impressive synthesis, however, is generated in *Walden*'s central essay, "The Ponds," when Thoreau stands "on the smooth sandy beach at the east end of the pond, in a calm September afternoon" (*W* 186), his eyes wandering over this magical body of water that is "intermediate in its nature between land and sky" (*W* 188–89). From his perspective, the physical and the metaphysical spheres, land and sky, merge and create the binary formula "Sky Water" (*W* 188). By making all these natural phenomena his own, Thoreau incorporates their integrative potential and conceives of himself as a bridger of duality rather than a victim of it (cf. Francis xi).

Thoreau between Liberalism and Communitarianism

Thoreau's drive for syntheses in observing nature, then, may prompt us to take a fresh, conciliating look at the liberalism-communitarianism debate. Just as Rawls, particularly through the publication of *Political Liberalism*, later conceives of himself as a "communitarian liberal" (Mulhall and Swift 461), or Walzer states that "I am a liberal communitarian" (interview), Thoreau can be regarded as a "connecting link," "a sort of hybrid product," somehow "intermediate in [his] nature" not only between detachment and commitment or the local and the global but also between the alleged antagonism of liberalism and communitarianism. He balanced the claims and needs of the self and society and established a stable in-betweenness first by discovering his community orientation within the liberal setting of democratic society and then by substantiating his liberal demand for self-culture and self-determination through community-directed reasoning. He thus provided his reader with "specific advice about ways in which the individual can achieve both microcosmic and macrocosmic fulfillment" (Francis 223). Through introspection and meditation, Thoreau uncovered his concern for community and its moral integrity. Simultaneously, he helped to sustain the liberal society by invoking a communally shared morality. He employed liberal and communitarian claims as reciprocal correctives and thus "initiate[d] a critical revision of liberalism that has profound affinities with communitarian thought" (Worley xi). As Antonio Casado da Rocha puts it, Thoreau "was not an anti-social anarchist, or even a pure liberal individualist, but . . . along with the main liberal themes of his thought there is also a democratic, even communitarian strand" (16). Thoreau's concept of individualism reveals that liberalism requires a communitarian counterweight, and community-directed thinking and acting presuppose a stable, autonomous self. Indeed, individual autonomy and self-determination are intrinsically linked to a functioning and stable system of democratic community within which autonomy can be claimed. Conversely, a stable democratic community is contingent upon the creative and curative potential of self-reliant individuals such as Thoreau. A democratic society is reliant on a dynamic interaction between self-determination and embeddedness. Detachment and social situatedness, then, are not mutually exclusive alternatives to each other, but they support and require each other.

Thoreau did not imagine a state or a community in which "the life of a civilized people [is turned into] an *institution*, in which the life of the individual is to a great extent absorbed, in order to preserve and perfect that of the race" (*W* 31–32, emphasis in original), in which individual integrity and autonomy are sacrificed to social cohesion or even social determinism. Rather, he attempted "to show at what a sacrifice this advantage is at present obtained, and to suggest that we may possibly so live as to secure all the advantage [social cohesion] without suffering any of the disadvantage [giving up autonomy]" (*W* 32). Thoreau envisaged a "really free and enlightened State" (*RP* 89) in which the individual and community coexist in mutual service. This state "can afford to be just to all men, and to treat the individual with respect as a neighbor"; it "would not think it inconsistent with its own repose, if a few were to lie aloof from it, not meddling with it, nor embraced by it." In return, the individual fulfills "all the duties of neighbors and fellow-men" (*RP* 89–90). How modern Thoreau's understanding of the relationship between self and democratic society is becomes apparent when we compare it with Walzer's "liberal communitarian" conception of the self-society relationship. Walzer states:

> I want to imagine a political community that is more open, open to departures, withdrawals, more loosely conceived, less demanding on its members. . . . The love of politics is only one possible human love; you cannot demand it of everybody. So politics is likely to be the work of people who enjoy political work. The great advantage of democracy is that it allows other people to come and go, to rush into the political arena when they have urgent interests, when they feel threatened, or when they have some aspiration, some sense of what can be accomplished. But it also allows people to withdraw. (interview)

Then, Walzer adds:

> It is easy to draw a picture . . . of an individualized, isolated self, so bereft of communal ties that he is incapable of forming and sustaining his relationships with other people. But that is a caricature of individualism. It is a caricature that gets at a certain tendency in individualist thought, which I think I want to resist. I am averse to the individual who says "I can do what I want with my life, with my body, with whatever power I have. I can do whatever I want without regard to other people." Rather, we are bound to other people. We come into the world since we come into a family, with commitments and obligations. We are never without those. (interview)

Communities must grant individuals room for self-determination; they must allow individuals to detach themselves from public space. Only if they are granted this leeway are individuals empowered to bring their social and political potentials to fruition, "to rush into the political arena when they have urgent interests, when they feel threatened, or when they have some aspiration, some sense of what can be accomplished." At the same time, however, this leeway must not be exploited to cut an individual's intersubjective ties, because this reduces liberalism *ad absurdum*. Despite its existence in a liberal matrix, the self never fully exists without the values and norms of a particular society, without the ends these values and norms generate, or without the conscience they shape. It is in the ends that the self embodies and the conscience that governs its behavior in moral space that the good promoted by a particular society lies. In that sense, the self is the holder of the communally shared and accepted notion of the good. This insight, then, helps to dissolve the question of whether justice and the right are superior to the common good or vice versa. The search for a hierarchy of the right and the good becomes meaningless once we discover the synthesis of the right-good relationship within the self, a synthesis for which Thoreau provided a vivid example. Although he probably did not experience the affective satisfactions within a community that communitarian ontology promises and that liberal ontology cannot provide, he did not perceive his social identity as an encumbrance but rather as a moral ground that he shared with his fellow Americans.

NOTE

1. The classification of communitarian approaches to liberalism as ontological, normative, and metaethical is suggested by Caney.

Part Three

THOREAU, LANGUAGE, AND THE WILD

DIETER SCHULZ
Nature, Knowledge, and the Method of Thoreau's Excursions

IN THE OPENING SECTION of "Autumnal Tints," one of his late natural history essays, Thoreau explains that he will be offering the reader extracts from notes he had compiled for a book he never managed to complete. The book would have consisted of colored reproductions of "a specimen leaf from each changing tree, shrub and herbaceous plant, when it had acquired its brightest characteristic color, in its transition from the green to the brown state. . . . What a memento such a book would be! You would need only to turn over its leaves to take a ramble through the Autumn woods whenever you pleased. Or if I could preserve the leaves themselves unfaded, it would be better still" (*Exc* 225). Thoreau's remarks correlate three notions that are central to his thought: walking ("a ramble"), reading, and nature. As Lawrence Buell pointed out some time ago, from *A Week on the Concord and Merrimack Rivers* to the late natural history essays, Thoreau's preferred genre was the excursion (*Literary Transcendentalism* 188–207). With few exceptions, the protagonist of his essays is a walker. Even where he doesn't announce a walk in the very title of a work (as he does, e.g., in "A Winter Walk," "A Walk to Wachusetts," "Walking"), the motif of walking pervades his writing just as it was his favorite activity in life.

Apart from physical pleasure, for Thoreau walking was a hermeneutical exercise. Nature should be studied much as one reads a book, for in a profound sense nature *is* a book—a web of signs, a text (literally, "that which is woven" or "web") to be deciphered. Conversely, books should be natural; the ideal book would reproduce and preserve the operations of nature. Such a notion harks back to the ancient topos of the book of nature, the *liber naturae*; from this perspective Thoreau offers yet another romantic version of a concept familiar from

classical antiquity on down through the Middle Ages to such early modern writers as Paracelsus and Jakob Boehme (St. Armand; D. Schulz). At the same time,
he anticipates some of the most exciting recent developments in linguistics, the
sciences, and philosophy. Some of these developments can only be touched upon
briefly here; for reasons of space, I will only indicate significant new departures
in linguistics and biology. In the major part of my argument, I will focus on the
walker-as-reader by analyzing the relationship between knowledge and method
as that relationship has been addressed in philosophical hermeneutics.

As Hans-Georg Gadamer, the key figure in modern hermeneutics, has reminded us in *Wahrheit und Methode* (1960), the Greek notion of method presupposes a fundamental unity of Being and Knowing (467–68 [*Truth and Method*
463–64]). Greek *methodos* originally means "following or accompanying something on its way"—a definition that captures Thoreau's philosophy of walking in
a nutshell. Gadamer invokes the ancient meaning of "method" in an attempt to
set the humanities off from the sciences, thus by implication widening the gap
between what C. P. Snow dubbed "the two cultures." But as Reinhard Schulz argues in *Naturwissenschaftshermeneutik* (Hermeneutics of the natural sciences),
the reach of Gadamer's reflections extends well beyond *Geisteswissenschaften*,
beyond the humanities and into the sciences; his approach has considerable
potential for overcoming the two-cultures dichotomy. If my claim for an affinity
between Gadamer and Thoreau makes sense, then, another look at Thoreau's
excursions promises far-reaching consequences.

Nature as Text, or, the Walker as Reader

The characteristic and perfectly legitimate response to Thoreau's imagined book
of specimen leaves in "Autumnal Tints" is summed up by William Rossi in
the introduction to his edition of the natural history essays when he refers to
Thoreau's "ironic dream of 'preserv[ing] the leaves unfaded' in a scrapbook"—
ironic because the specimen leaves inevitably would provide no more than "a
pale, ersatz 'memento'" of the original experience (Introduction xx–xxi). But
while the tone of Thoreau's remarks does suggest a heavy dose of facetiousness,
the passage also points to the innumerable and quite serious hints in his writings at a more profound affinity between writing or composing a book, on the
one hand, and the operations of nature, on the other.

Thoreau's plea for natural writing and a natural book derives much of its force from his conviction of the intrinsically linguistic features of nature. Echoing and expanding on Emerson's *Nature* (1836) and "The Poet," where Emerson had claimed that "things . . . are emblematic" (*CW* 1: 18) and that "things admit of being used as symbols because nature is a symbol, in the whole, and in every part" (*CW* 3: 8), Thoreau in *Walden* admonishes us to heed "the language which all things and events speak without metaphor, which alone is copious and standard" (111). Thoreau makes these remarks at the beginning of the "Sounds" essay, right after the essay "Reading," with its emphatic praise of the classics. The transition from "Reading" to "Sounds" may suggest a move away from books into nature, the former providing, like the scrapbook mentioned in "Autumnal Tints," merely a "pale, ersatz memento" of the real thing. Yet one can also envisage the link between the two essays as a transition from one book to another. (I wonder how many readers of *Walden* appreciate the technical and strictly linguistic meaning of such terms as "copious" and "standard.") In the famous sandbank passage of the "Spring" essay, the leaf patterns of the thawing sand are interpreted as signs used by nature to express itself: "No wonder that the earth expresses itself outwardly in leaves, it so labors with the idea inwardly" (*W* 306). Speculative and playful as his long reflections on the leaves may be, Thoreau insists not only on the legitimacy but also on the existential urgency of his endeavor by calling for a Champollion who will "decipher this hieroglyphic for us, that we may turn over a new leaf at last" (*W* 308).

Over and over Thoreau underscores the linguistic features of nature, its intrinsic bookishness, as it were, which makes the writer's task a job of translation; after perceiving the signs in nature, he then carries them over—"translates them"—onto the page. As he observes in "Walking," "Where is the literature which gives expression to Nature? He would be a poet who could impress the winds and streams into his service, to speak for him; who nailed words to their primitive senses, as farmers drive down stakes in the spring which the frost has heaved; who derived his words as often as he used them—transplanted them to his page with earth adhering to their roots" (*Exc* 208). The seemingly playful equation of the leaves of trees with the leaves of his scrapbook in "Autumnal Tints" thus contains a serious point; Thoreau conceives of nature not only by analogy to language but also as a language in literal terms, "without metaphor."

Linguistics and Biology

To echo the opening of Jane Austen's *Pride and Prejudice*, it is a truth universally acknowledged that the linguistic sign is arbitrary, that it is "unmotivated" by reality. That at any rate has been an axiom of modern linguistics. Thanks largely to Saussure, for a long time practically no self-respecting linguist would claim an intrinsic bond between words and things. From this perspective, Emerson's and Thoreau's belief in a language of nature or in its corollary, a natural language—the belief that drives the nineteenth-century obsession with etymologies so impressively documented by Michael West in *Transcendental Wordplay*—appears to be a hopelessly romantic, nostalgic illusion.

The Saussurian axiom is here to stay, but its reach has not gone unquestioned. As early as 1929, Edward Sapir tried to identify constraints on the arbitrariness principle by pointing to "a more fundamental, a psychologically primary, sort of symbolism" (226) at the phonetic level of language. Since the appearance of Roman Jakobson and Linda Waugh's *The Sound Shape of Language* (1979), phonosemantics (as this direction in linguistics calls itself) has produced an impressive amount of work suggesting an affinity between certain sound patterns and such notions as size (large vs. small) and distance (proximity vs. distance). In light of these studies, Thoreau's interpretations of sounds in *Walden* and elsewhere seem less facetious. Phonosemantics in turn is a branch of cognitive linguistics, specifically, iconicity studies. In addition to sounds, the latter include vocabulary, grammar, and syntax. One of its foundational figures, Charles Sanders Peirce, introduced the notion of the iconic sign, the sign that imitates certain features of reality. Iconicists define these features in physiological, psychological, and cognitive terms, challenging linguistics à la Saussure by arguing that language is motivated to a much higher degree than is commonly assumed (Nänny and Fischer; Givón).

Considering the relevance of modern linguistics to Thoreau, something can also be gained by a reversal of perspective. If iconicity studies move linguistics closer to Thoreau's engagement with language and nature, Thoreau himself moves in the direction of modern linguistics, including the hard-core Saussurean variety, inasmuch as his readings of nature emphasize relations rather than roots and essences. As Emerson had pointed out in "The Method of Nature" (1841), in nature "this refers to that, and that to the next, and the next to the third, and everything refers" (*CW* 1: 125). From "The Natural History of Massachusetts" down to the late "Wild Apples," "Huckleberries," and "Autumnal Tints," Thoreau offers paeans to the referential richness of nature. If the variety of natural objects emanates from and points to a principle of unity, of oneness, what interests him most in practical terms is the interplay of forces, of relations and influences that culminate in an autumn leaf, an apple, or a huckleberry. Without discarding the principle of identity and its linguistic corollary, metaphor, the later Journal and the natural history essays testify to a decided shift of attention from the vertical to the lateral axis of nature's text: from identity to contiguity, from metaphor to metonymy. How many factors have to come into play, how many things have to come into contact to produce the phenomena at hand! Thoreau would not have subscribed to the arbitrariness axiom, but his actual engagement with nature and his linguistic strategies envisage nature as a system of relational, interreferential signs whose meaning evolves from the context and con-tact of adjacent, contiguous objects and signs more than from any metaphysical grounding. Paradoxically, our knowledge of nature deepens as we learn to appreciate the richness of its surface.

If modern linguistics (both Saussurean and non- or anti-Saussurean) may have something to say to Thoreau, and if Thoreau may have something to offer that modern linguists (again both Saussurean and non- or anti-Saussurean) may find palatable, what about the modern discipline that would seem to either corroborate or compete with or perhaps leave behind Thoreau's nature studies? What about biology? Again, a few sketchy remarks must suffice. A major recent trend in biology goes quite far in the direction of a Thoreauvian reading of nature. Its driving impulse is neatly summed up in the title of a volume edited by John Cornwell: *Nature's Imagination* (1995). The essays in this collection share as their common concern a belief in the need, as Cornwell explains in the preface, "to put mind back into nature" (vii). According to so-called biosemiotics, evolutionist biology is right in assuming that nature is governed by stimulus-and-response patterns, but these patterns function not as linear cause-and-effect mechanisms so much as they operate in the manner of dialogic and aesthetic relationships. An organism creates not only itself but also its environment; both form part of a living unity. Francisco Varela counters what he considers to be the mechanistic reductions of mainstream evolutionary biologists by the concept of *autopoiesis*: a creative process in which the organism "reads" the signals of its surroundings in a reciprocal, vital relationship that shapes both sides through acts of interpretation and aesthetic, that is, disinterested, unselfish appreciation.

A linear cause-and-effect scheme fails to do justice to the ways in which organisms interpret the signals of their environment and thus create for themselves a world. In remarks that recall Emerson's comments on the "ecstatical state" in "The Method of Nature" (*CW* 1: 130), Andreas Weber finds "ecstasy" to be a key principle of nature. Organic life constantly "steps out of itself" by sending out signals advertising its presence and responds to the welter of signals around it (ch. 6; cf. Kerting 158–68). Both together produce a kind of concert. The Darwinian notion of a struggle for survival thus gives way to a holistic concept; nature is perceived as a living whole, a network or "meshwork" (Varela) of signifiers adding up to what the Greeks called *kosmos*; and *kosmos*, as readers of Emerson (*Nature*) and Thoreau ("Walking") recall, means "beauty" (*CW* 1: 12; *Exc* 217).

The developments I have indicated in my quick survey are still controversial. When the international Linguistic Iconism Association was formed in 1998, "many of its members wished to have their association with the group kept secret" (Magnus 26). As regards biology, at worst, colleagues in the field would smell a version of "intelligent design"; at best, they would pardon yet another whimsical fantasy about science of which people in the humanities are so fond. However, the trends I have noted have gained too much momentum to be brushed aside, and as Thoreauvians we may want to keep an eye on them as they parallel and support some of his central concerns.

Hermeneutics and Experience

Among the key tenets of modern philosophy is the idea that authentic knowledge is based on experience rather than authority and dogma. Francis Bacon, next to René Descartes perhaps the most influential representative of early modern philosophy, developed his theory of induction as the true way or method leading from ignorance to knowledge. The inductive method starts from careful and patient observation of nature, verifies its findings through experiments, and finally arrives at general laws, ideally mathematical, regarding the causes at work in nature. Knowledge of these causes and the laws governing them will in turn enable us to control nature, to gain mastery over it; for as Bacon announces in the headings of his *Novum Organum*, his work will deal "de interpretatione naturae et [Book I]/sive [Book II] de regno hominis"—that is, the ultimate goal of knowledge is power, the "reign of man."

Bacon provided the intellectual groundwork for empiricism, the philosophical underpinning of the sciences. One of his chief merits and one of his lasting (though unintended) contributions to hermeneutics is the demand that the interpretation of nature proceed gradually, *gradatim*, "step by step" (Gadamer 352–56 [346–50]). Bacon proposes a way, not a system, and he draws attention to the serious obstacles the mind faces on the road to knowledge. These include the errors or "idols" of dogma and authority (*idola theatri*), of conventional assumptions shared by the community (*idola fori*, or looking at things through the eyes of one's fellows), and of the preconceptions rooted in human nature (*idola tribus*, ideas motivated by our physiological and mental makeup). Due in part to these idols, the mind is beset by a penchant for "anticipation," for premature judging and hasty conclusions. Bacon exhorts us not to jump to conclusions but instead to observe our objects patiently and with great care.

Bacon's major contribution to the theory of experience is his emphasis on experience as process, a long-range process and a difficult one at that, as the mind needs to overcome the obstacles of anticipation and prejudice. At the same time, Bacon tends to vitiate the potential of his insights—and the potential of the sciences inspired by his principles—by shutting the case, as it were, just as he had opened it. Why should knowledge be equated with dominance? Why should the laws operating in nature be mathematical laws? What in the early modern era began as a liberating move against the widespread speculations about nature based on haphazard observation and the authorities over time developed its own brand of dogmatism by narrowing and eventually canceling the openness of the way Bacon had pointed out.

Moreover, and this is Gadamer's chief point of intervention, Bacon failed to develop his own insights into the hermeneutical structure of experience. First, Bacon's plea for objectivity in terms of quantitative analysis and mathematics ignores a fundamental aspect of any experience: that it is still *my* experience. Second, Bacon loses sight of the essential negativity of experience. By negativity, Gadamer (drawing on Aristotle and Hegel) means that experience always involves the frustration of something we thought we knew (356–62 [350–56]). In other words, there is no experience without anticipation and prejudice. When we learn something through experience, previous assumptions (conscious or unconscious) are *aufgehoben* in Hegel's triple sense of the word: they are "suspended," "saved or preserved," and "raised to a higher level." Something has happened to us, and the more "experienced" we become, the more we will be open to further adventures of this sort. An experienced person is not someone who knows a lot so much as someone who is flexible about the possibility that his or her assumptions may be shaken again at any time. Such openness, however, requires that we have preconceptions and expectations to begin with—that we are prejudiced.

While giving full credit to Bacon's claims for gradualism in the study of nature and his insight into the obstacles hindering experience, Gadamer redefines experience in hermeneutical terms by reinstating the subjectivity of the observer and of the very demons Bacon had felt obliged to exorcize for the sake of true knowledge: anticipation and prejudice. Indeed, knowledge requires patient and careful observation. "I have at all times endeavoured to look steadily at my subject": Wordsworth's remark from his preface to *Lyrical Ballads* (*William Wordsworth* 600) suggests an important continuity from Bacon's plea for a *gradatim* interpretation of nature to the romantic sensibility. But the ideal of objectivity ironically mistakes the very nature of its chief source of authentication, the nature of experience. Instead of futile attempts to eliminate subjectivity, hermeneutics à la Gadamer suggests that we include it in a dialogic concept. Experience affects the perceiver as well as the object; any conclusions achieved in such a process are necessarily provisional, as the dialogue between subject and object continues, but their very provisionality is needed to keep the process of experience open and to prevent a new kind of dogmatism.

Finally, the negativity of experience—the way in which experience flouts our preconceptions—also involves an act of faith: we can afford to tolerate and indeed welcome the tentative and inconclusive status of our findings because we can trust in the structural and ontological priority of Being. The world, including our body, precedes consciousness; our very organs of perception, the senses, antedate consciousness. Being always precedes and exceeds knowing. On the one hand, such an asymmetry alerts us to our limitations, including the ultimate limitation which is death. But, on the other hand, we can also feel grateful for being embedded in something that transcends our limits. Experience conceived as a hermeneutical venture may enable us to do justice to our sense of being-in-the-world—a sense that is not the result of knowledge but rather its fundamental precondition.

Lest these remarks appear to be wish-fulfillment fantasies on the part of a humanities person vis-à-vis the sciences, I will briefly draw attention to two writers whose primary interest was or is the natural sciences. The first is Hermann von Helmholtz (1821–94), professor of physiology and physics at a number of universities, including Heidelberg and Berlin, and very likely the most prominent German scientist in the second half of the nineteenth century. The author of groundbreaking contributions in mechanics, electromagnetism, and physiology, Helmholtz was one of the few scientists to reflect intensively on the epistemology and, mirabile dictu, the metaphysics of science. An *Universalgelehrter* familiar with the writings of Kant, Fichte, Schelling, and Goethe, he formulated a theory of scientific knowledge and of the experiment as the privileged mode of verifying such knowledge that reaches out to the humanities in order to overcome the constraints of a narrowly empiricist approach. The fragmentation of knowledge in the wake of the emergence of specialized disciplines calls for a metaphysical view of nature; only such a view can do justice to the whole of nature and to nature as a whole. Over and over Helmholtz expresses his admiration for Goethe's holistic vision and his thinking in analogies (an extraordinary appreciation on the part of a later nineteenth-century scientist). The inductive method—and here Helmholtz grapples not with Bacon so much as with John Stuart Mill—will never lead us to any substances that could be identified as the causes underlying and producing the phenomena we call nature. The very method of proof via induction is based on *Vertrauen*, on the act of faith that a law derived from an inevitably limited number of observations and experiments will apply to all relevant cases not yet observed. These and similar reflections prompt Helmholtz to call for a broad-minded concept of scientific research that would include, along with the Baconian, quantitative-mathematical variety, an approach informed by the Goethean principles of tact and analogy.

Helmholtz's fusion of epistemology and metaphysics provides important clues for anyone interested in a hermeneutics of both the humanities and the sciences. That, at any rate, is the claim of Reinhard Schulz (61–67, 154–59). According to Schulz, the sciences, just like the humanities, could benefit enormously from a hermeneutical revision of the concept of experience designed to overcome the crippling consequences of the Baconian tradition (181–91). Such a revision would include a notion Baconians have taken great pains to eliminate: the notion of interest. The scientific ideal of objectivity and the concomitant split between subject and object in the wake of Bacon and Descartes ignore the fact that we want and need to study nature because we are interested in it; interested not in a utilitarian sense (Bacon's "de regno hominis") but because our relationship with things is thoroughly mediated. In contrast to the objectivist stance, which puts the subject over against and separate from the objects of perception, the concept of interest (from Latin *inter-esse*) points to the degree to which we are always "in-between," involved with things and sharing their path. The latter phrase is not Schulz's but a variation of Emerson's definition of the imagination in "The Poet" as "a very high sort of seeing, which does not come by study, but by the intellect being where and what it sees, by sharing the path, or circuit of things through forms" (*CW* 3: 15).

"Sharing the path of things"—I can think of no better translation of Greek *methodos*. As hermeneutics à la Gadamer and a *Naturwissenschaftshermeneutik* à la Reinhard Schulz move beyond the constraints of the objectivity principle in favor of a dialogue with nature, they return us to the beginnings of Western philosophy, to the pre-Socratic notion of *nous*, of the mind as an awareness of being, not the expectation of anything specific but the miracle that there is being and not nothing. This insight, in turn, remains vital to our age thanks to its potential for overcoming the dichotomies informing our culture ever since the sciences developed from natural history into the various disciplines we know today.

Thoreau's Walking

In a polemical remark at the end of "The Natural History of Massachusetts," Thoreau explicitly denounces the sciences à la Bacon: "We do not learn by inference and deduction, and the application of mathematics to philosophy, but by direct intercourse and sympathy. It is with science as with ethics, we cannot know truth by contrivance and method; the Baconian is as false as any other" (*Exc* 28). In contrast to what he, like many of his contemporaries, took to be the "Baconian" way (Walls, *Seeing* 30–33), Thoreau's walks illustrate a notion of method that moves us back to the beginnings of Western thought. At the same time, Thoreau provides a modern alternative to the dominant traditions of scientific method by revising the concept of experience. Following Gadamer's lead, that revision can be described in terms of walking as an activity analogous to reading, a dialectic of prejudice and surprise, an adventure of rebirth.

Over and over Thoreau stresses the importance of being close to what we study, of befriending the plants and animals that have aroused our interest, the necessity of "familiarization" (Peck 124–25, 129) and "neighboring" (Cavell, *Senses* 102–10; cf. Specq, ch. 4). In order to study nature, we have to become a part of it, most notably by spending as much time as possible outdoors so as to align the self with the rhythms of the seasons. In "Wild Apples," in one of his many puns, Thoreau refers to the numerous influences that contribute to the apples' flavor. Only the walker gets the full benefit of nature's richest harvest; wind, frost, and rain have *seasoned* these apples, which "must be eaten in *season*, accordingly,—that is, out-of-doors" (*Exc* 280, emphasis in original). The same is true of huckleberries: "A huckleberry never reaches Boston" (*W* 173). The apodictic statement familiar from *Walden* is elaborated at length in "Huckleberries," an essay that climaxes in a veritable paean to the seasons and their healing potential as we submit ourselves, as walkers, to their influence: "Live in each season as it passes; breathe the air, drink the drink, taste the fruit, and resign yourself to the influences of each. . . . Be blown on by all the winds. Open all your pores and bathe in all the tides of nature, in all her streams and oceans, at all seasons. . . . Some men think that they are not well in spring or summer or autumn or winter; (if you will excuse the pun) it is only because they are not indeed *well*; that is, fairly *in* those seasons" (*WF* 238–39, emphasis in original).

Living "in season" in its turn involves constant acts of interpretation. Like the reader of a book, Thoreau tries to figure out what nature wants to express and what message it may have for him. Hence his repeated exhortations to improve the instruments of reading, the senses. Echoing Jesus (Matthew 11.15, 13.9, 43) he notes in his Journal of 1851, "He that hath ears to hear let him hear. Employ your senses" (*PJ* 3: 261). Christ's stress on the sense of hearing is broadened to include all senses. Another journal entry of the same year combines Matthew with Ecclesiastes (12.1) to lend religious urgency to a plea for comprehensive sensory refinement: "Remember thy creator in the days of thy youth. i.e. Lay up a store of natural influences—sing while you may before the evil days come—he that hath ears let him hear—see—hear—smell—taste—&c while these senses are fresh & pure" (*PJ* 3: 323). The Journal notes presume an original freshness of perception that needs to be restored. Earlier, in *A Week*, Thoreau had introduced an evolutionary perspective by arguing that our senses exhibit a rudimentary state in dire need of development to higher stages: "We need pray for no higher heaven than the pure senses can furnish, a *purely* sensuous life. Our present senses are but the rudiments of what they are destined to become. We are comparatively deaf and dumb and blind, and without smell or taste or feeling. . . . Is not Nature, rightly read, that of which she is commonly taken to be the symbol merely? . . . What is it, then, to educate but to develope these divine germs called the senses?" (*Wk* 382).

Nature, "rightly read," presupposes a perceiving subject equipped with first-rate senses. But unlike the reader of a book, the reader of the book of nature stays constantly in physical motion as part of a strategy of assimilation to the object of his interest, for one of the lessons Thoreau learned from Emerson and from his own experience was that nature involves motion and metamorphosis. The reader of nature, then, is first and foremost a walker. Thus the ancient correspondence of walking and thinking—a tradition dating as far back as the Greek *peripatos*—is supplemented by an approximation of the observer to nature as the activity of walking conforms to the principle of energy in motion—*natura naturans*—that pervades nature.

One of the dominant motifs in Thoreau's writing is surprise: surprise at discovering a new vista, new plants, or the blossoming of flowers at unexpected dates and in unexpected places. Surprise, however, presupposes familiarity and expectation. In view of his scorn for the beaten track and his praise of "extravagance" in the "Conclusion" of *Walden* (324), it needs emphasizing that Thoreau felt just as strongly about *natural* habits and routines as an enabling strategy. His daily walks represented such a strategy. The biggest surprises come when we cover familiar ground, or, rather, ground we thought was familiar. Habits set the stage for new discoveries, as when in "Autumnal Tints" he suddenly becomes aware of a large area of purple grasses and is overwhelmed by their beauty: "I had walked over those Great Fields so many Augusts, and never yet distinctly recognized these purple companions that I had there. I had brushed against them and trodden on them, forsooth; and now, at last, they, as it were, rose up and blessed me" (*Exc* 230).

Of course, surprises of this sort also presuppose openness on the part of the perceiver. The physical habit of walking goes hand in hand with a mind prepared for novelty. In remarks that may now have a Gadamerian ring, Thoreau reinstates the strategy of anticipation so odious to Bacon when he summarizes his observations in "Autumnal Tints": "All this you surely *will* see, and much more, if you are prepared to see it,—if you *look* for it. . . . There is just as much beauty visible to us in the landscape as we are prepared to appreciate,—not a grain more. . . . We cannot see anything until we are possessed with the idea of it, take it into our heads,—and then we can hardly see anything else. . . . A man sees only what concerns him" (*Exc* 256–57).

Any experience worth its name runs counter to (*durchkreuzt*) an expectation and at a deeper level reminds us of mortality, the ultimate frustration of desire (Gadamer 362–63 [356–57]). The religious overtones of the lines last quoted from "Autumnal Tints" underline, once again, the existential dimension of Thoreau's walks. A profound experience amounts to a radical realignment of our ideas and ourselves. Hence the emphatic tone of the opening paragraphs of "Walking," where Thoreau describes the setting out on a walk as a departure along the lines of Christ's exhortation to his followers to be "prepared to leave father and mother, and brother and sister, and wife and child and friends, and never see them again" (*Exc* 186). And the late essays link up with *A Week*, where Thoreau announces, "The traveller must be born again on the road" (306). As Paul learned on the road to Damascus, experience conceived in such radical terms involves the death of the old self and a new birth. Walking in this spirit puts into practice what Emerson, in a phrase already quoted from "The Method of Nature," called the "ecstatical state"—logically an oxymoron ("ecstasy" indicating a transitory moment as opposed to a "state") but for Thoreau a real-life possibility: as the walker "steps out of himself" (*ek-stasis*) and step after step joins himself to nature, he can triumphantly declare, as he does in *A Week*, "We are still being born" (385). Is not nature, after all, etymologically (from Latin *nasci*) and in fact that which is constantly in the process of being born?

The etymology of "nature" finally recalls the equally telling etymology of "experience" and its German equivalent. German *Erfahrung* has the advantage of revealing directly the link with traveling and walking; while *fahren* today usually refers to locomotion via train or car, the older meaning covers any kind of travel, including, for example, the quest of the knight in medieval romance ("die Fahrt des Ritters"). *Fahren* in turn goes with a fair amount of *Gefahr*, of danger. *Erfahrung* thus involves risks and adventures—a connotation surprisingly, though less obviously, contained in the English Latinate "experience," too. The Indo-European root **per* in "experience" combines the notions of travel (*per* is at the back of English "fare," as in "farewell" or "how did they fare") and danger or hazard ("peril").

The most elaborate scientific experiments should not blind us to the fact that, as Gadamer and Thoreau remind us, any experience worth its name eludes control; it embodies an encounter with truth *before* method, with being *before* consciousness. Such an insight transcends the boundaries of the sciences and the humanities; it provides a bridge across academic disciplines, including the gap between the "two cultures," as it enhances our sense of being-in-the-world. Thoreau managed to incorporate this insight into his daily activities with extraordinary clarity and intensity. Here, then, lies the gist of Thoreau's modernity for me. Physically and mentally he "walked" his way out of the state of alienation, which is one of the hallmarks of our contemporary malaise.

KRISTEN CASE

Thoreau's Radical Empiricism

THE KALENDAR, PRAGMATISM,
AND SCIENCE

THOREAU SCHOLAR PERRY MILLER once famously dismissed Thoreau's late Journal as "the tedious recordings of mere observations, of measurements, of statistics" attesting to "the dwindling of [Thoreau's] vitality" and the "exhaustion of the theory on which he commenced to be an author in the first place" ("Thoreau" 158–59). The theory Miller refers to here is the Transcendental idea that there is a discernible relation between natural phenomena and moral or spiritual laws. In Miller's view, Thoreau's statement "Let us not underrate the value of a fact; it will one day flower in a truth" is "a portent of his whole endeavor, even unto the disastrous end, when he was left abysmally with facts, when he had more and more to force them into stunted flowerings" (*Consciousness* 166). This judgment reflects what was for decades a critical consensus about Thoreau's career: that after *Walden*, Thoreau's work devolved from literature into mere empirical note-taking, of no value to literary scholars and dubious value to anyone.

In recent decades, however, Bradley P. Dean, William Rossi, H. Daniel Peck, Laura Dassow Walls, Michael Berger, and others have begun a reevaluation of Thoreau's late work, in particular the last years of the Journal. In large measure, these scholars have celebrated Thoreau's late works for the same reason earlier scholars dismissed them: in turning his attention more exclusively to the natural world, the later Thoreau began to write about nature not "for the sake of tropes and expressions" about human life (as he confesses to doing in *Walden*) but in an attempt to understand natural phenomena on their own terms (*W* 162). This reassessment of Thoreau's late writings has been central to the emergence of the ecocritical approach to literature in the past two decades.

In the final years of his life, Thoreau attempted to collect his observations of seasonal change over the years in a variety of lists and charts comprising a project he sometimes referred to as his "Kalendar." Robert D. Richardson has speculated that Thoreau's ultimate intent for these charts was to create "a grand calendar of Concord, the fullest possible account of a natural year in his hometown" ("Introduction" 9). Though it has received relatively little scholarly attention to date, the Kalendar project is, I believe, central to the ongoing reevaluation of the second half of Thoreau's career.

As Laura Dassow Walls has convincingly demonstrated, Thoreau's late work, both in its holistic, totalizing ambition and in its recognition of the interrelation of all things, places him squarely within the tradition of nineteenth-century philosophy and science. In particular, as Walls argues in *Seeing New Worlds*, the later Thoreau was profoundly influenced by what she identifies as the "empirical holism" of Alexander von Humboldt, a position that involves a recognition of the interrelation of mind and nature and that seeks to reconcile idealism and empiricism. Walls writes, "[Thoreau] finally could not accept the idealist move, to reach the universal by annihilating the restraints of the local and particular; nor did he accept the limited and methodically realized aims of the scientist's methods. Or rather—he *did* accept them both—by a process of reconciliation *modeled for him in much of the discourse of the time*, which sought to bring together polar opposites into new, progressive, higher unities" (*Seeing* 11, emphasis mine). Indeed, Thoreau's desire to create a "true & absolute account of things" (*PJ* 4: 174, qtd. in Peck 108), a comprehensive view of nature that would also honor each particular natural phenomenon, is remarkably similar to Humboldt's ambition in *Cosmos*. The Kalendar has other earlier important nineteenth-century sources as well, including Gilbert White's *Natural History of Selborne* and John Evelyn's *Kalendarium Hortensia*. As I will argue here, however, the Kalendar also points ahead to a recognition of the profound reorientations of both philosophy and science in the twentieth and twenty-first centuries.

When Thoreau began compiling the lists and charts that comprise the Kalendar, he had been interested in seasonal phenomena for some time. As he records in his Journal in 1856:

> I wanted to know my neighbors, if possible—to get a little nearer to them. I soon
> found myself observing when plants first blossomed and leafed, and I followed
> it up early and late, far and near, several years in succession, running to different

sides of the town and into the neighboring towns, often between twenty and thirty miles in a day. I often visited a particular plant four or five miles distant, half a dozen times within a fortnight, that I might know exactly when it opened, beside attending to a great many others in different directions and some of the equally distant, at the same time. (*J* IX: 157–58)

Both Thoreau's characterization of his endeavor as getting to "know his neighbors" and the intense *activity* involved in his particular brand of observation speak to the relational epistemology that the Kalendar project announces, an understanding of knowledge that anticipates twentieth-century developments, including pragmatism, ecological science, and science studies.

Some of the charts Thoreau created during these final years track individual seasonal phenomena, such as the flowering of plants. On these charts, individual species or phenomena are listed in a column on the left-hand side of the page, with the years (1852–60) listed in a row along the top (see figure 2). The date of a tree's first leafing is noted in the square corresponding to each year (Case 56).

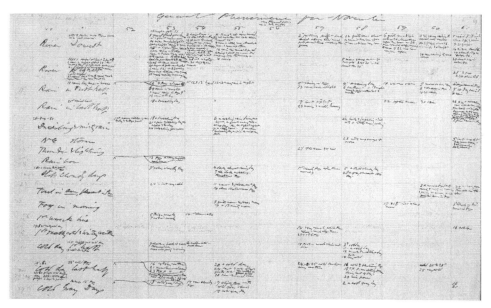

FIGURE 2. General Phenomena for November, page 3. Nature notes, charts, and tables: autograph manuscript, MA 610. The Pierpont Morgan Library, New York.

FIGURE 3. General Phenomena for May (list). Nature notes, charts, and tables: autograph manuscript, MA 610. The Pierpont Morgan Library, New York.

Boston University biologist Richard Primack has recently put these charts to use
in a study of the effects of global climate change on plants' flowering times and
birds' migratory habits in Concord. Primack's work, about which I'll have more
to say at the end of this essay, compares Thoreau's records, along with those of
later amateur naturalists, with his own field studies of Concord ecology (Miller-
Rushing and Primack).

My particular interest is in another set of charts, those in which Thoreau
collected his observations of "general phenomena" for individual months (see
figures 2 and 3). In these charts, Thoreau recorded the seasonal events ("phenomena," to use the word he preferred), often related to weather, that reflected
for him the essence of each month. Thoreau's process seems to have involved
a reorganization of the Journal's observations first into list form, with the seasonal phenomena listed chronologically by year and date, and then into the
charts, which allowed a comprehensive view of each month across the years
(roughly 1850–60). It is important to note that selection was involved at every
stage: Thoreau selected certain of the innumerable phenomena he observed to

record, then selected from among these observations for the lists, and then selected once more in compiling the charts. This process reflected Thoreau's belief
that each month was a season unto itself, with certain essential characteristics.
As Peck notes, "to delineate a season's beginning, middle and end phenomeno-
logically was, for Thoreau, to gather its essential features into a well-defined
frame for perception" (99).

Central to these charts is Thoreau himself, the gatherer of the phenomena,
present in such categories as "Sleep with window open" in May and "End of
sauntering walks" in November. In the monthly charts, Thoreau is less interested in an "objective" account of the natural world than he is in chronicling his
relation to it (figure 4). In 1859 he reflects on the meaning of seasonal phenomena for his own life: "They go publishing the 'chronological cycles' and 'movable
festivals of the Church' and the like from mere habit, but how insignificant are
these compared with the annual phenomena of your life, which fall within your
experience! The signs of the zodiac are not nearly of that significance to me that
the sight of a dead sucker in the spring is. That is the occasion for an *im*movable
festival in my church. Another kind of Lent . . ." (*J* XII: 390).

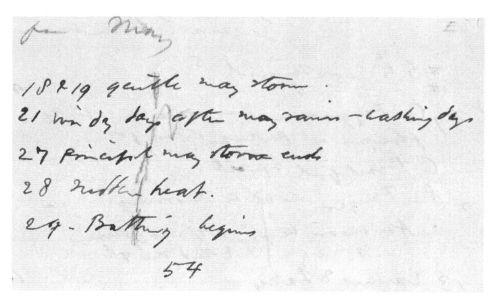

FIGURE 4. General Phenomena for May (list), detail. Nature notes, charts, and tables:
autograph manuscript, MA 610. The Pierpont Morgan Library, New York.

Thoreau does not, as some critics, notably Sharon Cameron, have argued, seek to banish the human from his observations of nature; rather, he takes the more radical step of reconceiving the human as part of nature. While the monthly charts of general phenomena form only one portion of this enormous incomplete project, they demonstrate Thoreau's evolving understanding of the human and the natural in his final years.[1] It is in these charts that Thoreau's anticipation of pragmatism can most clearly be seen.

The pragmatist conception of knowledge, articulated first by Charles Sanders Peirce in his 1878 paper "How to Make Our Ideas Clear" and expanded and popularized by William James in his 1906–7 lectures on pragmatism, entails a rethinking of knowledge within the context of evolution. As the second-generation pragmatist John Dewey explains in *Democracy and Education*, the pragmatist understanding of knowledge involves a new understanding of the relationship between self and environment: "The living creature," Dewey writes, "is a part of the world, sharing its vicissitudes and fortunes, and making itself secure in its precarious dependence only as it intellectually identifies itself with the things about it, and, forecasting the future consequences of what is going on, shapes its own activities accordingly. If the living, experiencing being is an intimate participant in the activities of the world to which it belongs, then knowledge is a mode of participation, valuable in the degree in which it is effective. It cannot be the idle view of an unconcerned spectator" (393). This new conception of knowledge as a mode of participation effectively dismantles the spectator view of knowledge, in which an interior subject passively beholds an exterior object. It is this new orientation that I believe Thoreau's late works, and in particular the charts of general phenomena, anticipate.

In 1857 Thoreau wrote in his Journal: "I think that the man of science makes this mistake, and the mass of mankind along with him: that you should coolly give your chief attention to the phenomenon which excites you as something independent on you, and not as it is related to you. . . . With regard to such objects, I find that it is not they themselves (with which the men of science deal) that concern me; the point of interest is somewhere *between* me and them (*i.e.* the objects)" (*J* X: 164–65). Here, Thoreau articulates a particular orientation toward the natural world, one in which the object of interest is neither a particular natural phenomenon nor the mind of the observer but rather *the relation between* the object and the observing self. In his attention to such relations,

Thoreau anticipates William James's call for a "radical empiricism." According to James, a thoroughgoing, or *radical*, empiricism would recognize that "*the relations between things, conjunctive as well as disjunctive, are as much a matter of direct particular experience, neither more nor less so, than the things themselves*" (*Essays* x, emphasis in original). Thoreau suggests that so-called modern science, by studying the "object" in isolation, stripped of its relations (including its relation to the observer), was actually insufficiently empirical. His relational approach to natural phenomena is wonderfully illustrated by his 1858 Journal entry about the striped bream, a species of fish he had recently discovered at Walden Pond: "In my account of this bream I cannot go a hair's breadth beyond the mere statement that it exists,—the miracle of its existence, my contemporary and neighbor, yet so different from me! I can only poise my thought there by its side and try to think like a bream for a moment" (*J* XI: 358–59). In recognizing that the bream is both "his contemporary and neighbor" and, as a member of another species, irreducibly different from himself, Thoreau suggests a new model for observation of the natural world, one that both includes the observer within the frame and preserves the natural context of the object observed. In the same entry, Thoreau objects that "a dead specimen of an animal, if it is only well preserved in alcohol, is just as good for science as a living one preserved in its native element." It is the living animal, "in its native element," that Thoreau wishes to know and through this knowledge gain, not dominance, but "a faint recognition of a living contemporary, a provoking mystery" (*J* XI: 360).

This new, relational view of knowledge emerged from Thoreau's careful attention to his experience of the natural world during the time at Walden and after and reflects his early grasp of the basic principles of evolution. As Bradley P. Dean notes in his introduction to Thoreau's important correspondence with Horace Greeley, "Thoreau was actively involved in what many consider the most important intellectual debate of the nineteenth century—that between progressivism, or special creation, and developmentalism, or evolution" ("Henry D. Thoreau" 630). Indeed, even before his 1860 reading of *On the Origin of Species*, Thoreau had already begun attacking the theory of special creation, whose most prominent proponent was Harvard zoologist Louis Agassiz. By 1856 Thoreau had developed his own theory that forest succession is driven by seed dispersal rather than "spontaneous creation." Thoreau's reading of *Origin* confirmed not only his theory of succession but also his general sense of the power and vitality of nature. "The development theory," he noted in his Journal on 18 October

1860, "implies a greater vital force in nature, because it is more flexible and accommodating, and equivalent to a sort of constant *new* creation" (*J* XIV: 147, emphasis in original). The charts of general phenomena, in particular, reflect the radical rethinking of the relationship of human beings to their environment demanded by the theory of evolution.

In addition to providing evidence of Thoreau's relational epistemology, the charts also provide a key to our understanding of the later Thoreau's method, about which William Rossi writes so compellingly elsewhere in this volume. After 1860, the charts become an intimate part of what Rossi calls "the whole lived and cumulative process" that constituted the Journal project, a process that included Thoreau's daily walks, writings in his field notebook, composition in the Journal, and finally transcription from the Journal to the lists and then the charts. Indeed, as I will illustrate below, the charts' complex intertextual relations to the Journal became clear as I began the work of attempting to read them, reinforcing my view that the Kalendar and the Journal are best under-stood as parts of a comprehensive process rather than as isolated works.

In attempting to decipher the charts of general phenomena, I often noted the dates for particularly illegible observations, then looked up the corresponding Journal entries in order to check my own transcriptions. On the chart of gen-eral phenomena for June, for instance, I noted a category that I guessed read "Blanched look of streets in morn." I was particularly interested in the subjective nature of this phrase as a category of observation. All the squares corresponding to this category were blank, except for the first one, under the year 1852. In this box, Thoreau did not include any observations but simply noted the date: 16. In order to test my hypothesis about the category, I turned to the Journal and looked up the entry for 16 June 1852, where I found the following extraordinary sentence: "The earth looks like a debauchee after the sultry night" (*PJ* 5: 102). The word I had taken for "blanched" was "debauched"; the category on the chart in fact reads "*Debauched* look of streets in morn"—a more radically subjective measure than I had imagined (my emphasis).[2] Clearly, Thoreau's interest here is at least as much the act of perception as it is the objects being observed. Though the chart contains only one entry under this category, Thoreau's designation of the category indicates that he believed that his sense of the streets' "debauched look" was a seasonal phenomenon, a typical June occurrence that might recur in subsequent years on 15 or 17 June. Here Thoreau suggests the centrality of his own perception to the reality of seasonal change, a suggestion that touches the heart of the entire Kalendar project. As H. Daniel Peck writes, "The larger goal toward which [the Kalendar] works is the restoration of the unity of self and world" (100).

Comparisons between Kalendar entries and their corresponding descriptions in the Journal also illustrate the way that, taken together, these two works achieve a double vision that, on the one hand, preserves the particulars of the individual moment in time and, on the other, places that moment within the recurring cycle of the seasons. One of the categories on the charts of general phenomena for November is "Seek sheltered places." Across from this heading, under the year 1857, Thoreau has written a date, "18," and two words: "rejoice in." The relevant passage from the Journal entry for 18 November reads as follows:

> The sunlight is a peculiarly thin and clear yellow falling on the pale-brown bleaching herbage of the fields at this season. There is no redness in it. This is November sunlight. Much cold slate-colored cloud, bare twigs seen gleaming toward the light like gossamer, pure green of pines whose old leaves have fallen, reddish or yellowish brown oak leaves rustling on the hillsides, very pale brown, bleaching, almost hoary fine grass or hay in the fields, akin to the frost which has killed it, and flakes of clear yellow sunlight falling on it here and there,—such is November.
>
> The fine grass killed by this frost, withered and bleached till it is almost silvery, has clothed the fields for a long time.
>
> Now, as in the spring, we rejoice in sheltered and sunny places. (*J* X: 186)

The particulars of this moment of November—its thin light, its bleached and frosted grass—are rendered in luminous detail within the streamlike chronological structure of the Journal, while the chart reflects that which represented, for Thoreau, the recurring essence embedded within this stream of particulars: the effect of the arrival of cold weather on the human inhabitants of the landscape. Taken together, the Journal entry and the Kalendar notation reflect a vision that, in Walls's terms, both aspires toward the "universal" and respects the integrity of the "local and particular" (*Seeing* 11). That the phenomena observed in this case—human rejoicing—should find its place among the other, more "objective" categories listed for November ("Rain," "Thunder and Lightning," etc.) reflects that the overarching project for Thoreau in these years was to restore the human to its rightful place within the context of the natural.

Thoreau's project of locating the human within the natural world was not confined to the monthly charts of general phenomena. Indeed, I believe that the entire project reflected a desire to recontextualize the human. While the lists and charts documenting leaf fall and flowering dates indicate the life Thoreau lived outdoors, immersed in the observation of nature, the charts also reflect, in their meticulous organizational schemes and their sheer quantity, a life still very much devoted to the uniquely human practice of writing. The intimate, reflexive relation between "outside" observation and "inside" documentation reflects Thoreau's evolving sense of the human and the natural: the act of observation informed what was documented, and the charts themselves often dictated what would next be observed. As he writes in his Journal in 1856, "I think we may detect that some sort of preparation and faint expectation preceded every discovery we have made. We blunder into no discovery but it will appear that we have prayed and disciplined ourselves for it" (*J* IX: 53). The act of recording *prepared* Thoreau for the act of observation, and vice versa. This dialectical process of observation and documentation became Thoreau's way of *being* in the natural world, his way of navigating and making sense of his environment. The structure of the project, with its movement away from prose description and toward a tracking of phenomena (human phenomena included) over time, suggests a growing interest in writing as a way of documenting *process* rather than as a way of producing a textual product.

Thoreau's final project touches directly the question of his modernity. As Walls has so thoroughly demonstrated, Thoreau's late work must be seen as exemplary of a particular, Humboldtian strain of nineteenth-century science. As she makes clear in *The Passage to Cosmos*, however, this position, somewhat paradoxically, makes Thoreau very much our contemporary, since we have only fairly recently begun to realize (or perhaps remember) something that Thoreau learned in the course of documenting his increasingly intimate relation to the natural world: that close observation is a mode of participation, that we are part of the world we would know. Insofar as "modernity" represents the division of the world into subjects and objects, culture and nature, Thoreau knew what we have only in recent decades begun to discover: that, as Bruno Latour insists, "we have never been modern."[3]

Here I would like to return to the work of Richard Primack, whose studies suggest the significance of Thoreau's phenological observations for contemporary scientists. As Primack and his colleague Abraham Miller-Rushing demonstrate, conventional studies of climate change, even long-term studies undertaken in the past few decades, have not been of sufficient duration to capture the overall picture of the effects of climate change in a particular region. Using Thoreau's charts, Primack and Miller-Rushing compared data about flowering times and birds' migratory patterns in Thoreau's time to their own field observations. Primack and Miller-Rushing have enlisted not only Thoreau's records but also those of amateur naturalists, some still living, in Thoreau's hometown. A recent study uses the diary of Rosie Corey, a seventy-seven-year-old former schoolteacher who kept accurate records of the behavior of local bird species for fifty-eight years. Ms. Corey describes her diary as "a very dull account of my daily life, that I did laundry or that someone called me up or that I went downtown shopping—or that I went walking and what I saw," adding, "if you have a sense of history and a sense of order, you like to keep a list" (Hotz 3).

Following up on their initial work published in *Ecology*, Primack and Miller-Rushing, along with a team of evolutionary biologists at Harvard led by Charles Davis, published a second study in the *Proceedings of the National Academy of Sciences* (Willis et al.). Primack, a conservation biologist, cautions that he was not correctly interpreting the data until he teamed up with Davis. In a profile in the *New York Times*, Primack notes that in the original study, "We just treated each individual species as a data point. . . . That was not the way to do it." Davis and two of his graduate students "began looking at the species data from an evolutionary perspective including, for example, the relationship between species traits and abundance." The new study, rather than just measuring the overall impact of climate change in Concord, provides a relational analysis. Climate change, Primack and his colleagues discovered, is affecting certain species more than others. According to Davis, "it's targeting certain branches in the tree of life" (Cornelia Dean 1–2).

In their reliance on the work of nonscientists, their focus on the interrelations between species within a particular geographical area, and their own intense and active fieldwork, Primack and Miller-Rushing embrace the spirit as well as the body of Thoreau's late work. Making use of the kind of knowledge that is particular to inhabitants, knowledge that emerges from daily observation not of a single object in isolation but of the network of relations that constitute a particular place, Primack and his colleagues have demonstrated what Thoreau's work has to offer contemporary science.

The question we're left with, then, is, what does this work offer the contemporary humanities? For one, I believe it offers us a way of beginning to see beyond or, rather, *work* beyond the nature/culture binary that has dominated humanist discussions of the environment for so long. Latour writes that "the human, as we now understand, cannot be grasped and saved unless that other part of itself, the share of things, is restored to it. So long as humanism is constructed through contrast with the object that has been abandoned to epistemology, neither the human nor the nonhuman can be understood" (*We Have Never* 136). What Thoreau's late work enacts is a new conception of the human, one in which we are defined by our relation to, rather than our separateness from, other organisms; in which we are allied, not opposed, to the material world; and in which human experience, including human emotion, is understood as empirical reality. This new conception restores the individual to his or her community, recognizing the essential embeddedness of human experience, its utter inextricability from the natural and social worlds in which it unfolds. It is characteristic of this orientation that it expresses itself as a method, a practice, rather than a law. Part of the reason there has been so little work on the Kalendar project by literary scholars is that much of the meaning in these charts and lists is so evidently located in Thoreau's process of compiling them, and reconstructing this process is an even more difficult undertaking than that of deciphering Thoreau's handwriting. Part of the reexamination of the function of the humanities currently undertaken by ecocriticism and other hybrid fields must be a new attention to the various functions of writing and a particular engagement with writing as a way of tracing, recording, and strengthening relations.

As Lawrence Buell notes in *The Environmental Imagination*, the recognition of the self as truly inseparable from its environment "implies the dissolution of plot and calls into question the authority of the superintending consciousness. . . . But what sort of literature remains possible if we relinquish the myth of human apartness? It must be a literature that abandons, or at least questions, what seems to be literature's basic foci: character, persona, narrative consciousness. What literature can survive under these conditions?" (145). A corollary question arises: What kind of methodology will best enable us to approach this literature? A critical task for literary scholars will be to find ways to talk about hybrid texts: texts that have been displaced or ignored because they have been caught between the "two cultures" of science and literature (Snow). These new approaches will draw on the strengths of literary studies—attention to language and, in particular, the role of metaphor in shaping our thinking—but they must also draw from the fields of science and science studies. As William Rossi's essay in this volume powerfully suggests, the lab studies of Latour and others may provide useful models.

In her earlier essay "Romancing the Real: Thoreau's Technology of Inscription," which also engages the parallels between Thoreau's work and Latour's lab studies, Laura Dassow Walls notes that in the Journal, Thoreau confronted "the choice of either erasing all the traces left by [his] local, partial, and arduous process, letting only the final inscription of truth remain; or of acknowledging the traces, letting his tracks show" (134). The Kalendar, like the Journal, is the richer for Thoreau's choice to let the traces of process remain. As we attempt to understand the Kalendar in its complex relations to Thoreau's other writings, our scholarly practice—observing, transcribing, moving back and forth between texts—will necessarily mirror Thoreau's "local, partial and arduous" practice of composition. Further study of the Kalendar will necessarily foreground the ways that process informs meaning in both Thoreau's work and our own.

NOTES

1. For a more complete description of this evolution, see David Robinson's essay in this volume.

2. As François Specq observed to me, the move from the Journal to the June chart clearly involved more than simple transcription: the "earth" of the Journal entry has become "streets" in the chart. Indeed, the original Journal sentence is a good deal more poetic than the category in the June chart. Here, as in the notation from the November chart described below, the lyricism and context of the original entry are sacrificed in the transfer from Journal to chart. As I explain elsewhere, I believe Thoreau saw the Kalendar as a complement to the Journal rather than a substitute for it—a way of picturing time as cyclical *in addition to* (not instead of) recording it as a forward-moving stream (Case). Here my analysis differs from that of H. Daniel Peck's in *Thoreau's Morning Work*.

3. See, especially, Latour's chapter "Redistribution," in *We Have Never Been Modern*.

MICHAEL JONIK

"The Maze of Phenomena"

PERCEPTION AND PARTICULAR
KNOWLEDGE IN THOREAU'S JOURNAL

"Slow Are the Beginnings of Philosophy"

A footnote from Kant's *Critique of Judgment* can serve as a provisional entry point to the set of questions concerning perception and particular scientific knowledge that Henry David Thoreau explores in his later Journal. While Kant's sarcasm is certainly pointed at Linnaeus, he also gives a warning to those who would systematize nature on the basis of particulars: "One may wonder whether Linnaeus could have hoped to design a system of nature if he had to worry that a stone which he found, and which he called granite, might differ in its inner character from any other stone even if it looked the same, so that all he could ever hope to find would be single things—isolated, as it were, for the understanding—but never a class of them that could be brought under concepts of genera and species" (216n24). Kant is in effect questioning the objectivity of Linnaeus's "artificial system," in which he "group[ed] individuals having the same appearance (for us) within the same species" (Huneman 5). Had Linnaeus questioned the inner character of every stone he found, even if they all looked like the piece of granite he was holding in his hands, in Kant's estimation he could never have constructed his *Systema Naturae* (1735). Thus Kant is here, as John Zammito shows, "[warning] against [making] overhasty inferences from empirical observations to general principles. . . . Linnaeus had fallen prey to error by taking the similarity of certain instances for a proof of the similarity of their fundamental principles. Such hasty generalization was not something a careful scientist permitted himself, but there were those 'so indiscriminate as to read their ideas into their observations.' Kant called such individuals 'rash sophists' [*rasche Vernünftler*]" (210).

To be sure, one goal of Kant's critical philosophy is to understand the *necessary* order of nature; for this reason he works to determine the a priori principles at the basis of all understandings of nature, principles that make understanding nature possible. This follows from his pronouncement that it is human understanding, not divine design or even nature itself, that legislates natural laws. Without understanding the structure of human understanding, we cannot understand the structure of nature, and there could be no natural science. Although the ability to divide nature—"to bring it under concepts of genera and species"—does not therefore rely per se on empirical knowledge, Kant insists that nature has order even in its particular rules, which we can know empirically (see also Kant, *Critique of Judgment* 185). Thus Kant does not dislocate the mind from the world but works to rigorously understand how the two are connected. He attempts to protect nature from those who would too easily or too hastily find fundamental principles for its organization. This is especially true, as he noted already in his *Critique of Pure Reason*, "if we bear in mind that in so great a multiplicity of things [as nature] there can never be much difficulty in finding similarities and approximations" (A668/B696).

Although there is not space to develop with any responsible thoroughness either Kant's thought on natural history or the detailed conceptual matrix Kant introduces in order to understand particular phenomena, suffice it to say that, generally, Kant's biological thought, often overshadowed by his earlier thought on physics, is of fundamental importance for understanding the romantic conception of life that developed in his wake, a conception that fundamentally inflects American Transcendentalism (see, e.g., Cavell, *Senses* 94–95). If not a direct reader of Kant, Thoreau inhabited the post-Kantian landscape, which had integrated, if selectively, elements of Kant, Goethe, and German *Naturphilosophie*. More specifically, Kant provides a philosophical point of departure for understanding Thoreau's approach to particularity. Like Kant's careful scientist, Thoreau seeks to avoid hasty judgments concerning observed phenomena. As he remarks in his Journal: "Ah give me pure mind—pure thought. Let me not be in haste to detect the *universal law*, let me see more clearly a particular instance" (*PJ* 4: 223). With Thoreau, one dwells with particulars. He works to cultivate a patient, "particularized" perceptual practice, to get to know the particular plants or animals or rocks or geographies of Concord and its environs through precise, careful observation. Already by his early essay "Natural History of Massachusetts," Thoreau posits slowness as essential to the dual enterprise of science and philosophy, a slowness necessary for a "fact" to "flower in a truth": "Let us not underrate the value of a fact; it will one day flower in a truth. . . . [I]t is much easier to discover than to see when the cover is off. . . . Wisdom does not inspect, but behold. We must look a long time before we can see. Slow are the beginnings of philosophy" (*Exc* 41). In *A Week on the Concord and Merrimack Rivers*, Thoreau details the importance of patience in encountering objects and in so doing explicitly links this patience to the writing of nature. There, he surmises, "a true account of the actual is the rarest poetry, for common sense always takes a hasty and superficial view" (*Wk* 265–66, 325).

To further his point, Thoreau turns, as does Emerson in *Representative Men*, not to Kant but to Goethe as his model:

> Though I am not much acquainted with the works of Goethe, I should say that it was one of his chief excellencies as a writer, that he was satisfied with giving an exact description of things as they appeared to him, and their effect upon him. . . . In his Italian Travels [*sic*] Goethe jogs along at a snail's pace, but always mindful that the earth is beneath and the heavens are above him. . . . He speaks as an unconcerned spectator, whose object is faithfully to describe what he sees, and that, for the most part, in the order in which he sees it. Even his reflections do not interfere with his descriptions. (*Wk* 325–26)

As such, to make a "true account of the actual" is not simply to report the real nor to indiscriminately read our ideas into another's observations. Rather, it is to see the world directly before us with the "cover off." It is to distill this world not by haste and superficiality but through slowed processes of seeing that act as counterforce to the fast complacencies of common sense. Like Kant, Thoreau will seek to avoid the "rash sophistry" of uncareful science and thus to protect individual natural forms from "unnecessary" generalization. Like Goethe, he will endeavor to jog at a snail's pace, to stay mindful of the earth beneath him and the heavens above him, to describe objects faithfully where he finds them— as, for example, along one of his walks. He follows the poet-scientist Goethe to the crossroads of the real and the ideal.[1] Thoreau effects a slow thinking *into* place in which place and mind become intimate, and perception becomes active and embodied.

For Stanley Cavell, this is a problem not only of perception but of knowledge as well. As he says of *Walden*: "Epistemologically, its motive is the recovery of the object, in the form in which Kant left that problem and the German idealists and Romantic poets picked it up, viz., a recovery of the thing-in-itself; in particular, of the relation between the subject of knowledge and its object" (*Senses* 95). The Journal project can be understood as both an extension and a transformation of this relationship, one that foregrounds the particularity of objects, how they are perceived, how they are understood scientifically and poetically. As such, Thoreau's emphasis shifts from the "recovery" of the object to its *relationality*. Relationality involves the approach to the object, to what occurs in what Laura Dassow Walls elsewhere in this volume calls the "transjective" interspace of subject-object, insofar as it is in this interspace that the relationship to the object becomes perceptible. In a central passage from November 1857, Thoreau restates the problem: "The philosopher for whom rainbows, etc, can be explained away never saw them. With regard to such objects, I find that it is not they themselves (with which the men of science deal) that concern me; the point of interest is somewhere *between* me and them (*i.e.* the objects)" (*J* X: 165). For Thoreau, in the dynamic, relational space between subject and object it is not only that the object must conform to our knowledge (as the Copernican turn insists) but also that our knowledge must acknowledge the resistant thingness of objects.[2] Thoreau becomes devoted to putting the facts of his natural science on a material basis. He turns away from his earlier idealism and Neoplatonism toward a broad, precise reckoning with the physical becoming of phenomena. In this way, he could be said to exacerbate Emerson's late movement in the same direction. Yet, unlike Emerson, Thoreau develops this relationship toward specific individual natural phenomena (and their complex interrelationships and metamorphoses) in terms of a carefully executed science. This becomes increasingly the case after an intense period of study of Carl Linnaeus, Georges Cuvier, Gilbert White, Alexander von Humboldt, John Evelyn, William Bartram, Louis Agassiz, Asa Gray, and Charles Darwin during the early 1850s (Richardson, *Life* 246, 254–56). After the publication of *Walden*, his commitment to observing, collecting, cataloging, and interpreting natural phenomena became an end in itself, the "literary expression" of which is his open-form, open-ended Journal project.

As "allied to life" (*PJ* 4: 459–60)—and, specifically, if complexly, to his own life—the Journal marks the natural processes he witnesses and those that suffuse and shape him. As was the case with *Walden*, this involved a detailed inventory of the "essential facts of life," which he undertook through a "perpetual instilling and drenching of the reality which surrounds us" (97). Yet the method of the Journal will be not to distill this material into an ordered narrative but to let it gradually expand out of its own situatedness. He sets as his task to get to know this situatedness: nature becomes a neighbor he wants to get to know (*J* IX: 157). In March 1856 he writes, "I seek acquaintance with Nature,—to know her moods and manners. Primitive Nature is the most interesting to me" (*J* VIII: 221). Or, again, the following year: "I am interested in each contemporary plant in my vicinity, and have attained to a certain acquaintance with the larger ones. They are cohabitants with me of this part of the planet, and they bear familiar names" (*J* IX: 406). They cohabit not only his "part of the planet" but the wild textual expanse of the Journal as it gradually opened before him throughout the 1850s and early 1860s. It takes a long time to get to know your neighbors, to get to know their names and moods and manners, their language: "Here I have been these forty years learning the language of these fields that I may the better express myself" (*J* X: 191; see also *J* XI: 137). The open form of the Journal befits such slow learning. It defers any resolution in how to perceive the world, allowing each new perception the potential to revise previous perceptions or developed categories for knowing. It respects the resistance of things and thus holds back before any universal law to open to our view new patterns of phenomena, to reveal incipient worlds of relation unfolding from our familiar world. This is the "constant endeavor . . . to get nearer and nearer *here*" (*J* XI: 275). This is the rarest poetry.

"The Maze of Phenomena"

As Thoreau's attention to particular phenomena increased, so did his awareness of the problems particular knowledge posed for how we understand science and natural description. On the one hand, he realized that attention to detailed specific knowledge could narrow the scope of knowledge. He registers this already in a Journal entry from August 1851, in which he writes, somewhat apprehensively, anticipating the work he would undertake throughout his final decade: "I fear that the character of my knowledge is from year to year becoming more distinct & scientific—That in exchange for views as wide as heaven's cope I am being narrowed down to the field of the microscope—I see details not wholes nor the shadow of the whole. I count some parts, & say 'I know'" (*PJ* 3: 380). There is in this passage an almost palpable lament: that without even the shadow of the whole to orient particular knowledge, we are left with knowledge that is only partial, incomplete. Does intense local knowledge condemn one to the backcountry of thought, in which one can never realize the true scope of its territory? Does particular knowledge risk repeating the dangerous assumption at the center of the Linnaean system, the generalization of knowledge or systematization of nature out of its parts? What does this mean for the process of journal writing as Thoreau now conceived it? Would too close attention to details obscure its larger framework?

On the other hand, as he became implicated in the details of Concord's natural life, Thoreau felt the danger of becoming overwhelmed by their sheer number, of being lost in the maze of myriad phenomena. As Kant warned, nature can be "infinitely diverse and [thus] beyond our ability to grasp" (*Critique of Judgment* 185). Nature in its vast swell of particulars exceeds knowledge, rendering it again partial or incomplete. As Thoreau reports on 7 June 1851, "I wonder that I even get 5 miles on my way—the walk is so crowded with events and phenomena" (*PJ* 3: 245). Or, looking back on the increasingly detailed and scientific character of his thought some years later, he writes: "I remember gazing with interest at the swamps about those days and wondering if I could ever attain to such familiarity with plants that I should know the species of every twig and leaf in them. . . . Though I knew most of the flowers, and there were not in any particular swamp more than half a dozen shrubs that I did not know, yet these made it seem like a maze to me, of a thousand strange species, and I even thought of commencing at one end and looking it faithfully and laboriously through till I knew it all" (*J* IX: 157).

Despite his familiarity with some of the plants of the swamp, it remains a world overflowing with particulars, a maze "of a thousand strange species." We are blinded by the surfeit of phenomena: "How much of beauty—of color, as well as form—on which our eyes daily rest goes unperceived by us!" (*J* XIV: 3). Thus how we encounter the particular is bound up with how we can perceive it within its tangle of relations. For Thoreau, a frequent visitor to swamps and other wild, overgrown "oases," to attain the level of specific knowledge he desires, to make sense of the maze, demands that it be "faithfully and laboriously" looked "through." As he will say in an entry from 1 November 1858, "Only the rich and such as are troubled with ennui are implicated in the maze of phenomena. You cannot see anything until you are clear of it." To see our way out of the enfolded immensities of nature requires a "doubl[ing] and distanc[ing]" of sight (*J* XI: 273).[3] It requires a type of perception that is no mere looking but an active, enactive perception that patiently pulls apart the tangle of particulars around us.

Thoreau's interest in the swamp not only underscores the systematic, if not obsessive, task he lays out for himself to specifically know his locality; it also reiterates his belief that modern scientific knowledge alone is inadequate for informing one's experience of the world. The experience of particular phenomena, unless *directly* experienced, is for Thoreau not yet true, not yet to be trusted. In *A Week* he insists that "each man can interpret another's experience only by his own" and that "knowledge is to be acquired only by a corresponding experience" (296). This points to a certain shortsightedness of scientific knowledge: in its reliance on universal laws, it forecloses the physical encounter with the particular, how it appears to us in its specificity, and how we can perceive it in its relations. Any seeing clearly of a phenomenon in the instance of its particularity instead depends on a perceptual restraint that holds back from expressing it in terms of a universal law. Any search for what Peck calls the world's "larger 'symmetry'" (61) depends on how we perceive the correspondences, likenesses, or relations in which a given particular is enfolded without becoming lost in the maze of phenomena (seeing no connections) or finding similarities and approximations all too easily (seeing connections everywhere). The success of our search depends on our mood, on the interest and attention we allow ourselves to invest, in order for things to become familiar to us—familiar enough that we can see them change, become unfamiliar and new. We rediscover the world in each instance of perceiving the world, in each moment of our dwelling in the world. Science can only lead us toward such rediscoveries but never wholly afford them to us. We need to be aware, attuned to the world, ready for it. Without such awareness, direct experiences cannot occur at all. We can be right before objects but still not see them, their beauty unperceived. As Thoreau writes in "Autumnal Tints," "Objects are concealed from our view, not so much because they are out of the course of our visual ray as because we do not bring our minds and eyes to bear on them. . . . A man sees only what concerns him" (*Exc* 256–57).[4] We must prepare ourselves to see by cultivating our attention. If Thoreau is often wary of novelty, we must keep in mind that the emphasis for Thoreau is to see more clearly what has been before us all along. Not to discover but to see with the cover off. To grind our perceptual lenses, like so many Spinozas, to a refined exactness.

So if Kant will critique Linnaeus's system on the basis that it makes an "overhasty inference from empirical observation to general law," for Thoreau the problem becomes determining the manner in which we are to dwell with particulars. Certainly, Linnaeus's "artificial system" of naming individual phenomena, including the sexual parts of plants, provided Thoreau with a guide for his own botanical experiences. But even the most detailed field guides cannot prepare us for the strangeness of an immersion in particulars. Whereas both the system of Linnaeus as well as the "natural" system of John Ray rendered more clearly the relationship between plants, as Thoreau surmised, the task still remains "to learn their relation to man—The poet does more for us in this department" (*PJ* 4: 353). The poet, like the taxonomist, is a namer who within every taxonomy or toponymy embeds a multiplex of implicit relations, a series of braided metonymies. Unlike Linnaeus, however, for Thoreau the poet-scientist will not understand names as markers for an all-encompassing theory of nature, one that will then inform all subsequent perceptions; the poet's task as namer is to put things perceived in relation to humanity, to detect new significant patterns in the dispersion of things, in which humans are themselves dispersed. Science, although it offers specific knowledge about phenomena, severs knowledge from the world of living relations. Thoreau laments when he kills a small turtle called a cistudo that "such actions are inconsistent with the poetic perception—however they may serve science—& will affect the quality of my observations" (*PJ* 8: 278). Through poetic perception we dwell with particulars, in the affinitive web of living relations in such a way that these relations can become significant. Poetic perception becomes a mode of active, imaginative cocreation and cocommunication of and with the living world. It becomes a means to reconnect the scientific observation of phenomena to its human significance, a task to which scientific perception alone is inadequate, if not blind: "One sentence of Perennial poetry would make me forget—would atone for volumes of mere science. The astronomer is as blind to the significant phenomena—or the significance of phenomena as the wood-sawyer who wears glasses to defend his eyes from sawdust— The question is not what you look at—but how you look & whether you see" (*PJ* 3: 354–55).

"Mere" science fails to see the connectedness of the object to the full extent of living relations. On this basis alone it cannot provide an adequate "description"

of a phenomenon, despite its avowed objectivity or desire for wholeness. "Significant" phenomena, though perhaps a highly subjective designation, depend
on the ability of the perceiver to understand that connection is something that
at all points exceeds subjectivity. Poetry, or poetic perception, makes no claims
to complete science or to provide convincing alternative types of description for
the same object. Rather, it underscores how the force of the creation of life—the
poiesis of life—exceeds the purview of scientific discourse. Scientific description is an incomplete endeavor insofar as it has to arrest the living object in
order to describe it; in so doing it sacrifices the living force fundamental to it.
Life stridently resists remaining captive to fixed systems of meaning. Thoreau
consequently works to understand nature on the basis of its processes, the transience of its forms, its seasonal and yearly variations. Science can count, analyze,
and measure the natural object, but it cannot truly account for this living force.
Rather, it is the "unmeasured and eloquent" description of our seeing a flower
open, the delightful participating in this living force, that is the truest description. "In proportion as we get and are near to our object," Thoreau will say later
in the same passage, "we do without the measured or scientific account." The
joy we feel in approaching the object, the joy of participating with it in a shared
living instant, becomes "complete and final in itself" (*J* XIV: 117, 119).

So if the Journal is "more simple" *and* "less artful" (*PJ* 4: 296), it is at once
more "unmeasured" (cf. Specq 75–76). Although Thoreau often celebrates and
practices methods of close scientific observation, and indeed the methods of
Humboldtian or Darwinian science, he at the same time scrutinizes these in
the name of poetry. This complicates easy characterizations of his later career
as that of an empirical scientist roving the fields, forests, and swamps of Concord collecting botanical data. As Thoreau asks, "This habit of close observation—   In Humboldt—Darwin & others. Is it to be kept up long—this science—   Do not tread on the heels of your experience   Be impressed without
making a minute of it. Poetry puts an interval between the impression & the
expression—waits till the seed germinates naturally" (*PJ* 3: 331; cf. Walls, *Seeing* 127). What is at stake in the close approach to phenomena is, to be sure,
how we perceive and *whether* we "see"; but, at the same time, so is how we dwell
in the *interval* between the instant of seeing and the instant of writing. In these
intervals, we hold back with Thoreau to see the particular more clearly, from
many perspectives and disjointed moments. It is a time of waiting and cultivation. "While I am abroad the ovipositors plant their seeds in me I am fly blown

with thought—& go home to hatch—& brood over them" (*PJ* 3: 330). "I succeed best," he writes on 5 May 1852, "when I *recur* to my experience not too late, but within a day or two—when there is some distance but enough of freshness" (*PJ* 5: 28). The Journal becomes built out of these intervals, as tiny seeds of perceptions and observations grow into its perennial poetry. Subsequent perceptions add new temporal textures and tessellations; objects remain novel and vivid as each time they are encountered with different eyes. In this way, each poetic interval becomes the near-far space of a multiplied perception—a doubling and distancing of sight. Perceptions perpetually undo perceptions by unseating previous perceptions. They assert new claims on the perceiver, burning holes in the fabric of experience. Each perception then does not harmonize poetry and science but arises from their unresolved *agon*. Throughout the Journal, poetry and science dance in an ever-expanding spiral, rising and falling on the breaths of winds, like Whitman's two dallying eagles. If Thoreau will go so far as to say that it is "impossible for the same person to see things from the poet's point of view and that of the man of science" (*PJ* 4: 356), his work will nonetheless constitute an attempt to see from both points of view, drawing the disparities into the binocular gaze of his perception. Perception in his work becomes less a catastrophic point where the poetic and scientific points of view disappear into a seamless whole than a *catastatic* point—a point where the two intersect and mutually intensify yet remain unresolved. As catastasis literally means, it is a "dwelling-in" or a "settling in," less an *ek-stasis* than a falling farther into the thing. In the idiom of tragic drama, catastasis refers to the part of the plot *before* the catastrophe, when things become raised to a fever pitch. In rhetoric, it is the exordium, when the orator is in full command of his or her topic, fully dwelling in its language or discourse. In Thoreau's poetic-scientific writing of the Journal, it refers to those unguarded moments when facts are in full bloom, bursting forth from the face of the page.

Ecological Perception

Thoreau's "dwelling-with particulars" is by no means static; as we have seen, it involves an ongoing movement among the myriad of natural phenomena, which Thoreau literalizes through his process of writing. This writing could be said to take place through the interactive navigation of landscape, mindscape, and textscape. As he notes in his Journal on New Year's Day, 1858: "I have lately been surveying the Walden woods so extensively and minutely that I now see it mapped in my mind's eye" (*J* X: 233). He becomes an intimate cartographer in which the thinking of place becomes an ongoing exploration of the terra nova of thought itself. To be sure, much of the critical work on later Thoreau, especially on his Journal, celebrates the vivid, multiform tropes of vision through which this presentation of nature becomes realized—the mapping in his mind's eye. To this end, Daniel Peck puts key emphasis on the role of visual perception: "That Thoreau is a preeminently visual writer has been obscured by comparisons with Emerson's famous ocularity. It is true that Thoreau's relation to nature is more broadly sentient, more aural and tactile, than Emerson's, but his spiritual vocation is, if anything, even more dependent on vision (that is, on real seeing) than that of his mentor. None of his writings show this more clearly than his mature Journal, which presents a complex picture of the world" (50). Peck reinforces this thought with a variety of visual examples, most prominently, those in which Thoreau draws analogies, correspondences between phenomena that share a visual likeness. On this basis he describes Thoreau's Journal project as "systematically searching the world for likeness, toward the discovery of its larger 'symmetry'" (61). Or again soon after, he adds: "While he sometimes uses his Journal to investigate organic (biological, geologic, or botanical) relationships among natural objects, the greatest number of its recorded observation of similitude are . . . achieved purely through visual means" (61).

The importance of visual perception in Thoreau's work is unquestionable and as such has been substantively developed in the literature. Yet if we dwell on—or dwell with—the manner in which Thoreau draws correspondences between the multiplicity of sensory events through nonvisual modes of perception, we can enrich our understanding of how perception operates more generally. This is to gauge how, in Peck's terms, "Thoreau's relation to nature is broadly sentient . . . aural, and tactile" (50; see also Friesen). In this regard, Thoreau follows the insight he attributes to the seventeenth-century natural historian John Gerard, namely, that by attending to the fullness of diverse sensory information one can better understand a particular phenomenon: "Gerard has not only heard of and seen and raised a plant, but felt and smelled and tasted it, applying all his senses to it. You are not distracted from the thing to the system or arrangement" (*J* XIV: 119). Attention to other forms of perception in addition to the visual gives us a richer understanding of perception in Thoreau's work and broadens how we understand his encounter with particulars-in-relation.[5] Thoreau, through his own sensitivity to the whole myriad of atmospheric stimuli, helps us cultivate our own attention to forms of particular knowledge. This expands the sensorium of thought. It proposes a thought that is not merely dependent on the sovereignty of the visible—the dominant paradigm of Western thinking—but draws on the diversity of sensual vocabulary, on all the "senses of Walden." This is not at the expense of the visible but at the expanse of the visible: the idea is that the senses mutually inhabit one another, and thus knowledge of the world is multiple and concurrent. Yet at the same time as the senses mutually inhabit one another, each provides unique information about particular phenomena—the senses do not present unified, synaesthetic knowledge but could be said to work together through their fundamental disunity. Through prolonged, intense attention to the natural distribution that each particular demands, Thoreau develops what could be called, after twentieth-century psychologist James J. Gibson, an "ecological perception"—a perception of connection and of the unsettling of connection that takes into account the multiform richness and particularity of sensation presented to us by our mobile world.

So to get a sense of Thoreau's ecological perception, let us turn again to particulars. To be sure, auditory perceptions resonate throughout Thoreau's writing. In "Natural History of Massachusetts," for example, he describes how "in May and June the woodland quire is in full tune, and given the immense spaces of hollow air, and this curious human ear, one does not see how the void could be better filled" (*Exc* 10–11). The season becomes marked by the birds; they transcribe the modulations from spring to summer: "As the season advances, and those birds which make us but a passing visit depart, the woods become silent again . . . the phœbe still sings in harmony with the sultry weather by the brink of the pond, nor are the desultory hours of noon in the midst of the village without their minstrel" (*Exc* 11). "Sounds" from *Walden* is nonetheless Thoreau's most profound meditation on how sound immerses the perceiver in the world of nature. The locomotive whistle draws a pointed commentary on the effects of commerce on the Massachusetts countryside as its timbers dart against the city walls, as "all the Indian huckleberry hills are stripped, all the cranberry meadows are raked" (*W* 116). Distant church bells play against the aeolian harp of the woods with a "vibratory hum," their echo becomes an "original sound," one "partly the voice of the wood" (*W* 123). As Thoreau states in "Winter Animals," the lowing of cows, the baying of dogs, the cackle of roosters, and the calls of screech owls and the loon likewise become the "*lingua vernacula* of Walden

Wood" (*W* 272). Each gives Thoreau "a new sense of the variety and capacity of that nature which is our common dwelling" (*W* 124). Like the language of the fields, which he slowly comes to speak, these sounds become "quite familiar to [him] at last" (*W* 272). Passages like these reverberate through the nearnesses and distances of the Journal, its familiar and unfamiliar settings: "When I stand more out of the wind, under the shelter of the hill beyond Clamshell, where there is not wind enough to make a noise on my person, I hear, or think that I hear, a very faint distant ring of toads, which, though I walk and walk all the afternoon, I never come nearer to" (*J* XIII: 241).

Yet if we turn to passages that foreground perceptions of smell and taste, we can perhaps get a fuller sense of what is at stake in considering ecological perception. Smell and taste further dislocate perception from a fixed subject-center into the heterogeneous, dispersive atmosphere of stimuli. Further, they can allow for a nearer approach: as Thoreau reports on 27 April 1852, at the first appearance of the "aments of the balm of Gilead," the bud "is filled with 'a fragrant, viscid, balsam' which is yellowish & difficult to wash from the fingers. It is an agreeable fragrance at this season. A nearer approach to leaves than in any tree?" (*PJ* 4: 495). In a passage from the preceding August, he marks how the sensorium pays tribute to "the royal month of August":

> In the fields I scent the sweet scented life everlasting which is half expanded. The grass is withered by the drought— . . .
>
> As my eye rested on the blossom of the meadow-sweet in a hedge I heard the note of an autumnal cricket—& was penetrated with the sense of autumn—was it sound? or was it form? or was it scent?, or was it flavor? It is now the royal month of August. When I hear this sound I am as dry as the rye which is every where cut & housed—though I am drunk with the seasons wine.
>
> The farmer is the most inoffensive of men with his barns & cattle & poultry & grain & grass—I like the smell of his hay well enough—though as grass it may be in my way. (*PJ* 3: 352–53)

The autumn onset does not merely index to the *chronochromie* of changing leaves but moves through the varied domains of sensation: the sweet scented life joins to the dry feeling of withered grass joins the eye resting on the blossom of a hedge joins the note of a cricket (itself a "dry" sound). Yet the "sense of autumn" that penetrates Thoreau remains as a series of uncertain sensual experiences: "Was it sound? Or was it form? Or was it scent? Or was it flavor?" The season's wine becomes inebriating, the drunk smell of fermenting hay. Walking is disoriented, as the high grass resists movement, like a slow slog through a swamp. We can note in passing that in the entries that follow this passage, among which are some of Thoreau's more memorable "moonlight passages," he develops this sensual disorientation: in the "faint diffused light in which there is light enough to travel and that is all" (*PJ* 3: 354), sight becomes dimmed, and a series of far-off night sounds betrays ready-made understandings. Thoreau thus accomplishes "clearer sight" of phenomena not only through figures of clarified vision but also through figures of obscurity, in a way that painters such as Cézanne and Picasso, composers Debussy and Schoenberg will unsettle perception and perspective in their work to open new modalities of perception, new *verklärte Nächte*.[6]

We can juxtapose this to another rich passage from the Journal, dated 23 May 1853, in which Thoreau details the particulars encountered in the evening light of Ministerial Swamp.[7] After listing a series of flowers animating the lively din of the windy May weather—the small veronica on the Cliffs, "Arenaria Serpyllifolia Thyme-leaved sandwort," etc.—he notes:

> As the Seasons revolve toward July. Every new flower that opens no doubt expresses a new mood of the human mind. Have I any dark or ripe orange yellow thoughts to correspond? The *flavor* of my thoughts begins to correspond. . . . For some time Dandelions & mouse ear have been seen gone to seed—autumnal sights. . . . As I rise the hill beyond geum meadow I perceive the sweet fragrance of the season—from over the turf—as if the vales were vast saucers full of strawberries—as if our walks were on the rim of such a saucer—   With this couple the fact that directly the fresh shoots of the firs & spruces will have the fragrance of strawberries. (*PJ* 6: 146–47)

As in the previous passage, Thoreau foregrounds his practice of phenology, his scientific transcription of the coming into view of phenomena. Yet in Thoreau's phenological practice the season is not just seen but heard, felt, tasted, and smelled. Even the thought he has out of season, the "autumnal sight" of the dandelion gone to seed, further registers a multiform phenology, if not phenomenology, of sensation. Such redolent passages are common throughout the Journal and the late natural history essays. "Wild Apples" abounds in sweet and sour passages. As Walls writes, "Part of the relish of the essay is Thoreau's elaborate connoisseurship of the flavors and textures of these scrubby, shrunken, sour, bitter, and cidery wild fruit, emphasizing that frontier contacts need not lack exquisite refinement" (*Seeing* 219). Indeed, Thoreau's text memorializes the diverse pleasures of the tastes of wild apples, now mainly extinct, as sweet commercial apples have almost wholly replaced them: the smell of wood smoke across the November twilight, the difference in smell of an apple and a muskmelon, the shift in spring perfumes toward a summer smell oncoming. Again these are not so much instances of synaesthesia as the perception of the relations of all the senses of a given instant, in a given approach to here. Taste perception becomes another way of knowing that exceeds the purview of sight-based science. Thoreau makes this explicit: "Science is often like the grub which, though it may have nestled in the germ of a fruit, has merely blighted or consumed it and never truly tasted it. Only that intellect makes any progress toward conceiving of the essence which at the same time perceives the effluence" (*J* XII: 23; see also Walls, *Seeing* 223).[8] Following the will of wildness, knowing by tasting becomes radicalized into a devouring raw. To live becomes "to live deep and suck out all the marrow of life" (*W* 91). "We are cheered when we observe the vulture feeding on the carrion which disgusts and disheartens us and deriving health and strength from the repast" (*W* 318). Animals come to know each other through eating: "Such is Nature, who gave one creature a taste or yearning for another's entrails as its favorite tidbit!!" (*J* XIII: 346; Richardson, *Life* 382).

Yet it is perhaps Thoreau's extended meditation on the European cranberry, *Vaccinium oxycoccus* (a name bestowed by Linnaeus), that most eloquently expresses his ecological perception in terms of tasting:

I have come out this afternoon a-cranberrying.[9] . . . This was a small object, yet not to be postponed, on account of imminent frosts—that is, if I would know this year the flavor of the European cranberry as compared with our larger kind. . . .

It is these comparatively cheap and private expeditions that substantiate our existence and batten our lives—as, where a vine touches the earth in its undulating course, it puts forth roots and thickens its stock. . . . Better for me, says my genius, to go cranberrying this afternoon for the *Vaccinium oxycoccus* in Gowing's Swamp, to get but a pocketful and learn its peculiar flavor—aye, and the flavor of Gowing's Swamp and of *life* in New England—than to go consul to Liverpool and get I don't know how many thousands dollars for it, with no such flavor. Many of our days should be spent, not in vain expectations and lying on our oars, but in carrying out deliberately and faithfully the hundred little purposes which every man's genius must have suggested to him. Let not your life be wholly without an object, though it be only to ascertain the flavor of a cranberry, for it will not be only the quality of an insignificant berry that you will have tasted, but the flavor of your life to that extent, and it will be such a sauce as no wealth can buy. (*WF* 165–66)

Here, an "insignificant berry" becomes significant through tasting. In every berry we taste the extent of our relatedness to the earth. In every berry we taste the flavor of our life.

Thoreau's "ecological" perception is an active perception insofar as it at once locates and dislocates notions of the place the perceiver is moving through. It is a mobile perception of a world itself in movement, rendering the familiar unfamiliar so that we might perceive it anew. This posits the perceiver as perpetually drawing on the living archive of the world. Instead of bare sensory input, the world serves as a kind of external memory for the perceiver. Thoreau's ecological perception, unlike that of Gibson or Alva Noë, will not locate his active perception only in invariant externalities, in what the world makes itself available to us—these cleave perceiver from perceived, subject from object, mind from earth, so to treat the latter in each case as an opportunity for use. Rather, as Thoreau famously asks in *Walden*, "Shall I not have intelligence with the earth? Am I not partly leaves and vegetable mould myself?" (138). This "with" is of fundamental significance. To Thoreau, ecological perception is another way of describing our poetic dwelling *with* particulars; it further highlights that to be among them is to bring them together in their differences, as they move and change, as we move and change in relation to them. Having intelligence *with* the earth is not merely treating the world as a space that we blindly tap our way through but to configure ourselves perpetually in approach to objects, in this "somewhere" between ourselves and them, in the evanescent, excited moments of feeling alive. For Thoreau, the process of perception becomes a negotiating of the nearnesses and distances, departures and returns that characterize our unmeasured approaches to phenomena. By emphasizing figures of proximity and remoteness—of "being-with"—Thoreau moves away from the absolute, ecstatic "Contact!" he describes atop Mount Katahdin. The "constant endeavor" of getting "nearer and nearer *here*" remains a perpetual approach. Phenomena are drawn intimately close yet remain distant in their resistant materiality; we hold back before facile generalizations or staged moments of cosmic union. To think with and within nature is to find ourselves gathered in this heterogeneous world of seeds and stones, flesh and fluid, friends and foreigners.[10] It is an attention to how place is continually shifting and becoming other. It is openness to multiform sensations, new atmospheres in which our heads can bathe.

In the final analysis, in the words of Norwegian philosopher Anstein Gregersen, "perception is an achievement" — or as Thoreau himself says, to perceive becomes our "greatest success" (*J* XII: 371).[11] But what kind of success? Does this mean that the success of perception is to interpret the hieroglyph of nature — its symbol, its correspondences? Is it to gain scientific certainty of a particular phenomenon? The conjecture here is that for Thoreau the success of a perception is not a hermeneutic success — the success of interpreting a symbol of nature and assigning it a meaning. Rather, the success of a perception is to remain in relation to the ineffable, to what is unexplainable, to resistant thingness. This is a sort of "negative capability." To hold back from assigning a given organism to a class or genera, species, or even *taxon*. To "not be in haste to detect the *universal law*" but to "see more clearly a particular instance." To remain poised in intimate extremity and extreme intimacy. To let the taste of difference linger in our mouth, unseasoned, wild as a hawk's wing.

NOTES

1. As Goethe writes in "Significant Help Given by an Ingenious Turn of Phrase," "My thinking is not separate from objects. . . . [T]he elements of the object, the perceptions of the object, flow into my thinking and are fully permeated by it . . . [M]y perception itself is a thinking, and my thinking a perception" (*Scientific Studies* 39). In Goethe's short piece on Kant, "Judgment through Intuitive Perception," the work of perception is to "penetrate the divine forces of nature" via an intuitive, imaginative movement from the empirical phenomenon to the archetypal (*Scientific Studies* 31–32).

2. This "somewhere between" becomes of fundamental importance: it comes to rhyme with what Thoreau calls the poetic "interval" between "impression and expression" (*PJ* 3: 331).

3. In the "Solitude" chapter of *Walden*, Thoreau explores a similar notion of "doubleness" (134–35); see Peck 85.

4. Or, from a related Journal passage from 4 November 1858: "There is as much beauty visible to us in the landscape as we are prepared to appreciate,—not a grain more" (*J* XI: 285).

5. Again, Thoreau circumscribes this point in his earlier work, yet extends and transforms it throughout the Journal. See also "Natural History of Massachusetts": "The true man of science will know nature better by his finer organization; he will smell, taste, see, hear, feel, better than other men. His will be a deeper and finer experience. We do not learn by inference and deduction, and the application of mathematics to philosophy, but by direct intercourse and sympathy. It is with science as with ethics, we cannot know truth by contrivance and method; the Baconian is as false as any other, and with all the helps of machinery and the arts, the most scientific will still be the healthiest and friendliest man, and possess a more perfect Indian wisdom" (*Exc* 28).

6. Likewise, in Thoreauvian terms, Debussy would offer us new *Claires de "loon."*

7. This passage comes the day before a somewhat infamous one that reads: "Talked or tried to talk with R. W. E. Lost my time—nay almost my identity—he assuming a false *op*-position where there was no difference of opinion—talked to the wind—told me what I knew & I lost my time trying to imagine myself somebody else to oppose him" (*PJ* 6: 149).

8. Parenthetically, one could note the importance of taste to Darwin's science. Despite its solemn longevity, the Galápagos tortoise isn't spared from Darwin's habit of taste testing the species he investigates, such as the rheas and armadillos he eats in Argentina. Of the tortoise, he remarks: "While staying in this upper region, [with a party of Spaniards on the Galápagos] we lived entirely on tortoise-meat. The breastplate roasted (as the Gauchos do *carne con cuero*), with the flesh attached to it, is very good; and the young tortoises make excellent soup" (*Voyage* 273). Likewise the lizards, which Darwin otherwise characterizes as torpid, dirty black, and half-stupid, don't escape his dinner table. "The meat of these animals when cooked . . . by those whose stomachs rise above all prejudices . . . is relished as very good food. Humboldt has remarked that in inter-tropical South America, all lizards which inhabit *dry* regions are esteemed delicacies for the table" (284). As Thoreau might add, "The science of Humboldt is one thing, poetry is another thing" ("Walking," *Exc* 208). Nonetheless, Thoreau cites Darwin to this effect: "Charles Darwin, in his *Voyage round the World*, speaks of finding wild potatoes on the islands of the Chronos Archipelago in South America. . . . The tubers . . . 'resembled in every respect and had the same smell as English potatoes; but when boiled they shrunk much and were watery and insipid, without any bitter taste'" (*WF* 118).

9. In the Journal, this passage occurs on 30 August 1856, yet Dean's text, *Wild Fruits*, includes it in a section dated 17 October 1859.

10. In this register we could think of Thoreau's formula from *Walden*: "Not till we are lost, in other words, not till we have lost the world, do we find ourselves, and realize where we are and the infinite extent of our relations" (171).

11. Or, as Thoreau writes in *Walden*: "If the day and the night are such that you greet them with joy, and life emits a fragrance like flowers and sweet-scented herbs, is more elastic, more starry, more immortal,—that is your success" (216).

FRANÇOIS SPECQ

Poetics of Thoreau's Journal and Postmodern Aesthetics

HENRY DAVID THOREAU'S JOURNAL, with its huge dimensions and sustained dedication to recording nature over the entire span of his adult life (it ranges from 22 October 1837 to 3 November 1861), was perhaps his most uncompromising enterprise. Mostly consisting of daily entries recording the protean sweep of nature in his hometown of Concord, Massachusetts, the Journal at first sight appears comparatively straightforward: much of it seems to have an obvious quality, indisputably part of a "natural" order, thus defying explanation. Many readers also feel challenged by their experience of this work as an open totality that can never achieve complete synthesis by virtue of its unstructured details and disjunctive mode of composition, which give it the appearance of an informal flux. Because of the difficulties of describing and analyzing the Journal, its apparent failure to achieve a coherent, cohesive literary space, and the seemingly limited range of Thoreau's interests, there was long a temptation to consider it as not only artless but devoid of artistic merit.[1]

The dedicated reader, however, soon comes to realize that the Journal is more than the sum of its parts and that Thoreau deliberately limited his formal means in order to focus on what he considered indispensable—thus writing what Wallace Stevens called "the poem of the mind in the act of finding / What will suffice" (239). Following this recognition, the literary dimension of Thoreau's Journal has been suggestively and creatively analyzed by a number of critics, starting with Sharon Cameron's pioneering *Writing Nature*. Cameron's study was decisive in its acknowledgment of the Journal's intrinsic importance and value, and it shed crucial light on the formal implications of Thoreau's efforts to "writ[e] nature" in a way that "subordinates human presence" (154).[2] H. Daniel

Peck added an important dimension through his emphasis on the idea that "in the very act of being written, the Journal dramatizes the condition of vital engagement that Emerson called 'the active soul,'" and he offered an analysis of time patterns in what he described as "a book of memory" keyed to a desire for "spatializing the temporal process" (160, 43, 46). Laura Dassow Walls gave yet another twist to our perception of Thoreau's Journal when she described it as a "technology of inscription . . . by which he would braid together self and nature through language, educing nature into discourse" ("Romancing" 125). This essay will situate itself in the wake of these classic studies of the Journal, but its focus and emphases will be somewhat different, as my own understanding of the Journal's dynamics is premised on a sense of its being primarily a living embodiment of Thoreau's aesthetic and philosophical stance. My reading will more particularly focus on the gravitational pull of Thoreau's thousands of pages, on the centrality of the passage of time rather than mastery of process, on his attunement to the enigma of the visible rather than on his desire for an underlying order or structure in the natural world, on his efforts to forever live at the edge between physical nature and human significance. As he offered meditations on the mysterious character of all things, Thoreau fundamentally made his Journal a workshop of being.

"Speak Though Your Thought Presupposes the Non Existence of Your Hearers"

What often disturbs readers of Thoreau's Journal is this work's almost exclusive focus on nature, as opposed to many journals that can be analyzed within the genre of the diary. With comparatively few exceptions—such as discussions of friendship—Thoreau's Journal is not in the genre of the personal diary, with its record of more or less intimate matters and personal ramblings (with complex varieties and degrees of self-display and self-concealment).[3] Instead, it precludes issues of self-expression: Thoreau was concerned not with the intricacies of individuality or subjectivity but with the mystery of the world. His journal is not about the self but, rather, strives to transcend the self—to liberate the self from the strictures of ordinary selfhood. Thoreau was less concerned with exploring his identity than with discovering and voicing the intimate otherness of nature—"express it without expressing yourself" was his motto (PJ 4: 158). He did not strive for self-expression and originality but, rather, for self-effacement, thus rendering traditional critical tools and concepts for the analysis of diaries ineffective. Many readers also find it difficult to accommodate the supreme concreteness of the work, which has often been read as a sign of dryness or unliterariness, all the more so since it nevertheless fails to deliver a stable image of the world. For a long time, the only satisfactory way of making sense of the Journal was to consider it as a literary notebook that the writer mined for his other works. But such an argument underestimates the logic, complexity, and intensity of Thoreau's poetic achievement: the Journal gained autonomy as a literary project as it moved away from repository or archive of discrete elements laid aside for their future flowering into truths, toward the realization of the intrinsic value of "facts" and of the self's immersion in temporality. As Thoreau reflected,

> I do not know but thoughts written down thus in a journal might be printed in the same form with greater advantage—than if the related ones were brought together into separate essays. They are now allied to life—& are seen by the reader not to be far fetched—   It is more simple—less artful—I feel that in the other case I should have no proper frame for my sketches. Mere facts & names & dates communicate more than we suspect—   Whether the flower looks better in the nosegay—than in the meadow where it grew—& we had to wet our feet to get it! Is the scholastic air any advantage? (*PJ* 4: 296)

The Journal of the 1850s, which is the focus of the present study, no longer was meant as a means to some literary end but, rather, represented or embodied a sustained process of perceiving and thinking.[4] The purpose of this essay, however, is not only to acknowledge the autonomy of the journal but to shed light on its paradoxical artfulness.

Thoreau's Journal may appear impersonal and divorced from humanity, as it did not strive for literary appeal—"Do not seek expressions—seek thoughts to be expressed," Thoreau solemnly declared (*PJ* 4: 223). It seems to have no desire to justify itself but, instead, offers itself for whatever its uniqueness is worth—as a straightforward, irrefutable, irreducible anthology of objective facts. In an era that has by and large been characterized by a poetics of disenchantment, Thoreau's unflagging devotion to observing nature is both fascinating and seemingly desperately old-fashioned, irremediably out of reach—to the point of appearing to the disheartened reader as "a kind of archaeological remnant" (Walls, "Romancing" 141). As a result of the Journal's almost exclusive focus on the emphatically nonhuman realm of nature, the reader may feel distanced from it—excluded from the world it depicts, literally *displaced*: instead of being the center of the world, of her or his world, the individual becomes peripheral, as though watching phenomena that entirely take place outside her or him.

The lack of literary appeal in an ordinary sense is further compounded by a certain "rawness" or "greenness" characterizing the Journal. Many entries offer only suggestions of perception, sketchy annotations, and minimal descriptions of the objects they mention. These so-called dry facts, which preserve the brief, summary, rough, and sketch-like qualities of the spontaneous observation in the Journal (although they may actually be processed field notes),[5] have often deterred or repelled readers while enthralling critics like Laura Dassow Walls, who beautifully describes it as "messy as a forest floor, lines crossing and crisscrossing, interfering with each other, dead-ending, tangling the clarity that truth commands" ("Romancing" 134).[6] Thoreau's Journal is threatening because it seems to lose readers in a maze of signs—to negate us entirely—and Sharon Cameron has cogently analyzed how it actually problematizes any way of quoting from it, thus rendering an adequate "representation" of this very literary object nearly impossible (16–23). My own way of addressing this impossibility, rather than concentrating on a detailed analysis of a few excerpts nonetheless, will be to propose a synthetic reconstruction of its internal dynamics that is analogous to the modeling practiced in the experimental sciences, in which a number of links and connections are established on the basis of observable "facts"—here, the reader's reading experience as well as Thoreau's own statements.

The reader feels destabilized by being powerfully confronted with a perception of the world as in a state of always having already commenced. With its strict, unremitting, chronological structure, the Journal seemingly imposes an enormous distance between itself and the reader, suggesting a monologue proceeding outside and in spite of us that in no way can become ours—Thoreau being quite different in this respect from Emerson, whom Lawrence Rosenwald describes as fundamentally "a dialogical diarist" (97). Thoreau was even led to conceive of his work as radically autonomous to the point of "speak[ing] though your thought presupposes the non existence of your hearers" (*PJ* 4: 224). That is further reinforced by Thoreau's play with the idea of the anonymity of the process of journalizing and his dream of an unmediated text, as though he were "a transparent eyeball" and mere scribe—an entirely neutral observer and writer ensuring that the Journal merely registers the world as it is. "I have no more distinctness or pointedness in my yearnings than an expanding bud—which does indeed point to flower & fruit to summer & autumn—but is aware of the warm sun & spring influence only" (*PJ* 3: 143). Thoreau unquestionably sought to coexist with rather than control the natural world: letting a thing come, rather than creating it, was his fundamental aesthetic stance—"Go not to the object   let it come to you" (*PJ* 5: 344).

To be sure, the reader who manages to go beyond the initial feeling of an unbridgeable distance between the world of the Journal and herself or himself is then confronted with the absence of true perspective into that world. The Journal is a huge work that precludes any sense of the appropriate point of view from which to read it—we are forever in the middle of things. This mode of writing either deters the reader or pulls her or him into a deep mental encounter with the work: there is no way of entering the Journal without confronting its sheer physicality and enormity. Reading is destabilized. By making it impossible to take in the whole within a limited time frame, the size of the Journal constructs a dimension that forces the motivated reader to get fully involved in the *work* of the book. Thoreau's Journal creates a literary space whose line of force rests in the intense exchange it calls for between the reader and the work. Readers must devise their own Ariadne's thread through its twists and turns. Although humanity seems to have been removed from the Journal because it is hardly figured anywhere—and rarely even as man reporting (on) nature—it is nevertheless intensely present in the person of the writer-perceiver and of the reader, for whom confronting the Journal offers a deep experience of intellectual and emotional response.

"Thoughts Accidentally Thrown Together"

A fascinated delight in the visual and sensory appearance of the world close at hand informs much of Thoreau's work. In the Journal, however, this inclusive encompassing of "ordinary landscape" and "details" of natural history is reinforced by a compositional mode that eschews hierarchy and integrative structuring. Journalizing turns the work into a repository for elements that are internally consistent but only loosely related: being purely accretive and disjunctive, if not disjointed, Thoreau's Journal is fundamentally organized around the rhetorical principle of parataxis (or juxtaposition), as opposed to hypotaxis (or subordination). The work's structure is not composed of a unified, homo-geneous frame, for the elements are not textually integrated, nor do they fully cohere conceptually. Buttressed together into a composite whole, they remain in tension—a creative, generative tension:

> Each thought that is welcomed and recorded is a nest egg—by the side of which more will be laid. Thoughts accidentally thrown together become a frame—in which more may be developed—& exhibited. Perhaps this is the main value of a habit of writing—of keeping a journal. That so we remember our best hours—& stimulate ourselves. My thoughts are my company—They have a certain indi-viduality & separate existence—aye personality. Having by chance recorded a few disconnected thoughts and then brought them into juxtaposition—they suggest a whole new field in which it was possible to labor & to think. Thought begat thought. (*PJ* 4: 277–78)

Thoreau's notations are accretive moments of inquiry or seemingly minor exer-cises in perception rather than virtuoso performances, and their power resides in their capacity to stimulate reflection and perception. His observations are humble and intimate, but they are a concrete embodiment of poetic pleasure and existential commitment. They testify to the fact that this commitment is one that accepts contingency rather than aspires to formal necessity. This low-key mode of writing seems to elude critical categories and tends to be detrimen-tal to an appreciation of the latter years of the Journal.

The structure establishes a disjunctive relation with the literary space as it builds up discontinuity as a central element in our reading experience. In the Journal, effects of displacement, truncation, and interference arise from the juxtaposition and reprise of discrete elements. The resulting idiosyncratic and far from seamless work disorients the reader: through its very structure and its intense and ever-renewed focus on the commonplace, in all its singularity, Thoreau's Journal is a powerful assault on all common fixed standpoints—even more so as it simultaneously seems to conform to the conventions of the pas-toral observer. Its paratactic complexity questions our competence as readers: it challenges our ability to make sense of things. Its discrepancies, determined by the lack of hierarchy and the fragmentation of our reading, not only stimu-late but fundamentally require and demand the participation of our intellect and entire being. What is involved here is thought: the Journal reaches out for our thoughts, not in any prescriptive way but as an open act of the mind—it "suggest[s] a whole new field in which it [is] possible to labor & to think" (*PJ* 4: 278). Thoreau constantly pushes the interpretative task back onto the reader, who cannot simply suspend disbelief and steep herself or himself in reverie and contemplation but is made aware of the involvement at the core of any act of both perceiving and reading. Although that may sound paradoxical in a work that seems to be so "natural," nothing is actually given to us in the Journal: *we* must participate in the work of reading in an immensely demanding way.

The text of Thoreau's Journal takes on a dense reality as a result of the interweaving and taut juxtaposition of elements presented as if in close-up. Its texture imbues this work with a presence and concreteness very different from the "remoteness" that Thoreau and the Transcendentalists found in fiction, which ensured that the world was kept at a safe distance, resulting in "dulness of sight" (*W* 105). Here there seems to be no buffer between world and reader, hence the intensity or even perhaps violence of the shock of recognition. Whatever the "fact," its transcription is positioned on the same plane as all the others, so that each summons us equally, as in nature itself—"in the true natural order the order or system is not insisted on. . . . The species and individuals of all the natural kingdoms ask our attention and admiration in a round robin" (*J* XIV: 119). The question of what is incidental, and what significant, is continually evaded in this deeply nonhierarchical work. Thoreau chose to preclude a reading of the work that privileges some elements over others, which thus become secondary, favoring radiant modes and clusters of words. He did not want to combine elements into an integrative whole. Rather, his journalizing focuses on specific objects or scenes, to which it gives equal importance compared with longer entries or descriptions—nothing is anecdotal. Each entry is monumental, but monumentality has nothing to do with size. It is asserted in the shorter entries as well as the longer ones and is always inferred from the dynamics of perception. The "insignificant" plant or animal trace suddenly becomes important and visible: Thoreau's Journal creates visibility.[7] To the extent that he considers that "in the true natural order the order or system is not insisted on," Thoreau primarily perceives his task as rescuing what would otherwise have gone unnoticed, as bringing the invisible to the fore—not in the sense of some behind-the-scenes reality but of what is commonly unseen because of practical concern, ignorance, or excess of knowledge, which all tend to (en)close reality the better to manage it. With the years his work became purer and barer, being sometimes reduced to juxtaposed "mere facts"—but Thoreau makes it clear that these are just as expressive in their apparent dryness as the more transcendental projections of the earlier period, and perhaps they are even more unsettling or disquieting because they are more "metaphysical" and hermetic—not transcendental mystery celebrated as such, but the immanent mystery of all that is.

The Journal does not purport to narrate a story: it eliminates plot/background distinctions in favor of the immediacy of a purely chronological flux. But through its apparent lack of depth, its absolute flatness, the Journal actually maintains and even brings to the fore the relationship between the world of nature and human consciousness:

> I live so much in my habitual thoughts—a routine of thought—that I forget there is any outside to the globe.—and am surprised when I behold it as now—yonder hills & river in the moon light, the monsters. Yet it is salutary to deal with the surface of things—   What are these rivers and hills—these hieroglyphics which my eyes behold? There is something invigorating in this air which I am peculiarly sensible is a real wind blowing from over the surface of a planet—   I look out at my eyes, I come to my window, & I feel & breathe the fresh air. It is a fact equally glorious with the most inward experience. Why have we ever slandered the outward? The perception of surfaces will always have the effect of miracle to a sane sense. (*PJ* 5: 309)

Thoreau eliminated all formal relationships from the Journal, adopting "a style in which the matter is all in all & the manner nothing at all" (*PJ* 4: 158) in order to better concentrate on external rather than internal relations, that is, on the relation between man and the world. Instead of being anomic and aloof, his Journal strikes one as vital and direct—"the first requisite and rule is that expression shall be vital and natural" (*J* XI: 386). Thus, instead of being a monologue developing outside us, or possibly even against us, Thoreau's Journal assumes a very lively and intimate dimension. It conveys a sense of closeness (but certainly not closure) and intimacy with the world, exposing the reader to a beauty that has become a stranger to our skeptical age. Thoreau's Journal conveys a heightened sense of presence: even brief entries have an assertive phenomenological presence. Thoreau's constant preoccupation was nature's coming to the fore: "That which presents itself to us this moment occupies the whole of the

present and rests on the very topmost point of the sphere, under the zenith"
(*J* XIV: 119).

"Something Complete and Final in Themselves"

Although Thoreau occasionally suggests that his writing has a destination, an
endpoint—"and at last I may make wholes of parts" (*PJ* 4: 277)—the Journal's
overall structuring through mere juxtaposition and accretion means that there
is no point where things come to a head: besides being nonhierarchical, Thoreau's Journal is also fundamentally nonteleological. It is deeply disturbing because it defies both the notion of artistic intent *and* the idea of practical pur-
posefulness: the Journal is a huge achievement of virtually no practical use or
value. Thus, although it seems to assume a somewhat mechanical nature—as
though it were merely an instrument (for) registering the objective appearance
of the world[8]—it intrinsically and conspicuously refuses to participate in an
economy of production: it is a venture without assignable end—"unconsidered
expressions of our delight which any natural object draws from us are something complete and final in themselves" (*J* XIV: 117). In this respect, the perfect
lack of *perfection*—completeness and flawlessness—involved in the purely accretive structuring of the Journal is, of course, a deliberate choice, allowing
Thoreau to preserve a degree of spontaneousness that can serve as a symbol
of authentic, nonalienated experience in an increasingly rational world that
brings the triumph of transitivity over intransitivity to its ultimate degree. His
approach may thus appear as a robust response to the overbearing, neutralizing
influences of the modern world.[9]

Thoreau refused to go beyond the momentary and the fragmentary to work
out an integrated structure, precisely because integration means neutraliza-
tion through subordination. Thoreau did not want to neutralize but to activate
and intensify—"We want no completeness but intensity of life" (*J* IX: 378). His
Journal possesses an indefiniteness, as if it were about to disintegrate, or rather
refused ever to cohere. Thoreau strove for *infinition* rather than definition—his
quarrel with definition runs throughout the Journal. To define is to subordi-
nate and impose order and logic on reality. On the contrary, in the Journal,
nature preserves its random openness: Thoreau (and the reader through the act
of reading) does not experience it as being defined in any particular way but

immerses herself or himself in its presence, coexists with it, without ever having—literally or symbolically—the final word. Thoreau's Journal is a book that
hypothetically might be extended without end: the term of this lifelong project can only coincide with the death of the writer—who ultimately, in a carefully crafted final entry late in 1861, can only imagine or hope that nature may
be self-registering—"All this is perfectly distinct to an observant eye, and yet
could easily pass unnoticed by most. Thus each wind is self-registering" (*J* XIV:
346). Thoreau recognized in the Journal a book that could not only generate
but regenerate itself, one that he could write over and over again without its
losing interest—in this sense it is close to *Leaves of Grass*, although the Journal's
expansiveness does not operate on the Whitmanian mode, whose rhythm patterns emphasize balance, repetition, and parallelism. Thoreau's central concern
is not to appropriate the world through either conceptualization or productive
activity but, on the contrary, to endlessly postpone the day of completion: his is
a perfectly antitotalizing stance. The nonteleological nature of the Journal was
not the result of a literary strategy (as it would tend to be for many postmodern
thinkers and artists) but of a conscious existential choice: living without end,
although purposefully.

For a writer like Thoreau, observation of the world raised more questions
than it answered, motivating endlessly renewed exploration or questioning. Although he also pursued scientific investigation, which arguably made him a
pioneer ecologist (as Thoreau scholarship has been eager to emphasize in recent
years),[10] his Journal is premised on the notion that nature is forever unknowable
in the sense that it resists fitting with or into boundaries and classifications. The
Journal structurally and thematically presents itself as an alternative to hierar-
chical and systematic organization of knowledge. Its capacity of resistance to
both narrative and scientific closure results in (and from) its ability to transform
and expand Thoreau's—and our—sense of reality. Nothing could be accepted
as definitive.[11] Indeed, every day renews perception and thus the need to write:
each entry becomes part of a series whose end is unthinkable because the exploration in which it participates is conceived of as endless—"but when my task [as
a surveyor] is done, with never-failing confidence I devote myself to the infinite
again" (*J* IX: 205). Thoreau thus devised a literary space that transcended the
human realm, at once intimate and infinite, because in this *entre-deux* lies our
ground for living, our motif of continued perception.[12]

The Journal forever fails to finally represent something, something stable, not because it anticipates postmodern skepticism but because what matters is process, the flow of energy. Thoreau does justice to nature by seeking to express its dynamic power: in the Journal it seems Nature is understood in its etymological sense, from the Latin *nasci*, "to be born"—nature, strictly speaking, is what is being born each day, each instant. Each perception takes on an ontological dimension because it originates the world, because it is lived by the poet as an act of origin—"How novel and original must be each new mans [*sic*] view of the universe—for though the world is so old—& so many books have been written—each object appears wholly undescribed to our experience—each field of thought wholly unexplored—   The whole world is an America—a *New World*" (*PJ* 4: 421). The world is being born, unfolds before our eyes in this book, which appears as an immense repository in which what has once lived stirs and lives again. The poet gathers up what cannot be exhausted, becoming what René Char called the "conservateur des infinis visages du vivant" (preserver of the infinite aspects of the living world) (195 [*Feuillets d'Hypnos*, no. 83]).

Around 1850, Thoreau came to reject the Neoplatonic cast of Emersonianism, notably, its belief in a teleological progression toward a suprareality (be it called the idea, truth, or beauty), and concomitantly swung to a celebration of becoming versus being. Thoreau's purpose is emphatically not to talk of essences. He came to resist the essentialist belief in a core reality within the manifold appearance of the world, or an all-enveloping truth beyond our immediate environment—what is of utmost concern to him, as it would be to Wallace Stevens, "is never the thing but the version of the thing" (332 ["The Pure Good of Theory"]). His Journal increasingly became preoccupied with *instancing*— "Ah give me pure mind—pure thought. Let me not be in haste to detect the *universal law*, let me see more clearly a particular instance" (*PJ* 4: 223). What matters is the process through which the spiritual engagement with the world turns *chronos* into *kairos*, that is, the crystallization of a time continuum into a single deeply resonant moment that is both timeless (the timelessness not of the concept but of the event perceived in its integrity) and timely. His journal writing, like music, makes time sensible. It dramatizes transitoriness, and to read Thoreau's Journal is to engage with duration, succession, and motion. This work is a constant disavowal of atemporality or immutability as illusion. Thoreau's Journal consistently refuses the temporal totalization promised by formal, conceptual, or symbolic synthesis—although he may also have sought after other forms of synthesis elsewhere, such as those favored by Humboldtian science, as suggested by his late writings, which attempted to fuse the synoptic and the micrologic.[13]

In spite of distant but persistent echoes from an already doomed natural theology—the Journal aping the irremediably lost Book of Nature—Thoreau does not work from an assumption of a preordained harmony of nature, nor does he give any credence to the notion of an eternally valid ordering scheme. "*Nature is a becoming*" (*J* XIII: 183), Thoreau was prompted to declare after his reading of Darwin's *Origin of Species*, which, to that extent, only confirmed what he had for some time been convinced of. Nor, above all, does he believe that writing has the power to transcend the terms of its own limited existence and arrive at a definitive interpretation of the cosmos. But, even though he turned his back on natural theology and embraced an abiding sense of instability or provisionality, Thoreau was no pioneer postmodernist either. Although a two-million-word endeavor, Thoreau's Journal does not celebrate an autonomous textuality, a world of words in which we were inevitably steeped. The vision encapsulated in Thoreau's Journal, although dislocated or fractured at heart, is not imbued with a sense of intrinsic fallibility, and in spite of its complex, active reflexivity, Thoreau's undertaking has nothing to do with the postmodern atomization or fragmentation of nature or with any form of irony. The correlation between firmness and fragility is the true hallmark of Thoreau's Journal, but this is only ontological fragility, not postmodern fallibility or fallacy.

Thoreau's Journal is also vastly different from postmodernist aesthetics because of his desire for absoluteness. It fundamentally evolved from a desire to transcend immediacy, to a reverence for immediacy's transcendency: the absolute was not to be achieved beyond but within experience, as kairos. The relative becomes the absolute only on condition that we commit ourselves to being entirely present to the here and now and to forever testing our presence to the world. Thoreau tried to achieve universality not at the expense of the relative but through and within the relative, which was metonymically related to the entire world.

It is through commitment—sensitivity born in the instant—that Thoreau develops his Journal. Beyond a simple possibility, only the process of perceiving truly constitutes reality. For him, the real is not so much an object or thing, in the sense of a reality already and forever there, as a source of inspiration, something both expected and unforeseen. His purpose was not to capture objects: it is rather, by a much more radical approach, the range of which is authentically "metaphysical" or ontological, to show the process whereby presence is established: this process is fundamentally one of differentiation. Awareness is very precisely the meeting place between reality and the possible, the unique means through which the absolute can become a possibility within life.

NOTES

1. For an insightful overview of critical approaches to Thoreau's Journal, see Neufeldt. Robinson's *Natural Life* provides fine accounts of the various phases of the Journal; see esp. 18–28 and 177–85.

2. Although I construe it somewhat differently, I entirely agree with Cameron's sense of the Journal as "literary experiment" (23) or experimental text.

3. Rosenwald rightly warns us against any temptation to regard diaries as transparent documents giving access to the truth of the "self" or of "character" and consistently dispels "the myth of the private diary" (14); Cameron proceeds from a similar assumption (16). Rosenwald chooses to use the term "diary" (or, rather, "utterance" [17]) for all known examples of daily record but does not discuss the reasons for his choice. I prefer to refer to Thoreau's diary as a journal not primarily because it is the standard term in the Thoreau corpus (probably because it is the word that is used in Thoreau's first entry [*PJ* 1: 5, 22 Oct. 1837]) but to reflect what I perceive to be a vastly different emphasis compared with, say, Pepys's *Diary*. For a general introduction to the nature and place of journals in Transcendentalism, see Sattelmeyer, "Journals."

4. It has often been emphasized that the major turning point was between 1849 and 1851, when Thoreau stopped cannibalizing his Journal for other works and increasingly focused on "nature." For an analysis of the transformation of Thoreau's Journal in the early 1850s, see the "Historical Introduction" to *PJ* 3 and 4; Neufeldt offers an insightful analysis of the complexities of Thoreau's Journal and of the difficulties inherent in editing it, which, he says, should be understood as "a form of translation" (53). Recent scholarly debate on Thoreau's Journal has mostly focused on the 1850s, following Cameron's challenging *Writing Nature*, which initiated a profound reconception of a previously neglected part of the Journal. We still lack a study of the entire range of Thoreau's Journal comparable to the full-scale study of Emerson's Journal offered by Rosenwald. Note that acknowledging its existence as an increasingly autonomous undertaking is not to deny that Thoreau's Journal of the 1850s was connected to several other projects, including the elaboration of a "Kalendar," and what has been edited by Bradley P. Dean

as *Faith in a Seed* and *Wild Fruits*. But my purpose here is to describe what I regard as the internal dynamics of Thoreau's Journal as a literary work in its own right. In this respect, although I share Neufeldt's warnings about the impossibility of fully "re-presenting Thoreau's Journal" (59), what I am intent on showing is comparatively independent of the way we choose to edit it: I believe that, although what it "is" is somewhat elusive, what it "does" is essentially the same whatever the edition is.

5. Thoreau often took notes during his walks and subsequently elaborated them in his Journal. The act of writing also sometimes involved rereading what he had written previously.

6. Here is one of countless examples of what may be described as "dry facts"—a sequence that also exemplifies the Journal's fundamental discontinuities:

Oct 3d Viola lanceolata in Moore's Swamp—

Oct 4th The maples are reddening—& birches yellowing The mouse ear
in the shade in the middle of the day—so hoary looks as if the frost
still lay on it—   Well it wears the frost Bumble bees are on the Aster
undulates & gnats are dancing in the air

Oct 5th The howling of the wind about the house just before a storm
tonight sounds extremely like a loon on the pond. How fit!

Oct 6 & 7th Windy—elms bare—(*PJ* 7: 100)

7. As Walls aptly puts it, "Like the self-registering winds of his final journal entry, none of this is significant *until someone makes it so* by observation and translation. That is, to observe is to make something that was *in*visible, *visible*, or significant and meaningful, by assigning it to a system" ("Romancing" 133)—although the latter remark may overstate the case, as the Journal rather seems to magnify the idea that "in the true natural order the order or system is not insisted on."

8. For an extended exploration of this idea, see Walls, "Romancing."

9. In that sense, what is seemingly postmodern in the Journal seems to border on antimodernism. Rosenwald also observes that "participation in the Concord cottage industry of journal keeping may be construed as a partial rejection of American mechanical and mercantile capitalism" (89).

10. Dean's reconstructions of Thoreau's unfinished manuscripts have gone a long way along this line as well as scholarly emphasis on the "Kalendar project." The most sustained exploration of Thoreau's relation to science has been pursued by Walls, notably in *Seeing New Worlds*.

11. The idea that there is no final truth or reality anticipates William James's notion of pragmatism. For James, pragmatism means turning "away from abstraction . . . , from verbal solutions . . . , from fixed principles, closed systems and pretended absolutes and origins" and "towards concreteness and adequacy, towards facts, towards action, and

towards power." That means also "the open air and possibilities of nature, as against dogma, artificiality, and the pretence of finality in truth" (*Pragmatism* 27). But the value of Thoreau's Journal is that it is no mere statement of philosophical ideas but their living embodiment.

12. Recent Thoreau scholarship may have overdrawn the case for a detranscendentalized Thoreau in the 1850s. In spite of his pursuit of such projects as "The Succession of Forest Trees" and *Wild Fruits*, I believe that the fundamental thrust of his relation to the world lay elsewhere. I here sympathize with Alan Hodder's analysis in *Thoreau's Ecstatic Witness*, which aims "to demonstrate that the late journal did not represent a repudiation of the past, but rather an extension and even progression of Thoreau's lifelong spiritual quest" (262). Lawrence Buell also analyzed Thoreau's description of what he takes to be a new species of bream in the late Journal (November 1858) as "the ultimate extension of the romantic dictum of discovering greater truths within particulars" (*Environmental Imagination* 264).

13. See Walls's notion of "empirical holism" in *Seeing New Worlds* and Michael Berger's concept of "synoptic vision" in *Thoreau's Late Career*.

DAVID DOWLING

Fraught Ecstasy

CONTEMPORARY ENCOUNTERS WITH
THOREAU'S POSTPRISTINE NATURE

CONTEMPORARY CANADIAN GRAPHIC design artist and experimental novelist Douglas Coupland shares grave concerns with Henry Thoreau for the devastating collision between the environment and the development of industrial capitalism—but not without an abundance of satirical irony exposing the dizzying contradictions within the culture that caused it. The ripple effects of this collision Coupland traces include social behaviors, consumption patterns, and attitudes toward nature in our postmodern culture, all of which he laments with arch irony and Thoreauvian skepticism, calling attention to the wasteful absurdities of the empty rituals that have become fixtures of daily life. In particular, Coupland sharply criticizes the way in which consumer culture and the pursuit of surplus capital and commodities have replaced authentic spirituality, especially as derived from nature. Thoreau's protopostmodern sensibility adumbrates Coupland's reverence for the redeeming power of nature as a balm for the rampant materialism and solipsistic individualism dominating contemporary culture. In response to the postmodern madness, a condition as defined by Satya Mohanty in which "all knowledge is seen as tied to the necessary miscognition of human subjects caught in a network of forces they cannot comprehend" (11), Coupland's characters, like Thoreau, flee to forests, deserts, and high mountain lakes to doff their professional identities and attempt to "drive life into a corner" to discover its true essence. While they do achieve transcendence in these sylvan settings, their epiphanies invariably bring deeper, more disturbing knowledge of industrial impact on the environment. I am not arguing that Thoreau was somehow transhistorically an antebellum postmodernist; instead, I detail his anticipation of Coupland's response to nature, which epitomizes one

234

type of postmodern ecological perspective. My objective is not to reconstruct either writer historically nor to advance a new understanding of theoretical periodicity. Rather, Thoreau functions in my argument as an invisible "line of force" (a concept Richard Poirier has used to explain Matthew Arnold's influence on Robert Frost [44]) prefiguring Coupland's environmentalist aesthetics.

Much of the inspiration for this essay comes from Laura Dassow Walls's moving observation that Thoreau believed the divine can indeed be accessed in nature however mitigated by the encroachments of civilization and despite how

> twentieth-century institutions assumed that nature was most valuable in its purest forms, and sadly devalued the environments in which ordinary human beings live and work. . . . [Thoreau] lived not in a pristine wilderness but on the outskirts of Boston, on land that had been cut over, farmed, and abused for generations. His ability to see beauty in that land—to make it stand, symbolically, for the principle of wild nature—can help twenty-first century generations to recover the desperately abused land they will inherit from us, and to see in it beauty, hope, regeneration. ("Thoreau's *Walden*" 16)

Seeing "such beauty in the everyday environment of a Boston suburb," according to Walls, transforms the Thoreauvian aesthetic encounter of nature from mere escape into a "call for social justice" ("Thoreau's *Walden*" 16). Developing this insight, I argue that finding such beauty in postpristine nature necessitates both a powerful romantic imagination and a realist's apprehension of industrial blight on the environment. Alternating between rapture and disgust, this tension Thoreau repeatedly identified pits the observer in an obtuse predicament common to postmodern literary landscapes such as those found in Coupland's novels. Further, a deep and full appreciation of nature's beauty as it stands in close proximity to industrial devastation ironically makes that postmodern experience more moving, both politically and aesthetically.

On Thoreau's "Realometer," Coupland would rank high, especially in novels such as *Shampoo Planet*, *Generation X*, and *Life after God*, where his characters fight through what he calls "Me-ism"—hodgepodge homemade spirituality inspired by consumer culture—and escape the prison of professional identity in the market in order to discover a deeper sense of self in nature. In a formulation that equally applies to Thoreau, Andrew Tate observed of Coupland that "for his postmodern cynicism and acute satires of the consumerist zeitgeist," he has confessed in his fiction and in interviews that "'I need God'" (*Douglas*

Coupland 326). Tate has usefully traced the epiphanic religious moments in Coupland and even parenthetically linked them to Thoreau. Coupland himself does not make his debts to Thoreau explicit, but they are readily evident, especially in "the desire to escape a pampered and preordained western life" and "the desire for an original relation to the universe by stripping away the burdens of history" (Tate, "'Now Here'" 330–31). Tate, however, does not expand on how those ecstatic moments articulate an environmental economic ethos, as I do here. The postmodern maladies Coupland identifies echo those of Thoreau's contemporaries in *Walden* and "Walking," which drive them into the wild for self-discovery, authenticity, and rebirth. Like Thoreau, Coupland's characters find that ecstatic immersion in nature brings them closer to human impact on nature, not farther from it. Thus their natural encounters are hard, riveting, and jarring, as they enact rituals to mourn the loss of nature—its clear-cut Canadian forests and polluted streams, like the land behind Walden Pond, scarred and lacerated by the new railroad—and reaffirm their opposition to the erosion of spiritual values that allowed this destruction.

The very essence of the natural process in Thoreau's writing, I want to argue, bears a distinctly protopostmodern sensibility, from self-referential pastiche to ecstatic, soaring visionary reveries that crash on the rocks of his neighbors' galling capitalistic exploitation of the environment. A sense of optimism always edges against the bizarre, even surreal, effects of economic sins that reify the environment as property and raid its resources of timber, ice, and fur to feed an insatiable demand for consumer goods. The villagers who run roughshod over the landscape for capital gain transform the woods into a site of laissez-faire capitalism unleashed, posing a direct threat to its value as source of spiritual sustenance. "For 'nature,'" according to Joe Jordan, "inhabits that curious niche between our systems, between use-value and exchange-value, where its value . . . can be traded and sold based on market forecasts, and our means of measuring its intrinsic worth is gone" (ix–x). Thoreau's mentor, Ralph Waldo Emerson, confirmed this sense of competing value systems in nature, noting that their collision brings about an absurd condition that nonetheless challenges, if not totally eclipses, visions of the divine in nature. "Is not the landscape, every glimpse of which hath a grandeur, a face of [God]?" he asks rhetorically (*CW* 1: 39). Emerson's qualification points precisely to the condition I am identifying as postmodern: "Yet this may show us what discord is between man and nature, for you cannot freely admire a noble landscape if laborers are digging in the field hard by. The poet finds something ridiculous in his delight until he is out of the sight of men" (*CW* 1: 39). Out of sight, however, does not mean out of mind; the tracks of industrial labor are inescapable during key phases in the development of capitalism, as claims on the land's profitability proliferate. Thoreau, like Coupland, does not flee "the digging in the field hard by" but examines such images of protopostmodern absurd mismatches in tones vacillating between darkly comic and crushingly somber. Unlike Emerson, Thoreau and Coupland are not content to just wait until they are out of sight of industry to find nature's beauty and instead behold its full essence in such a way that brings out its vulnerability. Both achieve such vision, but not before acknowledging the depth of the culture's larger crisis in spirituality and its roots in rampant materialism. Through this lens, the environment comes to signify a civilization dominated by an irresponsible commercial culture threatening to kill nothing less than the spirit that animates our relationship to nature, giving way, according to Coupland, to a spiritually vacuous life after God.

In 1991 Coupland published *Generation X: Tales for an Accelerated Culture*, the same year as Frederic Jameson's famous proclamation in *Postmodernism, or the Cultural Logic of Late Capitalism* that the "modern age" was increasingly showing signs of "the extinction of the sacred and the spiritual" (67). Within the next decade, both Coupland and Jameson would identify more explicitly an aching for some kind of spirituality to fill that void, calling into question the possibility that the spiritual could ever be extinguished. For example, Coupland's appropriately named Scout—who eventually scouts out his own nature through nature—observes in *Life after God* (1994) that "we are living creatures—we have religious impulses—we *must*—and yet into what cracks do these impulses flow in a world without religion. Sometimes I think it is the only thing I should be thinking about" (273–74). Jameson came to a similar conclusion in 1999, observing how "religion is once again very much on the agenda of any serious attempt to come to terms with the specificity of our time" ("Marx's Purloined Letter" 53). A century and a half prior to the specificity of Jameson's time, Thoreau observed how perfunctory and dutiful religion had become. He exposed how "unwillingly we say our prayers and commit ourselves to uncertainties" and to someone else's abstract vision of God when it is in the ever-transforming natural world connected to us wherein "all change is a miracle to contemplate" (*W* 11).

Nature would be the logical place for spiritual seekers of all stripes to look,

but increasingly those ardent searches render disillusioning evidence of capitalism's impact on the natural environment. When they are not a cathedral or
sylvan spectacle, the woods in *Walden* take on an almost noir atmosphere, like
the landscape of Jordan Fisher Smith's *Nature Noir: A Park Ranger's Patrol in
the Sierra* (2006), a site for the misdeeds of outlaws, for unspeakable treach-
ery and violence. The crimes against nature spring directly from the diseased
market culture Thoreau diagnoses in "Economy," the first chapter of *Walden*.
Most of the perpetrators are blind to their misdeeds, having rationalized their
actions according to a feverish pursuit of profit that sets their axes flying. To be
the watchman over this landscape puts Thoreau into a distinctly postmodern
situation, poised as he is at a key juncture in the development of capitalism to
witness one of the largest claims in American history laid upon the New England woodland while being virtually helpless to stop its seemingly inevitable
siege. In one Journal entry, Thoreau describes a farmer unwittingly killing off
seedlings by plowing his lot after clear-cutting it for a stand of winter rye. Short-
term profits squander the farmer's long-term financial gain and decimate the
future of the native pine and birch wood in the area. This double sin of bad business sense (Thoreau's antimaterialism never prevented him from admiring the
shrewd business sense that works with the environment) and the destruction of
nature urges Thoreau to cry out for "a guardian [to be] placed over" the scoun-
drel. "Forest wardens should be appointed by the town," he insists, as "overseers
of poor husband-men," in one of the earliest calls for environmental protection
in the form of park ranger law enforcement (*Faith* 173). The comment reflects
the odd circumstance of bearing witness to a crime metonymic of the culture's
larger economic ethos embedded in a legal system—no law to enforce means
no warden to enforce it—that has rendered his protests futile.

The crimes against nature Thoreau was helpless to stop anticipate Smith's
memoir, which extends the definition of Thoreau's postmodern environmental economics. The Frankfurt School represents some of the first radical environmental theorists to recognize this pattern, a major source of Thoreau's
anxiety concerning "how a market economy frames and shapes the ways in
which we appropriate the environment, a tradition that maintains that individual consciousness cannot directly counteract these larger forces," as Michael
Bennett explains (94). Smith's own tale of his acutely perceptive individual consciousness rendered powerless is all the more shocking since as an armed and
uniformed National Park Service ranger he is fully invested with the power to

enforce the law. Yet he is caught in an "accident of history" that led to the "delegation of armed rangers sent in to protect a piece of ground that could not be protected from the very government that employed them" (J. Smith 5). Thoreau would have been amused, if not crestfallen, at the scenario. Smith's assignment in 1986 to the Auburn Dam site in Northern California was fraught with Thoreauvian paradox rooted in a bizarre intersection of nature, government, and finance, with galling professional consequences for Smith. The ironic position, thus, of loving—"I hadn't expected how beautiful those canyons were," Smith confesses—and protecting something slated for destruction demystifies and complicates nature's transcendent power (6). Not only was it difficult to value land about to be flooded, and thus hard to make visitors comply with laws, but in a telling postmodern twist, courtroom judges began pardoning blasting and strip-mining violations, effectively transforming the land and its two majestic river canyons into "nature noir," a site for dumping murder victims, selling narcotics, and strip-mining, a place desecrated and violated in an abomination made more alarming since it was all perfectly legal.

Thoreau's darkness similarly comes from precisely this awareness of loving a natural world—of committing his faith in its miraculous power—slated for a process of destruction already well under way. Although the farmers at Flint's Pond are not to be confused with Smith's felons, Thoreau's tone of alarm and anger resonates with Smith's. A yearning for reenchantment in a culture so bent on breaking that faith is distinctive in both Coupland and Thoreau, who states his desire to return to a purity symbolized by birth's intimacy with the secrets of eternity in a famous line from *Walden*: "I always have been regretting that I was not so wise as the day I was born" (*W* 98). This thirst for enchantment exudes a sensibility consonant with Zygmunt Bauman's description of the postmodern condition: "All in all, postmodernity can be seen as restoring to the world what modernity presumptuously had taken away"; a reaction, like Thoreau's, to what is lost, a drive toward "a *re-enchantment* of the world that modernity tried hard to *dis-enchant*. It is the modern artifice," an echo of the market revolution's fabrications of Thoreau's antebellum era, which "has been dismantled; the modern conceit of meaning-legislating reason that has been exposed, condemned and put to shame. It is that artifice and reason," Bauman explains, "the reason of the artifice, that stands accused in the court of postmodernity" (x). And no one escapes the courtroom of Henry David Thoreau or of Douglas Coupland without a thorough cross-examination.

That desire for reenchantment is part of what makes Thoreau so appealing now, so inspiring and frequently cited (if not misquoted), as painstakingly
chronicled on the Internet today. Thoreau's burrowing into nature inspires a
lyricism where the "sandy bottom" of Walden Pond's "thin current slides away,
but eternity remains. I would drink deeper; fish in the sky, whose bottom is
pebbly with stars," at which point a return to a preverbal union with nature
is immanent: "I cannot count one. I know not the first letter of the alphabet"
(*W* 98). A dismantling of the pretenses and inefficiencies of market culture lead
him to demonstrate the details of his alternative economy, how he built his
house, how much lumber and how many nails it took, as the avenue toward
this ecstatic reenchantment with nature, however ephemeral or compromised
by traces of industrial impact. Herein lies the dynamic that enables Thoreau to
don the persona of "Buddha with a receipt from the hardware store" (McKibben
xii). Indeed, postmodernity is also associated with the promotion of or search
for such an alternative economy. In this spirit, Coupland's Tyler makes a living
off the dross of consumer and celebrity culture by creating an amusement park
out of landfill (called "History World") and selling Warholesque sketch imprints
from the commemorative stars embossed in the sidewalk of Hollywood Bou-
levard. Tyler's economy is as lean and idiosyncratic as Thoreau's quirky ledgers
and balance sheets.

Thoreau's nondenominational spiritualism, a passionate belief in God without Jesus, takes on a pantheistic universalist slant much in the way Coupland's
"emphasis on the need for the transcendent does not indicate the conversion of
the novelist to a kind of Evangelical Christianity or even an Emersonian belief
in an Oversoul," as Tate comments ("'Now Here'" 338). Yet I would argue that
Coupland's yearning for belief necessarily engages nature as a reaction to material prosperity's neglect of spiritual integrity and is rooted in a radical critique of
capitalism that can be described as Thoreauvian, though Coupland never pays
direct homage to him. Thoreau's penchant for parables with economic import,
usually dealing with material loss (such as the Indian basket, and the hound,
bay horse, and turtledove passages), bear a distinct resemblance to Coupland's.
For example, the Skeleton King's parable in *Polaroids from the Dead* allegorizes
the devastating East Bay fires of Northern California in the mid-1990s as a sort
of divine or mystical punishment for excessive materialism, a massive payback
for the culture's Faustian bargain of gold for spirit. "You live in mortal splendor,"
the Grateful Dead Skeleton King warns, "yet the price you pay for this comfort

is a collapsed vision of heaven—an inability to see any longer pictures in your heads of an afterlife" (*Polaroids* 60). That trade, according to the narrator of Coupland's *Life after God*, has resulted in "an inability to fully believe in love; instead we gained an irony that scorched everything it touched" (273). Thus in nature, Coupland's characters find a balm for their habitual ironic distance that at best constitutes fearless satiric swordplay and at worst a sneering hope- less skepticism. Such ironic distance uses humor for spiritual self-defense, a kind of survival mechanism in the face of rampant materialism not unlike Tho- reau's distance from Concord established by his hut at Walden Pond. Thoreau can sneer from a distance with bitter disgust, pointedly upbraiding readers in "Reading" and commercial farmers in "The Ponds." Yet he can also laugh at the folly of his own pursuits, as when he inadvertently drops his axe through the ice and resorts to fishing it out (also in "The Ponds"); he nearly burns down his own house in the appropriately named chapter, "House Warming," and fruitlessly chases the loon that mocks his every move in "Brute Neighbors." In "The Pond in Winter" he even imagines the pond itself reveling in droll retribution when an ice harvester slips through a crack and nearly dies. Ironic distance frames the comically absurd collision of trade and culture in that chapter's quintessentially Thoreauvian tableau of mesmerized onlookers gaping at a block of ice dropped in transit to market and lying in the road as if it were a huge gem gleaming in the sun. The market economy and commercial culture never look so bizarre to these authors as when they collide with nature, poke holes in it, endlessly pursue it, and leave its commodified remnants like so much trash in the street, an in- stance in which familiar nature—frozen pond water—is rendered like a garish Barnumesque curiosity in the heart of the marketplace.

Through this perspective, nature not only provides an unambiguous chan- nel for escape from commodities and professionalism but also displays the very signs of that market culture, usually in jarring juxtaposition. Specifically, the image of the railroad lacerating the landscape in *Walden* alerts us to the steely bulk, force, and momentum of the infrastructure of distribution that the loco- motive provided, its vital function for the spread of literacy and the attendant burgeoning of print culture. Thoreau observes that the vast majority of read- ing material that the railroad distributes for mass consumption is precisely the frivolous pap he decries in *Walden*. He laments the herculean efforts to advance media technology, such as the telegraph and daily mail delivery, only to distrib- ute utterly hollow messages. "I am sure that I never read any memorable news in a newspaper," he quips, since "to a philosopher all *news*, as it is called, is gossip" (*W* 94). The deadening effect of such reading can be traced back to how "we do not ride on the railroad; it rides upon us," effectively burying the spiritually moribund villagers: "The rails are laid on them, and they are covered with sand, and the cars run smoothly over them" (*W* 92). He famously questioned the great rush to construct a magnetic telegraph for communication between Maine and Texas without considering that "Maine and Texas, it may be, have nothing important to communicate" (*W* 52). All that feverish technological development comes prior to a satisfactory reason for its existence, resulting in a quagmire echoing a line that Coupland's Tyler felt-pens on a one-dollar bill: "LET'S JUST HOPE WE ACCIDENTALLY BUILD GOD" (*Shampoo* 219). As Tyler sarcastically suggests, heedless runaway industrial expansion, construction for its own sake without a moral compass, has inadvertently given rise to so many bizarre cultural fetishes that have shaped themselves around it that perhaps one random result may be the discovery of an authentic deity. His joke, like Thoreau's, hinges on the conspicuous absence of a higher ethical purpose in technological innovation conducted for the benefit of commercial interests.

Juxtaposed to the environment's function as a site of epiphany is Coupland's other nature—the sadder, bleaker one displaying the tracks of a postmodern economy bent on exploiting its bounty. Like Thoreau's own *nature noir*, the abuses Coupland finds in the environment reveal his deep distrust of consumerism and the development of technologies for their own sake regardless of use value. Coupland renders this postmodern environmental economy in the image of red numbers spray painted on the butt ends of Douglas fir logs assaulting the view from behind the giant trucks. "I wonder what these numbers and letters mean," Tyler, the Lancaster, Washington, youth says as he rides with his French girlfriend, Anna-Louise. They are on a pilgrimage to Glen Anna, a Canadian forest where they plan to perform a quirky ritual celebration of self and nature in which she cuts his hair and he takes her photographic portrait. This woodland is saturated with sacred significance Tyler had known as a child; his current hometown is dominated by a toxic waste dump and a crumbling mall. As they approach, the logging truck and the angry red "alpha numeric codes" emblazoned onto the ends of the freshly sheared trees serve as an ominous portent. Assault, violation, destruction, all in the name of selfish consumption, carry the meaning of the letters, which remind Tyler of the word "Divorce" scrawled on his mother's forehead in permanent marker, his stepfather's exceedingly cruel way of signaling the end of their marriage while she slept. Tyler ruminates further on the codes emblazoned on the trees, concluding that they "no doubt assist a value-added computer in Yokohama in converting the logs into chopsticks or paper towels." He comments to Anna-Louise how "tourists helicoptering in to view the Mount Saint Helen's eruption flew over clear-cuts and said, 'Oh my God, this is more horrible than any scenario I could have imagined.'" He adds that "there's a clear-cutting site . . . on Vancouver Island so dreadful, so horrifying and violated, it became known as the Black Hole, and even the loggers were sickened by what they had done and the area was closed off to all visitors." The logging truck turns out of sight but not out of mind. The economics of lumbering now give way to stunned mourning for the loss of nature: "The forest is gone and there are no words that I can say. . . . [T]here is nothing on the horizon. There are no birds or animals because there is nothing for the birds or animals." Coupland's veiled reference is to Rachel Carson's 1962 *Silent Spring*, a work at the forefront of ecocriticism and environmental activism. "The loss is absolute," as it is in Carson's birdless April, "bleeding orange tree rings" surrounding them, stumps "as large as a giant's dinner table in a prairie of grey mud." The experience leaves Tyler inconsolable. "Don't talk to me," he mutters to end the chapter (*Shampoo* 84–86).

Coupland's testimony of the violation of the landscape, which takes on genocidal proportions, is preceded by seamless and reverential unions with nature. Tyler and Anna-Louise have a silent interlude that leaves them "mellowed considerably." The pair climb out of the car after several hours of travel to stretch and play catch, "gorging on oxygen, like astronauts returning to earth . . . drinking in the trout-grey sky." "Playing catch like this is like dancing," a rhythmic intimacy unconsciously guiding their muscles, drawing the two deeper into the woods with each catch, "feeling seduced by a genetic secret, like a teenager learning to masturbate, not knowing what I'm doing, but continuing regardless, deeper into the forest, the ball miraculously managing to avoid the staid, butlerlike hemlocks and firs between us, the brush and undergrowth muffling all sound save for the beating of blood in my ears and the slap of the ball in our gloves." The connection with each other, organically and erotically charged, comes as a full immersion in nature, a kind of love-making with the environment and its processes that enables the sort of love Coupland's characters so often yearn for. It is on the "quiet, oh-so-quiet cool dry moss" that the two "move in on each other" until they meet. Coupland's syntax adopts the rhythms of the ball tossing back and forth between them and the almost gravitational pull that brings them, and nature, together, as the two reenter the car brushing "the hemlock needles off our bodies, needles that cover us everywhere" (*Shampoo* 82–83).

Thoreau's ecstatic natural reveries also precede bleak visions of capitalism's impact on the environment. At such moments, Thoreau's lyrical voice is quite distinct from his sober accounting as it rises to pitched, exalted notes usually aimed skyward toward the stars—"I prefer the natural sky to the opium eater's heaven" (*W* 217)—and clouds, as in the following reverie canoeing on Walden Pond: "In such transparent and seemingly bottomless water, reflecting the clouds, I seemed to be floating through the air as in a balloon, and their swimming impressed me as a kind of flight or hovering, as if they were a compact flock of birds passing just beneath my level on the right or left, their fins, like sails, set all around them" (*W* 189–90). This swirling and euphoric image poetically blends the lofty clouds, birds, and the fancy of his flight in a balloon over the reflected clouds on the water's surface, beneath which, in a near hallucinatory effect, swim "myriads of small perch" (*W* 189). The vitality and dynamism of the image is astonishing and, taken as lyricism, approaches a symphonic feel. Thoreau was well aware of the sound of his own poetic voice as much as he was acutely sensitive to the sounds of nature, which he enthusiastically pores over as a form of lyrical song in the chapter "Sounds."

Thoreau's own meditative paddling on the pond, as rhythmic and harmonious with nature as Tyler and Anna-Louise's in Coupland's vision, has him "dreaming awake" over that "sylvan spectacle" (*W* 191). Like the intrusive red code on the ends of the fir trees in Coupland, Thoreau's music gives way to the sound of wood-chopping, the sound of the free market intruding on his symphony. Significantly, his own alternative economy of deliberate living based on material subsistence to allow for such transcendent natural encounters is unceremoniously usurped by industrial capitalism's raid on natural resources to feed the debt-ridden consumers seeking to bulk up their already overloaded stocks of goods. Thus Thoreau refuses to regret the days he spent, or "wasted," according to conventional industrial values. Like the Coupland characters' dance with nature that began as a game of catch, a moment so totally pristine that it seems to step out of time altogether, Thoreau's wealth is in life, making him "rich, if not in money, in sunny hours and summer days," which he "spent . . . lavishly." It is after he leaves Walden Pond that the greater industrial designs on his sanctuary bring home the sobering truth: "Since I left those shores the woodchoppers have still further laid them waste, and the wood, with occasional vistas through which you can see the water. My Muse may be excused if she is silent henceforth. How can you expect the birds to sing when their groves are cut down?" he asks in the stultifying silence of the cleared forest (*W* 192), a silence that resembles Tyler and Anna-Louise as they sit, dumbstruck at the devastation, on their giant's table of a Douglas fir stump. Thoreau too depicts woodcutters who have "fatally injured Walden with an axe" and are "cutting down our woods more seriously than ever. . . . Thank God they cannot cut down the clouds" (*PJ* 4: 273).

Coupland's chopsticks and paper towels are a perfect match for Thoreau's pipeline from the pond to the village, a commodification of Walden's holy water, "sacred as the Ganges at least," to save the scant journey it would take to bathe or drink at the source. "We must go over space or we wither," wrote Charles Olson (114) in a line the ever-ambulant Thoreau would have heartily endorsed, covering ground on foot for up to four hours per day. Such a pilgrimage to the pond as a holy ritual in the pastime of living is lost on villagers now of the mindset that has them rooted at their desks, sedentary, working for weeks at a time to buy train tickets to visit towns easily accessible by foot. Thoreau's train is Coupland's logging truck, menacingly roaring through the wooded sanctuary with all the subtlety of a road grader. Thoreau blames the train for the felled lumber and destruction of nature's music: "That devilish Iron Horse, whose ear-rending neigh is heard throughout the town, has muddied the Boiling Spring with his foot, and he it is that has browsed off all the woods on Walden shore," going so far as to imagine jousting it to its death in the name of the countryside: "Where is the country's champion, the Moore of Moore Hall, to meet him at the Deep Cut and thrust an avenging lance between the ribs of the bloated pest?" (*W* 192).

Though he imagines himself as "the country's champion" here, Thoreau very much is the *people's* champion, who knows the stuff of redemption lies in even the most hardened of workers, "the engineers and firemen and brakemen," for they "see [Walden Pond] often, and are better men for the sight." Indeed, "the engineer does not forget at night, or his nature does not, that he has beheld this vision of serenity and purity once at least during the day. Though seen but once, it helps to wash out State-street and the engine soot." Playing along with the nomenclature of train stops reflecting speed and economy driven by schedules, transport, distribution, and delivery, Thoreau quips that the pond "be called 'God's Drop,'" a clever pun also alluding to the pond as a heavenly drop of water (*W* 193–94). By contrast, Coupland's faceless loggers hardly hold such redemptive capacity and instead bear identities that seamlessly merge with their trucks, like the tractor drivers in John Steinbeck's *The Grapes of Wrath*. Thoreau, however, would find the drivers capable of being touched by nature's beauty as well, much like the Canadian woodcutter in *Walden*. Thoreau's transcendental belief that the divine exists in all is thus far more democratic than Coupland's vilification of the truckers that excludes them from accessing natural beauty. Thoreau would characterize their witnessing of nature as he does that of the railway men: it may not necessarily be ecstatic, but it would leave them "better men for the sight" (*W* 193–94).

One mile east of Walden Pond lies Flint's Pond, a body of water that is higher and considerably larger than Walden but not nearly as deep or pure. Thoreau favors Walden in this way as a metaphor, for it lives "reserved and austere, like a hermit in the woods, so long, it has acquired such wonderful purity." For however much Walden's sanctity is threatened by capitalist enterprise, the pond nonetheless is resilient, constantly renewing itself, maintaining its godlike purity in the face of "the Irish [who] have built their sties by it, and the railroad [which] has infringed on its border, and the ice-men [who] have skimmed it once." Thoreau's fanciful renaming of Walden as "God's Drop" is followed by an intensely serious consideration of the pond as God's gift: "He rounded this water with his hand," directly reflecting its maker, who was "deepened and clarified in its thought, and in his will bequeathed it to Concord" (*W* 193–94). More than in any other ecstatic passage in *Walden*, Thoreau here explicitly witnesses nature not just as God's creation per se but, in a rhetorical formulation that equates the pond with the divine itself, vibrating with electric life and vitality, its dimensions of depth and purity carrying the keynote to his ode.

Opposite Walden, or "God's Drop," is the bigger yet shallower Flint's Pond, an apt metaphor for the economy of living that his neighbors have blindly embraced. Surface size alone, Thoreau reminds us, is no match for the dimension of depth. Whereas Walden's deeper, cleaner waters reflect the divine, the "unclean and stupid farmer" had "ruthlessly laid bare" Flint's shores, transforming its water into "the reflecting surface of a dollar, or a bright cent, in which [the admirer] could see his own brazen face." The appropriation of divine nature through its economic domination leads to tyranny over the land in which the corrupted yeoman farmer begins to play God, armed as he is with capital to justify a farm on which "nothing grows free, whose fields bear no crops, whose meadows no flowers, whose trees no fruits, but dollars; who loves not the beauty of his fruits, whose fruits are not ripe until they are turned to dollars" (*W* 196). Thoreau's spite in this famous passage is overwhelmingly directed at the transformation of farm into factory, a reification of living nature through crassly materialistic methods. This funneling of farming into ruthless economic acquisition results in a godlessness that Coupland precisely identifies in the postmodern condition of "life after God," in which "you are the first generation raised without religion" (*Life* 61). Thoreau's characterization of his neighbors at Flint's Pond reveals that Coupland's contemporaries were hardly the first generation to be raised without religion. The perfunctory Christianity masking the deeper materialistic values of Flint's farmers represents the historical precedent for the generation Coupland characterizes. The ethical erosion of the postmodern late twentieth century can, in this sense, be traced directly to the antebellum market revolution's impact on the environmental ethos. Indeed, where God is missing at Flint's Pond, there exists not only ruthless capitalist expansion but also a failure to find the divine in nature and perceive it as a gift and a privilege to be protected and loved through all the senses. Significantly, Thoreau's litany of the corrupted farmers' sins begins with his disdain for those "who never saw" nature's divine, rather than monetary, value. Next, failure to commune with the natural environment not as recreational entertainment but as a source of physical and spiritual purity ("who never bathed in it") misses the experiential merging with its processes that functions as a necessary precondition for activism ("who never protected it"). Thoreau ends the list by referencing his own rhetorical role as nature's missionary through his observation of how this missing chain of philosophical beliefs and actions renders the capitalist agrarian incapable of testifying on behalf of God's existence, for he had never witnessed the divine in nature in the first place, "never spoke a good word for it, nor thanked God that he had made it" (*W* 196). Gratitude and humility are often forgotten as essential components of this passage, which is otherwise known for its savage indictment and sweeping dismissal of a huge segment of the population spawned by market culture. Indeed, any arrogance characterizing Thoreau's impassioned venom should instead be understood as attributable to the capitalist ethos of economic narcissism practiced by the Flint's Pond farmers.

Coupland and Thoreau share an acute understanding not only of the depth and scope of the damage inflicted on the environment but of the bizarre attendant commodification of nature, from barcoded Douglas firs to crop leaves as dollar signs. Such a commodification of the wild gives rise to a *nature noir*, as

Smith describes it, a condition aptly characterized in the global economy on a multinational corporate level that has led to the overconsumption of the non-renewable resource of oil. Among the most alarming of today's industrial footprints on the environment is global warming, especially as portrayed through the lens of Al Gore's *An Inconvenient Truth*. On a local level, communities such as Boulder, Colorado, take pride in their aggressive protection of undeveloped land in open space programs; yet Boulder continues to struggle with human impact on native plant and animal species, as Denver's notorious brown cloud swells on its eastern horizon over the high plains toward Mexico City proportions. Industrial encroachment seems a historical inevitability in this mountain paradise. Other areas have, however, been progressing, such as Cleveland, Ohio's Cuyahoga River: the Cuyahoga was such a travesty of filth and waste in the 1970s that it literally caught fire, signaling an embarrassing all-time low in natural pollution. Though far from pristine, the waters around Cleveland have made a stunning recovery, and habitats around the river have literally come back to life. The beloved "Emerald Necklace" that dances in a byzantine loop from Lake Erie through northeastern Ohio and back still bears the taint of its days at the pinnacle of *nature noir*, but its regeneration offers a sterling example of the sort of environmental beauty and hope in which Thoreau was so deeply invested.

Visiting Walden Pond now brings about a sobering "inconvenient truth" of its own: the land's overuse, its polish and luster long gone with the wear of recreation seekers, its near destruction by developers prevented only at the last minute by the deus ex machina of rock star capital (provided by the Eagles' front man Don Henley, who would eventually found the Walden Woods Project). To avoid utter depression on the scale of a Douglas Coupland character, one must be mindful of how the nature that thrives, however compromised, symbolizes hope, beauty, and generation. Thoreau did not cling to Walden as a talismanic fetish, for what matters, as Martin Bickman so incisively observed, is not so much the particular natural object of attention—be it Whitman's live oak growing in Louisiana or Shelley's skylark—but the observer's spiritual appetite and "intensity of response to life" (121). For herein lies the key to a transcendence that has one foot in heaven and another firmly rooted in our fraught and beleaguered earth.

THOMAS PUGHE

Brute Neighbors

THE MODERNITY OF A METAPHOR

THE AIM OF THIS ESSAY is to study the implications of Thoreau's metaphor of neighborhood with animals in *Walden*. What does this anthropomorphic trope tell us about Thoreau's views on animality and on human-animal relations? Does the choice of "brute" rather than "animal" in "Brute Neighbors" express Thoreau's sense of human superiority or, on the contrary, his awareness that he, too, is animal? Though "brute" can simply be read as a synonym for "animal," it does bring out, by contrast, the anthropomorphism of "neighbors"—as if Thoreau wanted to make sure the reader would not miss the trope. It is indeed far from innocent. The concept of the "neighbor" is at the very heart of Christian morality. Implicitly, Thoreau seems to be extending the respectful and charitable treatment reserved for human neighbors to the animal world ("Love your non-human neighbor as yourself"). Is this trope, then, an expression of Thoreau's spiritualized concept of nature in *Walden*? Or does "neighborhood" suggest a sense of that continuity of life that Darwin was in the process of developing into a revolutionary theory? Clearly both. As Lawrence Buell has suggested, for Emerson, Thoreau, and their circle, "the rise of formal science did not so much discredit the notion of 'an occult relation between man and the vegetable,' in Emerson's quaint phrase, as translate it. Indeed, the evolutionary hypothesis intensified the claim of kinship by blurring the boundary between *Homo sapiens* and other species" (*Environmental Imagination* 188). The neighborhood trope, then, has roots both in natural theology and in naturalism.

Traditionally, anthropomorphic tropes have frequently been a way of "policing" the dividing line between human and animal (Soper 86). They are a symbolic burden we lay on animals, both in criticism and in praise, to help us describe human qualities and thereby to singularize the supposedly superior element of the human-animal opposition. "If man had not been his own classifier," Darwin dryly points out, "he would never have thought of founding a separate order for his own reception" (*Descent* 885). That separate order is frequently associated with what Derrida calls "pouvoir-avoir le logos" ("L'animal" 278), that is, the power that comes with naming and classifying: in Derrida's words, "[L]ogocentrism is first and foremost a thesis about animality" (278, my translation). Yet anthropomorphism, as the tradition of the beast fables attests, has always been a potentially subversive trope that blurs the dividing line between human and nonhuman animals at the same time as it tries to affirm it.[1] Such blurring is particularly noticeable from the romantic revolution onward. The primitivist current in poetry, for example, flows strong throughout the twentieth century (D. H. Lawrence and Robinson Jeffers, Gary Snyder and Ted Hughes come to mind). Of course, in much modern science, in Thoreau's time as still today, anthropomorphic tropes have been considered as a logical fallacy. They are also treated with suspicion by environmentalists and ecocritics, who tend to interpret them as symbolic exploitations of nonhuman nature (cf. Garrard 136–59). And yet, to many contemporary ethologists, sociobiologists, and anthropologists as well as to poets, such tropes suggest ways of representing human-animal relations beyond the traditional boundaries. In other words, rather than rejecting anthropomorphic tropes as epistemologically incorrect (Buell, *Environmental Imagination* 181), they can also be read as tension-filled semiotic fields suspended between exploitation and exploration, between dead and living metaphor, between the making and the unmaking of figurative language.

My argument in what follows will be that Thoreau was aware of such tensions and ambiguities and made use of them in his own rhetoric. More generally, the neighborhood metaphor in *Walden* (it also occurs in his other writings, e.g., the Journal) stands for his distinctive way of thinking about the ethical, scientific, and poetic consequences of a move from an anthropocentric to a biocentric idea of the world.[2] In that respect, it is highly significant to contemporary ecocriticism and animal studies.

"Brute Neighbor" or "Beast of Burden"?

At the beginning of the "Brute Neighbors" chapter in *Walden*, Thoreau uses the neighborhood metaphor to separate two different kinds of relationship between animals and humans: "Why do precisely these objects which we behold make a world? Why has man just these species of animals for neighbors; as if nothing but a mouse could have filled this crevice? I suspect that Pilpay & Co. have put animals to their best use, for they are all beasts of burden, in a sense, made to carry some portion of our thoughts" (*W* 225). The questions with which this passage begins concern Thoreau's observation of the interconnectedness of life forms at Walden. "Man" seems to him to be only one element within a whole. If humans have just this or that nonhuman animal as neighbor, it follows that they, too, have their allotted place in the larger order of things, an order one could then call bio- rather than anthropocentric. In Thoreau's neighborhood, "all the actors are not human," as Donna Haraway might say (*Haraway Reader* 127). But neighborhood does remain an anthropomorphic trope for all that, as does the *oikos* in "ecology." The biocentric neighborhood image in the above quotation is opposed to the more conventional kind where animals are symbolically exploited to carry the "burden" of human thought. The verb *made* ("made to carry some portion of our thoughts") can be understood in two different but related senses, depending on where the stress falls. If it falls on *made*, this implies that animals exist not for themselves but only to serve their human masters, as the Bible tells us; if it falls on *carry*, we are referred to traditional forms of anthropomorphism, for example, in the beast fables of "Pilpay & Co." Notice the rather flippant *& Co.*, surprising in a writer who, in a preceding chapter, has expressed his veneration of the classical literary canon.[3] Yet in speaking of animals as symbolic "beasts of burden," Thoreau expresses his awareness that by using the neighborhood metaphor he risks prolonging the very anthropocentric tradition he draws into question. The neighbor and the beast of burden are indeed both present in *Walden*. Though it is the former I intend to concentrate on because it plays a far more important part in Thoreau's thinking and writing, it cannot be dissociated from the latter.

Walden includes some examples of *theriomorphism*, that is, animal images used to express criticism of certain acts, kinds of behavior, or attitudes by bestializing them. In Thoreau's remarks about the squalid lives of the Irish Collins and Fields families, for example, these immigrant laborers' habit of sharing their home with their chickens is mentioned as an example of their supposedly lacking human dignity. In the Fields' farm, "the chickens, which had also taken shelter here from the rain, stalked about the room like members of the family, too humanized methought to roast well" (*W* 204). The proximity with the chickens bestializes the Irish immigrants. But, typically for Thoreau, the humanization of the chickens and, literally, their domestication are also criticized. We get a kind of blurring of the species boundaries that manifestly troubles Thoreau, as the reference to cannibalism and perhaps the stilted *methought* suggest. Though there are few examples of theriomorphism in *Walden*, it is nevertheless clear that Thoreau did not hesitate to criticize what he thought of as the "lower human instincts" by bestializing them. This is notably the case in "Higher Laws." Here Thoreau fears, for example, that his occasional craving for animal flesh may turn him into a savage beast or, at any rate, turn him away from the life of contemplation and poetry that he aspired to. Not only is the "animal within" *not* respected as a neighbor, it must even be eradicated: "We are conscious of an animal in us, which awakens in proportion as our higher nature slumbers. It is reptile and sensual, and perhaps cannot be wholly expelled" (*W* 219). Animality is referred to negatively to bring out by opposition Thoreau's preference of the life of the mind ("our higher nature") over that of the body, as if his craving for meat or his sexual desires were merely a question of that "sensuous and reptile" animal that is supposed to inhabit his body. Though Thoreau is speaking of instincts that humans share with animals, he bestializes the latter (not to mention associating them with the theme of original sin) to reinforce the species boundary. In these examples, in sum, Thoreau does not really refer to animals; it is *the animal*, in the most "speciesist" understanding of that term, that is being set up. Though this kind of "*bêtise*," to use Derrida's pun (*bête*, the root of *bêtise*, "foolishness," means "animal") (291), is not typical of Thoreau, it is one side of the anthropomorphic coin on whose other side is stamped the neighbor. Seen from this point of view, it seems significant that "Brute Neighbors," in which actual animals are referred to, should follow immediately upon "Higher Laws" like a kind of critical comment on such symbolic exploitation.

Already in *A Week on the Concord and Merrimack Rivers* Thoreau had insisted on the necessity of finding a nonanthropocentric way of looking at, thinking about, and representing animals, a way of moving, in his own terms, from the beast of burden to the neighbor. In the following passage, for example, he criticizes the exploitation of the Concord River's waterpower, which barred the shad population from migrating upstream to spawn so that it would eventually disappear from this environment: "Away with the superficial and selfish *philanthropy* of men,—who knows what admirable virtue of fishes may be below low-water mark, bearing up against a hard destiny, not admired by that fellow creature who alone can appreciate it! Who hears the fishes when they cry?" (*Wk* 37).[4] Humans, because of their unthinking anthropocentrism ("superficial and selfish"), are unwilling to consider the living conditions of a shad. At the same time, what makes us specifically human is our potential to appreciate the "virtue" or intrinsic quality of nonhuman animals; we alone, Thoreau argues, are "fellow creatures" capable of such empathy. Here, he seems to be specifically thinking of animal suffering ("the cry" of the fish) in terms he probably knew from Jeremy Bentham's famous remarks on the subject.[5] More profoundly, though, he defines the very essence of humanity in terms of empathy between human and nonhuman animals—in terms of particularity within continuity, one might say. It might be added here that several of the higher primates, as modern ethological studies have shown, *are* capable of empathy with the feelings of others, even across species boundaries. Of course, the shad passage, not least by its emotional appeal, is blatantly anthropomorphic, an example of what is sometimes called the "pathetic fallacy." The shad, too, are made to carry the burden of human thought. But here Thoreau is not concerned with reinforcing the species boundaries through symbolic appropriation; on the contrary, he tries to reach beyond "phil-anthropy." Such reaching beyond is represented by the metaphor of neighborhood with animals.

The ethical implications of this trope are succinctly summarized in Buell's comment on personification in nature writing from Thoreau to the present: "Ban[ning] pathetic fallacy—were such a thing possible—would be worse than accept[ing] its unavoidable excesses. For without it, environmental care might not find its voice" (*Environmental Imagination* 218). A rhetoric of empathy and care, Buell argues, unavoidably resorts to anthropomorphic tropes, though he is very careful to circumscribe such imagery: "The rhetoric of nature's personhood speaks merely to the nominal level; what counts is the underlying ethical orientation implied in the troping" (217). To rephrase this using Thoreau's images: even as neighbors, animals in *Walden* to some extent remain beasts of burden; their load is the "ethical orientation" (or reorientation) of Thoreau's thinking about nature. Yet, is neighborhood *only* a rhetorical device employed in the service of environmental care? Does it speak *merely* "to the nominal level," as Buell claims? In the second part of this essay, I want to argue that this trope stands for a way of representing animals and animality that foreshadows some of the discursive practices of modern ethology and, more generally, of contemporary animal and posthumanist studies. It can be described in terms of what ethologist Marc Bekoff calls "critical anthropomorphism" ("Wild Justice" 73), that is, anthropomorphism that questions its very quality as a trope.

Critical Anthropomorphism

Thoreau's insistence on neighborly relations with the nonhuman environment seems to express a certain dissatisfaction with the scientific disciplines of botany and zoology (though this is less evident in *Walden* itself). In an essay on Thoreau's relationship to systematic biology, Philip Cafaro (1998: 2), for instance, quotes an entry from the Journal that also contains the neighborhood trope: "Still I never studied botany, and do not to-day systematically, the most natural system is still so artificial. I wanted to know my neighbors, if possible,—to get a little nearer to them" (*J* IX: 157).[6] Thoreau here extends the concept of neighborhood to all living things, flora and fauna. (I will return to this extension of the trope in the conclusion to this essay.) The category of the neighbor is employed in contradistinction to a strictly scientific approach to nature. It underlines proximity or, even, intimacy as well as prudence ("to know my neighbors, if possible") rather than systematizing and classification. In this passage, Thoreau (like other romantic naturalists, e.g., Goethe) presents "hard" science as incomplete or artificial, despite his respect for modern biology and his use of certain of its methods (e.g., dissection). Knowing his neighbors, then, marks Thoreau's opposition to the traditional binary mode of thinking about nonhuman nature, animals in particular, that Derrida defines as the alternative between "appropriating projection" ("la projection appropriante," i.e., traditional anthropomorphism) and "severing interruption" ("l'interruption coupante," i.e., objectifying scientific discourse [Derrida, "L'animal" 269]). The neighborhood metaphor, by contrast, seems to combine scientific interest, environmental care, and aesthetic appreciation. It marks an attitude or a practice with respect to the natural world that refuses appropriation without accepting severance. In that respect, it is no longer "merely" a trope.

A comparable unmaking of metaphor occurs in the field of ethology. For primatologists like Jane Goodall, Barbara Smuts, and Frans de Waal, for example, the *personhood* of the animals they study is more than a simple rhetorical device expressing their scientific ethics. The notion of personhood defines their object of study and their relation to it. In the field of ethology, and in primate studies in particular, anthropomorphism is no longer universally considered "that worst of ethological sins" (Goodall 12). Bekoff speaks of the need for "cognitive empathy" with animals, which he defines thus: "As humans studying other animals, we cannot totally lose our anthropocentric perspective. But we can try as hard as possible to combine the animals' viewpoints to the ways in which we study, describe, interpret, and explain their behavior" (*Emotional Lives* 74).[7] Such an approach is also suggested by Thoreau's concept of neighborly relations with the animal world. There are numerous examples in *Walden* (and of course elsewhere in Thoreau's writings) that remind us of Bekoff's method of "combin[ing] the animal's viewpoint" with human representations of their behavior and thus of demonstrating "cognitive empathy."

In the following passage from the "Sounds" chapter, for example, Thoreau considers keeping a cockerel merely "for his music." But, then, a domesticated animal is, in a sense, no longer itself: "The note of this once wild Indian pheasant is certainly the most remarkable of any birds, and if they could be naturalized without being domesticated, it would soon become the most famous sound in our woods, surpassing the clangor of the goose and the hooting of the owl" (*W* 127). Notice in this passage the opposition between domestic and "naturalized" animals. How indeed can humans bring wild animals to adapt to human presence without denaturing them by domestication? While domestication implies raising and exploiting animals principally for food and labor, naturalizing the cockerel (i.e., settling the "once wild Indian pheasant" in the forests around Concord, an environment marked by human use), were such a thing still possible, would mean appreciating it for its intrinsic quality, that is, for its song. The naturalized cockerel, too, is exploited, but only inasmuch as its wild nature can give humans pleasure. Here Thoreau speaks especially of aesthetic pleasure, but in his argument in favor of neighborly relations with animals the aesthetic is only a part, though a crucial part, of a larger ethics that calls—as in the case, quoted earlier, of the Concord River shad—for an appreciation of animals on their own terms. The cockerel, in Thoreau's fantasy, is assimilated *and* wild at the same time. The burden of such a form of assimilation ultimately lies on humans, for the animal has not asked to be naturalized within their society.[8] In return for the proximity, knowledge, and pleasure they seek, humans must learn to appreciate and understand an animal's living conditions and habits. They, too, must become, so to speak, *nature-alized*. Such neighborhood demands a high degree of "cognitive empathy." One might add here that the distinction between domesticating and naturalizing could also be used to explain the difference between conventional anthropomorphism (the beast of burden) and Thoreau's critical brand (neighborhood).

It is to describe this kind of transformational relation with animals that cultural anthropologist Donna Haraway employs the term "significant otherness" (*Companion*, 3 passim), a relation contrasting radically with the conventional speciesism by dint of which the animal as nonperson defines the human-as-person. In the "naturecultural" world we inhabit, Haraway argues, humans and animals are always each other's "companion species," or, put differently, they are coconstitutive (32). Anthropomorphic tropes, then, may figure, even epitomize, our inevitably intermingled and interdependent relations with animals. Tropes of personhood, Haraway claims, are "necessary to keep the humans alert to the fact that somebody is at home" in the animals they encounter, study, or work with (50). There can be no doubt that for Thoreau "somebody is at home" when he goes to visit his "brute neighbors" and that those neighbors' otherness (e.g., the cockerel's crowing) is deeply significant to him. In the "Sounds" chapter, still, he goes so far as to describe his version of the *vita contemplativa*, which to ordinary human society might appear purely wasteful, as being in harmony with the lives of animals and plants: "As the sparrow had its trill, sitting on the hickory before my door, so had I my chuckle or suppressed warble which he might hear out of my nest. . . . This was sheer idleness to my fellow-townsmen, no doubt; but if the birds and the flowers had tried me by their standard, I should not have been found wanting" (*W* 112). Clearly, Thoreau is using animals here to criticize what he considered a life dominated by work, property, and other material concerns. His celebration of the "standard" that birds and even flowers would apply in order to judge the quality of life originates in a traditional satirical strategy, the kind Jonathan Swift employs in book 4 of *Gulliver's Travels*, for example. Yet here the implications of imagining human behavior from the nonhuman "other's" point of view (hence the reference to Thoreau's cabin as a "nest") goes well beyond Swift's satiric denunciation of instrumental reason in the name of horse sense (if the pun be allowed). Nonhuman nature is given a significant (i.e., signifying *and* important) role, for the person who has learned to appreciate its otherness thereby enriches the criteria by which he or she can make sense of his or her own life. Though Thoreau remains vague about the specific qualities of the nonhuman neighbors (the sparrow, the flowers) mentioned in this passage, the implications of making them judges of his behavior allow him to imagine their presence in terms of "significant otherness."

Relationships of "significant otherness," then, demand not only precise observation and appreciation of our fellow creatures' habits and habitats but also that we get to know them individually, not just as a group or species. Personalizing, or "naturalizing," the human-animal encounter in this manner implies a questioning of one's own (human) notion of personhood. Individualization and personalizing of animals is indeed frequent in *Walden*. One of the many examples is the loon that Thoreau describes as playing a prolonged game of hide-and-seek in the pond with him. The essence of Thoreau's evocation of this game concerns the way in which each player tries to anticipate the other's moves: "While he was thinking one thing in his brain, I was endeavoring to divine his thought in mine. It was a pretty game, played on the smooth surface of the pond, a man against a loon. Suddenly your adversary's checker disappears beneath the board and the problem is to place yours nearest to where his will appear again" (*W* 235). Thoreau describes the man and the animal as partners in a game whose rules they have laid down together and that they both respect. The game is a way of inviting the human player to *think like a loon* ("to divine his thought in mine"). He compares the pond's surface to the board in a game of checkers, a game in the course of which the personality of the loon, of *this* particular loon, emerges. Playing with the loon—as we might with a dog or cat—thus personalizes it or, in Vinciane Despret's term, transforms it into a "nonhuman person" ("devenir personne autre qu'humaine") (89). Despret develops her concept of nonanthropocentric personhood in trying to capture the effect of a series of portraits of great apes made by photographer Chris Herzfeld. These portraits—the anthropomorphic term is precisely to the point here—literally illustrate the work of ethologists like those mentioned earlier insofar as they at once individualize their subject and establish that subject as the product of a relation between observer and observed.[9] Though certainly more conventional than Herzfeld's photography, Thoreau's narrative about playing with a loon nevertheless serves, like the ape portraits, to individualize the animal and to try to think like or with it—an act of empathy that is for Thoreau always also a way of reflecting on the human. Several other examples of individual appreciation of an animal in *Walden*—arguably including even the victorious but terribly wounded black ant at the end of the ant battle—could be mentioned. Animals thus become "nonhuman persons" in Despret's sense. To use Cafaro's terms, Thoreau's representation of them embodies the essence of his naturalism: "(1) The existence and value of particular knowledge; and (2) the existence and value of acquaintance irrespective of knowledge" ("Thoreau on Science" 3).

Perhaps concepts like "significant otherness" and "nonhuman personhood" also help to throw further light on Thoreau's preference for wild (or, as we have seen, "naturalized") animals over domestic ones, which he considered denatured by human exploitation: "I kept neither dog, cat, cow, pig, nor hens, so that you would have said there was a deficiency of domestic sounds. . . . No cockerels to crow nor hens to cackle in the yard. No yard! but unfenced Nature reaching up to your very sills" (*W* 127–28). Domestic animals cannot be neighbors in the critical sense of that trope because they have been partly deprived of their otherness or, as Thoreau might have said, of their "virtues" (though many a cat or dog owner would object to this).[10] Personalizing a pet, as we so often do, does not entail the process of mutual assimilation and transformation envisioned by Thoreau. When he insists in describing his Walden neighborhood that "the nearest of blood to me and humanest was not a person nor a villager" (*W* 132), such blurring of the species boundary is not a question of preferring animals to humans or of shunning human society, let alone a question of wanting to extend to animals the "rights" that we reserve for our own species. What is at stake in Thoreau's preference of wild over domestic animals are "animal rites," to use Cary Wolfe's pun, and, extending that pun, "animal writes," that is, the ways we conceive of and represent animality in thinking of our human place in the order of things. (Perhaps we can take the ungrammatical "humanest" as an expression of the sense of exploration vehicled by such [w]rites.) Seen thus, the idea of a *wild* neighborhood is only seemingly paradoxical. As Haraway might say, Thoreau's wildness is "naturecultural."

Interspecies Translation

Finally, the notion under which we can perhaps subsume the examples mentioned in this discussion of "critical anthropomorphism" in *Walden* is that of translation. In adopting for our purposes the arguments of an essay by Elisabeth de Fontenay on "translating the language of beasts" ("traduire le parler des bêtes") we could represent Thoreau's efforts at establishing neighborly relations as a form of translation. Translation, too, is an anthropomorphic trope in this context but, like all the others, a trope that strains at its figurality. De Fontenay bases her argument in favor of interspecies translation on Walter Benjamin's reflections on the origins of language and on translation, in particular on his claim that the nature of things, be they animate or inanimate, reveals itself in language, "for it is of the essence of each thing to manifest its spiritual content. Seen thus, the word 'language' is by no means a metaphor" (*Sprache* 30).[11] On the contrary, for Benjamin the languages of all phenomena are interconnected. The nature of human beings is in their language: they speak in words and are therefore capable of naming things. In Benjamin's philosophy of language, translation holds a very particular status: it is "the passage from one language into another by a series of continual metamorphoses" (42). Such communication is an "uninterrupted flux [that] runs all through nature, from the lowest existing creatures to humans and from humans to God" (48). For Benjamin, a successful translation relies less on achieving a direct correspondence between signifiers than in suggesting what both the original and the target language have in common *as* language. Therefore, a successful translation is like an allegory of "pure language." It follows from this, according to de Fontenay, that human language, the most highly developed, can be considered as a translation of all the others: it is an expression of both singularity and of continuity. There are many passages in *Walden* that do indeed suggest an "uninterrupted flux" of communication and several that show us Thoreau as translator in de Fontenay's (and Benjamin's) sense. Here, for example, is Thoreau's representation of the cry of the cat-owl responding to the honking of geese (in "Winter Animals"): "Suddenly an unmistakable cat-owl from very near me, with the most harsh and tremendous voice I ever heard from an inhabitant of the woods, responded at regular intervals to the goose, as if determined to expose and disgrace this intruder from Hudson's Bay . . . and *boo-hoo* him out of Concord horizon. What do you mean by alarming the citadel at this time of night consecrated to me?" (*W* 272). This is not a scientific account of animal communication, it is a translation. Nor does Thoreau attempt to purge his text of the most obvious anthropomorphism. He does not pretend that he *knows* why the owl is hooting as it does, though experience and observation, always the basis of his writing, tell him he cannot be far off the mark. That is why his "translation" is preceded by *as if*. His intention here is to underline the necessity of a "discriminating ear": "If you had a discriminating ear, there were in [the hooting] the elements of a concord such as these plains never saw nor heard" (*W* 272). To a finely tuned ear the owl's cry represents the interconnectedness of life. It is, therefore, in "concord" with its environment, and Thoreau's effort at translating it expresses his will to represent himself as part of the flux. Translation is, then, a way of breaking the silence to which we condemned the lives of animals when, to return to Darwin's comment quoted at the beginning of this essay, "man [became] his own classifier," founding "a separate order for his own reception."[12] As employed by de Fontenay, translation as a trope *and* as an act of "cognitive empathy" (Bekoff) is on the cutting edge between separation and continuity: it is a kind of metatrope. As a result, the idea of translation seems to me to epitomize the development of "critical anthropomorphism" that I have tried to trace from Thoreau's neighborhood metaphor to contemporary animal studies.

But perhaps that is too harmonious a vision.[13] In Thoreau's practice, translating the cries of animals is an animal rite that may also suggest the risk and perhaps even the terror inherent in opening oneself to the animal other. It is useful at this point to recall Thoreau's wariness (analyzed in an earlier part of this article) concerning his animal instincts, metaphorically described as a "reptile and sensual" animal that lurked within him and that could cause havoc in a life devoted to spirituality. At any rate, translation for Thoreau, to use anthropologist Victor Turner's terminology, seems to be a "liminal experience," an experience that displaces borderlines. Turner employs the notion of liminality in his definition of the notion of ritual (or rite), which he also describes as a "transformative self-immolation of order" (164). If the rite of translation in Thoreau's *Walden* is such a liminal and transformative experience, then this would suggest that translation is less an act of transferring sense from one side (the animal) to another (the human) than of a double transformation in the course of which the target language is also transformed or, in this case, animalized. Consider, for example, the following passage in which Thoreau once more translates the cries of owls (screech owls in this case). "I love to hear their wailing," he tells us, "reminding me sometimes of music and singing birds; as if it were the dark and tearful side of music, the regrets and sighs that would fain be sung" (*W* 124). Here already the bird's cries seem to echo buried or concealed words in the human hearer that only music can otherwise evoke. Farther along in the same passage on the screech owls we read: "They give me a new sense of the variety and capacity of that nature which is our common dwelling. *Oh-o-o-o-o that I never had been bor-r-r-n!* sighs one on this side of the pond, and circles with the restlessness of despair to some new perch on the gray oaks. Then—*that I never had been bor-r-r-n!* echoes another on the farther side with tremulous sincerity, and—*bor-r-r-n!* comes faintly from far in the Lincoln woods" (*W* 124–25). Owls, Thoreau claims, summing up his observations on their cries, "represent the stark twilight and unsatisfied thoughts which all have"

(*W* 125). Though this sentence may read like a conventional anthropomorphic trope, it clearly is more than that in the context. The owls really do re-*present* something that is common to all living creatures. The word *bor-r-r-r-n!* is not an onomatopoeia but the translated language of nature (*natus*) itself. This is both exhilarating and terrifying—liminal, in Turner's term—so much so that Thoreau's relations with his "brute neighbors" will sometimes make him appeal to those "higher laws" that safely place certain of his instincts on the far side of the human-animal divide. The anthropomorphic coin will then be flipped from its neighborly to its theriomorphic face. Though poetically and ethically inspiring to Thoreau, neighborhood with animals is not always intellectually reassuring.

If Thoreau's representation of his "brute neighbors" in *Walden* seems to foreshadow contemporary debates about the lives of animals—Bekoff, Derrida, Haraway, and others were mentioned—this is the result of his sensitivity, noticeable throughout *Walden*, to the anthropomorphism that inevitably accompanies even the most Darwinian description of animals.[14] As the examples I have mentioned tend to show, Thoreau is keenly conscious of an ambiguity between symbolic exploitation and symbolic exploration. It is the latter path that he privileges, though the beast of burden and the neighbor cannot be clearly separated—on the contrary, the metaphor of the neighbor implies that of the beast of burden. In *Walden* this metaphor is the heart of a rhetoric of care and of fellowship with living creatures that does not try to conceal its artificiality. Nor does it conceal the influence of Christian morality. Such rhetoric can at times even be extended from animals to plants so as to embrace *all* living things. And yet, though neighborhood tends to be understood as all-embracing in *Walden*, animals do get to play a special part. It is in describing his neighborly relations with them that Thoreau seems to question the metaphorical value of his tropes in a way that invites comparison with the "critical anthropomorphism" of Bekoff and with such concepts as Despret's "nonanthropomorphic personhood." Perhaps by extending the kind of analysis proposed in this article to his other writings, especially the later ones, we could give a more solid grounding to the observation that Thoreau uses such tropes in a struggle to establish a nonanthropocentric point of vantage between the opposed extremes of symbolic appropriation of and objectivist separation from animals. That is at least what studies like Philip Cafaro's devoted to Thoreau's relationship to biology seem to suggest (see Cafaro, *Thoreau's Living Ethics*). Such an extension of my approach would have to include a comparison with Darwin, who was as keenly aware as Thoreau himself of the problem of anthropomorphism, especially in an evolutionary perspective. One could thus confirm that for Thoreau eco- or biocentrism was less a question of purging language of its "anthropocentric residue" (Norris 52) than of employing tropes critically. To put this differently, what is "modern" in Thoreau's use of tropes is the rapprochement between the poetic (or even mystical) and the scientific. Modern ethology has to some extent proved the poets—among whom one can include Thoreau—right. Finally, then, the effect of representing nonhuman animals as neighbors in *Walden* is to stress continuity or, conversely, to stress that humans are "literary animals," that is, animals whose particularity consists in telling stories to make sense of the ways we live together with other animals in our common neighborhood.[15]

NOTES

1. This ambiguity is exploited, for example, in Franz Kafka's beast fables such as "A Report to an Academy" and "The Metamorphosis." For insightful and relevant discussions of Kafka's beast fables, see Norris; Coetzee.

2. Margot Norris's study of twentieth-century biocentric discourse posits Darwin and Nietzsche as nineteenth-century precursors. The point of this essay is to show that Thoreau's practice (or poetics) of anthropomorphism, like that of Darwin and Nietzsche, makes of the animals in *Walden* (and elsewhere in his work) "beasts of the modern imagination" (cf. Norris, especially 26–52).

3. "Pilpay" is a reference to a famous collection of Hindu fables which, translated into various European languages, became one of the principal sources of inspiration of the genre of the beast fable from the Middle Ages to the eighteenth century (notably of La Fontaine's fables).

4. Thoreau's etymological use of the heavily connoted term *philanthropy* is of course ironic (the irony being indicated by the hyphen). Employed in this manner, "phil-anthropy" highlights the "discourse of species" and thus becomes almost synonymous with anthropocentrism. The first use of the latter term is recorded in the *OED* in 1863. This passage is extensively discussed by Cafaro, who singles it out as a significant example of Thoreau's emerging environmental ethics or "living ethics" (*Thoreau's Living Ethics* 139–74).

5. In his *Principles of Morals and Legislation* (1789), Bentham criticizes the idea of human superiority over animals in the following terms: "What else is it that should trace

the insuperable line? Is it the faculty of reason, or, perhaps, the faculty of discourse? But a full-grown horse or dog is beyond comparison a more rational, as well as more conversable animal, than an infant of a day, or a week, or even a month, old. But suppose the case were otherwise, what would it avail? The question is not, Can they *reason*? Nor, Can they *talk*? But, Can they *suffer*?" (from Kalof and Fitzgerald 9).

6. In this passage Thoreau reflects on the difference between systematic botanizing (with the help of scientific classification) and an approach that comes "naturally" to him and whose ideal is "attain[ing] to familiarity" with the plant world. Cafaro ("Thoreau on Science" 2–3) analyzes this passage as a typical example of Thoreau's "neighborly" and globalizing conception of nature study, developed to counter scientific approaches that tend to isolate the phenomena they study rather than trying to grasp them as parts of an environmental whole.

7. Bekoff also insists that "anthropomorphizing is an evolved perceptual strategy; we've been shaped by natural selection to view animals in this way" ("Wild Justice" 10).

8. It is noteworthy that in *On the Origin of Species* Darwin introduces the idea of natural selection in contradistinction to the domestic artificial form of selection employed by humans since the Paleolithic to "improve" certain qualities of the animals they raised for food, work, and companionship. As Ritvo puts it: "Over the past three centuries animal breeding has become a highly technical, self-conscious, and institutionalized process—a form of bioengineering before the fact" (136).

9. Despret's theoretical references also include such founding figures of modern ethology as Konrad Lorenz and Adolf Portman.

10. Antoine Cazé has pointed out to me that the result of Thoreau's (and many ecocritics') celebration of wilderness (and wildness) is to place the words "ecological" and "domestic" in opposition to each other, though they derive from the same idea: that of the dwelling, home, or hearth (*oikos* and *domus*). In the passage quoted above, the yard as a transitional space between wild nature and civilization is rejected by Thoreau, who prefers instead an imaginary continuity between the periphery ("unfenced nature") and the center ("your very sills").

11. The quotations from Benjamin in this paragraph are taken from the German original of the essays ("Über Sprache überhaupt und über die Sprache des Menschen" and "Die Aufgabe des Übersetzers"); the translations are my own. De Fontenay's study is based on the same passages from Benjamin, which she quotes in a French translation.

12. Why should we consider translating animal communication in the first place? De Fontenay's answer to this question seems to elaborate on Darwin's remark: "Because in nature as a whole and in animality in particular there is to be found a ubiquitous language of the mute, and because we cannot tell if the melancholy of animals is the result of their being mute or if their muteness is caused by the sad fact that they are named and

described by that human language they can never know. We have found in Benjamin's fragments a justification for submitting translation to a metaphorical and hyperbolical extension that grant it a consoling and quasi redemptive power" (33, my translation). For the wider philosophical background of de Fontenay's reflections on animality, see her monumental *Le silence des bêtes: La philosophie à l'épreuve de l'animalité* (Paris: Fayard, 1998).

13. A darker reading of the neighborhood trope is suggested by Michel Imbert's analysis of Thoreau's "tawny grammar" in "Walking" and in *Walden*. See Imbert's essay in this volume, whose influence on my own work I duly acknowledge here. In theoretical terms, the difference between Imbert's and my own approach could perhaps be summarized by the opposition between Deleuze's concept of "becoming animal" and Despret's of "becoming a nonhuman person." For a critical discussion of this opposition, see Haraway, *When Species Meet* 35–42.

14. Norris underlines the intense literary and critical sensitivity shown by Darwin with respect to the anthropocentric quality of his writing through "an awareness of the constraints placed upon scientific thought by a language whose very syntax permeates nature with the metaphysics of the subject ('It rains,' 'Es regnet,' 'Il pleut') and whose words for natural processes (selection, creation, affinity) must be continually purged of their anthropocentric residue" (52).

15. Thus the title of the collection of neo-Darwinian essays edited by Jonathan Gottschall and David Sloan Wilson, *The Literary Animal: Evolution and the Nature of Narrative* (Evanston, Ill.: Northwestern University Press, 2005). It is interesting to speculate on the correspondences between the neo-Darwinian idea of the "literary animal" and Benjamin's theory of translation, which posits human language and its capacity to name as a translation of all other forms of communication found in nature.

"Tawny Grammar"

WORDS IN THE WILD

THOREAU'S CALL IN "Walking" for the regeneration of European culture in the New World by regrounding it in wild nature can be interpreted within the context of contemporary discourse on America's Manifest Destiny. However, if Thoreau's call for a new ecology in this essay is decidedly "modern," it cannot, as nature, be reduced to the "nation's nature," in Perry Miller's words; on the contrary, it must be acknowledged as the unnameable nonhuman. Writing on wildness no longer meant reading through the Book of Nature and reinterpreting it in spiritual terms, as in Emerson's *Nature* (1836), but instead recognizing its significant otherness, which cannot be translated.

"I wish to speak a word for Nature, for absolute Freedom and Wildness" (*Exc* 185). In the opening sentence of "Walking," speaking for wildness means, ambiguously, speaking both on behalf of and instead of. How can wildness be advocated without being adulterated, by the same token, through the medium of words? In what sense can going wild be expressed without being reconfigured altogether? To what extent does language preclude wildness by containing it within a lexical system or a syntactical order? Or can wildness be spelled out precisely through the disruption of linguistic forms? In "Walking," Thoreau extols wildness in more or less conventional ways from a linguistic standpoint. He can praise it as a form of intense vitality through, for instance, a maxim like "Life consists with Wildness. The most alive is the wildest" (*Exc* 203)—a comparatively tame and abstract aphorism that asserts the compatibility between the two terms, which are ultimately equated. The writer's profession of faith may sound deceptively mild and mellow at first: "I believe in the forest, and in the meadow, and in the night in which the corn grows" (*Exc* 202).[1]

But then the text proceeds with an apparently factual statement that is incredibly graphic and gruesome in comparison: "The Hottentots eagerly devour the marrow of the Koodoo and other antelopes raw, as a matter of course" (*Exc* 202). The harshness of the act of devouring "the marrow of the koodoo" raw is compounded by the adverb "eagerly," which suggests in addition a form of obscene overindulgence. When Thoreau pleads for a return to a wildness that no civilization can face, he resorts again to the same forceful image to conjure up an unbearable sight, which this time involves the Western observer: "Give me a Wildness whose glance no civilization can endure,—as if we lived on the marrow of koodoos devoured raw" (*Exc* 202). Imagining ourselves feeding on raw meat like Hottentots leads to the final identification between our innermost selves and our estranged doubles: "We have a wild savage in us" (*Exc* 213). The phrasing gradually defamiliarizes and performs uncanny displacements between the far and the near, kin and kind. Ultimately, it is the boundary line between men and animals that gets blurred. Significantly enough, their bewildering conflation is rendered through the introduction of a puzzling foreign phrase, immediately translated literally into English: "*Gramatica parda*, tawny grammar": "There are other letters for the child to learn than those which Cadmus invented. The Spaniards have a good term to express this wild and dusky knowledge—*Gramatica parda*—tawny grammar—a kind of mother wit derived from the same leopard to which I have referred" (*Exc* 214).[2]

The passage Thoreau alludes to comes on the preceding page: "Here is this vast, savage, howling Mother of ours, Nature lying all around, with such beauty, and such affection for her children, as the leopard" (Exc 213). The expression "tawny grammar" reminds us that there is throughout *Walden* a pervasive obsession with alternative languages, including the sounds of "Brute Neighbors" and the physical marks made on thawing clay. It may hint at a language distinct from the two languages discriminated between in *Walden*: neither the abstract "father tongue" nor even the "mother tongue," properly speaking, but a language that dates back to an earlier stage than language learning, the language of animals and body language. English words in *Walden* tend to go wild again, turn tawny, as they aim at reinterpreting, translating nonverbal signs, animal sounds, or visual indexes of beastly bodies. They betray "the tonic of wildness" (*W* 317) and finally register the fury of the struggle for life in crude terms that are reminiscent of the previous quotations from "Walking": "We are cheered when we observe the vulture feeding on the carrion which disgusts and disheartens us and deriving health and strength from the repast" (*W* 318).

Higher Laws

In the chapter titled "Reading," Thoreau pits the oral mother tongue, characterized by its fluctuations, against the formality of the father tongue and likens reading, that is to say, the learning of the more chiseled and hieratic father tongue, to a kind of symbolic rebirth, learning to speak again in a sparse, crystal-clear style:

> Books must be read as deliberately and reservedly as they were written. It is not enough even to be able to speak the language of that nation by which they are written, for there is a memorable interval between the language heard and the language read. The one is commonly transitory, a sound, a tongue, a dialect merely, almost brutish, and we learn it unconsciously, like the brutes, from our mothers. The other is the maturity and experience of that; if that is our mother tongue, this is our father tongue, a reserved and select expression, too significant to be heard by the ear, which we must be born again in order to speak. (*W* 101)

Having imbibed the mother tongue "unconsciously" from early childhood onward, one's relationship to one's mother tongue is sensual, animal-like, almost "brutish" in his words, whereas the more "reserved" father tongue introduces the discipline of *logos*, rationalization and restraint. The father tongue raises and erases the mother tongue, sublimating it into a purer language. The transformation involves refining the coarse materiality of oral speech through the agency of choice words, "select expression."

The same logic of spiritualization and sublimation is at work in the chapter titled "Higher Laws." Thoreau acknowledges his dual attraction to savagery and spiritual life, the longing for elevation, and, conversely, the urge to go wild (Tissot 229). The chapter opens with the recognition of the enduring presence of animal instincts within the civilized self, but only to transcend them. It begins, tellingly enough, with the admission of an almost irrepressible urge to eat up a woodchuck raw and to derive "a strange thrill of savage delight" from the act: "I caught a glimpse of the woodchuck stealing across my path, and felt a strange thrill of savage delight, and was strongly tempted to seize and devour him raw; not that I was hungry then, except for that wildness which he represented" (*W* 210). The barbarity of the act is partly denied, though, as the narrator claims to hunger for a more abstract "wildness." Later on, Thoreau compares himself to a half-starved hound lying in wait for any kind of game, and he stipulates

again that his purpose was not to satisfy hunger but to take in wild life symbolically. In this respect, the text contains the explicit recognition of an underlying
beastliness in ourselves that cannot be evaded altogether, that surfaces in states
of unconsciousness: "We are conscious of an animal in us, which awakens in
proportion as our higher nature slumbers. Possibly, we may withdraw from it,
but never change its nature" (*W* 219). Nevertheless, the chapter ends with the
need to spiritualize "this slimy, beastly life" (*W* 218) and to purify the animal
self, "to let his mind descend into his body and redeem it" (*W* 222). Hence, the
effort to cleanse the body by means of strict self-discipline and, incidentally, by
following a strict vegetarian diet: "Nature is hard to overcome but she must be
overcome" (*W* 221).

Sounds

And yet, for all this self-discipline and despite the suppression of the mother
tongue in the name of the father tongue, Thoreau expresses his fascination for an
almost forgotten language, the nonverbal signs of nature prior to language that
is supposed to be metaphorical, at a second remove from the real thing: "We are
in danger of forgetting the language which all things and events speak without
metaphor, which alone is copious and standard" (*W* 111). Animal sounds or animal tracks, which are indexes, unmediated signals, point to an archaic stratum
of language more primeval than "written languages, which are themselves but
dialects and provincial" (*W* 111), subdued forms of the mother tongue. Animal
sounds are called "the very *lingua vernacula* of Walden Wood" (*W* 272).

It is tempting of course to reinterpret those natural signs through the prism
of our language and to assume they have a meaning, just as animal marks can
be described as typographical characters. Saying, for instance, "the fine print,
the small type of a deer mouse was to be seen" (*W* 267) amounts to likening the
Book of Nature to a printed page. Similarly, animal sounds can be rendered
through onomatopoeia and ascribed a meaning. The wailing of an owl is mock-
ingly rendered through an overdetermined sequence of sounds: "*Oh-o-o-o-o
that I never had been bor-r-r-n!*" (*W* 124), and it is supposed to spell out inexpressible suffering. The onomatopoeia can in their turn be retranslated into allegedly meaningful phrases: "*Hoo hoo hoo, hooer hoo*, sounded sonorously, and
the first three syllables accented somewhat like *how der do*" (*W* 272). Thoreau
resorts at times to anthropomorphic comparisons: "The hare in its extremity

cries like a child" (*W* 212); he depicts a squirrel "chiding all imaginary specta-
tors, soliloquizing and talking to all the universe at the same time" (*W* 274);
at one point, he even endows a cat-owl with speech through the use of proso-
popoeia (*W* 272).

It must be noted, however, that Thoreau also deliberately refrains from changing the beasts into talking animals and exposes himself to their uncanny foreign
language. Beasts are precisely tongue-tied creatures, endeavoring to express
themselves in vain. Their ill-fated babbling sounds, which remain unintelligible,
are particularly apt, therefore, to convey the "unsatisfied thoughts which all
have" (*W* 125). In the chapter titled "Winter Animals," Thoreau evokes strange
metamorphoses, foxes turned dogs as if they sought to find at last an adequate
way of expressing themselves: "Sometimes I heard the foxes as they ranged over
the snow crust, in moonlight nights, in search of a partridge or other game, barking raggedly and demoniacally like forest dogs, as if laboring with some anxiety,
or seeking expression, struggling for light and to be dogs outright" (*W* 273).
Thoreau, rather than resorting to onomatopoeia, may describe those sounds as
an odd combination of composite sounds, a whole "choir," half-human, half-
animal-like, sounds cluttered with eerie harmonics. He then proceeds to unfold
the complex train of thoughts triggered by those sounds:

> I was also serenaded by a hooting owl. Near at hand you could fancy it the most
> melancholy sound in Nature, as if she meant by this to stereotype and make per-
> manent in her choir the dying moans of a human being,—some poor weak relic
> of mortality who has left hope behind, and howls like an animal, yet with hu-
> man sobs, on entering the dark valley, made more awful by a certain gurgling
> melodiousness,—I find myself beginning with the letters gl when I try to imitate
> it,—expressive of a mind which has reached the gelatinous mildewy stage in the
> mortification of all healthy and courageous thought. It reminded me of ghouls
> and idiots and insane howlings. (*W* 125)

The sound of the owl, which is "the traditional bird of philosophy" (Cavell,
Senses 37), here is both dismal and musical; it is characterized by "a certain
gurgling melodiousness" and conjures up a mental state of despondency and a
heightened sense of decay, a far cry from Chanticleer's crowing (57). The ominous sound is tentatively rendered through a verbal equivalent, the word "gurgling," the combination of a guttural and a labial sound producing a sense of
sticky, viscous matter, a "gelatinous mildewy stage." Ultimately, the odd sound is

associated with the ravings and rantings of idiots and lunatics. The senseless animal sound is gradually internalized and seems to point to the wild man within, grown insane. The animal sound finally echoes an inner state of dementia that is inexpressible through the medium of articulate language (Susini 186–87). Eventually, animals seem to talk for men, to talk in their place, on behalf of their inner wildness. Animals act as spokespersons, as in fables, thus remedying the failure of language to convey the "wild savage in us": "I rejoice that there are owls. Let them do the idiotic and maniacal hooting for men" (*W* 125).

Loons

Significantly enough, Thoreau is especially attracted to the loon, "making the woods ring with his wild laughter" (*W* 233). The loon's fabled laugh is indescribable. It sounds like "a demoniac laughter," though actually it seems to partake of a wolf's howl: "He uttered a long-drawn unearthly howl, probably more like that of a wolf than any bird; as when a beast puts his muzzle to the ground and deliberately howls. This was his looning,—perhaps the wildest sound that is ever heard here, making the woods ring far and wide" (*W* 236). The "unearthly" sound provides clues that unsettle familiar taxonomies. It is at once that of a bird and of a wolf. It seems to dig into the earth and to be reverberated by the ground. The fabulous cry cannot be placed clearly. The outlandish unclassifiable sound is then reinterpreted in human terms but only to realize the unbridgeable gap that lies between the animal kingdom and the nature lover keen on tracking sounds. The loon lures on its pursuer but cannot be caught: "I concluded that he laughed in derision of my efforts, confident of his own resources" (*W* 236). Revealingly enough, the mysterious howls it utters are suddenly shrouded in mist, as if the loon's voice had been a kind of "prayer" to an unknown god (*W* 236) to be screened from sight. The loon's intractable otherness is emphasized, and, as Daniel Peck has argued (119–21), the hunt that sets up a man *against* an animal suggests that subjectivity comes into being against the backdrop of an unattainable object that emerges from the spatial background of the lake.

Still, the bird whose chief feature is "his wild laugh" (*W* 234) seems to voice a whole state of mind, "having thrown his voice into his head." The loon's untranslatable lingo becomes a trope for one's innermost idiolect and an incentive to introspective deep diving: "This of the loon—I do not mean its laugh, but its looning—is a long-drawn call, as it were, singularly human to my ear,—*hoo-*

hoo-ooooo, like the hallooing of a man on a very high key, having sometimes thrown his voice into his head. I have heard a sound exactly like it when breathing heavily through my own nostrils, half awake at ten at night, suggesting my affinity to the loon; as if its language were but a dialect of my own, after all" (*MW* 224–25). Hunting entails a weird nuptial dance between two estranged doubles, the hunter and the loon being birds of a feather somehow, as if chasing the bird on the surface of the pond involved as well chasing away the animal within (*W* 234–36). A game of hide-and-seek, "a man against a loon" (*W* 235), with a bird whose main characteristic is its cunning, its unpredictability, and its ability to elude rational calculation and thus to stand for the irrational depths that cannot be fathomed altogether by the observing subject: "He manœuvred so cunningly that I could not get within half a dozen rods of him" (*W* 234). The bird keeps diving and surfacing unexpectedly, "for again and again, when I was straining my eyes over the surface one way, I would suddenly be startled by his unearthly laugh behind me" (*W* 235). What is tantalizing about the sound of the loon is that it seems to sound hidden depths of the mind or to signal something at the back of one's mind that escapes attention. It is not by chance that the loon should alight at a very precise spot on the pond where it is particularly wide and deep, precisely at the point of intersection between its greatest length and width (*W* 289), as if the loon pointed to a depth that is crossed out even as the surveyor claims to be able to calculate it by triangulating the pond's length and its width (*W* 290). True, the loon is merely a loon, but, as such, being an animal, that is to say, the other par excellence, it embodies the wild that withstands men's grasp. Then, the unsuccessful hunt becomes a metaphor for attempting to capture wild life symbolically and for the failure to articulate the loon, which is but the double or the "doubloon" of the wild man within.

The Animal Spirit of Letters

Animal sounds signal wildness without and within. So do the grotesque and arabesque figures that can be made out across a bank of thawing clay in "Spring," which reads like the Book of Nature writ large. The episode seems to foreground the genesis of letters in continual gestation, word formation from their roots, fanciful etymological ramifications more or less derived from Charles Kraitsir's philological conjectures (Gura 134–35). True, "the sand foliage" suggests that letters, words blossom, germinate like vegetable leaves or beans, "making the

yellow soil express its summer thought in bean leaves" (*W* 157), but it also suggests that they grow organically and that the transformation of words through a
series of flexions is akin to the metamorphosis of a larva into a butterfly: "Thus,
also, you pass from the lumpish grub in the earth to the airy and fluttering butterfly. The very globe continually transcends and translates itself, and becomes
winged in its orbit" (*W* 306–7). "The vitals of the animal body" (*W* 305) loom
into view again as the earth is excavated. Grotesque shapes are excreted from
the bowels of the earth, laying bare the remains of the mother tongue straitjack-
eted by the father tongue. Glyphs are not merely globes and, by and by, glob-
ules but corrupt material, matter continually generated and wasted away. The
scatological overtones of the passage need not be overemphasized. The subdued
body surfaces obscenely. The sight transports the engrossed reader back to the
source of an archaic tongue, the aboriginal language of the body that surges up
again, complex-free, underlying the formation of linguistic units. Words such
as "lap, flap" are parsed, decomposed letter by letter, atomized till the body
contained underground by the institution of language is let loose again. Reading from the Book of Nature consists in doing away with the strict discipline
advocated in "Economy," giving free rein to extravagance in the dual sense of
reckless expenditure, and divagation, linguistic speculations that exceed the
bounds of reason (Richard 113–39). As in "Walking," the ending of the chapter
extols the squandering of lives, the never-ending process of mass destruction:
"I love to see that Nature is so rife with life that myriads can be afforded to be
sacrificed and suffered to prey on one another" (*W* 318). Similarly, the subter-
ranean linguistic delirium disrupts the manifest fixed forms and subverts lexical
meaning under cover of learned philological derivations. The fantastical designs across the bank, slantwise, give rise to a whole linguistic extravaganza that
in a sense burlesques the metadiscourse of scholars. "Labor," "labium," "lips,"
"lapse," "lobe," "globe" (*W* 306) may be paronomasias, but they are not cognate.
The whole drift of the passage sounds like mock philology, wildcat etymology,
nonsensical fantasizing rather than erudite, well-grounded "scientific" lexicol-
ogy. The free play of letters here, which is relatively unchecked by the rules
that govern word formation and sentence building, questions any authority. The
thaw that unearths wild life at its rawest unsettles the assumed authority of the
author encoded in Thoreau's family name. This final chapter is less a *mise-en-
abyme* of the laboratory of the Artist that foregrounds the raw material of the
man of letters than the disclosure of barbarian, inarticulate, and decomposed

linguistic remnants that are autonomous from any overall meaning. After all, "What is man but a mass of thawing clay?" (*W* 307). The vital upsurge of tawny grammar is proportionate to the falling into decay of standard linguistic forms.

To conclude, the writer's strategy partakes of the crafty tactics of hunting games in order to track down the animal body, the wild man within, to let it speak on its own, independently from the author's authority, to uncover a bewildering subtext that can only well up through the dislocation of ordinary language, whether it be the mother tongue or the father tongue. For all his indebtedness to Charles Kraitsir's philological assumptions on etymological roots and word formation, Thoreau's reverie on the generation of words, envisioning them no longer as fixed types but as animated shifting signs, subtly adumbrates the modern eagerness to recapture and give utterance to some suppressed animality and the unspeakable otherness it figures.

.

NOTES

1. Laura Dassow Walls comments on both statements in her essay "Believing in Nature" (15).

2. Gary Snyder has devoted an essay to the phrase *Gramática parda* in *The Practice of the Wild* (48–77), and so has Neill Matheson, who notes that "the Spanish idiom *gramática parda* implies an alternative, nonstandard mode of knowledge, something like slyness, cunning, or savvy" (629). Matheson emphasizes the fact that *Pardo* "can refer to such pard colors as brown or dun, and more specifically to dark or brown skin color, and so by extension to people of mixed race ancestry" (630). Significantly, according to Matheson, "Walking" calls for a darkening of white American culture, regrounded in wild nature. I thank William Rossi for calling attention to these two essays.

Bibliography

Alcott, A. Bronson. *Concord Days*. Boston: Roberts Brothers, 1872.

———. *The Journals of Bronson Alcott*. Ed. Odell Shepard. Boston: Little, Brown, 1938.

Alger, William Rounseville. "The Hermit of Concord." *Monthly Religious Magazine* 35.6 (1866): 382–89.

Angelo, Ray. *The Journal of Henry David Thoreau: Botanical Index*. Salt Lake City, Utah: Peregrine Smith, 1984.

Aristotle. *The Complete Works of Aristotle: The Revised Oxford Translation*. Ed. Jonathan Barnes. 2 vols. Princeton, N.J.: Princeton University Press, 1984.

Bacon, Francis. *The Works of Francis Bacon*. Ed. James Spedding et al. Vol. 1. Rpt. Stuttgart: Frommann-Holzboog, 1963.

Barfield, Owen. *What Coleridge Thought*. Middletown, Conn.: Wesleyan University Press, 1971.

Bartol, Cyrus A. "Modern Skepticism." *Christian Examiner* 49 (1850): 317–41.

Bauberot, Arnaud, and Florence Bourillon, eds. *Urbaphobie. La détestation de la ville aux XIXe et XXe siècles*. Pompignac: Éditions Bière, 2009.

Bauman, Zygmunt. *Intimations of Postmodernity*. London: Routledge, 1992.

Baym, Nina. "Thoreau's View of Science." *Journal of the History of Ideas* 26 (1965): 221–34.

Bekoff, Marc. *The Emotional Lives of Animals: A Leading Scientist Explores Animal Joy, Sorrow, and Empathy—and Why They Matter*. Novato, Calif.: New World Library, 2007.

———. "Wild Justice and Fair Play: Cooperation, Forgiveness, and Morality in Animals." *The Animals Reader: The Essential Classic and Contemporary Writings*. Ed. Linda Kalof and Amy Fitzgerald. Oxford: Berg, 2007. 72–90.

Benjamin, Walter. *Illuminations*. Ed. Hannah Arendt. New York: Schocken, 1968.

———. *Sprache und Geschichte: Philosophische Essays*. Stuttgart: Reclam, 1992.

Bennett, Michael. "Reconciling Green and Red." *Radical Relevance: Toward a Scholarship of the Whole Left*. Ed. Laura Gray-Rosendale and Steven Rosendale. Albany: State University of New York Press, 2005. 85–102.

Benson, Eugene. "Thoreau and His Writings, His Habits of Thought: *Cape Cod*." *New York Evening Post* 10 June 1866: 1.

Berger, Michael Benjamin. *Thoreau's Late Career and "The Dispersion of Seeds": The Saunterer's Synoptic Vision*. Rochester, N.Y.: Camden House, 2000.

Bhaskar, Roy. *A Realist Theory of Science*. Sussex: Harvester, 1978.

——— . *Reclaiming Reality: A Critical Introduction to Contemporary Philosophy*. London: Verso, 1989.

Bickman, Martin. *"Walden": Volatile Truths*. New York: Twayne, 1992.

Boghossian, Paul. *Fear of Knowledge: Against Relativism and Constructivism*. Oxford: Oxford University Press, 2006.

Borjesson, Gary. "A Sounding of *Walden*'s Philosophical Depth." *Philosophy and Literature* 18 (1994): 287–308.

Borst, Raymond R. *The Thoreau Log: A Documentary Life of Henry David Thoreau, 1817–1862*. New York: G. K. Hall, 1992.

Bosco, Ronald A., and Joel Myerson, eds. *The Emerson Brothers: A Fraternal Biography in Letters*. Oxford: Oxford University Press, 2006.

Bowen, Francis. "Philosophy of Cousin." *North American Review* 53 (1841): 1–40.

Brownson, Orestes A. "The Eclectic Philosophy." *Boston Quarterly Review* 2 (1839): 27–53.

——— . "Emerson's Prose Works." *Catholic World* 11 (1870): 202–11.

——— . "History of Philosophy." *Brownson's Quarterly Review* 1 (1844): 137–74.

——— . "Kant's *Critic of Pure Reason*." *Brownson's Quarterly Review* 1 (1844): 281–309, 417–49.

——— . "Protestantism Ends in Transcendentalism.—Concluded." *Brownson's Quarterly Review* 3 (1846): 369–99.

——— . "Two Articles from the Princeton Review." *Boston Quarterly Review* (1840): 265–323.

Bruce, Vicki, et al. *Visual Perception: Physiology, Psychology and Ecology*. Hove, U.K.: Psychology Press, 1996.

Buell, Lawrence. *The Environmental Imagination: Thoreau, Nature Writing, and the Formation of American Culture*. Cambridge, Mass.: Harvard University Press, 1995.

——— . *Literary Transcendentalism: Style and Vision in the American Renaissance*. Ithaca, N.Y.: Cornell University Press, 1973.

Bulfinch, Thomas. *The Age of Fable*. Boston: S. W. Tilton, 1855.

Bush, Harold K., Jr. *American Declarations: Rebellion and Repentance in American Cultural History*. Urbana: University of Illinois Press, 1999.

Bushman, Richard L. *The Refinement of America: Persons, Houses, Cities*. New York: Knopf, 1992.

Cafaro, Philip. "Thoreau on Science and System." 1998. *Paideia Archives*, 15 Apr. 2009. http://www.bu.edu/wcp/Papers/Envi/EnviCafa.htm.

——— . *Thoreau's Living Ethics: "Walden" and the Pursuit of Virtue*. Athens: University of Georgia Press, 2004.

Cameron, Sharon. *Writing Nature: Henry Thoreau's Journal.* New York: Oxford University Press, 1985.

Caney, Simon. "Liberalism and Communitarianism: A Misconceived Debate." *Political Studies* 40.2 (1992): 273–89.

Capper, Charles. "'A Little Beyond': The Problem of the Transcendentalist Movement in American History." *Transient and Permanent: The Transcendentalist Movement and Its Contexts.* Ed. Charles Capper and Conrad Edick Wright. Boston: Massachusetts Historical Society and Northeastern University Press, 1999. 3–48.

Carlyle, Thomas. *Sartor Resartus.* 1836. Notes and introduction by Rodger L. Tarr. Text established by Mark Engel and Rodger L. Tarr. The Norman and Charlotte Strouse Edition of the Works of Thomas Carlyle. Berkeley: University of California Press, 2000. http://www.nd.edu/~carlyle/sr.html.

Carroll, Joseph. *Literary Darwinism: Evolution, Human Nature, and Literature.* New York: Routledge, 2004.

Casado da Rocha, Antonio. "Towards a Reconciliation of Public and Private Autonomy in Thoreau's 'Hybrid' Politics." *Astrolabio: Revista Internacional de Filosofía* 8 (2009): 16–32.

Case, Kristen. "Henry Thoreau, Charles Olson and the Poetics of Place." *Concord Saunterer: A Journal of Thoreau Studies* ns 17 (2009): 44–72.

Cavell, Stanley. *The Claim of Reason: Wittgenstein, Skepticism, Morality, and Tragedy.* Oxford: Oxford University Press, 1999.

———. *In Quest of the Ordinary: Lines of Skepticism and Romanticism.* Chicago: University of Chicago Press, 1988.

———. "Night and Day: Heidegger and Thoreau." *Appropriating Heidegger.* Ed. J. Faulconer and M. Wrathall. Cambridge: Cambridge University Press, 2000. 30–49.

———. *The Senses of "Walden."* San Francisco: North Point Press, 1981.

Chambers, Robert. *Vestiges of the Natural History of Creation.* London: John Churchill, 1844.

Channing, William Ellery. *Dr. Channing's Note-Book.* Ed. Grace Ellery Channing. Boston: Houghton Mifflin, 1887.

———. "Likeness to God." *The Works of William Ellery E. Channing, D.D.* Boston: American Unitarian Association, 1896. 291–302.

Channing, William Henry. Translator's Preface. *Introduction to Ethics, by Théodore Jouffroy.* Boston: Hilliard, Gray, 1840. 1:vii–xix.

Char, René. *Œuvres complètes.* Paris: Gallimard, Bibliothèque de la Pléiade, 1983.

Christie, John Aldrich. *Thoreau as World Traveler.* New York: Columbia University Press, 1965.

Clarke, James Freeman. *Autobiography, Diary, and Correspondence.* Ed. Edward Everett Hale. Boston: Houghton Mifflin, 1891.

———. *The Ideas of the Apostle Paul*. Boston: Osgood, 1884.

Cleary, Marie Sally. "Bulfinch's Mythology." *Humanities* 8.1 (1987): 12–15.

———. *Myths for the Millions: Thomas Bulfinch, His America, and His Mythology Book*. Frankfurt am Main: Peter Lang, 2007.

Coetzee, J. M., et al. *The Lives of Animals*. Ed. Amy Gutmann. Princeton, N.J.: Princeton University Press, 1999.

Coleridge, Samuel Taylor. *Aids to Reflection*. Ed. John Beer. London: Routledge, 1993.

———. *Biographia Literaria*. Ed. Kathleen Coburn, Walter Jackson Bate, and James Engell. 2 vols. Princeton, N.J.: Princeton University Press, 1983.

———. *The Friend*. Ed. Barbara E. Rooke. 2 vols. London: Routledge and Kegan Paul, 1969.

———. *Lay Sermons*. Ed. R. J. White. London: Routledge and Kegan Paul, 1972.

———. *The Statesman's Manual*. Ed. R. J. White. London: Routledge and Kegan Paul, 1972.

Compagnon, Antoine. *Les antimodernes: De Joseph de Maistre à Roland Barthes*. Paris: Gallimard, 2005.

Cornwell, John, ed. *Nature's Imagination: The Frontiers of Scientific Vision*. Oxford: Oxford University Press, 1995.

Coupland, Douglas. *Generation X: Tales for an Accelerated Culture*. New York: St. Martin's Press, 1991.

———. *Life after God*. New York: Simon and Schuster, 1994.

———. *Polaroids from the Dead*. New York: HarperCollins, 1996.

———. *Shampoo Planet*. New York: Simon and Schuster, 1992.

Cousin, Victor. *Elements of Psychology: Included in a Critical Examination of Locke's Essay on the Human Understanding*. Ed. and trans. C. S. Henry. Hartford, Conn.: Cooke, 1834.

———. *Introduction to the History of Philosophy*. Trans. H. G. Linberg. Boston: Hilliard, Gray, Little and Wilkins, 1832.

Creuzer, Friedrich. 1810. *Symbolik und Mythologie der alten Völker, besonders der Griechen*. 4 vols. Leipzig: K. W. Leske, 1810–12.

Cruickshank, Helen, ed. *Thoreau on Birds*. New York: McGraw-Hill, 1964.

Darwin, Charles. *Descent of Man*. From *So Simple a Beginning: The Four Great Books of Charles Darwin: "The Voyage of the Beagle," "On the Origin of Species," "The Descent of Man," "The Expression of the Emotions in Man and Animals."* Ed. Edward O. Wilson. New York: Norton, 2006.

———. *On the Origin of Species*. London: John Murray, 1859.

———. *The Voyage of the Beagle*. New York: Modern Library, 2001.

Daston, Lorraine. "Objectivity and the Escape from Perspective." *The Science Studies Reader*. Ed. Mario Biagioli. New York: Routledge, 1999. 110–23.

Daston, Lorraine, and Peter Galison. *Objectivity*. New York: Zone, 2007.

Dean, Bradley P. "Henry D. Thoreau and Horace Greeley Exchange Letters on the 'Spontaneous Generation of Plants.'" *New England Quarterly* 66.4 (1993): 630–38.

——. Introduction. *Wild Fruits: Thoreau's Rediscovered Last Manuscript*. By Henry David Thoreau. Ed. Bradley P. Dean. New York: Norton, 2000. ix–xvii.

Dean, Bradley P., and Ronald Wesley Hoag. "Thoreau's Lectures after *Walden*: An Annotated Calendar." *Studies in the American Renaissance 1996*. Ed. Joel Myerson. Charlottesville: University Press of Virginia, 1996. 241–362.

——. "Thoreau's Lectures before *Walden*: An Annotated Calendar." *Studies in the American Renaissance 1995*. Ed. Joel Myerson. Charlottesville: University Press of Virginia, 1995. 127–228.

Dean, Cornelia. "Thoreau Is Rediscovered as Climatologist." *New York Times Online* 28 Oct. 2008. http://www.nytimes.com/2008/10/28/science/earth/28wald.html.

de Fontenay, Elisabeth. "Un rameau d'or pour traduire les bêtes." *Traduire le parler des bêtes*. Ed. Elisabeth de Fontenay and M.-C. Pasquier. Paris: Éditions de l'Herne, 2008. 10–37.

Deleuze, Gilles, and Félix Guattari. *A Thousand Plateaus: Capitalism and Schizophrenia*. Trans. Brian Massumi. Minneapolis: University of Minnesota Press, 1987.

Derrida, Jacques. *The Animal That Therefore I Am*. Ed. Marie-Louise Mallet. Trans. David Wills. New York: Fordham, 2008.

——. "L'animal que donc je suis." *L'animal autobiographique: Autour de Jacques Derrida*. Ed. Marie-Louise Mallet. Paris: Éditions Galilée, 1999. 251–301.

Despret, Vinciane. "Portrait de personne avec fourrure." *Les grands singes: L'humanité au fond des yeux*. Paris: Odile Jacob, 2005. 75–120.

Dewey, John. *Democracy and Education: An Introduction to the Philosophy of Education*. New York: Macmillan, 1916.

Dimock, Wai Chee. *Through Other Continents: American Literature across Deep Time*. Princeton, N.J.: Princeton University Press, 2006.

Dolis, John. *Tracking Thoreau: Double-Crossing Nature and Technology*. Madison, N.J.: Fairleigh Dickinson University Press, 2005.

Dowling, David. *Capital Letters: Authorship in the Antebellum Literary Market*. Iowa City: University of Iowa Press, 2009.

Eisenstadt, S. N. "Multiple Modernities." *Daedalus* 129.1 (2000): 1–29.

Ells, Stephen F. "Henry Thoreau and the Estabrook Country: A Historic and Personal Landscape." *Concord Saunterer* 4 (Fall 1996): 73–148.

Emerson, Mary Moody. *The Selected Letters of Mary Moody Emerson*. Ed. Nancy Craig Simmons. Athens: University of Georgia Press, 1993.

Emerson, Ralph Waldo. *The Collected Works of Ralph Waldo Emerson*. Ed. Joseph Slater et al. 10 vols. Cambridge, Mass.: Harvard University Press, 1971–.

———. *The Complete Works of Ralph Waldo Emerson.* Ed. Edward Waldo Emerson. Centenary Edition. 12 vols. Boston: Houghton Mifflin, 1903–4.

———. *The Early Lectures of Ralph Waldo Emerson.* Ed. Stephen E. Whicher, Robert E. Spiller, and Wallace E. Williams. 3 vols. Cambridge, Mass.: Harvard University Press, 1959–72.

———. *Emerson's Prose and Poetry.* Ed. Joel Porte and Saundra Morris. New York: Norton, 2001.

———. *The Journals and Miscellaneous Notebooks of Ralph Waldo Emerson.* Ed. William H. Gilman et al. 16 vols. Cambridge, Mass.: Harvard University Press, 1960–82.

———. *The Later Lectures of Ralph Waldo Emerson, 1843–1871.* Ed. Ronald A. Bosco and Joel Myerson. 2 vols. Athens: University of Georgia Press, 2001.

———. *The Letters of Ralph Waldo Emerson.* Ed. Ralph L. Rusk. 6 vols. New York: Columbia University Press, 1939.

———. "Thoreau." *Lectures and Biographical Sketches.* Boston: Houghton Mifflin, 1883. 419–52.

———. *The Topical Notebooks of Ralph Waldo Emerson.* Ed. Ralph H. Orth et al. 3 vols. Columbia: University of Missouri Press, 1990–94.

Etzioni, Amitai. *The Spirit of Community: Rights, Responsibilities, and the Communitarian Agenda.* New York: Crown, 1993.

Everett, Alexander. "History of Intellectual Philosophy." *North American Review* 29 (1829): 67–123.

Everett, Edward. "An Oration Delivered before the Municipal Authorities of the City of Boston on the 4th of July, 1860." *Littell's Living Age* 3rd ser. 10 (July, Aug., Sept. 1860): 286–96.

Feldman, Burton, and Robert D. Richardson. *The Rise of Modern Mythology, 1680–1860.* Bloomington: Indiana University Press, 1972.

Flaherty, Alice W. *The Midnight Disease: The Drive to Write, Writer's Block, and the Creative Brain.* Boston: Houghton Mifflin, 2004.

Foster, David R. *Thoreau's Country: A Journey through a Transformed Landscape.* Cambridge, Mass.: Harvard University Press, 1999.

Francis, Richard. *Transcendental Utopias: Individual and Community at Brook Farm, Fruitlands, and Walden.* Ithaca, N.Y.: Cornell University Press, 1997.

Friesen, Victor Carl. *The Spirit of the Huckleberry: Sensuousness in Henry Thoreau.* Edmonton: University of Alberta Press, 1984.

Fuller, Margaret. "Emerson's Essays." *Margaret Fuller, Critic: Writings from the "New York Tribune," 1844–1846.* Ed. Judith Mattson Bean and Joel Myerson. New York: Columbia University Press, 2000. 1–7.

———. *Summer on the Lakes, in 1843*. Urbana: University of Illinois Press, 1991.

Gadamer, Hans-Georg. *Truth and Method*. 2nd ed. Trans. Joel Weinsheimer and Donald G. Marshall. New York: Continuum, 2003.

———. *Wahrheit und Methode: Grundzüge einer philosophischen Hermeneutik*. 6th ed. Tübingen: J. C. B. Mohr, 1990.

Garber, Frederick. *Thoreau's Redemptive Imagination*. New York: New York University Press, 1977.

Garrard, Greg. *Ecocriticism*. London: Routledge, 2004.

Gérando, Joseph-Marie de. *Histoire comparée des systèmes de philosophie*. 4 vols. Paris: Alexis Eymery, 1822.

Gibson, James J. *The Ecological Approach to Visual Perception*. New York: Psychology Press, 1986.

Giles, Paul. *The Global Remapping of American Literature*. Princeton, N.J.: Princeton University Press, 2011.

Gilmore, Michael T. *Surface and Depth: The Quest for Legibility in American Culture*. Oxford: Oxford University Press, 2003.

Givón, Talmy. *Bio-linguistics*. Amsterdam: John Benjamins, 2002.

Goethe, Johann Wolfgang von. *Italian Journey*. Trans. W. H. Auden and Elizabeth Mayer. New York: Penguin, 1970.

———. *Scientific Studies*. Ed. and trans. Douglas Miller. New York: Suhrkamp, 1983.

Goetzmann, William H. "Introduction: The American Hegelians." *The American Hegelians: An Intellectual Episode in the History of Western America*. New York: Knopf, 1973. 3–18.

Goodall, Jane. "Chimpanzees—Bridging the Gap." *The Great Ape Project: Equality beyond Humanity*. Ed. Paola Cavalieri and Peter Singer. New York: St. Martin's Griffin, 1993. 10–18.

Goodman, Russell B. *American Philosophy and the Romantic Tradition*. New York: Cambridge University Press, 1990.

Gura, Philip F. *The Wisdom of Words: Language, Theology, and Literature in the New England Renaissance*. Middletown, Conn.: Wesleyan University Press, 1981.

Hamilton, William. "M. Cousin's *Course of Philosophy*." *Edinburgh Review* 50.99 (1830): 194–221.

Haraway, Donna. *The Companion Species Manifesto: Dogs, People and Significant Otherness*. Chicago: Prickly Paradigm Press, 2003.

———. *The Haraway Reader*. New York: Routledge, 2004.

———. *When Species Meet*. Minneapolis: University of Minnesota Press, 2008.

Harding, Walter. *The Days of Henry Thoreau*. 1965; Princeton, N.J.: Princeton University Press, 1993.

Hawthorne, Nathaniel. "Legends of the Province-House: II. Edward Randolph's Portrait." *Tales and Sketches*. New York: Library of America, 1982. 640–51.

Healey, Caroline W., ed. *Margaret and Her Friends, or Ten Conversations with Margaret Fuller upon the Mythology of the Greeks and Its Expression in Art . . . Beginning March 1, 1841, Reported by Catherine Healey*. Boston: Roberts Brothers, 1895.

Hedge, Frederic Henry. "Coleridge's Literary Character." *Christian Examiner* 14.1 (1833): 108–29.

———, ed. *Prose Writers of Germany*. Philadelphia: Carey and Hart, 1848.

Hegel, Georg Wilhelm Friedrich. *Hegel's Phenomenology of Spirit*. Trans. A. V. Miller. Oxford: Oxford University Press, 1977.

Helmholtz, Hermann von. "Ueber Goethe's naturwissenschaftliche Arbeiten" (1853); "Ueber das Verhältniss der Naturwissenschaften zur Gesammtheit der Wissenschaft" (1862); "Goethe's Vorahnungen kommender naturwissenschaftlicher Ideen" (1892). *Vorträge und Reden*. 5th ed. Braunschweig: Vieweg, 1903. Vol. 1: 23–47, 157–85; vol. 2: 335–61.

Hensley, Tim. "A Curious Tale: The Apple in North America." *The Best Apples to Buy and Grow*. New York: Brooklyn Botanic Garden, 2009. http://www.bbg.org/gar2/topics/kitchen/handbooks/apples/northamerica.htmlgardening/article/the_apple_in_north_america/.

Hessler, John. "From Ortelius to Champlain: The Lost Maps of Henry David Thoreau." *Concord Saunterer: A Journal of Thoreau Studies* ns 18 (2010): 1–26.

Hildebidle, John. *Thoreau: A Naturalist's Liberty*. Cambridge, Mass.: Harvard University Press, 1983.

Hodder, Alan D. *Thoreau's Ecstatic Witness*. New Haven, Conn.: Yale University Press, 2001.

"Hoop Petticoats and Crinoline." *Notes and Queries* (n.d.). Rpt. *Living Age* 28 Jan. 1860: 256. Cornell University Library, "Making of America." http://digital.library.cornell.edu/cgi/t/text/text-idx?c=livn;idno=livn0064-4.

Hotz, Eric Lee. "Another Thoreau Lesson." *Wall Street Journal* 13 June 2008: A10.

Howarth, William L. *The Book of Concord: Thoreau's Life as a Writer*. New York: Viking, 1982.

Humboldt, Alexander von. *Cosmos: A Sketch of the Physical Description of the Universe*. 2 vols. New York: Harper and Brothers, 1858; facsimile ed. Baltimore, Md.: Johns Hopkins University Press, 1997.

Huneman, Philippe, ed. *Understanding Purpose: Kant and the Philosophy of Biology*. NAKS Studies in Philosophy, vol. 8. Rochester, N.Y.: University of Rochester Press, 2007.

Ingram, Annie Merrill, et al., eds. *Coming into Contact: Explorations in Ecocritical Theory and Practice*. Athens: University of Georgia Press, 2007.

Jackson, Leon. *The Business of Letters: Authorial Economies in Antebellum America*. Stanford, Calif.: Stanford University Press, 2008.

Jager, Colin. *The Book of God: Secularization and Design in the Romantic Era*. Philadelphia: University of Pennsylvania Press, 2007.

Jakobson, Roman, and Linda R. Waugh. *The Sound Shape of Language*. London: Harvester Press, 1979.

James, William. *Essays in Radical Empiricism*. Ed. Ralph Barton Perry. New York: Longmans, Green, 1922.

———. "The Place of Affectional Facts in a World of Pure Experience." *Writings 1902–1910*. Ed. Bruce Kuklick. New York: Library of America, 1987. 1206–14.

———. *Pragmatism and Other Writings*. Ed. Giles Gunn. New York: Penguin, 2000.

———. *Writings: 1902–1910*. New York: Library of America, 1987.

Jameson, Frederic. "Marx's Purloined Letter." *Ghostly Demarcations: A Symposium on Jacques Derrida's Spectres of Marx*. Ed. Michael Sprinkler. London: Verso, 1999. 26–67.

———. *Postmodernism: or, the Cultural Logic of Late Capitalism*. London: Verso, 1991.

Jordan, Joe. *A Wilderness of Signs: Ethics, Beauty, and Environment after Postmodernism*. Newcastle, U.K.: Cambridge Scholars Publishing, 2006.

Kalof, Linda, and Amy Fitzgerald, eds. *The Animals Reader: The Essential Classic and Contemporary Writings*. Oxford: Berg, 2007.

Kant, Immanuel. *Critique of Judgment*. Trans. Werner S. Pluhar. Indianapolis, Ind.: Hackett, 1987.

———. *Critique of Pure Reason*. Trans. Paul Guyer and Allen Wood. Cambridge: Cambridge University Press, 1998.

———. *Metaphysical Foundations of Natural Science*. Trans. Michael Friedman. Cambridge: Cambridge University Press, 2004.

Kateb, George. *The Inner Ocean: Individualism and Democratic Culture*. Ithaca, N.Y.: Cornell University Press, 1992.

Kerting, Verena. *Henry David Thoreau's Aesthetics: A Modern Approach to the World*. Frankfurt am Main: Peter Lang, 2006.

King, Bradley Ray. "Thoreau's Rhetoric of Estrangement in Cape Cod: Looking at America through a Knot-hole." *Concord Saunterer: A Journal of Thoreau Studies* ns 18 (2010): 27–45.

Latour, Bruno. *Pandora's Hope: Essays on the Reality of Science Studies*. Cambridge, Mass.: Harvard University Press, 1999.

———. *We Have Never Been Modern*. Cambridge, Mass.: Harvard University Press, 1993.

Lebeaux, Richard. *Thoreau's Seasons*. Amherst: University of Massachusetts Press, 1984.

Louis, Margot Kathleen. "Gods and Mysteries: The Revival of Paganism and the Remaking of Mythography through the Nineteenth Century." *Victorian Studies* 47.3 (2005): 329–61.

Lowell Daily Citizen and News. 9 Dec. 1865.

Magnus, Margaret. "What's in a Word? Studies in Phonosemantics." Diss. University of Trondheim, Trondheim, Norway. 2001. http://www.trismegistos.com/Dissertation/dissertation.pdf.

Marsh, James. "Preliminary Essay to Aids to Reflection." *Aids to Reflection, by Samuel Taylor Coleridge.* Ed. John B. Beer. London: Routledge, 1993. 487–529.

Matheson, Neill. "Thoreau's *Gramática Parda*: Conjugating Race and Nature." *"Walden," "Civil Disobedience" and Other Writings* by Henry David Thoreau. Ed. William Rossi. Norton Critical Edition. 3rd ed. New York: Norton, 2008. 613–31.

McGregor, Robert Kuhn. *A Wider View of the Universe: Henry Thoreau's Study of Nature.* Urbana: University of Illinois Press, 1997.

McIntosh, James. *Thoreau as Romantic Naturalist: His Shifting Stance toward Nature.* Ithaca, N.Y.: Cornell University Press, 1974.

McKibben, Bill. Introduction. *Walden.* Boston: Beacon Press, 2004. vii–xxiii.

Milder, Robert. *Reimagining Thoreau.* Cambridge: Cambridge University Press, 1995.

Miller, Perry. *Consciousness in Concord: The Text of Thoreau's Hitherto "Lost Journal," 1840–1841.* Boston: Houghton Mifflin, 1958.

———. "Thoreau in the Context of International Romanticism." *New England Quarterly* 34.2 (1961): 147–59.

———, ed. *The Transcendentalists: An Anthology.* Cambridge, Mass.: Harvard University Press, 1950.

Miller-Rushing, Abraham J., and Richard B. Primack. "Global Warming and Flowering Times in Thoreau's Concord: A Community Perspective." *Ecology* 89.2 (2008): 332–41.

Mohanty, Satya. *Literary Theory and the Claims of History: Postmodernism, Objectivity, Multicultural Politics.* Ithaca, N.Y.: Cornell University Press, 1997.

Moller, Mary Elkins. *Thoreau in the Human Community.* Amherst: University of Massachusetts Press, 1980.

Morgan, Adrian. *Toads and Toadstools: The Natural History, Folklore, and Cultural Oddities of a Strange Association.* Berkeley, Calif.: Celestial Arts, 1995.

Morton, Timothy. *Ecology without Nature: Rethinking Environmental Aesthetics.* Cambridge, Mass.: Harvard University Press, 2007.

Mulhall, Stephen, and Adam Swift. "Rawls and Communitarianism." *The Cambridge Companion to Rawls.* Ed. Samuel Freeman. Cambridge: Cambridge University Press, 2003. 460–87.

Murdock, James. *Sketches of Modern Philosophy, Especially among the Germans.* Hartford, Conn.: J. C. Wells, 1842.

Myerson, Joel, ed. *Emerson and Thoreau: The Contemporary Reviews.* Cambridge: Cambridge University Press, 1992.

Nänny, Max, and Olga Fischer, eds. *Form Miming Meaning: Iconicity in Language and Literature*. Amsterdam: John Benjamins, 1999.

Nelson, Richard K. *The Island Within*. New York: Vintage, 1991.

Neufeldt, Leonard. "'*Praetextus*' as Text: Editor-Critic Responses to Thoreau's Journal." *Arizona Quarterly* 46.4 (1990): 27–72.

Newman, Lance. *Our Common Dwelling: Henry Thoreau, Transcendentalism, and the Class Politics of Nature*. New York: Palgrave Macmillan, 2005.

———. "Thoreau's Materialism: From *Walden* to *Wild Fruits*." *More Day to Dawn: Thoreau's "Walden" for the Twenty-First Century*. Ed. Sandra Harbert Petrulionis and Laura Dassow Walls. Amherst: University of Massachusetts Press, 2007. 100–126.

Noë, Alva. *Action in Perception*. Cambridge, Mass.: MIT Press, 2005.

Norris, Margot. *Beasts of the Modern Imagination: Darwin, Nietzsche, Kafka, Ernst, and Lawrence*. Baltimore, Md.: Johns Hopkins University Press, 1985.

Nye, David E. *American Technological Sublime*. Cambridge, Mass.: MIT Press, 1994.

Olson, Charles. *Call Me Ishmael*. San Francisco: City Lights, 1947.

Parker, Theodore. "Ackermann's *The Christian in Plato*." *Christian Examiner* 25.3 (1839): 367–84.

———. "Cudworth's True Intellectual System." *Christian Examiner* 27.3 (1840): 289–319.

———. *A Discourse on the Transient and Permanent in Christianity*. Boston: Author, 1841.

———. "More's Works." *Christian Examiner* 27.1 (1839): 48–71.

———. "Transcendentalism." *The World of Matter and the Spirit of Man*. Ed. George Willis Cooke. Boston: American Unitarian Association, 1907. 1–38.

Paul, Sherman. *The Shores of America: Thoreau's Inward Exploration*. 1958; Urbana: University of Illinois Press, 1972.

Peck, H. Daniel. *Thoreau's Morning Work: Memory and Perception in "A Week on the Concord and Merrimack Rivers," the Journal, and "Walden."* New Haven, Conn.: Yale University Press, 1990.

Peirce, Charles Sanders. "How to Make Our Ideas Clear." *The Essential Peirce, Volume 1 (1867–1893)*. Ed. Nathan Houser and Christian Kloesel. Bloomington: Indiana University Press, 1992. 124–41.

Poirier, Richard. *Robert Frost: The Work of Knowing*. Stanford, Calif.: Stanford University Press, 1990.

Porte, Joel. *Emerson in His Journals*. Cambridge, Mass.: Harvard University Press, 1982.

Rawls, John. *Political Liberalism*. New York: Columbia University Press, 1993.

———. *A Theory of Justice*. Cambridge, Mass.: Harvard University Press, 1971.

Reinhold, Meyer. *Classica Americana: The Greek and Roman Heritage in the United States*. Detroit: Wayne State University Press, 1984.

Richard, Claude. "Henry David Thoreau: L'hydrodynamique de la lettre." *Lettres améri-caines*. Aix-en-Provence: Alinea, 1987. 113–39.

Richardson, Robert D., Jr. *Henry Thoreau: A Life of the Mind*. Berkeley: University of California Press, 1986.

———. "Introduction: Thoreau's Broken Task." *Faith in a Seed: The Dispersion of Seeds and Other Late Natural History Writings* by Henry D. Thoreau. Ed. Bradley P. Dean. Washington, D.C.: Island Press, 1993. 3–17.

Ripley, George. *Discourses on the Philosophy of Religion: Addresses to Doubters Who Wish to Believe*. Boston: James Munroe, 1836.

———, ed. *Philosophical Miscellanies, Translated from the French of Cousin, Jouffroy, and B. Constant*. 2 vols. Boston: Hilliard, Gray, 1838.

Ritvo, Harriet. "Animal Planet." *The Animals Reader: The Essential Classic and Contemporary Writings*. Ed. Linda Kalof and Amy Fitzgerald. Oxford: Berg, 2007. 129–40.

Robinson, David M. *Natural Life: Thoreau's Worldly Transcendentalism*. Ithaca, N.Y.: Cornell University Press, 2004.

———. "Thoreau and Idealism: 'Face to Face to a Fact.'" *More Day to Dawn: Thoreau's "Walden" for the Twenty-First Century*. Ed. Sandra Harbert Petrulionis and Laura Dassow Walls. Amherst: University of Massachusetts Press, 2007. 41–59.

Rorty, Richard. *Philosophy and the Mirror of Nature*. Oxford: Blackwell, 1980.

Rosenblum, Nancy L. *Another Liberalism: Romanticism and the Reconstruction of Liberal Thought*. Cambridge, Mass.: Harvard University Press, 1987.

———. "Strange Attractors: How Individualists Connect to Form Democratic Unity." *Political Theory* 18.4 (1990): 576–86.

Rosenwald, Lawrence. *Emerson and the Art of the Diary*. New York: Oxford University Press, 1988.

Rossi, William. "Following Thoreau's Instincts." *More Day to Dawn: Thoreau's "Walden" for the Twenty-First Century*. Ed. Sandra Harbert Petrulionis and Laura Dassow Walls. Amherst: University of Massachusetts Press, 2007. 82–99.

———. Introduction. *"Wild Apples" and Other Natural History Essays by Henry D. Thoreau*. Ed. William Rossi. Athens: University of Georgia Press, 2002. vii–xxiv.

———. "The Journal and *Walden*." *"Walden," "Civil Disobedience," and Other Writings* by Henry David Thoreau. 3rd ed. Ed. William Rossi. Norton Critical Edition. New York: Norton, 2008. 313–18.

———. "Thoreau's Transcendental Ecocentrism." *Thoreau's Sense of Place: Essays in American Environmental Writing*. Ed. Richard J. Schneider. Iowa City: University of Iowa Press, 2000. 28–43.

Sandel, Michael J. *Liberalism and the Limits of Justice*. Cambridge: Cambridge University Press, 2006.

Sapir, Edward. "A Study in Phonetic Symbolism." *Journal of Experimental Psychology* 12 (1929): 225–39.

Sattelmeyer, Robert. "Depopulation, Deforestation, and the Actual Walden Pond." *Thoreau's Sense of Place: Essays in American Environmental Writing.* Ed. Richard J. Schneider. Iowa City: University of Iowa Press, 2000. 235–43.

———. Introduction. *Henry David Thoreau, the Natural History Essays.* Layton, Utah: Gibbs M. Smith Publishers, 1980. vii–xxxiv.

———. "Journals." *The Oxford Handbook of Transcendentalism.* Ed. Joel Myerson, Sandra Harbert Petrulionis, and Laura Dassow Walls. New York: Oxford University Press, 2010. 291–308.

———. "The Remaking of *Walden.*" *Writing the American Classics.* Ed. James Barbour and Tom Quirk. Chapel Hill: University of North Carolina Press, 1990. 53–78.

———. *Thoreau's Reading: A Study in Intellectual History.* Princeton, N.J.: Princeton University Press, 1988.

Scharnhorst, Gary. *A Literary Biography of William Rounseville Alger (1822–1905): A Neglected Member of the Concord Circle.* Lewiston, N.Y.: Mellen, 1990.

Schlegel, Friedrich von. 1800. *Dialogue on Poetry and Literary Aphorisms.* Trans. Ernst Behler and Roman Struc. University Park: Pennsylvania State University Press, 1968.

Schneider, Herbert W. "American Transcendentalism's Escape from Phenomenology." *Transcendentalism and Its Legacy.* Ed. Myron Simon and Thornton H. Parsons. Ann Arbor: University of Michigan Press, 1966. 215–26.

Schulz, Dieter. "Thoreaus Wildäpfel, Berkeley und die Sprache der Natur." *Ex Praeteritis Praesentia: Sprach-, literatur- und kulturwissenschaftliche Studien zu Wort- und Stoffgeschichten. Festschrift zum 70. Geburtstag von Theo Stemmler.* Ed. Matthias Eitelmann and Nadyne Stritzke. Heidelberg: Winter, 2006. 275–94.

Schulz, Reinhard. *Naturwissenschaftshermeneutik: Eine Philosophie der Endlichkeit in historischer, systematischer und angewandter Hinsicht.* Würzburg: Königshausen und Neumann, 2004.

Serres, Michel, and Bruno Latour. *Conversations on Science, Culture, and Time.* Trans. Roxanne Lapidus. Ann Arbor: University of Michigan Press, 1995.

Seybold, Ethel. *Thoreau: The Quest and the Classics.* New Haven, Conn.: Yale University Press, 1951.

Shanley, J. Lyndon. *The Making of "Walden" with the Text of the First Edition.* Chicago: University of Chicago Press, 1957.

Sikes, Wirt. *British Goblins: Welsh Folk-Lore, Fairy Mythology, Legends and Traditions.* London: S. Low, Marston, Searle and Rivington, 1880.

Smith, Barbara Herrnstein. *Scandalous Knowledge: Science, Truth, and the Human.* Durham, N.C.: Duke University Press, 2006.

Smith, Jordan Fisher. *Nature Noir: A Park Ranger's Patrol in the Sierra*. Boston: Houghton Mifflin, 2006.

Snow, C. P. *The Two Cultures*. Cambridge: Cambridge University Press, 1993.

Snyder, Gary. "Tawny Grammar." *The Practice of the Wild*. San Francisco: North Point Press, 1990. 48–77.

Soper, Kate. *What Is Nature? Culture, Politics and the Non-Human*. Oxford: Blackwell, 1995.

Specq, François. *Transcendence: Seekers and Seers in the Age of Thoreau*. Higganum, Conn.: Higganum Hill Books, 2006.

Sperber, Michael A. *Henry David Thoreau: Cycles and Psyche*. Higganum, Conn.: Higganum Hill Books, 2004.

Spivak, Gayatri Chakravorty. *Death of a Discipline*. New York: Columbia University Press, 2003.

St. Armand, Barton Levi. "The Book of Nature and American Nature Writing." *ISLE: Interdisciplinary Studies in Literature and the Environment* 4 (1997): 29–42.

Stevens, Wallace. *The Collected Poems of Wallace Stevens*. New York: Knopf, 1981.

Susini, Christian. "La 'folie' Walden: Raison et déraison dans *Walden*." *Henry D. Thoreau, Cahier de l'Herne n° 65*. Ed. Michel Granger. Paris: Éditions de l'Herne, 1994. 175–87.

Tate, Andrew. *Douglas Coupland*. Manchester, U.K.: Manchester University Press, 2007.

———. "'Now—Here Is My Secret': Ritual and Epiphany in Douglas Coupland's Fiction." *Literature and Theology* 16.3 (2002): 326–38.

Tauber, Alfred I. *Henry David Thoreau and the Moral Agency of Knowing*. Berkeley: University of California Press, 2001.

Taylor, Charles. "Atomism." *Philosophy and the Human Sciences: Philosophical Papers 2*. Cambridge: Cambridge University Press, 1985. 187–210.

———. "Overcoming Epistemology." *Philosophical Arguments*. Cambridge, Mass.: Harvard University Press, 1995. 1–19.

———. *A Secular Age*. Cambridge, Mass.: Harvard University Press, 2007.

Teichgraeber, Richard F. *Sublime Thoughts/Penny Wisdom: Situating Emerson and Thoreau in the American Market*. Baltimore, Md.: Johns Hopkins University Press, 1995.

Thoreau, Henry David. *Cape Cod*. Ed. Joseph J. Moldenhauer. Princeton, N.J.: Princeton University Press, 1988.

———. *The Correspondence of Henry David Thoreau*. Ed. Walter Harding and Carl Bode. New York: New York University Press, 1958.

———. *Early Essays and Miscellanies*. Ed. Joseph J. Moldenhauer and Edwin Moser, with Alexander Kern. Princeton, N.J.: Princeton University Press, 1975.

———. *Excursions*. Ed. Joseph J. Moldenhauer. Princeton, N.J.: Princeton University Press, 2007.

———. *Faith in a Seed: The Dispersion of Seeds and Other Late Natural History Writings*. Ed. Bradley P. Dean. Washington, D.C.: Island Press, 1993.

———. *Journal. The Writings of Henry D. Thoreau*. Ed. Elizabeth Hall Witherell et al. 8 vols. to date. Princeton, N.J.: Princeton University Press, 1981–.

———. *The Journal of Henry David Thoreau*. 14 vols. Ed. Bradford Torrey and Francis H. Allen. Boston: Houghton Mifflin, 1906; New York: Dover, 1962. [The Dover edition is fourteen volumes bound in two: vols. I–VII, 1837–October 1855, and vols. VIII–XIV, November 1855–61.]

———. *Letters to a Spiritual Seeker*. Ed. Bradley P. Dean. New York: Norton, 2004.

———. *The Maine Woods*. Ed. Joseph J. Moldenhauer. Princeton, N.J.: Princeton University Press, 1972.

———. "Nature Notes, Charts and Tables: Autograph Manuscript." 1851–60. MA 610. Pierpont Morgan Library, New York.

———. Online Journal Transcripts. The Thoreau Edition, Elizabeth Witherell, editor in chief. http://thoreau.library.ucsb.edu/writings_journals.html.

———. *Reform Papers*. Ed. Wendell Glick. Princeton, N.J.: Princeton University Press, 1973.

———. *Walden*. Ed. J. Lyndon Shanley. Princeton, N.J.: Princeton University Press, 1971.

———. *A Week on the Concord and Merrimack Rivers*. Ed. Carl F. Hovde, William L. Howarth, and Elizabeth H. Witherell. Princeton, N.J.: Princeton University Press, 1980.

———. *Wild Fruits: Thoreau's Rediscovered Last Manuscript*. Ed. Bradley P. Dean. New York: Norton, 2000.

Tissot, Roland. "'Un étrange frisson de délices sauvages': L'animalité." *Henry D. Thoreau, Cahier de l'Herne n° 65*. Ed. Michel Granger. Paris: Éditions de l'Herne, 1994. 223–31.

Turner, Victor. "Social Dramas and Stories about Them." *Critical Inquiry* 7.1 (1980): 141–68.

Van Leer, David. *Emerson's Epistemology: The Argument of the Essays*. Cambridge: Cambridge University Press, 1986.

Varela, Francisco J. "Organism: A Meshwork of Selfless Selves." *Organism and the Origins of Self*. Ed. Alfred I. Tauber. Dordrecht: Kluwer, 1991. 79–107.

Very, Jones. *Poems and Essays by Jones Very: Complete and Revised Edition*. Ed. James Freeman Clarke. Boston: Houghton Mifflin, 1886.

Walker, James. "Foundations of Faith." *Christian Examiner* 17.1 (1834): 1–15.

———. "Spiritual Discernment." *Reason, Faith, and Duty*. Boston: Roberts, 1876. 202–21.

Walls, Laura Dassow. "Believing in Nature: Wilderness and Wildness in Thoreauvian Science." *Thoreau's Sense of Place: Essays in American Environmental Writing*. Ed. Richard J. Schneider. Iowa City: University of Iowa Press, 2000. 15–27.

———. "A Constant New Creation: Thoreau and the Politics of Darwin." Presentation, Thoreau Society Annual Gathering, 11 July 2008, Concord, Mass.

———. "From the Modern to the Ecological: Latour on Walden Pond." *Ecocritical Theory: New European Approaches*. Ed. Axel Goodbody and Kate Rigby. Charlottesville: University of Virginia Press, 2011. 98–110.

———, ed. *Material Faith: Thoreau on Science*. Foreword by Edward O. Wilson. Boston: Houghton Mifflin, 1999.

———. *The Passage to Cosmos: Alexander von Humboldt and the Shaping of America*. Chicago: University of Chicago Press, 2009.

———. "Romancing the Real: Thoreau's Technology of Inscription." *A Historical Guide to Henry David Thoreau*. Ed. William Cain. New York: Oxford University Press, 2000. 123–51.

———. *Seeing New Worlds: Henry David Thoreau and Nineteenth-Century Natural Science*. Madison: University of Wisconsin Press, 1995.

———. "Textbooks and Texts from the Brooks: Inventing Scientific Authority in America." *American Quarterly* 49.1 (1997): 1–25.

———. "Thoreau's *Walden* in the Twenty-First Century." *Concord Saunterer* 12–13 (2004–5): 15–16.

Walzer, Michael. Interview by Christian Maul, Princeton, N.J., 6 Oct. 2008.

———. *Spheres of Justice: A Defense of Pluralism and Equality*. New York: Basic Books, 1983.

Weber, Andreas. *Natur als Bedeutung: Versuch einer semiotischen Theorie des Lebendigen*. Würzburg: Königshausen und Neumann, 2003.

Wellek, René. "Emerson and German Philosophy." *New England Quarterly* 16 (1943): 41–62.

———. "The Minor Transcendentalists and German Philosophy." *New England Quarterly* 15 (1942): 652–80.

West, Cornel. *The American Evasion of Philosophy: A Genealogy of Pragmatism*. London: Macmillan, 1989.

West, Michael. *Transcendental Wordplay: America's Romantic Punsters and the Search for the Language of Nature*. Athens: Ohio University Press, 2000.

Willis, Charles G., Brad Ruhfel, Richard B. Primack, Abraham J. Miller-Rushing, and Charles C. Davis. "Phylogenetic Patterns of Species Loss in Thoreau's Woods Are Driven by Climate Change." *Proceedings of the National Academy of Sciences* 4 Nov. 2008: 17029–33.

Wilshire, Bruce W. *The Primal Roots of American Philosophy: Pragmatism, Phenomenology, and Native American Thought*. University Park: Pennsylvania State University Press, 2000.

Winterer, Caroline. "Classical Oratory and Fears of Demagoguery in the Antebellum Era." *Classical Antiquity and the Politics of America, from George Washington to George W. Bush*. Ed. Michael Meckler. Waco, Tex.: Baylor University Press, 2006. 41–54.

——. *The Culture of Classicism: Ancient Greece and Rome in American Intellectual Life, 1780–1910*. Baltimore, Md.: Johns Hopkins University Press, 2002.

Wolfe, Cary. *Animal Rites: American Culture, the Discourse of Species, and Posthumanist Theory*. Chicago: University of Chicago Press, 2003.

Wood, Mark. "Another World Is Possible." *Radical Relevance: Toward a Scholarship of the Whole Left*. Ed. Laura Gray-Rosendale and Steven Rosendale. Albany: State University of New York Press, 2005. 213–37.

Wordsworth, William. *William Wordsworth*. Ed. Stephen Gill. Oxford: Oxford University Press, 1984.

——. "The world is too much with us." *Poetical Works*. Rev. ed. Oxford: Oxford University Press, 1969. 206.

Worley, Sam McGuire. *Emerson, Thoreau, and the Role of the Cultural Critic*. Albany: State University of New York Press, 2001.

Zammito, John H. *The Genesis of Kant's Critique of Judgment*. Chicago: University of Chicago Press, 1992.

Contributors

KRISTEN CASE is assistant professor of English at the University of Maine at Farmington. She has published articles on Henry David Thoreau, Robert Frost, and Ezra Pound and is the author of *American Pragmatism and Poetic Practice: Crosscurrents from Emerson to Susan Howe* (Camden House, 2011). She is director of Thoreau's Kalendar: A Digital Archive of the Phenological Manuscripts of Henry David Thoreau and incoming editor of the *Concord Saunterer: A Journal of Thoreau Studies*.

RANDALL CONRAD, an independent scholar in Lexington, Massachusetts, has contributed Thoreau studies to the *Concord Saunterer*, the *Thoreau Society Bulletin*, *ATQ*, and other publications. He is the translator of François Specq's *Transcendence* (2006) and tends the Thoreau Project website at www.calliope.org/thoreau/.

DAVID DOWLING, assistant professor in the School of Journalism and Mass Communication at the University of Iowa, has published numerous books and articles on media and publishing in nineteenth-century American history and contemporary culture. His books include *Literary Partnerships and the Marketplace: Writers and Mentors in Nineteenth Century America* (LSU), *The Business of Literary Circles in Nineteenth-Century America* (Palgrave), *Chasing the White Whale: The Moby-Dick Marathon; or, What Melville Means Today* (Iowa), and *Capital Letters: Authorship in the Antebellum Literary Market* (Iowa).

MICHEL GRANGER is professor emeritus of American literature at the University of Lyon (Lyon 2). He is the author of *Henry D. Thoreau. Narcisse à Walden* (Lyon: Presses Universitaires de Lyon, 1991), and *Henry David Thoreau. Paradoxes d'excentrique* (Paris: Belin, 1999). He has edited collections of essays on Thoreau, including *"Cahier de l'Herne": Henry D. Thoreau* (Paris: L'Herne, 1994) and *Henry D. Thoreau. Désobéir* (Paris: 10/18, 1997). He has introduced and edited several new translations of Thoreau's works: *Essais* (translated by N. Mallet; Marseille: Le Mot et le Reste, 2007), *Walden* (translated by Brice Matthieussent; Marseille: Le Mot et le Reste, 2010), and *Résistance au gouvernement civil et autres textes* (translated by N. Mallet; Marseille: Le Mot et le Reste, 2011) and is currently preparing a selection of extracts from Thoreau's Journal. Prof. Granger is a former president of the French Association for American Studies and a former editor of *Revue Française d'Études Américaines*.

MICHEL IMBERT is associate professor at the University of Paris VII (Denis Diderot). His articles deal mainly with Herman Melville and nineteenth-century American literature. His more recent publications include two articles on Thoreau: "L'ensauvagement du savoir, de Henry Lewis Morgan à Henry David Thoreau (*League of the Iroquois, The Maine Woods*)," in *La fabrique du sauvage dans la culture nord-américaine*, edited by Véronique Beghain and Lionel Larré (PU Bordeaux, 2009), and "Le seuil de résistance dans Resistance to Civil Government," in *Littérature et politique en Nouvelle-Angleterre*, edited by Thomas Constantinesco and Antoine Traisnel, *Actes de la recherche à l'ENS*, no. 7 (2011).

MICHAEL JONIK is lecturer at the University of Sussex in the School of English and American Studies. He was previously a Mellon Postdoctoral Fellow in the Society for the Humanities and visiting assistant professor in the Department of English at Cornell University. His research and teaching examine seventeenth- through nineteenth-century American and transatlantic literary and intellectual history in relationship to the history of science, religious studies, and philosophy. He has recently published essays on Melville in the *Oxford Literary Review* and *Leviathan* and is completing two books: *A Natural History of the Mind: Science, Form, and Perception from Cotton Mather to William James* and *Melville's Uncemented Stones: Character, Impersonality, and the Politics of Singularity*.

CHRISTIAN MAUL studied English and German literature and linguistics at the University of Heidelberg and at San Francisco State University. He graduated in April 2006 and subsequently pursued a master's degree in American studies at the Heidelberg Center for American Studies. He worked as a teaching assistant at the English Department of the University of Heidelberg and as a trainer for Business English. Dr. Maul is currently teaching English and German at a public *Gymnasium* near Heidelberg. His PhD dissertation, *From Self-Culture to Militancy, from Conscience to Intervention: Henry David Thoreau between Liberalism and Communitarianism* (Trier: Wissenschaftlicher Vertrag Trier, 2011), aims to shed new light on Thoreau's concept of individualism from a communitarian perspective.

BRUNO MONFORT is professor of American literature at Université Charles de Gaulle–Lille 3; he has published on Melville, Hawthorne, and nineteenth-century American literature. He has recently translated into French (with Ronald Jenn), edited, and annotated a collection of Hawthorne's stories about sculpture (*La semblance du vivant: Contes d'image et d'effigies*) and, with Agnès Derail, a selection of Melville's late poetry (*Derniers poèmes*), both at Éditions Rue d'Ulm, Paris.

HENRIK OTTERBERG is an economist at the Chalmers Science Park of Chalmers University in Gothenburg. His publications, focusing on hermeneutics and reception history, include a monograph on Thoreau, *Hound, Bay Horse, and Turtle-Dove: Obscurity and*

Authority in Thoreau's Walden (2005), and a Nordic cultural history of animals, *Bernströms bestiarium: En djurens nordiska kulturhistoria* (2008). He is currently at work on a collection of essays regarding zoontologies in classic to modern literature as well as a reception history of interpretations of prehistoric parietal art.

THOMAS PUGHE teaches English at the University of Orléans (France). He received his PhD from the University of Basel in Switzerland. His main research interests include contemporary British and American literature and ecocriticism. He has published two books on contemporary American fiction as well as articles on ecocriticism and, more particularly, the representation of animals and animality.

DAVID M. ROBINSON is Oregon Professor of English and director of the Center for the Humanities at Oregon State University. He is author of *Emerson and the Conduct of Life* (Cambridge, 1993) and *Natural Life: Thoreau's Worldly Transcendentalism* (Cornell, 2004). He authored the chapter on "Emerson, Thoreau, Fuller and Transcendentalism" for the annual *American Literary Scholarship* from 1988 to 2008. His current projects include work on Margaret Fuller and Stanley Cavell.

WILLIAM ROSSI is professor of English and director of undergraduate studies at the University of Oregon. He is the author of essays on Thoreau, Ralph Waldo Emerson, and nineteenth-century natural science and coeditor most recently of *Emerson and Thoreau: Figures of Friendship* (Indiana, 2010) with John T. Lysaker.

DIETER SCHULZ is professor and chair emeritus of English and American studies at Ruprecht-Karls-University of Heidelberg. After completing his studies of English and Russian at the University of Marburg (Dr.phil. 1968), he spent three years as a post-doctoral research fellow in American studies at Yale University. He has taught at the Universities of Stuttgart and Wuppertal and has held visiting professorships at Oregon State University and the University of New Mexico. His book publications include *Suche und Abenteuer* (1981), a study of quest patterns in English and American romantic fiction; *E. L. Doctorow: A Democracy of Perception* (1988; coedited with Herwig Friedl); and *Amerikanischer Transzendentalismus: Ralph Waldo Emerson, Henry David Thoreau, Margaret Fuller* (1997). Over the last twelve years he has published some twenty articles on Emerson and Thoreau, specifically on the intellectual roots of Transcendentalism and its impact on twentieth-century developments in the arts and philosophy.

FRANÇOIS SPECQ is professor of American literature and culture at the École Normale Supérieure de Lyon (Université de Lyon) and a researcher affiliated with the CNRS (Centre National de la Recherche Scientifique, UMR LIRE). He has published critical studies and translations of works by Henry David Thoreau, Ralph Waldo Emerson, Herman Melville, Frederick Douglass, Margaret Fuller, and Mary Austin.

JOSEPH URBAS is professor of nineteenth-century American literature at the Université Michel de Montaigne–Bordeaux III and member of the philosophy research group Sciences, Philosophie, Humanités (http://www.sph.u-bordeaux.fr/). He has recently published articles on Emerson in the *Southwest Philosophy Review* and the *European Journal of Pragmatism and American Philosophy*. He is currently preparing a book on Emerson's metaphysics.

LAURA DASSOW WALLS is the William P. and Hazel B. White Professor of English at the University of Notre Dame, where she also teaches in the History and Philosophy of Science Program. She has published widely on Thoreau, Emerson, and Alexander von Humboldt, including *Seeing New Worlds: Henry David Thoreau and Nineteenth-Century Natural Science* (Wisconsin, 1995), *Emerson's Life in Science: The Culture of Truth* (Cornell, 2003), and, most recently, *The Passage to Cosmos: Alexander von Humboldt and the Shaping of America* (Chicago, 2009), which won the Merle Curti Award from the Organization of American Historians and the James Russell Lowell Prize from the Modern Language Association. Currently, she is at work on a new biography of Thoreau, for which she received a Guggenheim fellowship in 2010–11.

Index

Note: *Walden* and the Journal, massively cited in this volume, have no index entries of their own. See specific topics (e.g., Journal writing, HDT's; loon, at Walden Pond, etc.).

208, 209, 227; etymological meaning of, 185; and frustration, 179, 185; gap between, and knowledge, 60; and hermeneutics, 178–81; as inner life, 59; inscription of, 59–60, 62–64, 64–66, 134, 174; knowledge grounded in, 120; of nature, 49, 60, 77, 79–80, 193, 206, 227; sensual, 212; subjective, 162; theory of, 179, 180–82; and walking, 185; writing rooted in, 114–15, 120, 127, 129
"Experience" (R. W. Emerson), 35

fact(s), 209; "essential facts of life" (*Walden*), 204; "flower in a truth," 132, 187, 202, 209; HDT's concept of, 133; recorded in later Journal, 75, 225–26, 232n6; strong writing grounded in, 114
fairy rings, 86
Faith in a Seed (HDT), 77–78, 132
Fall, the, in Christian tradition, 92, 135, 252
fate, 24, 56, 144, 147
Feldman, Burton, 139, 142
Fichte, Johann Gottlieb, 110, 181
Flint's Pond, 246–47
"Following Thoreau's Instincts" (Rossi), 120
Friend, The (Coleridge), 110, 123n5
Fuller, Margaret, 22, 24, 113; death of, on Cape Cod, 37; interest of, in mythology, 146; in Italian revolution, 37

Gadamer, Hans-Georg, 174, 180, 182, 184–85
Gandhi, Mohandas K., 69
gardening, 148–49
generativity, 91
Genesis, book of, 92

Gérando, Joseph-Marie, 119
Gerard, John, 210
German philosophers, 110–11, 138. *See also specific philosophers*
Gettysburg address (Lincoln), 94
Gibson, James J., 211, 215
Giles, Paul, 23
Gilpin, William, 81n4
globalization, 23, 34, 101n29
global warming, 31, 190, 196–97, 248
God (Christian divinity), 87, 92, 108, 114, 150, 235, 242, 246; Calvinist, 147; for Emerson, 236; "God's Drop," 245, 246; HDT's belief in, 240; human likeness to, 119; and language, 259; modern extinction of, 237, 247; and nature (for HDT), 130–31, 237, 246; as object of reason, 123; permanence of, 114; and special creation, 78
gods, 150; ancient Greek and Roman, 87, 139, 146; as human projections, 147; of native peoples, 148
Goethe, J. W. von, 181, 201–2, 254; on Kant, 216n1
golden age, 96–97
Goodall, Jane, 254–55
Gray, Asa, 203
Greeley, Horace, 193
Gregersen, Anstein, 216
Grimm, Jacob and Wilhelm, 143

Hamilton, William, 123n5
Haraway, Donna, 251, 256, 258, 261
Harper's Magazine, 63
Hawthorne, Nathaniel, 23–24, 142, 143; "Edward Randolph's Portrait," 143–44; mythological tales by, 143
Healey, Caroline, 146

phonosemantics, 53; *Sound Shape of Language* (Jakobson and Waugh), 176
Pindar, 119
Pinkham Notch (N.H.), 83, 88, 100n28
planetarity, 23, 25–27, 37, 40; in Dimock, 40n3
Plato and (neo-)Platonism, 10, 84, 109, 111, 114, 115–16, 117, 119, 128, 203, 229
Poe, Edgar Allan, 22
"Poet, The" (R. W. Emerson), 175, 182
poet, the, and poetic perception, 40, 182, 216n2, 229; poetics of Journal, 219–33 passim; versus scientific perception, 59, 120, 207–8
Poetics (Aristotle), 127–28
poet-scientist: Goethe as, 202; HDT as, 207
Poirier, Richard, 235
Polis, Joe, 28
Pomey, François, 142
postmodernism, 40, 42n16, 134, 230, 232n9, 234–35, 238, 239; protopostmodern sensibility in HDT, 236
pragmatism (philosophy), 187–99 passim, 232–33n11
Pratt, Minott, 90
premodernism, literary, of HDT, 51–52, 213
Prescott, William H., 22
Primack, Richard, 190, 196–97
progress: HDT's antimodern rejection of, 44, 46, 47, 49, 66; moral and spiritual, for HDT, 46; "religion of," 148; westward, 32
prose style: Elizabethan, 129; embodies author's character, 127–29; HDT's, 82–101 passim; HDT's view of, 129, 130; Montaigne's, 115, 116; poetics of

HDT's, 40, 83; Raleigh's, 128–29. *See also* Journal writing, HDT's; rhetoric; writing
Prose Writers of Germany (Hedge), 110–11
Puck, 87
Punkatasset Hill (Concord), 90
Putnam's Monthly Magazine, 63

"Questionings" (Hedge), 107–8

railroad, 34, 241; dominance of, 242; HDT's ambivalence toward, 47, 56; HDT's mythologizing of (*see* mythopoeia); symbolism of, for HDT, 56, 147. *See also* train
Raleigh, Walter, 115, 135; heroic character of, for HDT, 128–29
Rawls, John, 159–63 passim; as "communitarian liberal," 167; versus communitarians, 159–62; *Theory of Justice*, 153
Ray, John, 207
realism (philosophical), 118, 122n3, 125n16; Emerson's, 115; ontological, 107, 112–14, 116–18
reason, 107, 109, 117, 122–23n5, 168, 239, 256, 262–63n5
Reinhold, Meyer, 139
relationality, 28, 203. *See also* transjectivity
religion, 107, 112, 113, 123–24n8, 156, 185; challenged by Darwinism, 72–73, 80; for Coleridge and Marsh, 109–10; comparative, study of, 139; doctrines and traditions of, 73, 84; and epiphanies, 235; freedom of, 160; for HDT, 73; human need for, 114, 237; modern loss

individual and society, 159; influenced by German natural philosophy, 231n3; and Journal writing, 231n3; ontology and realism in, 105–25 passim

transjectivity, 23, 27, 29–31; in *Cape Cod*, 32; relationality, 28, 203. *See also* object/subject dichotomy

translation, 4; of animal communication, 258–61; of natural data, 61, 63; of signs in nature, 175

Tudor, Frederic, 99n11

Turner, Victor, 260, 261

Twain, Mark, 22

"two cultures" dilemma, 174, 186, 198

Van Leer, David, 105

Varela, Francisco, 177–78

vascularity, 23, 27, 30–31, 40, 115, 125n14

Very, Jones, 116, 117, 121

vision, 85, 86, 95, 206; "intentions of the eye," 95–96

Waal, Frans de, 254

Walden pond and woods, 27, 28–29, 34, 37, 38, 74, 76, 90, 133, 163, 240–41, 244–46, 248

—pond: as antimodern refuge, 70, 72, 240; HDT's map of, 28, 41n11; house at, 39, 90; loon at (*see* loon, at Walden Pond); natural history of, 31, 193; pure waters of, 71, 245, 246; thawing sandbank near, 167

—woods: animal language of, 211–12, 268; botanizing in, 90; damaged by railroad, 236, 245; ecology of, 251, 258; surveying in, 210; Walden Woods Project, 248

Walker, James, 113, 119

walking: as method, 182; like reading, 182; theme in HDT, 173, 213

"Walking" (HDT), 21, 31–39 passim, 152, 173, 178, 185, 265–66, 272

Walls, Laura Dassow, 187; "A Constant New Creation," 98; *Passage to Cosmos*, 196; "Romancing the Real," 199, 220–22; *Seeing New Worlds*, 40, 59, 182, 188, 195, 213–15; "Thoreau's *Walden* in the Twenty-First Century," 235

Walzer, Michael, 40n3, 161, 167

Waugh, Linda, 176

Week on the Concord and Merrimack Rivers, A (HDT), 185, 202; antianthropomorphism in (cry of the shad), 252–53; discusses knowledge, 65–66; evolutionary perspective in, 183; and excursion genre, 173; experience in, 206; meaning of nature in, 22; as memorial to brother, 34, 76; myth in, 139; syntheses in, 167

Wellek, René, 123n5

west (direction), 32, 35, 39; America's "rhizomatic West," 42n14. *See also* Manifest Destiny

West, Michael, 176

White, Gilbert, 188, 203

Whitman, Walt, 25, 209, 228, 248

wild, the, and wildness, 32, 37, 79, 96, 149, 214, 258, 263n10, 265–73 passim

"Wild Apples" (HDT), 177, 183, 213–14

Wilderness Society, 32

Wild Fruits (HDT), 132

Wilkes Expedition, 22, 23

Williams, Terry Tempest, 59

Winterer, Caroline, 140

Wolfe, Cary, 258